T0406335

Religion and the Science of Human Nature in the Scottish Enlightenment

"Robin Mills' new book is a comprehensive and insightful account of the academic study of religion by philosophers in the Scottish Enlightenment. It is especially valuable for its attention to figures who are not well known today, but who were influential in the eighteenth century."

—Dr. James Foster, *University of Sioux Falls*

"There has been a lot of scholarly interest in the Scottish Enlightenment's thinking on religion, but surprisingly little has been written on the links between this writing and the Scots' famous 'Science of Man'. In this excellent volume Robin Mills sets out to remedy this by offering a survey of the social scientific examination of religion by a range of key Scottish thinkers of the time. Clear, concise, and elegantly written, it is a welcome addition to the literature."

—Professor Craig Smith, *University of Glasgow*

"Absorbing and thoughtful, Robin Mills's book on the natural history of religion in the Scottish Enlightenment fills a conspicuous gap in the history of ideas. With remarkable erudition and no little finesse, he brings home the originality and distinctiveness of the Scottish endeavour to produce a naturalistic account of religion in the second half of the eighteenth century. What is particularly refreshing about Mills's study, however, is his unfashionable insistence that this venture represented a rupture with previous approaches to the study of religion, inaugurating a recognisably modern outlook."

—Dr. Niall O'Flaherty, *King's College London*

R. J. W. Mills

Religion and the Science of Human Nature in the Scottish Enlightenment

palgrave macmillan

R. J. W. Mills
Institute of Intellectual History
University of St Andrews
London/St Andrews, UK

ISBN 978-3-031-49030-9   ISBN 978-3-031-49031-6 (eBook)
https://doi.org/10.1007/978-3-031-49031-6

© The Editor(s) (if applicable) and The Author(s), under exclusive license to Springer Nature Switzerland AG 2023

This work is subject to copyright. All rights are solely and exclusively licensed by the Publisher, whether the whole or part of the material is concerned, specifically the rights of translation, reprinting, reuse of illustrations, recitation, broadcasting, reproduction on microfilms or in any other physical way, and transmission or information storage and retrieval, electronic adaptation, computer software, or by similar or dissimilar methodology now known or hereafter developed.
The use of general descriptive names, registered names, trademarks, service marks, etc. in this publication does not imply, even in the absence of a specific statement, that such names are exempt from the relevant protective laws and regulations and therefore free for general use.
The publisher, the authors, and the editors are safe to assume that the advice and information in this book are believed to be true and accurate at the date of publication. Neither the publisher nor the authors or the editors give a warranty, expressed or implied, with respect to the material contained herein or for any errors or omissions that may have been made. The publisher remains neutral with regard to jurisdictional claims in published maps and institutional affiliations.

Cover illustration: © Melisa Hasan

This Palgrave Macmillan imprint is published by the registered company Springer Nature Switzerland AG
The registered company address is: Gewerbestrasse 11, 6330 Cham, Switzerland

Paper in this product is recyclable.

Dedicated to Kerenza, Wolf, Bear and Pig

Acknowledgements

With loved ones exiting and entering this world, and the necessary realignments about what matters that result, this is not the book that I set out to write. It was composed in brief quiet moments in between close family members waking up and falling asleep and is offered to the reader here not as a fully polished work. I have, all the same, accumulated several debts in its composition, which I have great pleasure in mentioning here. My doctoral supervisor Richard Serjeantson was an exemplar of judicious scholarship and scholarly joie de vivre. I am grateful to Felicity Loughlin, who has been working concurrently to me on very similar themes but from a different interpretative angle, and who generously shared her research and commented on mine. I encourage readers interested in this subject to read her work. James Alder provided vital diversion, especially when I needed it, and Barnaby Crowcroft, vital enthusiasm, often greater than my own. Angus Gowland is a sound, calm voice in an academic world where the table-talk is usually not calm. Ian Stewart, Silvia Sebastiani, Paul Wood, Thomas Ahnert, and Niall O'Flaherty commented on much earlier attempts at individual chapters, making my work much better than it was. Craig Smith read a first draft of an initial whole draft (and the Adam Ferguson section twice) and helped me polish the material. As did Chris Berry, who has been unstinting in his helpful criticism and moral support Richard Whatmore kindly helped secure me an institutional base at St Andrews that helped me finish writing. If I could have had two dedications, I would have also dedicated this book, from afar, to Paul Sagar. Kerenza Davis is lovely, and I love her. All mistakes of argument and composition that remain are my responsibility alone.

Contents

1	**Introduction**	1
	Religion and Precursors to the Scottish "Science of Man"	18
	References	30
2	**Religion and the Start of the Science of Human Nature: Campbell, Turnbull and Hume**	37
	George Turnbull on Religion and the "Moral Anatomy" of the Mind	38
	Archibald Campbell on Mythography and the Science of Man	45
	David Hume's Treatise *and the "Science of Man"*	51
	References	53
3	**David Hume and the Emptiness of Natural Religion**	57
	Religion, Imagination and the Passions	63
	The Psychology of Miracles	71
	Religion's Relationship with Philosophy: Past and Future	75
	The Practical Consequences of Hume's Study of Religion	80
	References	88
4	**Adam Smith on Religious Psychology in Society**	91
	The Histories of Philosophy and of Physics	93
	The Psychology of Religion in the Theory of Moral Sentiments *(1759)*	99

	Religious Sects and Social Stability in the Wealth of Nations	107
	The Decline and Fall of Medieval Catholicism	112
	References	117
5	**Henry Home, Lord Kames on Mechanistic Human Nature**	121
	Kames's Essays on the Principles of Morality and Natural Religion *(1751)*	122
	The Sketches of the History of Man *(1774) and the "Sense of Deity"*	129
	Kames on the Improvement of Theology	131
	On the Character of Religious Worship	134
	Religion and Morality	136
	Allegory and Myth as Childish Fictions	140
	References	146
6	**David Hume's "Natural History of Religion" (1757)**	149
	Human Nature and the Lack of Universality	152
	The "Natural Progress" of Religion?	157
	References	167
7	**William Robertson on Revelation and the Limits of Progress**	169
	Robertson's Necessity of Revelation at the Time of Christ's Mission	173
	True Religion and the Necessity of Social Progress	176
	Superstition's Role in Limiting of Progress: The History of America *(1777)*	180
	The Natural Progress of Religion and the Necessity of Revelation	190
	References	195
8	**Adam Ferguson, Stoicism and the Individual Alone**	199
	Ferguson and the Naturalness of Religion	203
	Ferguson on the Link Between Religion, Happiness and Society	208
	The Primacy of Theism and the Power of Superstition	215
	References	220

9	George Campbell on Miracles and the Weakness of Hume's "Science of Man"	223
	References	233
10	John Gregory on Human Nature, Happiness and Religious Devotion	235
	Speculative Theology and Effective Affective Preaching	238
	Anti-Scepticism	245
	References	249
11	James Dunbar on Climate and Civil Religion	251
	References	256
12	James Burnett, Lord Monboddo on Egyptian Daemons	257
	Monboddo's Curious "History of Man"	260
	Monboddo's Two Accounts of Religion	264
	References	272
13	The Radicalism of James Hutton	273
	Philosophers and the Science of Religion	275
	Hutton on the Natural Progress of Religion	279
	The Alignment of "Christianity" and Philosophy	282
	References	285
14	Dugald Stewart, Religion and the End of the "Science of Human Nature"	287
	References	296
15	Conclusion	297
	References	309

Appendix 1: Two and a Half 'Four Stage' Theories of Religion	313
Appendix 2: Alexander Gerard and the Inadequacies of Progressive Histories of Religion	321
Index	329

Abbreviations

I follow the standard practice of referring to Smith and Hume's texts using abbreviations and in the below form. Where possible, citations are to book, chapter, and paragraph.

Adam Smith

- TMS *The Theory of Moral Sentiments* (1759/1790), ed. Knud Haakonssen (Cambridge: Cambridge University Press, 2002)
- WN   *An Inquiry in the Nature and Causes of the Wealth of Nations* (1776), eds. R. H. Campbell, A. S. Skinner and W. B. Todd (Oxford: Oxford University Press, 1976).

David Hume

I have used the Hume Texts Online website (davidhume.org) developed by Amyas Merivale and Peter Millican

- DNR *Dialogues concerning Natural Religion* (London, 1779)
- EHU *An Enquiry concerning Human understanding* (1748) in *Essays and Treatises* (London, 1777)
- EPM *An Enquiry concerning the Principles of Morals* (1751) in *Essays and Treatises* (London, 1777)
- H   *The History of England* (London, [1754–62) 1778)

NHR	"The Natural History of Religion" (1757) in *Essays and Treatises* (London, 1777)
P	"A Dissertation on the Passions" (1757) in *Essays and Treatise* (London, 1777)
T	*Treatise of Human Nature* (London, 3 vols., 1739–40)

The abbreviations for the below Hume essays are used, citing David Hume, *Essays, Moral, Political and Literary*, ed. Eugene F. Miller (Indianapolis, ID: Liberty Fund, 1987).

BG	"Whether the British Government inclines more to Absolute Monarchy, or to a Republic" (1741)
NC	"Of National Characters" (1748)
PG	"Of Parties in General" (1741)
Sc	"The Sceptic" (1742)
SE	"Of Superstition and Enthusiasm" (1741)

CHAPTER 1

Introduction

Abstract This book surveys the main contributions of the enlightened Scottish "science of man" that examined the relationship between human nature, society and religious belief and practice. The introduction briefly outlines what the Scottish "science of human nature" was, how its discussion of religion differed from other genres and other enlightened approaches to the study of religion and how it related to earlier iterations of the "science of man" as applied to religion. It stakes a claim for a distinctly Scottish contribution to the Enlightenment's discussion of religion.

Keywords Scottish Enlightenment · "Science of man" · "History of mankind" · History of idolatry · Mythography · David Hume

Two passages from the work of David Hume (1711–1776) set the agenda for this expository survey and analysis of the Scottish Enlightenment's treatment of religion. In his *Treatise of Human Nature* (1739–1740), Hume claimed that knowledge of "natural religion" was in "some measure dependent on the science of man,"[1] while in the opening section of his "Natural History of Religion" (1757; hereafter NHR), he

[1] T 0.1.

distinguished between the two central topics of natural religion: "that concerning [religion's] foundation in reason, and that concerning its origin in human nature."[2] In contrast to the general tenor of existing scholarship, the following discussion takes seriously the many contributions of the Scottish "science of man" to the examination of the second of Hume's themes: the relationship between human nature and religion.[3] In doing so, I will demonstrate the origins and development of religion to be as much a part of the Scots' common conversation about human nature as other more well-studied topics.[4] Such a position runs against an impression that, besides Hume's NHR, Henry Home, Lord Kames's (1696–1782) *Sketches of the History of Man* (1774), and some passages in Adam Smith's (1723–1790) juvenile essays, the Scottish Enlightenment's contribution to the Europe-wide burgeoning naturalistic study of religion was minimal. Instead, I want to claim that the Scots authored social scientific theories of the origin and development of religion that set them at the forefront of the emerging enlightened study of religion, and these need to be incorporated both into our studies of the Scottish Enlightenment and in more general accounts of the emergence of non-theological studies of religion.[5]

While there are many studies on the thought of individual Scots, especially Hume and Smith, the following is the first book-length account of the Scottish Enlightenment's treatment of the origins and development of religion.[6] The focus is on the social theorists of the High Scottish Enlightenment, and especially those who can be classified as practising the "science of human nature." This covers two to three generations of

---

[2] NHR 1.

[3] For overviews of enlightened Scottish thought on religion, see Harris (2014, Chs. 25–27), Suderman (2015, esp. §IV) and Stewart (2019). Suderman notes that the Scots were interested in the question of "how much then was religion a human construct or a function of man's propensity for social organization," thought he limits his discussion to this specific question to Kames. Yandell (1990, esp. xiv) argues that scholarship has tended to examine Hume's *Dialogues* to the detriment of our understanding of Hume's 'Natural History of Religion,' despite the latter's centrality to Hume's religious thought.

[4] Spadafora (1990, p. 372) claimed that the only Scottish authors to write about the 'natural history of religion' were Ferguson, Kames and Hume.

[5] For studies on the emergence of the science of religion see, for example, Byrne (1998), Kippenberg (2001), Wheeler-Barclay (2010) and Nongbri (2013). See also Harrison (2015).

[6] See Berry (1997, 2000) for overviews.

thinkers, primarily academic philosophers and theologians, running from Archibald Campbell (1691–1756) to Dugald Stewart (1753–1828), or from the 1740s to the 1820s. My starting point is 1739–1740, when works published by Hume, Campbell and George Turnbull (1698–1748) publicly inaugurated the Scots' "science of human nature," and in ways that directly commented on the relationship between religion and human nature. This is not to deny the importance of developments prior to the middle of the eighteenth century, but it is to argue that there is a qualitative difference in the works published by earlier eighteenth-century Scottish philosophers and the "scientists of man" who published in the mid-century, not least because of their increased sense of, to borrow Silvia Sebastiani's wording, the "variety and historicity" of human nature and human societies.[7] It is the self-conscious aim of writing the "science of man," and within that science, the "history of mankind," that distinguishes the authors discussed below. Nor is it to say that the authors discussed in subsequent chapters constitute all the significant thinkers who make up the "Scottish Enlightenment," only that attempts to reclassify the Scots as "late humanists" falls flat when extended to the social theorists covered in this book.[8]

The "science of human nature" involved adopting and adapting the methods of recent natural philosophy to the study of human nature.[9] Most of the thinkers discussed below shared the view of Hume, as expressed in the *Treatise*, that "moral philosophy is in the same condition as natural, with regard to astronomy before the time of Copernicus."[10] New vistas for the study of moral philosophy, which incorporated the study of human nature, were opened up by conceiving of the subject as potentially subject to the same approaches as natural philosophy. These included studies reflecting on the internal operations of the human mind, developing what Hume termed in the *Treatise* an "accurate anatomy of human nature," and more predominantly amongst enlightened Scottish thought than principally English predecessors in the emerging "science

---

[7] Sebastiani (2022).

[8] Cf. Kidd (2018). George Turnbull was an exception to this.

[9] For overviews, see Phillipson (1981), Wood (1996), Frasca-Spada (1999), Taylor (2013), Schabas (2014), Berry (2015) and Broadie (2015). See also the essays in Jones (1989), Fox, Porter and Wokler (1995) and the special issue of the *Archives de philosophie* (2015) dedicated to the topic.

[10] T 2.1.3.6–7.

of man," studies examining how human nature functioned in social contexts.[11]

The emergence of the "human sciences" was another stage of the "scientific revolution," involving the abandonment of theological and scriptural explanations and their replacement by appeals to amassed historical evidence and inductive, and occasionally conjectural, reasoning based on that evidence.[12] The Scots were engaged, as Chris Berry puts it, in a "scientific enterprise as they understood it."[13] I have included discussion of sections from narrative histories that are usually classified as "philosophical history," such as the major works of William Robertson (1721–1793) or Hume's *History of England*, but which contained material that exemplifies the approach of the "science of man."[14] This move is informed partly by Hume's claim in the *Enquiring Concerning Human Understanding* (1748) that the "chief use" of history is to "discover the constant and universal principles of human nature by showing men in all varieties and circumstances and situations and furnishing us with materials from which we may form our observations and became acquainted with the regular springs of human action and behaviour."[15] Historical facts are "so many collections of experiments by which the politician or moral philosopher fixes the principles of his science; in the same manner as the physician or natural philosopher becomes acquainted with the nature of plants, minerals and other external objects."[16] It was these very findings about human nature that emerged out of the "history of mankind" that were then applied scientifically, in turn, to make judgements about the likely causes and effects of past historical events.

The enlightened Scots were interested in what passions, capabilities and propensities existed in human nature that helped create and inform religious belief and behaviour, but they differed over what these were, how they worked and to what extent they were affected by exogenous factors.

---

[11] T 1.4.6.23.

[12] Gaukroger (2016).

[13] Berry (1997, p. 52).

[14] On philosophical history, see Trevor-Roper (2010, pp. 1–16) and Salber Phillips (2000, p. 171). For a helpful overview of eighteenth-century Scottish historical writing, see Allan (1993).

[15] EPH 8.7.

[16] EPH 8.7.

They analysed how religions change over time but disputed whether this was a linear transition from a primordial polytheism to a refined monotheism, or whether the progress of religion was uneven, could be stalled or, indeed, whether change warranted the name "progress" or "improvement" at all. They contested the issue of whether religious development was linked to changes in society's means of subsistence or the extent of civic stability, or whether physical causes such as climate, had a determinative influence. They debated whether religious progress occurred in tandem with improvements in the arts and sciences, and whether improved religious knowledge for the elite resulted in improved piety for the multitude. Indeed, they debated whether the multitude were capable of religious improvement or whether they were inherently superstitious, and how to manage them if that was the case. They debated how to respond to religious diversity and rivalry within societies, and whether established churches or religious competition had the most beneficial moral and social effects. Finally, they grappled with how their new naturalised understandings of human nature and religion related to established beliefs in revelation and miracles, especially concerning the issue of testimony.

The enlightened Scottish theories of religion were not the handmaidens of traditional Christian studies, epitomised by historical inquiries into the origins of idolatry. Instead, the Scots were participating in a separate field of inquiry, the "science of human nature," studied on its own terms and for its own reasons. There is also something stark and sudden about the emergence of the new science, in Scotland at least, compared to the usual emphasis on the gradual emancipation of naturalised studies of religion from revealed religion.[17] It is this epistemological rupture that has frequently led to the major thinkers of the Scottish Enlightenment being held by subsequent social scientists as the precursors, sometimes originators, of their field. The key feature, in published works from the 1750s, is the emphasis on the progressive quality of human nature and of society, and the attempt to comprehend human and social diversity within the frameworks of change over the *longue durée*.[18]

Two caveats are necessary, however. Firstly, the Scots did not pursue a distinct "science of religion," as religion was one topic amongst many

---

[17] Cf. Apps (2010, p. xiii).

[18] Emerson (1984).

under the large umbrella of the "science of man" or the "history of man." This means they are not the progenitors of the subject as it emerged in the following century. But the fact that religion was one topic amongst many in a "science of human nature" also distances the enlightened Scots from the advances in the historical study of religion of the early modern period, in that what they were doing was not a continuation of earlier genres. Charges that what came during the Enlightenment plagiarised what came before, when applied to the enlightened Scots, miss the mark. Evidence and specific arguments were repeated perhaps, but the overall interpretative framing of such evidence and arguments had changed. Moreover, the authors discussed in the following did not share the same philological talents, antiquarian sensibilities or even broad-based knowledge that practitioners of the earlier study of religion had. This applies even, or perhaps I should say, most illustratively, to Hume's NHR.

Secondly, while the Scottish scientists of human nature separated their studies from the framework of mythography and adherence to the biblical framework of human history, most retained a deeply theistic understanding of what constituted religion and why it should be studied. This included the continued use of the Christian definition of religion itself, one that drew upon Saint Augustine and ultimately Cicero: that the essence of religion was belief in a supreme being and an immortal soul, and for some also, belief in future rewards and punishments. While the enlightened Scots did not privilege Christian concepts or biblical history, they were interested in discussing the implications for understanding what true religion was from the application of the "science of man" to religion.[19] One recurrent theme in the chapters that follow is a split between those Scots who quietly set Christianity aside and those who believed the "science of man" could support it. All, however, were involved in the move away from the mythography. This did not entail an abandonment of religious concerns, but the continued shift away from overtly theological explanatory models and Christian historical frameworks and towards naturalistic explanations of human nature and societal function and change. In several senses, the naturalistic study of religion could still be a theological enterprise, such as when divine intervention was discussed as one cause amongst many for social change, when the findings of the "history of man" were seen to demonstrate the truth of a specific form of

---

[19] But see the contrasting analysis in Loughlin (2020).

religion or when the religion of everyday life was emphasised as superior to speculative theology and self-mortification.

Taken as a whole, the enlightened Scots discussed in the following chapters were not theorists of paganism or idolatry, but of a category of human behaviour termed "religion." The gradual emergence in the early modern period of a neutral category of religion, of religion as an anthropological datum, as something separate to (a) older uses of *religio* referring to a reverential stance and worship towards God and (b) the distinction between Abrahamic "religions" and "paganism," and thus a category as applicable to Christianity as to other religions, cannot detain us here.[20] But the Scots lie atop that development and contribute to its consolidation: religion was treated as one factor amongst many in the history of society and in the scientific investigation of human nature. The historical moment discussed in this book is not one in which the participants of a Christian Enlightenment thought about paganism in new ways that modified earlier histories of idolatry and mythology. That is, when most of the enlightened Scots confront the Gods, to use Frank Manuel's phrasing, they were seeking to understand, in recognisably naturalistic ways, something called "religion"—though they might distinguish, most clearly in the case of Kames, between "theology" and "worship." We lose sight of what is new and what is different in the enlightened Scottish discussion of religion should we downplay the secularising aspects of their theories.[21]

Somewhat surprisingly, the role of enlightened eighteenth-century studies of religion has been downplayed by historians of the study of religion, who have either held that the modern study of religion was born in either the seventeenth or the nineteenth centuries. One celebrated contribution to the field has, for example, claimed that the seventeenth century

---

[20] See Nongbri (2013) and Harrison (2015). The Scottish Enlightenment is absent from the two major historical studies on the history of the concept of religion in the eighteenth century: Despland (1979) and Feil (2012). David Hume is mentioned in Feil (2012, pp. 279–292), but is taken as a representative of freethinking discussion in England. He wasn't.

[21] As Roger Emerson noted, "complete secularization" of enlightened Scottish sociohistorical thought "was yet a step away because the 'spontaneous order' generated in every age by a myriad of human actors was still the providence of God displayed in secondary causes." It did mean, however, that the "manifestation of the divine in history" was *more* intelligible to the "moralists using the proper methods" than the theologian. See Emerson (1989, p. 84).

was an "era of innovation," while the eighteenth was one of "synthesis."[22] I do not want to be read as arguing that this accolade for inaugurating the modern study of religion should be given instead to the eighteenth century, only that such "centuryism" belies the ongoing transformation of the study of religion between c. 1600 and c. 1900 and has missed out on significant developments in the intervening period. I want to argue, by contrast, that the enlightened Scottish account of religion was characteristic of an increasingly naturalised study of religion emerging across Europe, though one with its own unique stamp and emerging for its own specific reasons. The Scots have a strong claim in contributing a significant and coherent body of work that shifted the study of religion towards a more recognisably modern form compared to earlier Christianised studies. They inherited from the seventeenth century an understanding of the multiplicity of systems of religious belief and practice, but they cut off much of the explanatory apparatus of earlier generations of historians of idolatry and shifted to a progressive method of explanation. This significance extends beyond Hume's NHR, despite the dominant position in the literature being that Hume's dissertation was an outlier or that it contained "decisive step" away from declinist theories of theism's descent into polytheism and a "complete reversal" of how enlightened Europe thought about religion.[23]

Still, the enlightened Scots' discussion of religion was part of an epistemological rupture about how to think about human nature, and which led to the emergence of new discourses (the "science of human nature" and the "history of mankind"). It was quite possible for the enlightened Scots to not avowedly and significantly engage with that "complex set of empirical and theoretical developments that occurred throughout the seventeenth century, and which no writer could ignore if they wanted their views on the nature of world religions to be taken seriously."[24] The argument that the legacy of seventeenth-century comparative studies of paganism fundamentally framed Enlightened European understandings of

---

[22] Stroumsa (2010, p. 2). See also Stroumsa (2021). Manuel (1959) adopts a similar position. On early modern studies of paganism, idolatry and mythology, see Miller (2001), Mulsow (2005), Rubiés (2006), Ossa-Richardson (2013), Stroumsa (2015) and Levitin (2012, 2018, 2022).

[23] Schmidt (1987, p. 21). Also cf. Preus (1987) and Harrison (1990).

[24] Levitin (2018, p. 97).

religion, especially via the conduit of Pierre Bayle, is a significant improvement on the somewhat *ex nihilo* treatments of Enlightenment studies of religion.[25] So much of what is deemed radical or subversive in the hands of eighteenth-century *philosophes* had precursors in Christian scholars trying to understand religious diversity in the seventeenth. Still, when the argument is made that Hume's NHR essentially reiterated Bayle's view that all "paganism" was to be understood as "quasi-atheistic monism" and that Hume's examples were all drawn from Bayle, we have possibly abandoned interpreting the eighteenth century on its own terms.[26] The problem I think with this approach is that it collapses a separate intellectual enterprise, the "science of man," into an established practice of the Christian study of idolatry or "mythography". Superficial similarities set aside, Hume's NHR and the majority of the texts discussed in the following were engaged in a separate endeavour to their seventeenth-century predecessors. Not to understand the actual history of religion, but to understand the relationship between human nature, religion and society.

Between the mid-eighteenth and mid-nineteenth centuries, the human and moral sciences reached an unprecedented level of methodological coherence, explanatory power and social importance. Stephen Gaukroger has described this process as resulting in the explanatory framework for best understanding humanity within the natural world was no longer Christianity, but the new and independent human sciences.[27] The naturalised, social scientific approach to religion undertaken by Scottish scientists of human nature distinguishes them from contemporary Scottish and wider European works of mythography. Indeed, one of my main arguments is that most of the "scientists of man" argued in ways that were distinct from the traditional forms of evidence and argument that characterise the study of religion undertaken by biblical scholars, mythographers, antiquarians and philologists. This is true even of the Scottish contemporaries of Hume, Smith, Robertson, Ferguson and the other leading thinkers of the High Scottish Enlightenment. There is something qualitatively different between Hume's NHR and Henry Home, Lord Kames's *Sketches of the History of Man* (1774), and James Geddes' *Essay on*

---

[25] Levitin (2012).
[26] Levitin (2018, p. 97).
[27] Gaukroger (2016).

the Composition and Manner of Writing of the Ancients, Particularly Plato (1748), Duncan Shaw's *The History and Philosophy of Judaism* (1787), George Campbell's edition of *The Four Gospels* (1789) or Alexander Geddes' *Critical Remarks on the Hebrew Scriptures* (1800).[28] This is not to say that certain texts in the latter group were not influenced by the concerns and findings of the "science of human nature"—thus Shaw, for example, repeatedly turns to "human nature and the history of mankind" to substantiate his observations—only that the temporal framework, methods and authorial goals substantially different.[29] Shaw or the two Geddes, characteristic of this separation, wished to best defend and better understand Christianity, and did so using the tools of philology—in the case of Shaw, he wrote against Hume's insinuations in various essays that come under the banner of the "science of man." The authors I am interested in, however, wanted to understand the relationship between human nature religion and society. This might still lead to conclusions about providentially arranged final causes, but whether these were bound up with apologia for Christianity has to be assessed on a case-by-case basis.

Aiming for broad coverage, in the following short chapters I have given space to several of the lesser lights of the Scottish Enlightenment. It is not the case, however, that what follows is the sum of all original or substantial thinking on how to think about religious change emerging out of eighteenth-century Scotland.[30] A case in point here is the Aberdonian philosopher and first Professor of Greek, then Principal of Marischal College, Aberdeen, Thomas Blackwell (1701–1757).[31] In his *Enquiry into the Life and Writings of Homer* (1735), he explained the genius of Homer in terms of the societal context in which the poet lived. The *Enquiry* has been viewed, not entirely persuasively, as one of the progenitors of Scottish social theory.[32] In the *Letters concerning Mythology* (1748), for which Blackwell wrote the bulk of the letters, mythology

---

[28] For thoughtful readings of enlightened Scottish discussions of religion that stress continuity rather than discontinuity with earlier histories of idolatry, see Loughlin (2016, 2019, 2020). I am grateful to Dr. Loughlin for letting me read these papers in draft.

[29] Shaw (1787, p. 47).

[30] One prominent absence is the discussion of the changing position and power of the clergy in John Millar's *An Historical View of the English Government* (1787; expanded edition, 1803).

[31] Loughlin (2016).

[32] Coltharp (1995).

was viewed as a "great work" used by sage pagans to civilise the "rude tribes of uninstructed men" at the dawn of human history.[33] Blackwell treated ancient mythology with a respect and seriousness unlike many of his contemporary mythographers.

We can briefly examine Blackwell's *Letters* to demonstrate how he was not a participant in the "science of man," and in the process illuminate further what that science was concerned with. Blackwell did not narrate trajectories of religious progress resulting from the interplay of the religious propensities of human nature and societal conditions. He was not explicitly inspired by recent achievements in natural philosophy to apply "scientific" methods to the study of human nature. When he broke up history into a series of stages, they were not socio-economic ones based on the means of subsistence but were taken from the Roman philosopher Varro's division of human history into "the unknown, the fabulous, and the historical."[34] Blackwell did not seek to understand the "unknown" phase of human history through examining contemporary travel literature for accounts of "savage" peoples. Similarly, when describing the fabulous age, and expressing a view that Lord Kames would mock as ridiculous, Blackwell maintained that "the first Priests and Poets" were "fathers of wisdom [who] knew more and thought deeper" than scoffers (like Kames) at ancient myth understood.[35] Blackwell was a scholar demonstrating considerable philological erudition (and "abstruse speculation") concerning the texts of antiquity; he innovated within the existing study of ancient myth.[36] His book was received by mid-eighteenth-century readers as provocative because it challenged shibboleths about the precise importance of ancient myth, not because he had revolutionised the way of interpreting such myth.

In terms of the *Letters* at least, attempts to classify Blackwell as a participant in the enlightened Scottish branch of the "science of man," indeed as one of its main progenitors, or as exemplifying the "conjectural history" approach to man and society are unpersuasive.[37] A good example of the distance between Blackwell and the Scottish scientists of

---

[33] Blackwell (1748, p. 82).

[34] Blackwell (1748, p. 192).

[35] Blackwell (1748, p. 118).

[36] Simonsuuri (1979, p. 101).

[37] E.g. Emerson (1984, p. 79) and Coltharp (1995, p. 58).

human nature is the former's explanation of the origin of myth. Certainly, Blackwell shared with the latter group a belief that rationally grounded philosophy could not convince the multitude and that it was necessary for a political or clerical elite to mould a civic religion that aided social stability and moral behaviour. But he described the creation of this civic religion purely in terms of the benign influence of the "first poets and philosophers," who understood the truths of monotheism and sought to translate these in digestible ways beneath the cloak of myth to the multitude.[38] What Blackwell did not do, from the perspective of the "science of man," was explain how society developed to a point where it was possible to have poets and philosophers in the first place, who not only had the leisure to decipher truths about the universe but also the authority to dictate these to the rest of mankind. The appeal to sages assumed what it needed to explain.

There is even greater distance between our enlightened Scottish scientists of human nature and the key questions and themes of contemporary historians of religion, both the mythographer and "freethinking" or "deist" critic. On the whole, the enlightened Scots did not seek to, for example, (a) establish connections between Noah's progeny or the Lost Twelve Tribes of Israel and newly discovered peoples in the extra-European world in an effort to explain the peopling of the planet; (b) develop highly-complicated systems of chronology to incorporate other civilisations into biblical time, such as the attempt to align biblical chronology with that of the Chinese annals; (c) perform sophisticated acts of biblical criticism to explain (or explain away) apparent contradictions in the bible; (d) seek to use non-Christian religious traditions to prove the existence of a primitive or natural religion, subsequently corrupted by either sin or scheming priests; (e) demonstrate, similarly, the existence of a *prisca theologia* or *philosophia perennis* which could be identified in all religions, passed on by the recipients of esoteric religious wisdom; (f) rely upon supernatural explanations, such as the influence of daemons; (g) explain the links between paganism and ancient Greek philosophy; or (h) explain the character of Catholicism in terms of Roman paganism. There are exceptions, as in the cases of Archibald Campbell's *Necessity of Revelation* (1739), George Turnbull's *Principles of Moral and Christian Philosophy* (1740) and James Burnett, Lord Monboddo's (1714–1799)

---

[38] Loughlin (2016).

discussion of religion in his "History of Man." But these exceptions all help clarify what was distinct about the Scottish "science of man." To a great extent, the authors discussed in the following had been liberated from the concerns of early modern historians of idolatry and paganism and the methods associated with them, jettisoning (for good or bad) several centuries of increasingly sophisticated philological methods and well-resourced research. Indeed, the Scots can look distinctly uninterested in issues of detail and precision about the content of the religions they were surveying. And when they were interested in the differences and subtleties of pagan religion, these were subordinated to the societal contextualist reasoning the Scottish Enlightenment is known for.

So while there are exceptions, in profound ways the Scottish study of religion captured here was fundamentally different to the Christian study of paganism and idolatry that was established in the preceding century and which endured into the eighteenth.[39] In the place of the traditional concerns of humanist, apologetic and freethinking scholarship on paganism, the Scots were concerned with understanding religion as one factor amongst many in a totalising science of man and society. Thus, the study of religion exhibited similar qualities to the other subjects studied by the enlightened Scottish scientists of man. The majority assumed a universal human nature with inherent characteristics, which manifested themselves in specific ways under the influence of specific local circumstances.[40] The most commonplace form discussion of religion took was what scholars have variously termed the "natural," "conjectural" or "stadial" history of religion.[41] Usually, but not always, this was predicated on a sense of a trajectory from primitive to civilised society. These histories were farsighted theories of human development across long periods of time, though the precise temporal parameters might change according to the particular study—compare Smith's account of the decline of Catholicism with Kames's stadial history of theological systems. Altogether, however, this form of history was, according to Dugald Stewart, the

---

[39] Something painstakingly demonstrated in Kidd (2016).

[40] Berry (1982).

[41] Wood (1990) encourages us to clearly delineate between 'natural history' and 'conjectural history', the former being the more prominent analytical method in the Scottish Enlightenment. Contrast this with Emerson's more capacious use of 'conjectural history' (1984).

"peculiar glory of the latter half of the eighteenth century," and nowhere more so than in Scotland.[42]

Such an approach quickly created tensions with religious orthodoxy. This was just as often the case of avowedly Christian authors trying to render their histories of religion compatible with their Christian beliefs as it was authors who were making claims about human nature and society that had subversive implications for Christianity and, in the case of Hume, all religion beyond a "minimal theism." One fault line emerging from the following author studies is that between those Scots whose professed Christianity was either very unorthodox, just for show in a censorious society or actively ironic (Hume, Smith, Kames, Ferguson, Monboddo, Hutton and Stewart) and those believers who used the "science of man" to defend or better understand Christianity (Archibald Campbell, Robertson, Gregory, George Campbell, Dunbar and Gerard). To argue for the widespread "resilience of the basic contours of the Mosaic paradigm within the Scottish Enlightenment" is to downplay the existence of the former group, who skirted around whether their theories tallied with scripture or established doctrine.[43] Certainly, the Scottish Enlightenment was a form of "religious enlightenment," in the sense that no major figure was an atheist of the French type—though Hume came closest.[44] But using the adjective "religious" can occlude the challenge being posed to Christianity by the more deistic Scottish social theorists.[45]

While sharing with the general shift towards naturalistic explanations of religious change over the longue durée with many of their Parisian counterparts, the Scottish science of human nature was different in its character to many of the leading studies emerging out of the High French Enlightenment.[46] Certainly, many prominent works on the history of religion in the wider European Enlightenment shared a desire to set aside Christian theological explanations and biblical time. And we might think about the Scottish discussion of religion as a local variation, with local characteristics, of a continental development with some general characteristics. But there is a qualitative difference. Many leading works, especially in the

---

[42] Stewart (1854–1860, vol. i, p. 70).

[43] Cf. Kidd (1999, p. 49).

[44] On enlightened French atheism, see, recently, Devellennes (2021).

[45] Cf. Ahnert (2015, pp. 1–2).

[46] Manuel (1959).

French Enlightenment, were philological endeavours, not interested in the conjectural or "natural" development of religion and characterised more by a continuation of the level of erudition of previous generations of historians of religion, but with an increasingly naturalistic and often irreligious bent.[47] The works associated with the Académie des inscriptions, one of the key intellectual centres for French studies of religion and of which there is no Scottish counterpart, involved in-depth research into the origins, belief systems and socio-political functions of the various forms of ancient paganism.[48] One such text emerging out of the Académie, Charles de Brosses's (1709–1777) *Du culte des dieux fétiches ou parallèle de l'ancienne religion de l'Égypte avec la religion actuelle de la Nigritie*, was a work of erudition, demonstrating de Brosses's learning in both the fields of ancient history and contemporary ethnography.[49] Though de Brosses engaged fulsomely with Hume's NHR, his own work was methodologically very different to Hume's light-touch erudition, psychological reasoning and use of humour.[50] A similar judgement could be made of Charles-François Dupuis's (1742–1809) *Origine de tous les cultures, ou Religion universeslle* (1795).[51] Admittedly, we find in France a move, during the Revolutionary 1790s, towards schematic trajectories of religious change, such as in Volney's *Les ruines ou meditations sur les revolutions des empires* (1791) and Condorcet's *Esquisse d'un tableau historique des progres de l'esprit humain* (1795). These are not related so much to socio-economic context, however, but to the gradual liberation of man towards true rational religion—matched in Scotland only, perhaps, by the radically deistic James Hutton and, in certain lights, Kames. Another difference is the continued appeal in France to a theory of decline from an original true monotheism due the powers of priestcraft, regardless of whether that original religion was tied to Christianity or not.[52] The essence of enlightened French studies of religion, moreover,

---

[47] The former use of 'natural' here means the expected developed of a human phenomenon or institution, the latter use of 'naturalistic' means explanations emerging purely out of the natural world.

[48] See Apps (2010), Harvey (2014), Matytsin (2022) and Nicolì (2022). See also Stroumsa (2021, Ch. 2).

[49] Piettre, (2015).

[50] David (1974). But see also Faria (2021).

[51] Kidd (2016).

[52] Nicolì (2022).

is regularly identified as intentionally, and often aggressively, subversive of Christianity.

Modern scholars of the emerging study of religion tend to agree that learning about non-Christian religions meant that "traditional European worldview and even Christianity itself were in danger of being relativized, destabilized and marginalized."[53] It is argued that the study of non-Christian religions led to a sense of: (a) the parochialism of Christianity's unique claims to religious truth, with concomitant increases in interest in, tolerance of and accommodation with other religions; and (b) the sense of some underlying natural religion shared by all religions, discernible beneath each parochial religion's specific characteristics.[54] The case study of the High Scottish Enlightenment's "science of man" as applied to religion suggests such a summary is too narrow. Several of the avowedly Christian authors (especially Archibald Campbell, Robertson and Dunbar) found that their growing knowledge of the history of religions demonstrated the truth of Christianity or, at least, that they could fashion this historical material into plausible apologia for Christianity. Others found that trajectories of religious development led to conclusions that undermined Christianity, such that the phenomenon of appealing to revelation was a vestige of a more primitive age (Kames, Hutton and, in his more "optimistic" moments, Hume) or that popular Christianity had a lot in common with popular paganism (Hume). We cannot say, however, that their conclusions led to them developing any sense of European marginalisation. Often the reverse is true: that such studies often led to a newfound sense of European superiority. The point here is that there was no *necessary* "devaluation of Christianity" resulting from the study of religious diversity, though such a devaluation was possible, and that the response depended very much of the pre-existing beliefs of the social theorist in question.[55] Certainly, we can find instances of such devaluation, as when Kames maintained that he did not believe that Christianity was the only way to heaven and, likewise, argued that diversity of religious opinion seemed to have been the deliberate design of providence. Moreover, with some of the Scots (especially Hutton), there is a possibility that Christianity was being reconceived in new ways, less rigidly pinned

---

[53] Apps (2010), p. 2).
[54] Stroumsa (2010, p. 6).
[55] Stroumsa (2010, p. 6). See also Hunt et al. (2010).

to biblical history, rites and ceremonies or theological dogma, and more associated with the religion's moral content.

One of the long-standing issues in scholarship on the purported emergence of the proto-social sciences during the European Enlightenment is whether aspects supposed to be innovative in the 1750s were actually instances of ways of thinking that had long been present in Western thought. With reference to the Scottish context, Roger Emerson reminded us that instances of conjectural or stadial historical thinking are easily discernible in ancient thought and that such instances are often clearly the sources of High Scottish Enlightenment thinking.[56] The point is well taken, but there is still the residual fact that the enlightened Scots were studying something called "human nature" in philosophical historical perspective, and this was something new, not least generically. The Scots could even claim to have moved the argument on from earlier practitioners of the "science of human nature." One not entirely arbitrary starting point of the application of the science of man to the study of religion would be Chapter XII of Thomas Hobbes's *Leviathan* (1651). But Hobbes's analysis was not undertaken in the social and historical manner, charting developments over the *longue durée*. I am arguing that a new discourse over the origin and development of religion emerged around the middle of the eighteenth century, that it used different theoretical frameworks from those of earlier accounts of the origin of religion and indeed required the theorists involved, especially those writing the "history of mankind," to break with earlier approaches, and instead innovative with new ways of accumulating and presenting evidence for claims about human nature and religion. It was informed more by Hume's *Treatise*, Montesquieu's *Spirit of the Laws* (1748) or Buffon's *De la manière d'étudier l'histoire naturelle* and *Histoire naturelle de l'homme* (1749) than by G. J. Vossius's *De theologia gentili* or Thomas Hyde's *Historia religionis veterum Persarum, eorumque magorum* (1700). The "science of man" was an epistemological rupture, one that can be assessed by reading Blackwell's letter on the origin of paganism against Hume's or Kames's treatment of the origin of religion—a rupture of which many of the *literati* were well aware.[57]

---

[56] Emerson (1984).

[57] On the claim that the Scottish social theorists were self-consciously aware of the newness of their studies, see Eriksson (1993). See also the thoughtful discussion in Kidd (2018).

While it is certainly true that we must accept the "continuing importance of theological languages in Enlightenment thought" if we are to understand eighteenth-century intellectual culture, the language of the science of human nature clearly encouraged readers to think about religion in naturalistic terms.[58] This is true even of those enlightened Scots who were leading ministers in the Church of Scotland or avowedly defending the truth of Christianity. A little unfashionably, amongst intellectual historians at least, I am thus reasserting the relationship between Scottish Enlightenment thought and modernity; and also that, at least in terms of naturalistic theories of religion, there is indeed an intellectual throughline to nineteenth-century disenchantment and scepticism, even if the Scots cannot be said to have established an enduring "school." But if this is too much for some readers, what I am primarily doing is seeking to demonstrate that religion has been largely ignored in discussions of the proto-social scientific study of the Scottish Enlightenment and that this is an oversight worthy of correction given that, when taken together, the Scots provided an innovative and distinct body of work as part of the wider European Enlightenment's debate over religion and human nature.

Religion and Precursors to the Scottish "Science of Man"

The application of the "science of human nature" and the resulting progressivist histories of religion that emerged in mid-eighteenth-century Scotland have very little to do with the transformations of the history of religion in the seventeenth to the early eighteenth centuries, nor by the simplistic account of the emergence of comparative religion as a "battle between philosophical rationalists and the 'undiscriminating bigots of orthodoxy'."[59] The "conjectural" histories of religion that emerged in the published writings of Hume, Kames, Robertson, Hutton, Monboddo and Stewart were all outgrowths not from the earlier study of religion, but from the "science of man" considered in a historical frame, or what became the "history of mankind." I will end this introduction with a survey, necessarily incomplete and light-touch, of the treatment of the origin and development of religion in the pre-1740s "science of man," as it was defined by several of the Scots themselves.

---

[58] Ahnert (2015, p. 3).
[59] Critiqued in Levitin (2012), here quoting Hugh Trevor-Roper (p. 46).

The "science of human nature" was not of Scottish creation and, similarly, not of eighteenth-century origin. In his *Treatise*, Hume listed "some late philosophers in England" as having "put the science of man on a new footing," with the implication of the passage being that they had applied the methods of Francis Bacon to the study of human nature. Hume's list of philosophers ran: Locke, Shaftesbury, Mandeville, Hutcheson and Butler. In his "Letter to the Edinburgh Review" (1755), Adam Smith held that English philosophers had "led the way not only in natural philosophy" but also in "morals, metaphysics and part of the abstract sciences."[60] His list included Hobbes, Locke, Mandeville, Shaftesbury, Butler, Clarke and Hutcheson. We can set aside Samuel Clarke as principally a rationalist theologian, and someone criticised by several of the enlightened Scots for failing to incorporate an understanding of human nature into his natural theology. The remainder, however, all pursued investigation into, as Joseph Butler put it in the Preface of his *Fifteen Sermons Preached at the Rolls Chapel* (1726), "what the particular nature of man is."[61] We should not overlook the overlap between Hume and Smith's near identical lists—Smith, noticeably, included Hobbes, an author that Hume did not include but whom some commentators have seen as heavily informing Hume's *Treatise*.[62] Nor should we overlook Smith's view, and Hume's implied view, that, in Smith's words, the "abstract science of human nature was but in its infancy" until the end of the seventeenth century.[63] Clarke aside, each of Hume and Smith's practitioners of the new science contributed an account of the relationship between human nature and religion.[64]

Hobbes was one of the principal intellectual stimuli of the Enlightenment's debate over humanity's unsocial sociability.[65] The reception of Hobbes in terms of the emergence of the "science of man," however, is usually framed as a primarily negative one which prompted the Scots to

---

[60] Smith (1982, p. 250).

[61] Butler, (2006, p. 37).

[62] E.g. Russell (2008). See also Sagar (2018).

[63] TMS VII.iii.2.5.

[64] My glosses here necessarily trample roughshod over the large, sophisticated literature on Hobbes and Locke's thought on these issues. By contrast, discussion of the relationship between religion and human nature in Shaftesbury, Hutcheson, Mandeville and Butler is limited.

[65] For a recent discussion, see Sagar (2018).

develop their social contextualism.[66] This is epitomised by Adam Ferguson's criticism that state of nature theorists tended to select "one or a few particulars on which to establish a theory." Thus, Hobbes, to the Scots, reduced complex human nature and the complex interactions between humans and society, down to a view of men as irreducibly self-interested creatures.[67] Such theorists had failed, Ferguson held, to use the methods of the "natural historian" who collected "facts" from "observations and experiments" and induced general truths about man and society from these facts.[68] The theorists of the state of nature relied upon conjecture at the expense of the principle of induction and thus failed the tests of the "science of man." Similarly, Hobbes conceived of the state of nature as explaining how atomised individuals would interact with each other. The Scottish social theorists responded critically to such simplistic visions of pre-social human nature and the argument that political authority was the creation of a social contract, and developed in response their sense that society and its institutions developed in complex and interrelated ways over long periods of time.

Hobbes's claims about how human nature informed the origin of religion, however, were likely stimulating to the theorists of the High Scottish Enlightenment. While a theme that Hobbes returned to throughout his oeuvre, Chapter 12 of *Leviathan* (1651) serves as a key text to summarise those claims of Hobbes that his eighteenth-century Scottish readers may have drawn upon given their praise of him as a scientist of man. Hobbes summarised four "natural seeds of religion" as being "opinion of ghosts," "ignorance of second causes," "devotion towards what men fear" and "taking of things casual for prognostics."[69] While the "pursuit of causes" by the disinterested observer of nature will eventually lead to acknowledgement of a "first and an eternal cause of all things," most people are motivated by fearful "solicitude" about their futures.[70] Such motivation "gives occasion of feigning of as many Gods, as there by men that feign them."[71] In many of Hobbes's writings, likewise, we find

---

[66] See, for example, the mentions *passim* of Hobbes in Berry (1997, 2013).
[67] Ferguson (1996, p. 8).
[68] Ferguson (1996, p. 8).
[69] Hobbes (1996, p. 79).
[70] Hobbes (1996, p. 77).
[71] Hobbes (1996, p. 77).

the argument that speculative inquiry on subjects that exceed the limits of human experience and reason, as is often the case in religious matters, leads to incorrect and often dangerous beliefs. Such activity, however, is inevitable as, Hobbes claimed, all men are concerned with the "causes of their own good and evil fortune."[72] Likewise, all men attribute causes to effects they observe and "when he cannot assure himself of the true cause of things," he depends on either "such as his own fancy suggests; or trusts to the authority of other men."[73] The Scottish scientists of human nature "develop[ed] the problem of fear," understood as a principal motivation behind so much human behaviour, "as a function of time," but while starting from a Hobbesian position, they provided a developmental account in which the influence of fear changed according to other factors.[74]

Locke's conceptualisations of the state of nature and a social contract too were criticised by the Scots for their lack of empirical grounding. The principal influence of Locke on the Scottish "science of man," however, was the emphasis that all knowledge comes from sense experience or reflection upon that experience, or what Locke described as his "short and ... true history of the first beginnings of human knowledge."[75] This opened up the sense of behaviour and beliefs being the result of social context, and with a sense of the malleability of social context, likewise the malleability of human nature. The Scots took from Locke a sense of the development of human knowledge as resulting from the accumulation of experience and reflection. This informed the commonplace analogy of children developing into adults with "savage" societies developing into "civilised" ones. The key idea was that the development in both cases, from children/savages to adults/the civilised, was the move from a mental landscape of immediate particulars to that of abstract notions.[76] What the Scots served to do is situate this Lockean sense of the influence of

[72] Hobbes (1996, p. 76).

[73] Hobbes (1996, p. 76).

[74] Iacono (1994, p. 674).

[75] Locke (1690, 2.12.15). See also Wood (1996) and, with specific reference to religion, Berry (2000).

[76] Berry (1997, p. 114).

experience on belief and behaviour into contexts of social interaction and societal change.[77]

While not securing total victory, Locke's *Essay concerning Human Understanding* (1690) was an influential text that framed debate at the beginning of the eighteenth century over the origin of religious beliefs. Famously, in Book I of the *Essay*, Locke exploded the commonplace doctrine that asserted the existence of innate ideas and principles engraved into human nature. The testimony of human history demonstrated, however, that the universal consent over religious tenets one would expect from innate religious belief did not exist. Religious diversity not universality was the norm and those apologists who appealed to universal consent lazily conflated both polytheistic and monotheistic popular religions as demonstrating the universal belief in a single God. The existence of God was a belief that emerged upon a concerted act of reasoned consideration and the religious error that littered human history demonstrated that most people did not undertake such work. Locke distinguished between the "wise and considerate," who gain their "true notions" of God through the exercise of their reason, and the "lazy and inconsiderate," who take their notions from "chance … common tradition and vulgar conceptions."[78] Most of humankind lazily received their religious notions from tradition and custom. Locke's legacy to the debate over religious innatism included not only the most concerted contemporary critique against innate ideas, but also arguments strengthening the view that true religion was passed down by tradition only. In the *Reasonableness of Christianity* (1695), Locke was explicitly sceptical about the ability of natural reason to develop full knowledge of natural religion.[79] Christianity was absolutely necessary as Jesus revealed two truths otherwise unattainable by natural reasons: the existence of an afterlife with rewards and punishments and God's mercy to the repentant. The history of pagan societies demonstrated that "it is too hard a thing for unassisted reason" of both the vulgar and the learned to come to knowledge of basic religious truths.[80] The Gospel was the necessary dissemination of true religion in a form intelligible to the multitude.

---

[77] Again, see Berry (1997) and Berry (2013), *passim*.
[78] Locke (1690, i.iii.16).
[79] See Lucci (2021).
[80] Locke (1695, p. 265).

In the wake of the controversy over the first formation of religious ideas of which Locke's *Essay* was a key component, a number of Scottish and Irish moral philosophers provided a new description of the origins of religious belief within human nature.[81] The *Essay* had helped discredit the commonplace doctrine of innate religious ideas and principles. Concerned about the sceptical implications of Locke's argument and desiring to reassert the natural foundations of religious belief, Anthony Ashley Cooper, the Third Earl of Shaftesbury, Francis Hutcheson and their successors set out a new account of religious nativism in this light. This new description of humanity's psychological capabilities and processes retained the position of earlier religious nativists, such as the Cambridge Platonists, that exogenous factors affected the formation of their natural religious ideas. The primary explanatory model, however, was no longer innate ideas, but a newly discovered set of internal senses, such as the sense of beauty or the moral sense, which lead to the development of basic religious beliefs and feelings upon interaction with the natural world. Humans are predisposed to form religious notions, but the accuracy of these beliefs depends on the external contexts in which those notions are formed. While similar in many ways, the Shaftesbury-Hutcheson argument involved a move away from reasoned proofs and innate ideas and towards sentiments and feelings.

Influenced by the Third Earl of Shaftesbury's *Characteristicks* (1711) and driven forward by Hutcheson, from the 1720s onwards a new argument emerged that emphasised the pre- or non-rational propensities of human nature in framing religious notions and sentiments. The internal senses of harmony, beauty and order and the related moral sense provided the mental means by which the basic tenets of natural religion were formed in the mind. Shaftesbury put forward a teleological account of human nature in which a worshipful, theistic religious belief was one of the natural ends of the human species. The frequent if disjointed discussion in the *Characteristicks* positioned "religion" as a "natural affection" or "natural passion."[82] Religious belief and devotion was the result of an instinctive experience of wonderment upon the perception of the "numbers, harmony, proportion, and beauty of every kind" observable in the

---

[81] See Mills (2021).

[82] The most forthright statement appears in Miscellaneous Reflections No. II. See Shaftesbury (2001, vol. iii, p. 23). See also vol. i, p. 31, vol. ii, pp. 43, 88 and vol. iii, p. 24. On Shaftesbury's religious thought, see Rivers (2000, Ch. 2).

natural world.[83] These "naturally captivate[] the heart, and raises the imagination to an opinion or conceit of something majestic and divine."[84] This "passion" or "natural affection" Shaftesbury positioned as part of human nature, and thus, "it is evident that religion itself is of the kind and must therefore be natural to man."[85] However, the religious affections of human nature were not sufficient on their own to form true theistic notions. The innate propensity to find the natural world wonderful required refinement via the exercise of humanity's "rational part." For Shaftesbury, reason was prompted by this instinctive wonderment into encouraging the individual to consider their "immediate relation to the universal system and principle of order and intelligence."[86] The "natural affection" of religion drives human nature forward, but humans require lengthy thinking on the natural world to come to true religion. The first prompt and directive to religiosity, however, was the affections or passions.

While Shaftesbury did not articulate a systematic theory about the origins of religious belief, the argument that we are pushed towards religion not by reason but by non-rational means was developed further by Francis Hutcheson. As Benjamin Crowe has shown, Hutcheson maintained that basic religious notions were not the result of long deductions of reason but due to a number of internal senses.[87] In his *An Essay on the Nature and the Conduct of the Passions and the Affections* (1728), Hutcheson argued that "ideas of divinity arise from the internal senses"; humanity's natural "apprehensions of a deity" first arose from non-rational origins. The belief in God was a "natural effect" of our constitutions. The process was twofold but instantaneous. First, our "internal sense" leads us to immediately perceive "grandeur, beauty, order, [and] harmony" upon observation of the natural world. Second, whenever this happens we immediately "raise an opinion of a mind, of design, and wisdom."[88]

---

[83] Shaftesbury (2001, vol. iii, p. 20).
[84] Shaftesbury (2001, vol. iii, p. 20).
[85] Shaftesbury (2001, vol. iii, p. 23).
[86] Shaftesbury (2001, vol. iii, p. 137).
[87] See Crowe (2010, 2011) and, more generally, Harris (2008).
[88] Hutcheson (2002, p. 116).

For Hutcheson, humans were naturally religious prior to any chain of abstract reasoning.[89] The instantaneous apprehension of a cause of the harmony, beauty and order of the universe was a determination of the mind "more natural" than any other; similarly, the resulting notion of a deity is an "effect more universal" than any other.[90] And as soon as we have an idea of a "superior mind," then an "inward devotion arises."[91] Hutcheson described the formation of a worshipful disposition towards the deity in a similar two-step process to the perception of the existence of a deity. Experience of the natural word raises the idea of a deity, which in turn raises the passion of devotion. Thus, the "disposition in mankind to religion"—in terms of both belief in God and worship of God—was undeniable.[92] The tendency to "devotion, or love and gratitude to some governing mind" is one of those "dispositions and actions" which are "part of our constitution" and is "antecedent[ ] to any volition of our will."[93] Humans are "naturally inclined" to be religious, and they arrive at belief "as universally and with as much uniformity as they do a certain stature and shape."[94] This framing of human nature demonstrated that "to be the perfection of our kind" is, in part, "to know, love and reverence the great author of all things."[95] Humans, for Hutcheson, were religious animals by nature.[96]

While Hutcheson rejected the elitism of Shaftesbury's *Characteristicks*, he shared the Earl's argument that the perfection of human nature involved developing a set of theistic beliefs. Whereas religious knowledge was to be refined through the use of reason, the first formation and the real driving force of religious belief were the non-rational aspects of human nature: the internal senses of beauty, harmony and order and the correlate moral sense. The process was described as immediate or instinctual. In Regent at Marischal College, Aberdeen, David Fordyce's influential framing of the position, "it does not appear, from any true

---

[89] Compare with Harris (2004, p. 233).
[90] Hutcheson (2002, p. 116).
[91] Hutcheson (2002, p. 117).
[92] Hutcheson (2002, p. 116).
[93] Hutcheson (2002, p. 130).
[94] Hutcheson (2002, p. 130).
[95] Hutcheson (2002, p. 131).
[96] On the prominence of this position in Scottish moral philosophy, see Mills (2015).

history or experience of the mind's progress, that any man by any formal deduction of his discursive powers, ever reasoned himself into the belief of a God."[97] This immediate belief in God was companioned by an immediate belief in the necessity of worshipping that God. Shaftesbury and Hutcheson, and many of the Scots discussed below, rejected the view that all humans could, or did, come to knowledge of the existence and attributes of God through a chain of reasoning alone. Aside from the elitist Shaftesbury, this group held that the problem with the rationalist position was that it was fundamentally a philosopher's religion far out of the mental reach of the generality of humankind. Happily, however, human nature had been providentially arranged not to need logic and ratiocination, but sense and intuition, to believe in God. Thus, the internal sense theorists offered a new account explanation of the origin of religious notions.

This set Hutcheson apart from Joseph Butler. While Hume wrote to Hutcheson in January 1743 opining that the latter's "moral sense" was near identical to Joseph Butler's "conscience," Butler had no truck with the idea that human nature had innate capabilities for the easy formation of the basics of theism.[98] In *The Analogy of Religion* (1736), and arguing against a deistic notion of the primacy of a simple theism easily known by the light of nature, Joseph Butler maintained that the truths of religion were known due to an initial revelation subsequently diffused throughout the world. The "whole system of belief" in one creator god, to whom "mankind is in a state of religion," was "received in the first ages."[99] The system was not "first reasoned out" but was "taught first by revelation," and its appearance in the "first ages of the world" confirms its truth. The fact that it "has been professed in all ages and countries" was evidence that the system of revealed religion was "conformed to the common sense of mankind," but Butler rejected the idea that monotheistic belief was "natural, obvious, and forces itself upon the mind."[100] The historical primacy of monotheism, given "how unapt for speculation rude

---

[97] Fordyce (2003, p. 108). See also pp. 37, 147.

[98] Greig (1932, vol. i, p. 47).

[99] Butler (2006, p. 210).

[100] Butler's position here is illustrative of the continued prominence in early eighteenth-century theological writings, despite Locke's purportedly successful explosion of the *consensus gentium* argument in *Essay*, that while there were no innate religious ideas, there was universal agreement about the existence of God.

and uncultivatzed minds are," demonstrates it must be the result of revelation. In Lockean vein, Butler argued that the "state of religion in the heathen world" and the "natural inattention and ignorance of mankind in general" demonstrated that the "light of nature" alone was not sufficient to reach the truths of religion. Butler maintained that only the historical accuracy of the scriptural account of humanity's origins could explain the existence of theism.

The author from Hume and Smith's lists who most anticipated Scottish social theory was the Anglo-Dutch physician Bernard Mandeville.[101] Indeed, many of the commonplaces in what follows are to be found in Mandeville's later works. In Part I of *The Fable of the Bees* (1723), Mandeville had provided conjectural histories of the origins of society and morality, viewing both as conventional developments that resulted when politicians encouraged the multitude to accept the restraints required by social life by flattery and manipulation, creating a standard of virtues. In the second part of the *Fable* (1729), and in *An Enquiry into the Origin of Honour* (1732), Mandeville turned his initial histories into substantial conjectural histories explaining how human institutions had gradually developed over time. Importantly for our concerns, in the Fifth Dialogue of *Part II*, Mandeville set out a "natural history" of the development of religious belief and religious institutions within primitive societies. He treated religion outside of biblical time and solely as a human phenomenon. Unlike the other early "scientists of man" identified by Hume and Smith, and while he clearly was utilising Hobbes's account in *Leviathan*, Mandeville outlined how religious belief developed over time as a result of the interaction between human nature, the improvement of knowledge and the power of priests.

Religious belief originated in the passion of fear provoked by inexplicable and threatening natural events, and not either a natural religious disposition or ratiocination on the natural world. Primordial religion took the form of a rudimentary anthropomorphic polytheism that only concerns the "savage," who is wholly employed in staying alive, when there are "immediate obstacles" to that goal.[102] Religious belief develops over time due to two influences, but both are the result of improvements

---

[101] See Simonazzi (2015). On Mandeville as a scientist of man, see also Castiglione (1986) and Hundert (1994).

[102] Mandeville (1924, vol. ii, pp. 209–213).

in society. The first is the improvement of human reasoning capability, as man becomes "more perfect in the labour of the brain, and the exercise of their highest faculty" (e.g. reason). At least amongst the learned, the anthropomorphic polytheistic elements of belief are replaced by a notion of an "infinite and eternal being," though this theism still contains the "most miserable, unworthy, and extravagant notions of the supreme being."[103] Priestcraft is the second cause behind the formation of systems of religion in response to the experience of diversity of religious opinion within early societies. Mandeville's realist view of human nature held that while systems of idolatry were introduced as the consequence of "the Roguery of designing Priests" who "invented those Lies, and made Fables for their own Advantage," priests were only able to do this because the multitude were fools fearful about futurity and who willingly believed those priests who claimed to be "friends" with the gods.[104] The deist hypothesis that religion was a purely political creation failed to appreciate that such priestcraft could never have occurred without the overpowering influence of fear over men. What Mandeville encouraged his readers to understand was that religion will always be with us and was a societal factor that politicians had to manage through manipulation of the passions of the multitude.[105]

Many of the themes of the embryonic "science of man" were expanded upon by the thinkers of the High Scottish Enlightenment. But as John Dunn and Daniel Carey have argued, one key shift from Locke, Shaftesbury and Hutcheson to Hume, Kames and Smith was a historicisation of investigations into human nature.[106] Mandeville is an interesting bridging case here, and arguably, the significance of his conjectural histories of society, morals and religion, especially in his later writings, has been underemphasised in our current literature on the Scottish Enlightenment, as opposed to an overriding emphasis on what Smith termed his "licentious system."[107] Still, Mandeville did not exhibit the concern with historical facts that characterised the discussion of religious change of the High Scottish Enlightenment. But more than just placing the issue of the

---

[103] Mandeville (1924, vol. ii, pp. 207–208, 213, 215).

[104] Mandeville (1924, vol. ii, pp. 213–214, 210, 218).

[105] Branchi (2022).

[106] Dunn (1983), Carey (2006). See also Mills (2015).

[107] For an interesting discussion, however, see Hurtado-Prieto (2006).

relationship between religion and human nature into historical and societal context, the enlightened Scots viewed the subject as one of the key components of the "science of man" and the "history of mankind." It is time we updated our account of the Scottish Enlightenment to reflect that fact.

* * *

Finally, a few words on structure. The following is a diachronic account that brings together discussion of individual Scottish thinkers' contribution to the application of the "science of man" and the "history of mankind" to religion. I have not heavily embedded the discussion into the context of eighteenth-century Scotland, though I have paused to do so when especially relevant. Scholarship on the Scottish Enlightenment has often viewed its key members as professionally and personally linked to each other, and engaged in the same questions, using the same methods and differing more in the detail than in overall theory. Something to this effect inspired the anthropologist Edward Evans-Pritchard's droll assessment that "all the Scottish moral philosophers wrote the same books."[108] Informed by this sense of a shared research proect, the following stands apart from the more commonplace framing of the study of intellectual history, at least in Anglophone academia, as a series of controversies or vigorous debates in which the authorial intentions of specific authors are to be garnered from situating their texts in the wider contexts to which they were responding. There are indeed chronological elements in what follows: the public inauguration of the "science of man" in 1739–1740; the importance of Kames, Hume and Smith in setting the agenda for studying the relationship between religion and human nature; the deepening of the historical detail and the refinement of established opinions in the texts that follow; the Aberdonian response to the Humean challenge, though we find less unity of approach in Northern Scotland than might be expected; the appearance of authors by the 1790s who seem to be moving away from the science's initial positions; and Dugald Stewart's surprising return to the staple arguments of seventeenth-century natural theology. There is a strong sense, however, of the thematic continuity of the conversation and the concepts throughout the period covered, and each author is discussed in terms of the innovative quality of their contribution to that shared conversation.

[108] Evans-Pritchard (1981, p. 15).

References

Ahnert, Thomas. 2015. *The Moral Culture of the Scottish Enlightenment*. London: Yale University Press.

Allan, David. 1993. *Virtue, Learning, and the Scottish Enlightenment: Ideas of Scholarship in Early Modern History*. Edinburgh: Edinburgh University Press.

Apps, Urs. 2010. *The Birth of Orientalism*. Philadelphia, PA: University of Pennsylvania Press.

Berry, Christopher J. 1982. *Hume, Hegel and Human Nature*. The Hague, NL: Martinus Nijhoff.

———. 1997. *The Social Theory of the Scottish Enlightenment*. Edinburgh: Edinburgh University Press.

———. 2000. Rude Religion: The Psychology of Polytheism in the Scottish Enlightenment. In *The Scottish Enlightenment: Essays in Reinterpretation*, ed. Paul Wood, 315–334. New York, NY: University of Rochester Press.

———. 2013. *The Idea of Commercial Society in the Scottish Enlightenment*. Edinburgh: Edinburgh University Press.

———. 2015. The Rise of the Human Sciences. In *Scottish Philosophy in the Eighteenth Century. Volume I: Morals, Politics, Art, Religion*, ed. Aaron Garrett and James Harris, 283–322. Oxford: Oxford University Press.

Blackwell, Thomas. 1748. *Letters Concerning Mythology*. London.

Branchi, Andrea. 2022. *Pride, Manners, and Morals: Bernard Mandeville's Anatomy of Honour*. Leiden, NL: Brill.

Broadie, Alexander. 2015. Scotland's Science of Man. In *The Enlightenment in Scotland: National and International Perspectives*, ed. Jean-Francois. Dunyach and Ann Thomson, 85–105. Oxford: Voltaire Foundation.

Butler, Joseph. 2006. *The Works of Joseph Butler*, ed. David E. White. Rochester, NY: University of Rochester Press.

Byrne, Peter. 1998. The Foundations of the Study of Religion in the British Context. In *Religion in the Making: The Emergence of the Science of Religion*, ed. Arie L. Molendijk and Peter Bels, 45–65. Leiden: Brill.

Castiglione, Dario. 1986. Considering Things Minutely: Reflections on Mandeville and the Eighteenth-Century Science of Man. *History of Political Thought* 7: 463–488.

Carey, Daniel. 2006. *Locke, Shaftesbury, and Hutcheson: Contesting Diversity in the Enlightenment and Beyond*. Cambridge: Cambridge University Press.

Coltharp, Duane. 1995. History and the Primitive: Homer, Blackwell and the Scottish Enlightenment. *Eighteenth-Century Life* 19: 57–69.

Crowe, Benjamin D. 2010. Religion and the 'Sensitive Branch of Human Nature.' *Religious Studies* 46: 251–263.

———. 2011. Hutcheson on Natural Religion. *British Journal for the History of Philosophy* 19: 711–740.

David, Madeleine V. 1974. Histoire des religions et philosophie au xviiie siècle: le président de Brosses, David Hume et Diderot'. *Revue philosophique de la France et de l'étranger* 164: 145–160.

Despland, Michel. 1979. *La religion en Occident: évolution des idées et du vécu*. Paris: Cerf.

Devellennes, Charles. 2021. *Positive Atheism: Bayle, Meslier, d'Holbach, Diderot*. Edinburgh: Edinburgh University Press.

Dunn, John. 1983. From Applied Theology to Social Analysis: The Break Between John Locke and the Scottish Enlightenment. In *Wealth and Virtue: The Shaping of Political Economy in the Scottish Enlightenment*, ed. Istvan Hont and Michael Ignatieff, 119–135. Cambridge: Cambridge University Press.

Emerson, Roger L. 1984. Conjectural History and Scottish Philosophers. *Historical Papers/Communications Historiques* 19: 63–90.

———. 1989. The Religious, The Secular and the Worldly: Scotland 1680–1800. In *Religion, Secularization and Political Thought: Thomas Hobbes to J. S. Mill*, ed. James E. Crimmins, 68–89. London: Routledge.

Eriksson, Björn. 1993. The First Formulation of Sociology: A Discursive Innovation of the 18th Century. *European Journal of Sociology/Archives Européennes de Sociologie/Europäisches Archiv Für Soziologie* 34: 251–76.

Evans-Pritchard, Edward. 1981. *A History of Anthropological Thought*, 1981. London: Faber & Faber.

Faria, Pedro. 2021. David Hume, the Académie des inscriptions and the Nature of Historical Evidence in the Early Eighteenth Century. *Modern Intellectual History* 18: 299–322.

Feil, Ernst. 2012. *Religion, Band 4. Die Geschichte eines neuzeitlichen Grundgegriffs im 18. und frühen 19. Jahrundert*. Göttingen: Vandenhoek & Ruprecht.

Ferguson, Adam. [1767] 1996. *An Essay on the History of Civil Society*, ed. Fania Oz-Salzberger. Cambridge: Cambridge University Press.

Fordyce, David. [1748] 2003. *The Elements of Moral Philosophy*, ed. Thomas Kennedy. Indianapolis, IN: Liberty Fund.

Fox, Christopher, Roy Porter, and Robert Wokler, eds. 1995. *Inventing Human Science: Eighteenth Century Domains*. Berkeley CA: University of California Press.

Frasca-Spada, Marina. 1999. The Science and Conversation of Human Nature. In *The Sciences in Enlightened Europe*, ed. W. Clark, J. Golinski, and S. Shcaffer, 218–245. Chicago, IL: Chicago University Press.

Gaukroger, Stephen. 2016. *The Natural and the Human: Science and the Shaping of Modernity, 1739–1841*. Oxford: Oxford University Press.

Greig, J.Y.T. ed. 1932. *The Letters of David Hume*, 2 vols. Oxford: Clarendon Press.

Harris, James. 2004. Answering Bayle's Question: Religious Belief in the Moral Philosophy of the Scottish Enlightenment. In *Oxford Studies in Early Modern Philosophy*, vol. 1, ed. Daniel Garber and Steven Nadler, 229–253. Oxford: Oxford University Press.

———. 2008. Religion in Hutcheson's Moral Philosophy. *Journal of the History of Philosophy* 46: 205–222.

———. ed. 2014. *The Oxford Handbook of British Philosophy in the Eighteenth Century*. Oxford: Oxford University Press.

Harrison, Peter. 1990. *'Religion' and the Religions in the English Enlightenment*. Cambridge: Cambridge University Press.

———. 2015. *The Territories of Science and Religion*. London: University of Chicago Press.

Harvey, David Allen. 2014. The Rise of Modern Paganism? French Enlightenment Perspectives on Polytheism and the History of Religions. *Historical Reflections* 40: 34–55.

Hobbes, Thomas. [1651] 1996. *Leviathan*, ed. Richard Tuck. Cambridge: Cambridge University Press.

Hundert, E. J. 1994. *The Enlightenment's Fable: Bernard Mandeville and the Discovery of Society*. Cambridge: Cambridge University Press.

Hunt, Lynn, Margaret Jacob, and Wijnand Mijnhardt. 2010. *The Book That Changed Europe: Picart and Bernard's Religious Ceremonies of the World*. London: Belknap Press.

Hurtado-Prieto, Jimena. 2006. The Mercantilist Foundations of 'Dr Mandeville's Licentious System': Adam Smith on Bernard Mandeville. In *New Voices on Adam Smith*, ed. Leonidas Montes, 247–270. London: Routledge.

Hutcheson, Francis. [1742] 2002. *An Essay on the Nature and Conduct of the Passions and Affections, with Illustrations on the Moral Sense*, ed. Aaron Garrett. Indianapolis, IN: Liberty Fund.

Iacono, Alfonso M. 1994. The American Indians and the Ancients of Europe: The Idea of Comparison and the Construction of Historical Time in the 18th Century. In *European Images of the Americas and the Classical Tradition*, 2 parts, eds. Wolfgang Haase and Reinhold Meyer, 658–691. New York, NY: De Gruyter.

Jones, Peter, ed. 1989. *The Science of Man in the Scottish Enlightenment*. Edinburgh: Edinburgh University Press.

Kidd, Colin. 1999. *British Identities Before Nationalism: Ethnicity and Nationhood in the Atlantic World 1600–1800*. Cambridge: Cambridge University Press.

———. 2016. *The World of Mr Casaubon: Britain's Wars of Mythography, 1700–1870*. Cambridge: Cambridge University Press.

———. 2018. The Scottish Enlightenment and the Matter of Troy. *Journal of the British Academy* 6: 97–130.

Kippenberg, H.G. 2001. *Discovering Religious History in the Modern Age*. Princeton, NJ: Princeton University Press.

Levitin, D. 2012. From Sacred History to the History of Religion: Paganism, Judaism, and Christianity in European Historiography From Reformation to "Enlightenment." *The Historical Journal*. 55: 1117–1160.

———. 2018. What Was the Comparative History of Religions in 17th-Century Europe (and Beyond)? Pagan Monotheism/Pagan Animism, from T'ien to Tylor. In *Regimes of Comparatism: Frameworks of Comparison in History, Religion and Anthropology*, 49–115. Leiden, NL: Brill.

———. 2022. *The Kingdom of Darkness: Bayle, Newton, and the Emancipation of the European Mind from Philosophy*. Cambridge: Cambridge University Press.

Locke, John. 1690. *An Essay Concerning Humane Understanding*. London.

———. 1695. *The Reasonableness of Christianity*. London.

Loughlin, Felicity. 2016. The Study of Pagan Religions in Enlightenment Scotland: The Case of Thomas Blackwell (1701–1757). *Records of the Scottish Church History Society* 45: 82–98.

———. 2019. Socrates and Religious Debate in the Scottish Enlightenment. In *Brill's Companion to the Reception of Socrates*, ed. Christopher Moore, 658–681. Leiden: Brill.

———. 2020. The Pagan Supernatural in the Scottish Enlightenment. In *The Supernatural in Early Modern Scotland*, ed. Julian Goodcare and Martha McGill.

Lucci, Diego. 2021. *John Locke's Christianity*. Cambridge: Cambridge University Press.

Mandeville, Bernard. [1723–1729] 1924. *The Fable of the Bees*, 2 vols, ed. F.B. Kaye. Oxford: Oxford University Press.

Manuel, Frank E. 1959. *The Eighteenth Century Confronts the Gods*. London: Harvard University Press.

Matytsin, A. 2022. Enlightenment and Erudition: Writing Cultural History at the Académie des inscriptions. *Modern Intellectual History* 19: 323–348.

Miller, Peter N. 2001. Taking Paganism Seriously: Anthropology and Antiquarianism in the Early Seventeenth-Century Histories of Religion. *Archiv für Religionsgeschichte* 3: 183–209.

Mills, R.J.W. 2015. Lord Kames's Analysis of the Natural Origins of Religion: The *Essays on the Principles of Morality and Natural Religion* (1751). *Historical Research* 89: 751–775.

———. 2021. *The Religious Innatism Debate in Early Modern Britain: Intellectual Change Beyond Locke*. Basingstoke: Palgrave-Macmillan.

Mulsow, Martin. 2005. Antiquarianism and Idolatry: The Historia of Religions in the Seventeenth Century. In *Historia: Empiricism and Erudition in Early Modern Europe*, ed. G. Pomata and N.G. Siraisi, 181–210. Cambridge, MA: MIT Press.

Nicolì, Laura. 2022. *Les Philosophes et les Dieux. Le Polythéisme en debate dans la France des Lumières (1704–1770)*. Paris: Honoré Champion.
Nongbri, Brent. 2013. *Before Religion: A History of a Modern Concept*. Yale, CT: Yale University Press.
Ossa-Richardson, Anthony. 2013. *The Devil's Tabernacle: The Pagan Oracles in Early Modern Thought*. Oxford: Princeton University Press.
Phillipson, Nicholas. 1981. The Scottish Enlightenment and the Science of Man. *Theoretische Gechiedenis* 8: 3–19.
Piettre, Renée Koch. 2015. President de Brosses's Modern and Post-Modern Fetishes in the Historiography and History of Religions. In *History and Religion: Narrating a Religious Past*, ed. Bernd-Christian. Otto, Susanne Rau, and Jörg. Rüpke, 393–405. Berlin: De Gruyter.
Preus, J. Samuel. 1987. *Explaining Religion: Criticism and Theory from Bodin to Freud*. New Haven, NJ: Yale University Press.
Rivers, Isabel. 1991–2000. *Reason, Grace, and Sentiment: A Study of the Language of Religion and Ethics in England, 1660–1780*, 2 vols. Cambridge: Cambridge University Press.
Russell, Paul. 2008. *The Riddle of Hume's Treatise*. Oxford: Oxford University Press.
Sagar, Paul. 2018. *The Opinion of Mankind: Sociability and the Theory of the State from Hobbes to Smith*. Princeton, NJ: Princeton University Press.
Salber Phillips, Mark. 2000. *Society and Sentiment: Genres of Historical Writing in Britain, 1740–1820*. Princeton, NJ: Princeton University Press.
Schabas, Margaret. 2014. Philosophy of the Human Sciences. In *The Routledge Companion to Eighteenth Century Philosophy*, ed. Aaron Garrett, 731–752. Abingdon: Routledge.
Schmidt, Francis. 1987. Polytheisms: Degeneration or Progress? In *The Inconceivable Polytheism: Studies in Religious Historiography*, ed. Francis Schmidt, 9–60. London: Harwood Academic.
Sebastiani, Silvia. 2022. Monboddo's 'Ugly Tail': The Question of Evidence in Enlightenment Sciences of Man. *History of European Ideas* 48: 45–65.
Shaftesbury, Lord, Anthony Ashley Cooper. [1711] 2001. *Characteristicks of Men, Manners, Opinions, Times*, ed. Douglas den Uyl, 3 vols. Indianapolis, IN: Liberty Fund.
Shaw, Duncan. 1787. *The History and Philosophy of Judaism*. Edinburgh.
Simonazzi, Mauro. 2015. Atheism, Religion and Society in Mandeville's Thought. In *Bernard de Mandeville's Tropology of Paradoxes: Morals, Politics, Economics, and Therapy*, ed. Edmundo Balsemão and Joaquim Braga. Dordrecht: Springer.
Simonsuuri, Kirsti. 1979. *Homer's Original Genius: Eighteenth-Century Notions of the Early Greek Epic (1688–1798)*. Cambridge: Cambridge University Press.

Smith, Adam. [1795] 1982. *Essays on Philosophical Subjects, with Dugald Stewart's Account of Adam Smith*, eds. W.P.D. Wightman, J.C. Bryce and I.S. Ross. Indianapolis, IN: Liberty Fund.

Spadafora, David. 1990. *The Idea of Progress in Eighteenth-Century Britain*. London: Yale University Press.

Stewart, Dugald. 1854–1860. *The Collected Works of Dugald Stewart*, 11 vols, ed. William Hamilton. Edinburgh.

Stewart, M.A. 2019. Religion and Rational Theology. In *The Cambridge Companion to the Scottish Enlightenment*, 2nd ed., ed. Alexander Broadie and Craig Smith, 33–59. Cambridge: Cambridge University Press.

Stroumsa, Guy. 2010. *A New Science: The Discovery of Religion in the Age of Reason*. London: Harvard University Press.

———. 2015. The Scholarly Discovery of Religion in Early Modern Times. In *The Cambridge World History*, ed. Jeffrey H. Bentley, Sanjay Subrahmanyam and Merry E. Wiesner-Hanks, 313–333. Cambridge: Cambridge University Press.

———. 2021. *The Idea of Semitic Monotheism: The Rise and Fall of a Scholarly Myth*. Oxford: Oxford University Press.

Suderman, Jeffrey. 2015. Religion and Philosophy. In *Scottish Philosophy in the Eighteenth Century. Volume I: Morals, Politics, Art, Religion*, ed. Aaron Garrett and James Harris, 196–238. Oxford: Oxford University Press.

Taylor, Jacqueline. 2013. The Idea of a Science of Human Nature. In *The Oxford Handbook of British Philosophy in the Eighteenth Century*, ed. James Harris, 65–83. Oxford: Oxford University Press.

Trevor-Roper, Hugh. 2010. *History and the Enlightenment*, ed. John Robertson. London: Yale University Press.

Wheeler-Barclay, Marjorie. 2010. *The Science of Religion in Britain, 1860–1915*. London: University of Virginia Press.

Wood, Paul B. 1990. The Natural History of Man in the Scottish Enlightenment. *History of Science* 18: 89–123.

———. 1996. The Science of Man. In *Cultures of Natural History*, eds. Nicholas Jardin, J.A. Secord and Emma C. Spary, 197–210. Cambridge: Cambridge University Press.

Yandell, Keith. 1990. *Hume's Inexplicable Mystery: His Views on Religion*. Philadelphia, PA: Temple University Press.

CHAPTER 2

Religion and the Start of the Science of Human Nature: Campbell, Turnbull and Hume

Abstract This opening chapter argues that religion, far from being of secondary importance to the High Scottish Enlightenment's (1740–1800) "science of man," was a central topic. The focus is on the first three major publications of that science: Archibald Campbell's *The Necessity of Revelation* (1739), David Hume's *Treatise of Human Nature* (1739–1740) and George Turnbull's *The Principles of Moral and Christian Philosophy* (1740). All claimed, though in differing ways, that moral philosophers and theologians could apply the methods of recent natural philosophy to the study of human nature, including man's religious propensities. It was Hume's approach in the *Treatise*, however, that set the foundations for subsequent discussion.

Keywords David Hume · Archibald Campbell · George Turnbull · "Science of man" · Natural philosophy · Scottish Enlightenment

The relationship between religion, human nature and society is not usually treated as a central theme in the Scottish "science of man," and what has been seen as significant instead is the Scots' "rational theology." Far from religion being of cursory importance in the High Scottish Enlightenment, c. 1740–c.1800, the period actually began with a series of texts that made it clear that the science of human nature was fundamentally intertwined with religious topics. This can be demonstrated from examining those works, published in quick succession, that argued in different ways for the application of natural philosophical methods to topics relating to religion: Archibald Campbell's *The Necessity of Revelation* (1739), David Hume's *Treatise of Human Nature* (1739–1740) and George Turnbull's *The Principles of Moral and Christian Philosophy* (1740). Each of these authors claimed that moral philosophers and theologians could apply the methods of recent natural philosophy to the study of human nature, including the man's religious propensities. The idea that the methods of recent natural philosophy could be applied to human nature and society were not new to these publications, and the idea had been present in the Scottish universities for some decades, while Turnbull had already suggested it in a small publication in 1726. The concurrence of these three publications in 1739–1740, however, marked a shift into print and into wider Scottish intellectual life. While the differing methodological approaches of Campbell, Hume and Turnbull suggest a plurality of possible "sciences of human nature," as we shall see in subsequent chapters, it was the approach of Hume exhibited first in the *Treatise* and developed further in later writings that exemplified and informed many of the central themes and questions of the enlightened Scottish study of religion.

George Turnbull on Religion and the "Moral Anatomy" of the Mind

The Aberdonian academic theologian Turnbull was the first Scottish Enlightenment thinker to publish calls that the study of human nature be informed by recent advances in natural philosophy.[1] He did so in the belief it would improve our natural theological knowledge. Yet the expositions presented by Turnbull of the possible benefits of studying natural philosophy in two graduation theses given while a regent at Marischal College, Aberdeen, in the 1720s, did not contain a substantial outline of the future "science of man." In his *Philosophical Theses on the Association of Natural Science with Moral Philosophy* (1723), Turnbull claimed that the more we learn about the attributes of God from the study of the natural

---

[1] For an overview see Ahnert (2007).

world, the more we can know "by the light of nature our duty towards him and the worship which is acceptable to him."[2] Recent advances by Bacon and Newton had shown the way: we learn about creation not by "fanciful hypotheses or unfounded conjectures," but by "mathematical reasoning or clear and certain experiments and analogy."[3]

In 1723, Turnbull was not recommending the application of natural philosophical methods to the study of human nature or society, but rather encouraging his Christian readers to observe the "beautiful association and analogy of physiology [i.e. the laws of nature] with ethics."[4] Natural philosophy had shown that the world is characterised by elegance and order, so likewise God created man with a "share in reason" and a "social sense" that pursues the "common good of all intelligence beings" in ways that lead to a beneficent social order.[5] Just as the natural world is characterised by beauty and harmony, so we should pursue the "just and regular moderation" of our passions to achieve similar harmony in our conduct.[6] Study of natural philosophy also encourages us to "take a broader view" of our lives, "fashions us to modesty and magnanimity" in the face of creation and induces a "humane and sociable frame of mind."[7] Contemplation of a beautiful, orderly, harmonious natural world created by a wise, benevolent lawgiver encourages virtuous, pious behaviour in the observer. It thereby serves to reduce what Turnbull viewed as the superstitious attribution of "wonderful effects to [mere] natural causes."[8]

Turnbull reiterated this position in *Academical Theses on the Most Beautiful Structure of the Material and Rational World* (1726). Knowledge of man's duty to their fellow human and to their God emerged from study of the natural world, and it is knowledge gained from this study that must "underpin moral philosophy."[9] Turnbull then turned *briefly* to the idea that we can learn about human nature directly by utilising the methods

[2] Turnbull (2014, p. 53).
[3] Turnbull (2014, p. 59).
[4] Turnbull (2014, p. 55).
[5] Turnbull (2014, p. 54).
[6] Turnbull (2014, p. 55).
[7] Turnbull (2014, p. 55).
[8] Turnbull (2014, p. 56).
[9] Turnbull (2014, p. 73).

of natural philosophy, rather than just drawing an analogy with the findings of natural philosophy with moral philosophy. Just as Bacon and Newton had studied the natural world through "collating and comparing" its phenomena to "distinguish the order in that structure from the aberrations," so moral philosophers can collate and compare the facts of man to understand the "perfection of human nature."[10] We could study "the force, the use, and the mutual relations" of the "faculties" of human nature to learn how they were intended to work by our maker.[11] Unlike the *literati* who followed, Turnbull understood this proposed science of human nature in narrowly psychological, rather than social, terms.

A more extensive argument about the benefits of studying human nature scientifically appeared in Turnbull's *Principles of Christian and Moral Philosophy* (1740), but in ways that demonstrated the chasm between his understanding of a prospective "science of human nature" and that of Hume's. To Turnbull, the study of natural philosophy, including the study of man, helps us identify the laws of nature that produce the "good, perfection and beauty" found in the natural world.[12] Here, a Ciceronian claim, that we can observe the beauty, elegance and harmony of the natural world, is undergirded by an appeal to the investigative potential of new scientific methods associated with Bacon, Newton, Robert Boyle and others, to identify the laws of nature, including the laws of human nature.[13] Moreover, the pursuit of natural philosophy is really part of the study of moral philosophy, because it ultimately teaches us about God and his creation, including man's duty to himself, his fellow humans and his God.

Turnbull's *Principles* was intended to be a contribution to a debate that was not front and centre of High Scottish Enlightenment concerns: the relationship between natural and revealed religion. Turnbull's ultimate purpose in the *Principles* was to demonstrate that the findings of the science of morals were completely aligned with, and certainly did not supersede, the doctrines found in revealed religion. He positioned himself as following a middle path between recent theologians who "depress and vilify human understanding" and stress the necessity

---

[10] Turnbull (2014, p. 65).
[11] Turnbull (2014, p. 65).
[12] Turnbull (2005, vol. i, p. 48). See Demeter (2016, pp. 16–17).
[13] Cicero, *De officiis* 1.4.

of revelation to understand all our moral and religious duties, and those freethinkers who believed that scripture provided only a "very imperfect account" of humanity and its relationship to God and claimed that unassisted reason should be the ultimate judge of the content of those same duties.[14] Turnbull was engaged in an apologetic exercise of demonstrating the theological legitimacy of the natural philosophical study of man and nature and its harmonious relationship with revelation, as well as drawing out the theological conclusions of that study.

Moral philosophy is the "science" of studying minds.[15] It takes the form of a "moral anatomy" of the mind's various "faculties, powers, dispositions and affections," resulting from "reflexion on the mind itself and its inward operations."[16] The moral philosopher must proceed first by reducing the "appearances or facts in the moral world to general laws," inspired by the sense that they will be analogous to the laws of nature discovered by natural philosophy.[17] From here, the moral philosopher must identify the "wise and good final causes of those general laws" and demonstrate how these final causes align with "scripture doctrine concerning God, providence, human nature, virtue or human perfection, and a future state."[18] Both natural philosophy (or the study of corporeal objects) and moral philosophy (or the study of sensible objects) had the same goal of identifying God's fixed laws of nature. But as Turnbull would note, natural philosophy was a form of moral philosophy, because it was ultimately a study of God. Turnbull thus saw the study of human nature as one branch of a general moral philosophy, which incorporated the laws of both corporeal and spiritual beings, with the goal of understanding God's arranged final causes.[19] In this, Turnbull was fundamentally at odds with Hume's concept of the "science of man," as we will see, as the foundational science upon which all others were built.

Recent "improvements in natural philosophy" had demonstrated that the only basis of "real knowledge" was "experiment and fact," and the "science" of mind involved the same process of "investigation, induction,

---

[14] Turnbull (2005, vol. ii, p. 471).

[15] Turnbull (2005, vol. i, p. 47).

[16] Turnbull (2005, vol. i, pp. 7, 23, 47).

[17] Turnbull (2005, vol. ii, p. 469).

[18] Turnbull (2005, vol. ii, p. 471).

[19] Demeter (2016, p. 39).

and reasoning" as science of corporeal objects.[20] Turnbull's approach to the study of human nature involved something more, however, than a "collection of facts discovered by experience."[21] He described his method as "mixed moral philosophy," meaning the use of "principles inferred from immediate observation, and others deduced from such principles, by reasoning from ideas or definitions."[22] As Tamas Demeter as suggested, this sees Turnbull imitating Newtonian "mixed mathematics," as found in the *Principia*.[23] The study of morals involves both a priori reasoning from definitions of terms relating to human nature and drawing inferences from accumulated observations of human action. To understand our nature and purpose, the moral philosophy proceeds in Newtonian fashion of "reasoning from principles to effects and effects to principles."[24] This meant that once an accumulation of observations demonstrated the truth of a particular principle, then it was possible, without reference to further observation, to extrapolate from that principle other effects.

Natural philosophy, including its application to human nature, had its limits. As Thomas Ahnert has discussed, across several publications Turnbull argued that it was from revealed religion alone that we learn the doctrine of our future existence, and rewards and punishments. The frame of the natural world and human nature demonstrated order and harmony, from which we can confidently infer the providential government of a benevolent deity.[25] Yet the doctrine of future rewards and punishments in an afterlife was not something demonstrable by reason alone. Thus, Turnbull claimed, in his anti-deist pamphlet *Christianity Neither False Nor Useless, Tho' Not as Old as the Creation* (1731), scripture "sets before us certain truths," such as the future fate of our immortal souls, "which are powerful motives to moral obedience" but which "the Law, or Light of Nature, cannot discover."[26] Without this doctrine, the dictates of moral obligation lack sufficient weight to compel the bulk of mankind to act. In arguing for the necessity of revelation for understanding the core tenets of

---

[20] Turnbull (2005, vol. i, pp. 8, 47).
[21] Turnbull (2005, vol. i, p. 62).
[22] Turnbull (2005, vol. i, p. 65).
[23] See Demeter (2016, pp. 37–38). E.g. Turnbull (2005, vol. i, p. 63).
[24] Demeter (2016, p. 38).
[25] Ahnert (2015, p. 87).
[26] Turnbull (1731, p. 43) and Ahnert (2015, p. 44).

religion, Turnbull was reflective of a recurrent position within the enlightened Scottish study of religion, and one particularly prominent amongst its Aberdonian strand.

When it came to the question of the natural origins of religion, Turnbull's position combined both the older doctrine of innate religious ideas, associated with Cartesianism and which still had purchase at the Aberdeen colleges in the early eighteenth century, and the new approach found in moral sense theory, associated with Anthony Ashley Cooper, the Third Earl of Shaftesbury and Francis Hutcheson. This set out a two-stage process, first Cartesian then Shaftesburian, for the formation of the idea of God. Firstly, upon consideration of the natural world, the mind "cannot escape from forming" the idea of a "creating and sustaining power or principle."[27] The idea of God, understood as an "intelligible form or conception," was "innate" and "occurs to everyone."[28] The fact that our idea of God is the result of innate propensity of the mind explained, Turnbull claimed, how we can have an idea of an immaterial being of which we have no direct sense experience. Secondly, once our innate idea of God is realised, our innate moral sense "naturally disposes us" to ascribe to God "intelligence, … love of order and benignity of temper."[29] From here, our moral sense frames us to immediately admire the author of nature. Citing the passage from Hutcheson's *Essay on the Nature and the Conduct of the Passions*, Turnbull summarised that "disposition to religion," in both belief in and worship of God, is as natural to man as the "connexion between the sexes."[30] It was this sort of argument that Hume would reject as disproven by the evidence of ancient history and travel literature at the beginning of his "Natural History of Religion" (1757).

For Turnbull, the fact that forming an idea of God was a natural propensity of human nature was evidence of the existence of that God. But, while human nature had a "natural capacity" to be religious, true religion required the cultivation of habit and education.[31] This in turn involved acts willed by individuals. We must first habitually pay attention to the natural world around us, which prompts the intuitions of our

---

[27] Turnbull (2005, vol. i, p. 230).
[28] Turnbull (2005, vol. i, p. 235).
[29] Turnbull (2005, vol. i, p. 235).
[30] Turnbull (2005, vol. i, p. 235).
[31] Turnbull (2005, vol. i, p. 145).

innate religious propensities. But it was also the "great business of reason [to] cultivate, improve and then preserve in due force" the dictates of our moral sense to our God.[32] All humans have it "in our power to improve all our faculties, powers, and affections; and to grow daily in wisdom and in virtue."[33] It is the God-given end of human nature to prepare ourselves for "great moral happiness, arising from a well-cultivated and improved mind suitably placed."[34] Central to this was contemplation of the "manifest tokens of infinite intelligence, power and goodness, shining so visibly" in God's works.[35]

Just as Turnbull discussed the religious propensities of human nature in terms of the pious behaviour of an individual, he explained the origin of false religion and irreligious behaviour in terms of the degeneration of our natural propensity to belief and worship of God by bad habits and the influence of bad priests. The existence, power, wisdom and goodness of God are knowable to anyone who pays even the slightest attention to the "beauty, order, and benevolence" evident in the structure of the universe.[36] Lack of attention direct to the natural order leads humans to setting up "fictitious gods," usually in the form of polytheistic worship of "corruptible man, birds, beasts, and insects."[37] Our reason is also corrupted by "superstitious practices" and by vice-filled living, leaving our minds "unwilling" and "unable to behold the light."[38] The corruption of religion, however, was as much "promoted by tyranny" as it was by immorality.[39] Princely and priestly tyrants spread the "deification of tyrants and heroes," first bringing idolatry into the world, as a means to secure their power and devour their "prey," the rest of humanity.[40] Turnbull's source here was not an erudite work in the history of idolatry, but the third epistle of Alexander Pope's *Essay on Man* (1734).[41]

[32] Turnbull (2005, vol. ii, p. 579).
[33] Turnbull (2005, vol. ii, p. 580).
[34] Turnbull (2005, vol. ii, p. 584).
[35] Turnbull (2005, vol. ii, p. 610).
[36] Turnbull (2005, vol. ii, p. 530).
[37] Turnbull (2005, vol. ii, p. 530).
[38] Turnbull (2005, vol. ii, p. 530).
[39] Turnbull (2005, vol. i, p. 237).
[40] Turnbull (2005, vol. i, p. 238).
[41] Turnbull (2005, vol. i, pp. 289–290).

Turnbull's views about the degeneration of man's natural theism into polytheism and idolatry, due to the combined influence of flawed human nature or priestcraft, were characteristic of much mainstream Protestant thought. And it contrasted substantially with the socio-historical discussions of religion that emerged from the 1750s, from which Turnbull stands at quite a distance's remove. He did make what became the commonplace Baconian call that we must accumulate facts from which to make informed claims about human nature, but lacked any explicit sense of historical diversity and what that might mean for comprehending human nature. Turnbull's concern, however, was not to understand the workings of society or to chart the origin and progress of human institutions, but to demonstrate the truths of moral philosophy and their harmony with revealed religion. He utilised the "moral sense" theory of Shaftesbury and Hutcheson but, like them, did not incorporate a strong socio-historical component explaining how man's internal senses worked in different contexts.[42] Turnbull's discussion of the relationship between human nature and religion, especially in terms of idolatry and polytheism, exhibited the commonplace declinist positions of the previous century, rather than the advances of the next few decades.

Archibald Campbell on Mythography and the Science of Man

Archibald Campbell's *The Necessity of Revelation* (1739) was a highly innovative text. Campbell, Professor of Divinity and Ecclesiastical History at St Andrews from 1733 until his death in 1756, viewed the methods of the science of human nature as useful tools in religious controversy. Campbell's book contained a strikingly clear application of natural philosophical methods to the study of pagan religion and, like Turnbull's *Principles*, was a contribution to early eighteenth-century Britain's ongoing controversy over the relationship between natural and revealed religion.[43] Against the "English Deists," but also against orthodox Presbyterianism who accused Campbell himself of "deism," Campbell sought to demonstrate that true religion depended on knowledge derived from revelation alone, without which unassisted human reason was impotent.

---

[42] See Carey (2006).
[43] On this see Mills (2021).

Like Turnbull, he did so for apologetic purposes. Unlike Turnbull, Campbell did so precisely because he wished to challenge the belief of both orthodox Presbyterianism in Scotland and contemporary English "deist" thinking that maintained, to Campbell, a naïve belief in the powers of unassisted human reason to come to the truths of natural religion.[44]

As Thomas Ahnert has shown, part of the emergence of Moderatism within the Church of Scotland involved a sceptical reclassification of the capacity of unassisted reason to achieve epistemic certainty in doctrinal matters.[45] Most of the enlightened Scots, Campbell amongst them, went against the Kirk's position that the heathens were through the exercise of their reason alone to come to an understanding of the moral law— including the existence of God and the immortality of the soul. More generally, Campbell was going against the long-standing position within Christianity that the study of natural theology was independent to and sequentially prior to study of revealed religion, even if it would only teach the basics of theism and gave no insight into doctrines, say, of salvation or grace. Campbell accepted his view, that natural religion was dependent on revealed religion, would appear as a "paradox" to his readers.[46] Thus, while broadly persuasive, Ahnert's recent bringing together of Turnbull and Campbell as reflective of a certain heterodox position within Scottish Presbyterianism in the early eighteenth century glosses over the major gap between Turnbull and Campbell on which tenets of true religion could be discerned by reason alone. In his *Necessity*, Campbell wrote a whole book challenging the sort of religious nativism that Turnbull professed.

Campbell deployed the methods of recent natural philosophy to demonstrate that reason alone could not come to belief in the two essential tenets of religion: the existence of God and the immortality of the soul. He collected facts about pagan theological doctrines, usually in the form of the opinions of past philosophers, and he induced conclusions about the relationship between human nature and religion from those facts. In sum, the erroneous beliefs across the ancient pagan world demonstrated that true religion was known only at moments of specific revelation, such as when received by Noah and subsequently transmitted by tradition, though this was easily corrupted under the weight of human

---

[44] For a more detail discussion of the context of Campbell's work, see Mills (2015).
[45] Ahnert (2015).
[46] Campbell (1739, p. 383).

frailty. Campbell did not deny that, once the core tenets of true religion were known, the study of natural theology could build on them. But he stressed that the study of pagan religion demonstrated that without stable knowledge of truths disseminated via revelation, humans could not come to true religion nor build valid systems of natural theology. Campbell's eminently "enlightened" application of the methods of natural philosophy to the study of human nature and society defended, like Turnbull, the less obviously "enlightened" conclusion that revelation was the foundation of all religious knowledge, "natural" as much as revealed.

Campbell believed that the principal external threat to revealed religion in early eighteenth-century Britain came from "deism," or the belief in the self-sufficiency of human reason to come to the truths of religion and the subordination of revealed religion to the tests of that reason. It was this challenge that provoked Turnbull and Campbell to innovate, though in different ways. To the deists, natural religion and revealed religion were of equal value, given that a good God would not demand his flock to believe things they could not understand and would not have left knowledge of religion up to the transmission of tradition alone. But unlike Turnbull, Campbell argued that the orthodox Presbyterianism's appeal to the power of the light of nature to come to knowledge of the two core tenets of religion aligned too closely to the "deist" argument, and undermined Christianity's claim to uniqueness.

It is in context of needing new arguments to (a) thwart the "deist" assault on Christianity and (b) rebuke charges from orthodox Presbyterians in the Kirk that he was wrong on the question of the powers of the light of nature that Campbell innovated with a new methodological approach to the study of the origin of man's basic religious notions. Campbell's central conclusion—that knowledge of the foundational tenets of religion stemmed from revelation and was transmitted by tradition alone—was not new. While we can find intellectual antecedents prior to then, such as John Selden, the argument had gained traction in Britain from the 1690s in response to the emerging "deist" threat. But Campbell draped his position in appeals to the leading discussions of the weakness of unassisted reason and the absence of innate religious ideas found not only in the writings of Pierre Bayle and John Locke, but a plethora of recent authors including Antoine Arnauld, Jean-Pierre de Crousaz, Samuel Parker and Thomas Halyburton.

More originally, he adopted explicitly Baconian and Newtonian methods to study the powers of the unassisted light of nature (the cause) by analysis of the religious opinions of ancient heathens (the effects). He claimed to argue "from the effect to the cause," to show that "God has actually favoured mankind with the blessing of revelation."[47] Campbell remained consistent throughout the 1730s in his view that the light of nature *can* teach humans what is necessary for a happy life, but only after it had been informed by axiomatic principles found in revelation alone.[48] What he changed in *Necessity of Revelation* was to clad his position on the weakness of human nature in the language, concepts and associated glory of natural philosophy. He used both the intellectual standing of natural philosophy and its methods to give his arguments increased weight and rhetorical power.

To make credible claims about the capabilities of unassisted reason to reach true religious notions, Campbell argued we must undertake a "course of experiments" that established "particular facts really existing."[49] The systematic collation and analysis of pagan religious opinions would lead to the establishment of facts about ancient heathenism that had validity comparable to those established by recent natural philosophy. Just as the "course of repeated experiments" resulted in discovering "certain knowledge in matters of natural philosophy," so the same could be expected in the study of the "religious powers and abilities of intelligent beings."[50] In Lockean fashion, Campbell opined that so many religious notions were felt to be natural because "we are trained up from our youth in our common philosophy, and which appears very plausible, almost demonstrably true in speculation."[51] Much of the "deist" picture of natural religion was merely a "romance."[52] What was needed was a genuinely empirical study of the "religious powers of human nature," and this required examination of the theological opinions of Greco-Roman philosophers and wider society.[53] The pagan philosophers were the first thinkers to have fully forgotten the teachings of revelation. In contrast

[47] Campbell (1739, p. 386).
[48] Campbell (1730, pp. v–xiii; 1733a, pp. xxviii–xxix; 1733b, esp. pp. 23, 31–32, 34).
[49] Campbell (1739, pp. 16, 23).
[50] Campbell (1739, pp. 28–29).
[51] Campbell (1739, pp. 11–12). See also Campbell (1736, pp. 37–38).
[52] Campbell (1739, p. 24).
[53] Campbell (1739, p. 64). See also pp. 25, 29, 30.

to the social theorists who came after him, who were profoundly interested in a pre-social "primordial man" at the beginning of human history, Campbell rejected the existence of such a "state of nature" as contradicted by biblical account.[54] The pagan sages of ancient Greece and Rome could serve as the test subjects of the deist and orthodox Presbyterian position that humans are capable to come to knowledge of natural religion by dint of the light of nature alone.

The ultimate conclusions that Campbell derived from his empirical study of pagan religion were that (a) "it appears *in fact*" that knowledge of God "came originally from revelation" and was passed on "by tradition" and that (b) it was a "fact" that humans "left to themselves" are incapable of coming to true notions about the existence of God and the immortal soul.[55] There was no consensus of the wise or of all peoples about basic religious tenets, and those heathen philosophers who did believe in God or an immortal soul were recipients of vestiges of "sacred traditions," as acknowledged by many pagan philosophers themselves.[56] Far from being instances of a universal natural religion, paganism was "at an infinite distance" from true religion.[57] It was a "matter of fact," drawn from the "experiments I have made," that the natural religion of unassisted humankind was astrolatry, or worship of the heavenly bodies.[58] The most commonplace religious systems in the pagan world were polytheistic. This was partly because pagan philosophers were not true natural philosophers, lacking any "sure way of purchasing knowledge, by following a long train of experiments," meaning their theologies were built on "fancy and imagination," "abstract reasoning" and "hypotheses [made] at random."[59]

The *Necessity of Revelation* was a contribution to the well-established genre of histories of idolatry newly strengthened in the language of recent natural and sceptical philosophy. Certainly, Campbell's account

---

[54] Campbell (1739, pp. 81–82, esp. fn. B, pp. 169–170; and, most fully, pp. 183–186 fn. C).

[55] Campbell (1739, pp. 71–72, 388). See also p. 191. For thoughtful discussion of Campbell's work, see Loughlin (2019, 2020).

[56] Campbell (1739, pp. 102, 340). See also pp. 100–101.

[57] Campbell (1739, pp. 221, 262). See also pp. 228, 281.

[58] Campbell (1739, pp. 200, 206).

[59] Campbell (1739, p. 262). See also pp. 286, 346.

of a fall away from an initial theism based on revelation, due to the consequences of human inattention, forgetting, sin and priestcraft, was a staple of contemporary mythography. But he utilised the scientific language of collecting "observations" and described the act of extrapolating conclusions from these examples as "experiments" and the conclusions themselves as demonstrable "matters of fact."[60] The appeals to Bacon and Newton in *Necessity of Revelation* are some of the most direct and extensive found during the Scottish Enlightenment, but Campbell was participating in religious controversy and had co-opted the burgeoning "science of human nature" to give lustre to long-held arguments. The book was no dispassionate social scientific study of religion but a combative polemic; Campbell was conducting a scientific study of human nature but did not describe himself as writing a "science of man."

As with Turnbull, Campbell's application of natural philosophical methods to the study of human nature was different to the natural histories of religion of the social theorists of the High Scottish Enlightenment. But Campbell's innovative scientific framing set him apart from Turnbull's humanist leanings; the former wrote as a modern, the latter's arguments were replete with citations of the ancients.[61] Campbell's evidence base was limited to pagan societies and philosophers in the centuries between the Flood and the coming of Christ, though he believed he was drawing conclusions of universal applicability and pointed to recent studies of Eastern and New World religion as proving his claims. Campbell did not write a conjectural or stadial history of religious development. Religious change was understood in terms of degeneration, not progress, with decline explained in terms of both distance from the Noachite moment of direct revelation and the weakness of reason. Socio-politico-economic contexts were not relevant: Campbell treated his ancient philosophers *en masse*.

Despite the innovative scientific framing of *Necessity of Revelation*, the work was out of step with the enlightened discussions of religion that followed, and no mention of Campbell's methods can be found amongst the texts of the High Scottish Enlightenment's science of man. The lack of influence of the *Necessity* in the succeeding decades, despite its

[60] E.g. Campbell (1739, pp. 23–30, 199–200, 219, 262, 292, 359).

[61] Indeed, for all the commentary on Turnbull's 'Newtonianism,' the most cited author, by some distance, is Cicero.

methodological innovation, reflects how the social theorists of the High Scottish Enlightenment were not participating in theological controversies, at least not directly. They pursued a separate study: the "science of man" and, subsequently, its correlate, the "history of mankind." Campbell's methodological framing was new, but the genre he was contributing to (histories of idolatry) and the conclusion he drew (the necessity of revelation) were not. Campbell reiterated the commonplace early modern argument that the pagans were entirely incapable of achieving knowledge of theism when they did not have access to revelation or because they had forgotten the Noachite tradition. He did so, similarly, on the equally well-established grounds of the absolute limits of postlapsarian reason. But he supported these positions with a new "scientism" inspired by recent sceptical philosophy and Baconian and Newtonian natural philosophy.

DAVID HUME'S *TREATISE* AND THE "SCIENCE OF MAN"

Hume's *Treatise of Human Nature* is the third of our Scottish philosophical works published c. 1739–1740 which articulated a new scientific approach to the study of religion and human nature. Hume's philosophical output from 1739 onwards as containing a strong degree of consistency and of many of the arguments on religious topics existing in outline or by implication in the *Treatise*. More generally, the Scottish science of man, especially when it came to the discussion of the relationship between religion and human nature, ultimately owed considerably more to Hume's *Treatise* than it did either Turnbull's *Principles* or Campbell's *Necessity*. Much of the High Scottish Enlightenment discussion on religion consisted of responses to Hume's "Of Miracles," "Of a Particular Providence and a Future State" and the NHR. These texts, in various ways, can be traced back to the *Treatise*.

Seeing the *Treatise* as key to the Scottish "science of human nature's" discussion of religion involves first substantiating the claim that Hume's *Treatise* was concerned with religious topics. Despite Hume's famous claim in the Introduction that the "science of man" should be the basis of all other sciences, including that of "natural religion," the *Treatise* has often been read as devoid of religious implications.[62] Instead, the conclusions about human nature that Hume drew in the *Treatise* were only

---

[62] T 0.4.

subsequently applied to religious topics in his later writings. Certainly, this reading fits in with our understanding of some of Hume's thought processes when composing the *Treatise*. In December 1737, Hume told Henry Home, Lord Kames, that he had cut off the "noble parts" of the *Treatise* that were sceptical of the reality of miracles and, possibly, also removed a section equally sceptical about the immortality of the soul, in an effort to "give as little offence" to religious readers as possible.[63] This still left the space open for the offence Hume deemed necessary, and the irreligious implications of his arguments would have been obvious to any attentive reader versed in early modern European philosophy—that is, the *Treatise*'s intended audience.[64] In March 1738, Hume wrote again to Kames, expressing his belief that adoption of Hume's "principles" would "produce almost a total alteration in philosophy."[65] Such an alteration would include a transformation of the understanding of early modern European philosophy's principal focus: natural theology. Situating Hume's *Treatise* into the context of contemporary philosophy, the commonality of subject matter and irreligious implications of Hume's arguments are clear. Arguments that view the *Treatise* as being devoid of religious implications necessarily are ones that read it outside of its cultural and intellectual context.[66]

Even after Hume's gutting of its most controversial elements, there are several textual indications that the *Treatise* spoke to religious themes. Hume signalled to his readers that the "science of man" would have profound implications for our knowledge about the "nature of superior powers" and their "disposition towards us, and our duties towards them."[67] He was offering a "foundation almost entirely new" upon which the "system of sciences" should be rebuilt.[68] Natural religion was one of those sciences that would have to be thought about in new ways. Like other species of "philosophy," it involved the process of "assigning new

[63] Hume to Henry Home, 2 December 1737, Greig (1932, vol. i, p. 24).

[64] Russell (2008) and Wright (2009, p. 30). Guimarães (2009) is less persuasive because it infers a naturalistic account of religion from the *Treatise*.

[65] Hume to Henry Home, 13 February 1939, Greig (1932, vol. i, p. 26).

[66] The idea that the *Treatise* lacked religious significance cannot explain, for example, the campaign to prevent Hume from being appointed to the chair of philosophy at Edinburgh in 1745. See Emerson (1994) and Stewart (2022, Ch. 5).

[67] T 0.4.

[68] T 0.6.

causes and principles to phenomena, which appear in the visible world."[69] Philosophers needed to become "thoroughly acquainted with the extent and force of human understanding, ... the nature of ideas we employ, and the operations we perform in our reasonings."[70] Hume's profound if often implicit message in the *Treatise*, drawn out in later writings, was that human reason was profoundly inadequate for acquiring natural theological knowledge.

While many of the concepts and arguments found in the *Treatise* appeared in Hume's later writings and in the contributions of other enlightened Scots, we should not view Hume as fixing the parameters of the study of religion that followed. Key innovations were to come from other authors. Notably, what is absent from those passages explicitly and implicitly referencing religion in the *Treatise* is the sense of the progress of religion over time in changing societal surroundings. The benefits of such an approach to the study of religion might be inferred from a reading of Book III of the *Treatise*. This assessment could be extended to Hume's writings in the 1740s too, with a shift in his approach towards a more historicised understanding of human nature occurring in the late 1740s and early 1750s.[71] Indeed, it was Hume's relative and intellectual interlocutor Kames who, with the *Principles*, published the High Scottish Enlightenment's first treatment of religion that emphasised the singular importance societal context, though not yet with the historical detail of the "history of mankind."

REFERENCES

Ahnert, Thomas. 2007. The 'Science of Man' in the Moral and Political Philosophy of George Turnbull (1698–1748). *Acta Philosophica Fennica* 83: 89–104.

———. 2015. *The Moral Culture of the Scottish Enlightenment*. London: Yale University Press.

Baumstark, Mortiz. 2008. David Hume: The Making of a Philosophical History: A Reconsideration. PhD thesis, University of Edinburgh.

---

[69] T 1.4.7.13.

[70] T 0.4.

[71] See Baumstark (2008) and Harris (2015, p. 252). For an argument that Hume's philosophical thinking was underpinned by conjectural historical analyses from the *Treatise* onwards, see Faria (2022).

Campbell, Archibald. 1730. *Discourse Proving That the Apostles Were No Enthusiasts*, 2nd ed. London.
———. 1733a. *An Enquiry into the Original of Moral Virtue*. Edinburgh.
———. 1733b. *Oratio de vanitate luminis naturae*. Edinburgh.
———. 1736. *Professor Campbell's Further Explications*. Edinburgh.
———. 1739. *The Necessity of Revelation*. London.
Carey, Daniel. 2006. *Locke, Shaftesbury, and Hutcheson: Contesting Diversity in the Enlightenment and Beyond*. Cambridge: Cambridge University Press.
Demeter, Tamás. 2016. *David Hume and the Culture of Scottish Newtonianism: Methodology and Ideology in Enlightenment Inquiry*. Leiden, NL: Brill.
Emerson, Roger L. 1994. The 'Affair' at Edinburgh and the 'Project' at Glasgow: The Politics of Hume's Attempts to Become a Professor. In *Hume and Hume's Connexions*, ed. M.A. Stewart and John P. Wright, 1–22. Edinburgh: Edinburgh University Press.
Faria, Pedro. 2022. The Structure of Hume's Historical Thought Before the *History of England*. *Intellectual History Review*. https://doi.org/10.1080/17496977.2022.2154998 [Accessed on 21 December 2022].
Greig, J. Y. T., ed. 1932. *The Letters of David Hume*, 2 vols. Oxford: Clarendon Press.
Guimarães, Livia. 2009. Skepticism and Religious Belief in *A Treatise of Human Nature*. In *Skepticism in the Modern Age: Building on the Work of Richard Popkin*, ed. Maia Neto, José Raimundo, Gianni Paganini, and John Christian Laursen, 345–364. Leiden: Brill.
Harris, James. 2015. *David Hume: An Intellectual Biography*. Cambridge: Cambridge University Press.
Loughlin, Felicity. 2019. Socrates and Religious Debate in the Scottish Enlightenment. In *Brill's Companion to the Reception of Socrates*, ed. Christopher Moore, 658–681. Leiden: Brill.
———. 2020. The Pagan Supernatural in the Scottish Enlightenment. In *The Supernatural in Early Modern Scotland*, ed. Julian Goodcare and Martha McGill. Manchester: Manchester University Press.
Mills, R.J.W. 2015. Archibald Campbell's *Necessity of Revelation* (1739)—The Science of Human Nature's First Study of Religion. *History of European Ideas* 41: 728–746.
———. 2021. *The Religious Innatism Debate in Early Modern Britain: Intellectual Change Beyond Locke*. Basingstoke: Palgrave Macmillan.
Russell, Paul. 2008. *The Riddle of Hume's Treatise*. Oxford: Oxford University Press.
Stewart, M.A. 2022. *Hume's Philosophy in Historical Perspective*. Oxford: Oxford University Press.
Turnbull, George. 1731. *Christianity Neither False Nor Useless, Tho' Not as Old as the Creation*. London.

———. [1740] 2005. *The Principles of Moral and Christian Philosophy*, 2 vols., ed. Alexander Broadie. Indianapolis, IN: Liberty Fund.

———. 2014. *Education for Life. Correspondence and Writings on Religion and Practical Philosophy*, ed. M.A. Stewart and Paul B. Wood. Indianapolis, IN: Liberty Fund.

Wright, John P. 2009. *Hume's 'A Treatise of Human Nature': An Introduction*. Cambridge: Cambridge University Press.

CHAPTER 3

David Hume and the Emptiness of Natural Religion

Abstract This chapter surveys Hume's discussion of the relationship between religious belief and human nature in works aside from the "Natural History of Religion" (1757). The religious consequences of Hume's arguments in the *Treatise of Human Nature* (1739–1740) were largely left implicit. From his *Essays, Moral and Political* (1741–1742) onwards, Hume provided a deeply sceptical, provocative account about natural religion, which set the philosophical agenda of the High Scottish Enlightenment's discussion of religion. The conclusions Hume drew were profound: the limits of reason and experience meant that religious belief could not legitimately extend beyond a minimal theism; belief in revealed religion was irrational; that religion was usually detrimental to individual and societal well-being; and yet religious belief was a permanent feature of life.

Keywords David Hume · Sceptical philosophy · "Science of man" · Minimal theism · Natural religion · Scottish Enlightenment

Hume's "science of man" as set out in the *Treatise* would inform the High Scottish Enlightenment's discussion of religion, with much of what followed in oblique, though sometimes explicit, dialogue with Hume's theories.[1] The conclusions Hume drew from his philosophy of human nature were profound in their implications: the limits of reason and experience meant that belief in natural religion beyond a minimal theism and revealed religion were non-rational and often irrational, but the same characteristics of human nature meant that religious belief was a permanent feature of life. He wanted "dogmatical reasoners" to realise the "strange infirmities of human understanding" and, suitably humbled, to back off from bigotry and persecution.[2] The traditional understanding of moral philosophy tied it to the God's book of nature and the view that, ultimately, the study of morality told us about God's creation and intentions for man. Hume's study of human nature sought to replace, to borrow Tamas Demeter's phrase, the "dominant ideology of enquiry" that made sense of man with ultimate reference to God and replace it with "secular methodological standards."[3]

Likewise, we can extend Stephen Buckle's conclusion about Hume's *Enquiry concerning Human Understanding* to all Hume's writings on human nature: "to complete the revolution in philosophy," by extending the methods of "mechanical principles to human functioning," would mean nothing less than the "end for the Christian religion," as least in terms of its philosophical credibility.[4] Still, if Hume had the goals of (a) detaching the study of human nature from God and (b) undermining the credibility of Christian theology, then the chapters that follow this one indicate that, to some degree, Hume's efforts were in vain.

The central text of Hume's examination of the relationship between human nature and religion was his "Natural History of Religion" (1757), discussed in a subsequent chapter, but the concepts and arguments used in that dissertation appeared in Hume's earlier writings. Examining Hume's study of the relationship between religion and human nature involves setting aside a distinction Hume drew in the NHR between the origin of religion in reason and the origin of religion in human nature. While useful for demarcating the specific focus of the NHR, and for distinguishing between the ontological enterprise of demonstrating (or not)

---

[1] The large scholarship on Hume's religious thought has covered the topics discussed below in detail. I do not claim originality and owe particular debts to Russell (1995, 2008, 2021) and Holden (2010), though both might disagree with what I am arguing.

[2] EHU 12.24.

[3] Demeter (2016, p. 7). See also Russell (1995).

[4] Buckle (2004, p. 53).

the existence of God and the anthropological enterprise of anatomising human nature, the distinction ran against Hume's claim that "reason is, and ought only to be, the slave of the passions."[5] Much of Hume's philosophy guides us through how our thinking and behaviour are informed by non-rational facets of human nature. Hume's critique of the arguments for natural and revealed religion take the form of exposing how purportedly rational claims are informed by precisely such non-rational aspects of our natures—that is, there is no simple "origin" of religion in reason alone and arguments drawn purportedly from reason often betray the influence of other aspects of human nature.

One underlying message of the *Treatise*, drawn out clearly in the *Enquiry into Human Understanding* (1748), and reiterated in the *Dialogues*, was that nearly all of the claims of natural theology were philosophically unjustifiable. There were no sources of knowledge for the existence and attributes of God or the soul: the "science of man" effectively taught that the "science" of natural theology did not exist and was instead the result of "rash arrogance," "lofty pretensions" and "superstitious credulity."[6] All we can legitimately believe is what Philo in the *Dialogues* termed "philosophical theism," or the proposition that "the cause or causes of order in the universe probably bear some remote analogy to human intelligence."[7] Aside from this very weak rendering of the first cause argument, nothing further could be inferred about either the attributes of or how (indeed, if) man should act towards the cause or causes of order in the universe. All religious belief that went beyond this "minimal theism," and all religious worship per se, was grounded on something other than sound reason and had something other than the first cause as its object. An observation David Berman made of the *Dialogues* can be extended to much of Hume's writings, that he "gradually but devastatingly strips the concept of God of religious meaning."[8]

---

[5] T 2.3.3.4.

[6] EHU 5.1.

[7] DNR 12.34. See also Gaskin (1983). Harris cautions against equating Philo with Hume's own position: "the point of the *Dialogues* was not for Hume to establish a position of his own, for, properly speaking, he had not position to advocate. It was, rather, to present the case for theism [via Cleanthes], and to show it crumbles almost into nothing under rational examination [by Philo]," see Harris (2015, p. 447).

[8] Berman (1988, p. 103).

Hume leaves us, as Robert Fogelin puts it, "with an anaemic deity no theist would find acceptable."[9]

A couple of remarks in the *Dialogues*, moreover, suggest that "philosophical theism" might be one of those beliefs that human nature is framed to develop instinctively and without resort to reasoning. Hume has Cleanthes, in the vein of Shaftesbury, Hutcheson and especially Kames, ask Philo whether "from your own feeling … if the idea of a contriver does not immediately flow in upon you with a force like that of a sensation."[10] Certainly Philo goes on to reject that any such sensation has any validity as evidence for the existence of God such as the religious nativist argument of early modern apologetics would hold. But he does, at the end of the *Dialogues*, concur with Cleanthes that belief in some invisible intelligent power behind the effects observed in nature is instinctive and that "suspense of judgement" is impossible.[11] The issue was clearly on Hume's mind in the early 1750s, when both the *Dialogues* and NHR were composed. In his 10 March 1751 letter to Gilbert Elliot of Minto, Hume drew a distinction between this instinctive sense of providential creation and the anthropomorphic pareidolia that characterises most religious belief.[12] At first blush, there is a contradiction with the argument made in the NHR, where Hume claimed that the "universal propensity to believe in invisible intelligent power" was not an "original instinct."[13] But what is being discussed in the *Dialogues* is a concerted moment of considering the universe, whereas the NHR discusses the formation of belief an inevitable aspect of the normal working of human nature. For our concerns in this chapter, we can note that, for Philo and unlike the

---

[9] Fogelin (2017, p. 124).

[10] DNR 3.7. There is a certainly a temptation to conjecture that, given Hume's *Dialogues* was written around the time that Kames's *Principles* was published, Cleanthes was based to some degree on Kames. For a suitably cautious but informative discussion see Stewart (2022, p. 297–302), arguing that Cleanthes might a composite figure reflecting the "enlightened experimental theism" of the 1750s, of which Kames was a prominent proponent. Still, in terms of contextualising Hume's *Dialogues* and NHR, commentators have largely overlooked the possible significance of Kames's *Principles* for both texts.

[11] DNR 12.6.

[12] Hume to Gilbert Elliot of Minto, 10 March 1751, Greig (1932, vol. I, pp. 153–154). See also Fosl (2019, pp. 240–241).

[13] NHR 15.5.

tradition of providentailist naturalism associated with Kames, the instinctive belief in a cause behind creation tells us next to nothing about that cause.

Hume's philosophy of human nature taught that natural religion was an outlier in the "complete system of the sciences."[14] While the focus of the "science of man" should be the fields of "common life," in the realm of natural religion, as Philo puts it in the *Dialogues*, "we are like foreigners in a strange country."[15] In the *Treatise*, Hume stated that when we go beyond the "narrow compass" of our experience and think about the "heavens," we enter a "world of its own," full of "scenes, and beings, and objects, which are altogether new."[16] As we have no experience of the heavens, however, this world exists only in the "universe of the imagination."[17] In *EHU*, Hume held many of the key themes of natural religion—the "origin of worlds," the "economy of the intellectual system" and the "region of spirits"—were all "beyond the reach of humanity capacity."[18] Anatomising human nature teaches us that there are extensive, absolute limits to our knowledge of the traditional themes of natural theology. Theologians and philosophers who stretch beyond these limits when discussing "so remote and incomprehensible" a topic often, Hume claimed in language distinctly reminiscent of Thomas Hobbes, "savours more of flattery and panegyric than of just reasoning, and sound philosophy."[19]

In the *Treatise*, though his Introduction had alerted readers to their presence, the irreligious consequences of Hume's account of human nature for the central concepts of natural theology remained implicit. His treatment of notions of absolute time, absolute space, notions of infinity and the soul, however, turned on the limits of our experience. At root, "we can never have reason to believe that any object exists, of which we cannot form an idea," and we have no ideas on any of these objects.[20]

---

[14] T 0.6.

[15] DNR 1.10.

[16] T 1.2.6.8.

[17] T 1.2.6.8.

[18] EHU 8.1.

[19] EHU 11.27. For a discussion stressing the strong similarities between Hobbes and Hume see Russell (2008). See also Sagar (2018).

[20] T 1.3.14.36.

Each was absolutely essential to natural theology, but each was empty of cognitive content.[21] The irreligious implications of Hume's "science of man" were made clearer in the *EHU*, especially in the essays "Of Miracles" and "Of a Particular Providence and of a Future State." Hume stated that the tools of "experience and observation and analogy" leave us with little knowledge of the first cause.[22] The natural and revealed foundations of Christianity cannot be supported using the "principles of human reason."[23] Towards the end of *EHU* Hume would write that, indeed, "divinity or theology" had a "foundation in reason," but only "so far as it is supported by experience."[24] Hume's reader would have not forgotten that we have no experience of pretty much all the concepts central to early modern Christian theology.

The end of Hume's *EHU* contained several statements that were especially provocative in their implications. Famously, Hume made the bold injunction that if a work of "divinity or school metaphysics" contained neither mathematical nor experiential reasoning it consisted of "nothing but sophistry and illusion" and could be committed "to the flames."[25] In their place, Hume encouraged his readers to confine their judgements to "common life, and to such subjects as fall under daily practice and experience."[26] This reiterated the message of the *Treatise*, that philosophy should be our "guide," in "preference to superstition of every kind or denomination."[27] The human mind, constantly agitating, does not rest on the objects of common life, but if we set aside theology for philosophy, adopt "mild and moderate sentiments" and turn the concerns of our inquiries into "objects of a cold and general speculation," we might avoid the excesses of superstition.[28] We might still develop erroneous beliefs, but while "errors in religion and dangerous; those in philosophy [are] only ridiculous."[29]

---

[21] For deeper discussion see Yandell (1990), Russell (2008), Holden (2010) and Yoder (2011).

[22] EHU 11.30.

[23] EHU 10.40.

[24] EHU 12.32.

[25] EHU 12.34.

[26] EHU 12.25.

[27] T 1.4.7.13.

[28] T 1.4.7.13.

[29] T 1.4.7.13.

Religion, Imagination and the Passions

Hume maintained that the passions and the imagination were the principal factors involved in framing religious belief. We are concerned about futurity, yet we lack any experiential "foundation to rest upon" to judge.[30] It is the "vivacity" of our impressions and ideas that is the "requisite circumstance" to inform our passions.[31] But our notions of futurity or supernatural power have no real content, and we are thus never able to be rest easy in our beliefs. The lack of concrete evidence, combined with our natural concern about the future, excites our passions, hope and fear, and these take control of our thinking. Specifically, the passions influence the imagination, leaving us prone to create superstitious fictions that, by turns, quell and inflame our anxieties. Similarly, without experience of supernatural power that might guide our notions of futurity, our passions direct us to undertake a "narrow and more natural survey of their object," transferring our attention towards worldly objects.[32] We are natural idolators.

Any attempt to discern a fixed notion of God is unsustainable and causes mental anguish. Inevitably, we are drawn to forms of belief and worship that are informed by (a) the senses and non-rational parts of human nature encouraging a focus on (b) objects in the natural world. In the *Treatise*, Hume noted that Catholics used sensual aids to contemplateGod, given that notions of such "distant and immaterial objects" otherwise "decay away."[33] A few years later, in the essay "The Sceptic" (1742), Hume claimed that all "popular superstition" dealt with our inability to comprehend an "abstract, invisible object" by providing worldly objects that affect "the senses and imagination."[34] The "philosophical devotion" of the theologian is no different. As epitomised by the individual captured in "The Platonist" essay that precedes "The Sceptic," such moments of supposed religious clarity are only ever the "transitory

---

[30] P 1.13.

[31] T 2.3.6.10.

[32] EHU 8.34.

[33] T 1.3.8.4. See also EHU 5.16.

[34] Sc 23. I acknowledge the need for scepticism about the complete identification of the figure of the "Sceptic" with Hume's own position, e.g., Watkins (2019, pp. 102–103), but view the essay as clearly in line with Hume's arguments as expressed elsewhere. See also Holden (2010, pp. 61–62) and Stewart (2022, pp. 94–95).

effect of high spirits, great leisure, a fine genius, and a habit of study or contemplation."[35] The devotion of the theologian reflects a state of enthusiasm, believing that God is directly communicating with them, developed in very specific circumstances, rather than the actual identification of a clear idea of God. It is characteristic of how all religion has the essential character of resulting from humans attempting to paper over their limitations.

Focused consideration on supernatural power was impossible; idolatry was inevitable result of this impossibility and needed to be managed, as it could never be extirpated. In the *History of England*, Hume described how attempts by the Church of Scotland in the early seventeenth century to limit worship to "contemplation of that divine essence, which discovers itself to the understanding only," inevitably collapsed into a peculiar form of idolatry.[36] Such a "species of devotion" was "little suitable to human frailty," leading to anxiety and a variety of self-destructive and socially dangerous behaviours, such as obsessional inner contemplation, self-deceiving rapture and withdrawal from society.[37] The Kirk having banned all sensual aids to worship but unable to eradicate the need within human nature to have an experiential locus for religious sentiment, led to its ministers to idolatrise their "own mystical comments on the scriptures."[38] If we wish to maintain our religious devotion, Hume's Sceptic stated, we must "find some method of affecting the senses and the imagination," as reason and experience were not fit for the purpose.[39] Failing to appreciate the idolatry-prone quality of human nature would lead to misguided attempts to stop sensual worship, leading to the pressures of fixing on some tangible object bleeding out into other locations or behaviours.

Hume had explained in the *Treatise* how the same arguments held for belief in an immaterial, immortal soul subject to future rewards and punishments.[40] The notion of a "future state is so far removed from our comprehension" that, whatever arguments we can develop for

---

[35] Sc 23.

[36] H 5:47.34.

[37] H 5:47.34.

[38] H 5:47.34.

[39] Sc 23.

[40] Here influenced by Russell (2008, pp. 141–142). I acknowledge the criticism of Russell's account of the *Treatise*, e.g. Harris (2015, p. 499 fn. 163), that it includes a "determined effort to find 'irreligion' on almost every page." It's only found on *some* pages.

its existence, the idea never has "sufficient authority and force."[41] We do not actually believe in the immortality of the soul and, regardless of our professions about its existence, the idea does not influence our behaviour. The weakness of the analogy between our present life and a future one after bodily death "entirely destroys belief" in the existence of an immortal soul.[42] The fact we have no direct experience of either soul or afterlife, and the analogy between our life in the here and now and any future one was so weak, explained why the "bulk of mankind" were practical atheists, motivated by immediate pleasure and pain alone.[43] "Eminent theologians" claim that the multitude are "really infidels in their hearts," but Hume responded it was not sinfulness that was the problem but that the notions involved were too obscure to affect behaviour.[44] No-one can hold belief in immortality or afterlife with a "true and established judgement," all we can attain is a "faint idea ... of our future condition."[45] Without vivacity, notions of soul and afterlife have no "authority" over either our passions or will.[46]

We thus find in the *Treatise* hints of Hume's argument in later writings that certain religious tenets did not influence day to day behaviour. We are naturally incredulous about life after death due to the "want of resemblance to the present life."[47] What most people spend their time worrying about is not the state of their immortal souls, but "what may happen after their death, provided it regard *this* world."[48] Hume's other example here further illuminates his position that even the most zealous "really do not believe what they affirm concerning a future state."[49] The sensible amongst the Roman Catholics share the same disgust at the cruelty and barbarity of the Gunpowder Plot or the St Bartholomew's Day Massacre as their Protestant counterparts. But these Protestants are the same people that they "without any scruple ... condemn to eternal and

[41] T 1.3.9.13.
[42] T. 1.3.9.14.
[43] T 1.3.9.13.
[44] T 1.3.9.13.
[45] T 1.3.9.13.
[46] T 1.3.9.14.
[47] T 1.3.9.13.
[48] T 1.3.9.14. My italics.
[49] T 1.3.9.14.

infinite punishments"—unless, as Hume wryly notes, they do not actually believe in the reality of those punishments.[50] If people truly believed the teachings of their religion, they would have to believe their neighbours were going to burn in hell, but their day to day interactions suggested they do not, *really*, believe this. Moreover, in the *Treatise* and the *EPM*, Hume's account of moral philosophy is a purely secular affair in which, to borrow phrasing from Thomas Holden, the "promise of divine sanctions and rewards is both ineffective and unnecessary."[51]

The power of religious ideas, however, seems to alternate, depending on the circumstances, between belief and disbelief.[52] The superstitious beliefs that do have "authority" over us emerge out of several non-rational facets and principles of human nature responding to the very real human lot of temporal suffering and natural theological ignorance. These were the passions of hope and fear, the workings of the imagination, man's anthropomorphic tendencies and our quickness to vehemence in disputes over speculative matters. In "Of the Passions" (1757), Hume claimed that the "production and conduct of the passions" was subject to a "certain regular mechanism" comparable to the general laws of natural discovered by natural philosophy.[53] This dissertation, streamlining the analysis of Book II of the *Treatise*, outlined how the direct passions of hope and fear are "derived from the probability of any good or evil" resulting from an unexpected or unexplained natural event.[54] The mind is "incessantly tossed" between the two over the outcome of a future event.[55] But ultimately uncertainty has a stronger "connection with fear," and similarly "everything that is unexpected affrights us," and thus, it is fear which dominates our mental worlds.[56] The workings of the direct passion of fear are especially relevant for understanding the superstitious tendencies of human nature. Our experience of the sensation of fear "naturally

---

[50] T 1.3.9.14.

[51] Holden (2020, p. 239).

[52] Guimarães (2009, p. 361).

[53] P 6.19. This was one of Hume's *Four Dissertations* (1757), on which see Harris (2015, pp. 354–368) and Merivale (2018).

[54] P 1.8.

[55] P 1.8.

[56] P 1.19; T 2.3.9.26.

converts into the thing itself, and gives us a real apprehension of evil."[57] We attribute the fear we experience to the actually existing fearfulness of some external object: the mind "always forms its judgements more from its present disposition than from the nature of its objects."[58]

Our passions, aroused by the sudden or threatening events experienced in nature, motivate the mind to form beliefs about supposed supernatural power. It is the faculty of the imagination, however, that forms these beliefs. The "imagination of man [is] delighted with whatever is remote and extraordinary" and quickly runs "without control" away from daily experience.[59] Motivated by the passions, the imagination creates fictions about the existence, character and motivations of supposed invisible, intelligent power. Informing this process is the imagination's propensity to rest on touchable or viewable objects when we are in a state of agitated confusion. The mind is directed away from obscure notions of invisible power and towards vivid ones of "sensible objects," as the latter "have always a greater influence on the fancy."[60]

Informing the imagination's creation of superstitious fictions was the anthropomorphic tendency of the human mind. Hume identified this in the *Treatise* as the "great propensity" of the mind "to spread itself on external objects, and to conjoin with them any internal impressions, which they occasion."[61] We "bestow on external objects the same emotions, which [human nature] observes in itself; and to find everywhere those ideas, which are most present to it."[62] Our inherent anthropomorphism, Hume opined in a 1743 letter to William Mure, enabled most believers to degrade God "into a resemblance of themselves, and by that means render him more comprehensible."[63] In *EHU*, Hume criticised theologians for their tendency to consider themselves "in the place of the supreme being" when making their purely speculative judgements of God's attributes and conduct.[64] Similarly, Philo observed in the *Dialogues* how the multitude

[57] T 2.3.9.26.
[58] T 2.3.9.26.
[59] EHU 12.25.
[60] T 1.3.8.4.
[61] T 1.3.14.25.
[62] T 1.4.3.11.
[63] Hume to William Mure June 1743, Greig (1932, vol. I, p. 51).
[64] EHU 11.27.

at best view their god(s) as having "human passions," and at worst they depress "the Deity far below the condition of mankind."[65]

The most significant of these three was the influence of the passions. Whenever fear or hope "enter into religion," as Philo puts it in the *Dialogues*, they form a "species of divinity, suitable to itself."[66] This was a partial reiteration of the analysis in Hume's "Of Superstition and Enthusiasm" (1741).[67] Here, he had argued that if fear dominated an individual's thoughts about religion the result was superstition, or the dread-infused belief in "infinite unknown evils."[68] If hope dominated then the result was enthusiasm, or the belief in the "immediate inspiration of that divine being, who is the object of devotion."[69] Which passion dominated depended on an individual's character or their life circumstances. Superstition and fanaticism were not fixed aspects, Philo noted, an individual could "run into the other extreme" as their life changed.[70] Man is "subject to certain unaccountable terrors and apprehensions," resulting from unhappy life circumstances, ill health, "a gloomy and melancholic disposition" or a combination of these three.[71] The melancholic, dejected individual broods upon the "terrors of the invisible world" and thereby plunges "himself still deeper in affliction."[72] When there are no "real objects of terror" present, we find "imaginary ones, to whose power and malevolence" our minds set "no limits."[73] Enthusiasm resulted from a similar aetiology. In moments of "unaccountable elevation and presumption," and feelings of pride, strength and power, the quotidian objects of common life seem inadequate to explain such sentiments.[74] Instead,

[65] DNR 12.31, 12.32.

[66] DNR 12.29.

[67] Nick Phillipson described this essay as "the starting point for nearly all subsequent secular thinking about the history of religion." See Phillipson (2011). But it was also an instance of common type of article that appeared in the British magazines and periodicals in the early eighteenth century.

[68] SE 2.

[69] SE 3.

[70] DNR 12.29.

[71] SE 2.

[72] DNR 12.29.

[73] SE 2.

[74] SE 3.

the imagination indulges in "raptures, transports and surprising flights of fancy," and thus "swells with great, but confused conceptions," which the enthusiast attributes to the "immediate inspiration" of God.[75]

Of the two, hope and fear, it is "terror," as Philo puts it when trying to convince Cleanthes of the social disutility of religion, that is the "primary principle of religion."[76] When the imagination is assisted by fear, we readily project imagined fictions onto the world. We are scared by threatening events or about our futures, but we lack direct supernatural objects onto which we can latch our fears. Instead, we raise up "imaginary enemies" and "daemons" out of our fancy, Philo explains, and these "haunt [man] with superstitions terrors."[77] "Superstition" molests the "anxious breast of wretched mortals."[78] Humans do not find "consolation in religion" and are inherently "gloomy and melancholy" about their future.[79] The prospect of death is so "shocking to nature" that we can only think of it with gloom, and it is this gloom that influences most people's sense of life after death as something characterised by "devils and torrents of fire and brimstone."[80] Religion is not only ineffective in bringing us happiness; it actively reduces it. In arguing that religion neither consoled nor is essential to the moral life, Hume, at least in the guise of Philo, differed profoundly with his contemporaries.

Another principle of human nature is relevant here. Hume identified an innate tendency in man to be "shocked and disturbed" by worldviews contrary to our own. We quickly engage in disputation over even "the most speculative and indifferent opinions."[81] This principle, Hume noted in "Of Parties in General" (1741), was the "origin of all religious wars and divisions," exaggerated by the fact that we are sensitive to the very shaky foundations our religious beliefs are built on.[82] In the *History of England*, Hume recited the views of the Elizabethan defender of religious toleration, Cardinal Pole, that "polemical divines" treated their opponents with

---

[75] SE 3.
[76] DNR 12.29.
[77] DNR 10.11.
[78] DNR 10.11.
[79] DNR 10.27.
[80] DNR 10.28.
[81] PG 12.
[82] PG 13.

"impatience."[83] They did so, Hume noted, because they held theological beliefs they "neither clearly comprehend, nor entirely believe," and respond with "zealotry and persecution" when easily "shaken in their imagined faith."[84] We hold our theological beliefs, that we do not and cannot understand, as sacrosanct and respond with vituperation against those who we believe dispute those beliefs. As discussed more later, Hume viewed the establishment of Christianity, as the perversion of philosophy into theology, as leading to the continued excitation of this inherent principle to disputation.

Whereas the non-rational elements of human nature are behind the formation of most religious beliefs, all beliefs, including presumably those of natural religion, that stem from "very refined reflections have little or no influence upon us."[85] The "conclusions" of such reflections "vanish" as soon as we "leave our closet and engage in the common affairs of life."[86] Unlike the other authors discussed in this book, Hume did not believe that, as James Harris puts it, the "doctrines of natural religion are able to counteract feelings of resentment and despair."[87] Imagining a case where a man who is being tortured, Hume notes dryly in the *EHU* that "you would surely more irritate than appease" him if you recommended he to take comfort from a sense of providential order in the universe.[88] It is tempting to think that John Gregory had this passage in mind when, as discussed later on, he suggested that the sceptical philosopher would only cause further distress should their disseminate their views—that we cannot prove the existence of God, the soul or the afterlife—to recently bereaved parents.

Hume's argument here raises two questions about his account of the origin and character of religious beliefs. First, the claim that abstract reasoning does not inform our belief or action for long raises the question of whether Hume believed his science of man would change the theological opinions of his readers. But, while admitting the possibility that the arguments of the *Treatise* might have no effect, Hume forbore

---

[83] H 3:37.2.

[84] H 3:37.2.

[85] T 1.4.7.7. Here I am drawing on Harris (2004, esp. 247–251) and Harris (2005).

[86] T 3.1.1.1.

[87] Harris (2004, p. 248).

[88] EHU 8.34.

giving up on his own chains of reasoning, given that to do so would "cut off entirely all science and philosophy," and he believed the new science of man could establish a "system or set of opinions [that] might stand the test of the most critical examination."[89] Second, given that sustained changes of reasoning do not inform our belief for long, why should we be concerned about speculative theology or commonplace religious errors? Hume's answer seems to be that popular superstitions tend to rouse the violent passions; speculative theology, more appositely, becomes a problem when the theologian exits their closet and expects the world to adhere to their newly developed views.[90] The problem is thus the power that the theologian has within a society, for their beliefs would be as harmless as the philosophers without such power and an accompanying expectation that they should use it.

The Psychology of Miracles

So far, we have been examining how Hume believed that the limits of human nature prevented the formation of rationally-grounded religious beliefs. In this he could share the stage with theologians who ridiculed the vanity of human reason and stressed the necessity of revelation for our knowledge of true religion. Moreover, as commentators regularly note, Hume frequently struck a fideist note in his writings, such as when he ended the *EHU* claiming that the "best and most solid foundation" of "divinity or theology" is "faith and divine revelation," rather than appeals to reason and experience.[91] Such posturing could have acted as a defence against accusations of impiety or worse, but equally, as in the case of "Of Miracles," allowed Hume to indulged in some ribbing of his religious readers.[92] But Hume extended his scepticism to revealed religion too—indeed, in the very same *EHU* where he claimed revelation should be the basis of theology—and on the same grounds that the inherent tendencies of human nature informed our easy susceptibility to ridiculous

---

[89] T 1.4.7.9, 1.4.7.14.

[90] Costelloe (2018, pp. 272–273).

[91] EHU 12.32.

[92] For an example of discussion of Hume using fideism as a pre-emptive defence see Box (1990, p. 212). On the issue of ridicule, compare the analyses of Harris (2015, pp. 231–232) and Ahnert (2019). For an account of why Hume was not a fideist see Fogelin (2017, esp. pp. 107–112).

accounts of miraculous events. History is riddled with "forged miracles, and prophecies, and supernatural events," which demonstrated the existence of a "strong propensity of mankind to the extraordinary and the marvellous."[93]

Despite his "castration" that removed discussion of miracles from Book I of the *Treatise*, several claims appeared in that work hinted at the argument of the subsequent "Of Miracles" (1748).[94] The passions of "admiration and surprize" are aroused by "miraculous relations" and spread "over the whole soul."[95] The ideas received from these relations, despite them coming from "quacks and projectors," gain a vivacity that make them resemble "inferences we draw from experience," encouraging us to give such relations more credit than their deserve.[96] In "Of Miracles," Hume expanded on these passing remarks.[97] There is a tendency in human nature to abandon our usual means of reasoning on the "ground of the greatest number of past observations," when faced with something "utterly absurd," and to accept the testimony precisely because it is so unbelievable.[98] The passions aroused by hearing tales of miracles form an "agreeable emotion," which creates a "sensible tendency" to believe said accounts, enjoyable all the more precisely because such testimony seems absurd.[99] Pleasure is also behind the active dissemination of miraculous stories, as tellers experience "pride and delight in exciting the admiration" of those to whom they are telling tales.[100] Likewise, enjoyment is behind the "greediness" of travellers reporting "wonderful adventures, strange men, and uncouth manners."[101]

---

[93] EHU 10.19. I have used Wootton (1990), Siebert (1990), Yandell (1990) and Stewart (2022, Ch. 12).

[94] See Stewart (2022, esp. p. 327).

[95] T 1.3.10.4.

[96] T 1.3.10.4.

[97] James Harris has suggested that "Of Miracles" the work by Hume "which had the biggest impact on his contemporaries." See Harris (2022, p. 6). Similarly, see Fergusson (2019).

[98] EHU 10.16.

[99] EHU 10.16.

[100] EHU 10.16.

[101] EHU 10.17.

3 DAVID HUME AND THE EMPTINESS OF NATURAL RELIGION   73

It is the multitude who spread gossip about miracles, because they are most susceptible to falling for religious imposture. To Hume, the vulgar are ignorant, stupid and primarily motivated by pleasure rather than reason and are all too happy to lap up tales of miracles. By contrast, the learned tend to ignore the same reports—at least initially. Philosophers deem such stories as "too inconsiderable to deserve their attention."[102] But in the absence of learned scrutiny accurate records of the supposed miraculous events perish "beyond recovery," and the supposed truth of the miracle becomes entrenched amongst the "deluded multitude."[103] Another key factor is the relative development of knowledge within a society, with miracles treated as ridiculous populations in refined societies often being accepted as true by peoples further away in less civilised societies.

The "violations of truth" contained within miracle testimony also tells us much about the psychology of the religious enthusiast and their gullible audiences.[104] The credibility of the enthusiast is always doubtful because they tend to be under the influence of "vanity and a heated imagination."[105] Fanaticism can make the believer both "imagine he sees what has no reality" and lie "for the sake of promoting so holy a cause."[106] But equally often the fanatic is not knowingly lying, but actually enters "seriously into the delusion," with the line between truth and falsehood blurred in their mind.[107] Moreover, the fanatic is subject to the great "temptation" to present themselves as an "ambassador from heaven."[108] Hume's discussion indicates an easy blurring of the lines between imposture and fanaticism, where the liar begins to believe their own lies, but he also notes how a fanatic can be influenced by motives, such as pride or greed, beyond their own enthusiasm. A similar assessment can be found in *History of England*. When discussing puritan fanatics, Hume holds that pure religious imposture was "impossible to counterfeit [for] long" because religion is "congenial to the human mind," and thus the imposter

[102] EHU 10.33.
[103] EHU 10.33.
[104] EHU 10.38.
[105] EHU 10.29.
[106] EHU 10.17.
[107] EHU 10.29.
[108] EHU 10.29.

comes to believe to their claims; and that, similarly, fanaticism is easily "warped by those more familiar motives of interest and ambition."[109]

The opinions of the enthusiast's audience are equally dubious. The multitude allow "passion" and a "heated imagination" to "disturb the regularity" of their minds.[110] Explicitly echoing Lucretius, Hume states that the multitude "receive greedily" any report that "sooths superstition"—the adverb "greedily" being the particularly sensuous one that Hume regularly uses when describing the religious follies of the vulgar.[111] Further dangers arise if the enthusiast deploys eloquence that appeals to their "gross and vulgar passions."[112]

The assessment of reports of miracles must be judged against the "known and natural principles of credulity and delusion," as taught by the science of human nature.[113] Nearly all reports of miraculous events come from the vulgar, who are not capable of applying the "fine" methods of detecting religious imposture.[114] Any claim of miraculous happenings was to be doubted because the "knavery and folly of men are such common phenomena," and hence, reported miracles were infinitely more likely to be the result of such credulity than actual violations of the law of nature.[115] Another lesson from the study of man was that the practice of securing power through religious imposture was present in "all ages," as was the fact that the multitude are "much imposed on by ridiculous stories."[116]

The broad lesson of the science of human nature, as applied to accounts of miracles, was that Christian revelation cannot be defended "on the principles of human reason," but must be held on faith alone.[117] That faith could seem increasingly ridiculous if we examined scripture through the lens of the "science of human nature." Scripture was a

---

[109] H 55.100n108. See also Siebert (1990, pp. 101–102).
[110] EHU 10.17.
[111] EHU 10.30; Lucretius, *De rerum natura* 4.593–594.
[112] EHU 10.18.
[113] EHU 10.31.
[114] EHU 10.34.
[115] EHU 10.37.
[116] EHU 10.38.
[117] EHU 10.40.

tissue of marvellous stories first composed by a "barbarous and ignorant people," who would be prone to explaining unusual phenomena by appeals to supernatural power.[118] Similarly, scripture was composed "long after the facts which it relates," meaning it was neither subjected to learned scrutiny at the time nor can it be subject to proper historical criticism now.[119] The only evidence of scripture's miracles was presented by passionate and deluded individuals who either wished their accounts were true or who were pretending they were. The fact that the miracles of scripture resemble those "fabulous accounts which every nation gives of its origin," speaks to the general tendencies of ignorant peoples to make up and to fervently believe their own stories about supernatural power.[120]

Religion's Relationship with Philosophy: Past and Future

Underpinning Hume's recommendation, implicit in the *Treatise* and more explicit in later writings, that his readers abandon natural theology, was his historical claim that Christianity had colonised the practice of philosophy.[121] Pagan philosophy, characterised by the pursuit of truth, was corrupted by Christian theology, which aimed to explain and defend the Christian religion. The core problem for Hume was that theologians are not concerned with the "discovery of truth," but are apologists for their established beliefs who "refute any hypothesis" on the pretext of its "dangerous consequences to religion and morality."[122] This "method of reasoning" was "more common" than any other when it came to theology.[123] In the process, theism had covered up virtue in a "dismal dress."[124] The ability of philosophy to reach the truth required wresting back control from the theologians, and detaching philosophy from the interests of theology.

---

[118] EHU 10.40.
[119] EHU 10.40.
[120] EHU 10.40.
[121] See Livingston (1998, Ch. 5).
[122] T 2.3.2.3. Similarly, EHU 8.26.
[123] T 2.3.2.3.
[124] EPM 9.5; Holden (2020).

Key here were the "accidental causes" in the story of Christianity's rise.[125] The first was the new religion's colonisation of philosophy. Christianity appeared as a belief system in a pagan world in which philosophy was dominant. To persuade potential converts and to defend the new religion, Christian preachers had to be more persuasive than their pagan philosopher critics. The preachers were "obliged to form a system of speculative opinions" and defend their doctrines with "all the subtility of argument and science."[126] The preachers were defending a pre-established set of tenets rather than a way of studying the world, meaning that with the spread of Christianity, the pursuit of truth was abandoned for theology's peculiar combination of self-deception and motivated reasoning. Another accidental cause in the rise of Christianity was that the new religion developed independently and initially in opposition to the "polite part of the world," and to Roman political authority.[127] The result of such independence was the rule of "priestly government" over the new religion and the "separation of the ecclesiastical and civil powers," even when Christianity became the established religion of the Roman Empire.[128] Unfettered by the constraints of political necessity which might push for unity and tolerance, independent ecclesiastical power engendered a "spirit of persecution" against any political or religious rival who challenged the Christian priesthood.[129] Unlike most ancient religions, early Christianity was not a civil theology subordinate to the political needs of society, but demanded to be the inverse.

The rise of speculative theology brought about by Christianity's takeover of philosophy exacerbated the universal propensity of human nature to feel disputatious with those who hold different beliefs. Hume framed this in a broadly progressive context of the spread of philosophy, set out first in the essay "Of Parties in General" (1741) and then reiterated in EHU and in the NHR.[130] In "barbarous and uninstructed" societies, when mankind were "wholly illiterate," rulers and multitude

---

[125] PG 13.
[126] PG 14.
[127] PG 13.
[128] PG 13, PG 14.
[129] PG 13.
[130] EHU 11.3, NHR 11.2.

alike accepted "every pious tale or fiction."[131] Primitive religion mainly consisted in "traditional tales," consumed without "much reasoning or disputation."[132] The mythopoetic beliefs of different sects differed, but this did not bother anyone; similarly, no sect concerned themselves with demonstrating the truth of their traditionary tales, as they were not interested in proving, with certainty, their truth.[133] Subsequently, "philosophy ... spread over the world," with the implication being that it is only at a certain stage of literacy and philosophical development that religious faction emerges.[134] In the *History of England*, Hume claimed that "in all former ages ... religious sects and heresies and schisms" were considered dangerous, "not wholly excepting even those of Greece and Rome."[135] Religious factionalism did not begin with Christianity's takeover of philosophy, only that it reached an unprecedent of vehemence at this point; similarly, the sects of philosophy in the ancient world disputed vehemently over the truth.[136] Rather, it was in the context of a literate, philosophical pagan culture that Christianity had to establish itself. In the process of doing so, the content of popular religion shifted from mythology (stories) to doctrine (tenets), and philosophy was subordinated to theology, and humanity's inherent principle of disputativeness came to the fore. "Keenness in dispute" and "mutual hatred and antipathy" were endemic to early Christian sects, leading to the "greatest misery and devastation."[137] Any "primitive Christianity" that existed was quickly subsumed into the philosophical theology of an insurgent religion, developed to secure victory over established philosophy and religious rivals.[138]

The rise of Christianity was a civilisational turn with disastrous consequences, the theocratisation of the pagan world and, with it, the normalisation of "artificial lives," as normal moral behaviour was crowded out by the demands of ascetic, unsocial Christianity.[139] In the "Dialogue"

[131] PG 13, EHU 11.3.
[132] PG 14.
[133] See Pocock (2001, p. 194).
[134] PG 14.
[135] H App 4.12.
[136] Merrill (2015, p. 143).
[137] PG 14.
[138] Cf. Buckle (2004, p. 52).
[139] EPM D.52–53. See also Herdt (2013).

that ends the *Enquiry concerning the Principles of Morals* (1751), and foreshadowing Hume's argument in the NHR, Palamedes speaks of how ancient paganism had "very little influence on common life," with religion constituted solely of "sacrifices and prayers."[140] During antiquity, the regulation of morals and mores was the "business of philosophy alone," while the practice of superstition was practiced by the "vulgar and illiterate."[141] Philosophy might have initially taken on enthusiastic forms, but soon lost its rough edges as it became commonplace. In the Christian world, however, theology not only took over from philosophy, but also theism took over polytheism as the popular religion. The result was the emergence of "pertinacious bigotry."[142] Christianity had prescribed a "universal rule to our actions, to our words, to our very thoughts and inclinations," backed up by the threat of future punishment.[143] These universal rules, however, were based on abstract speculations beyond the ken of human nature and experience. Palamedes's unnamed interlocutor, usually identified with a fictional Hume, states that "illusions of religious superstition [and] philosophical enthusiasm" involve departing from the "maxims of common reason" and the "natural principles of [the] mind," and lead to the living of "artificial lives" which are "in a different element from the rest of mankind."[144]

Not only did the spread of Christianity direct people towards unnaturalness in their belief and behaviour, but the new religion also placed a fetter on the development of human knowledge that endured until the revival of letters.[145] Theology "bends every branch of knowledge to its own purpose, without much regard to the phenomena of nature or to the

---

[140] EPM D.53. See also Livingston (1998, pp. 91–101).

[141] EPM D.53.

[142] EHU 11.3.

[143] EPM D.53.

[144] EPM D.57.

[145] As part of a reading of the High Scottish Enlightenment as the self-aware inheritors of Reformation theology, Suderman (2015, §2) views the Scots as claiming that the revival of European learning resulted from the Reformation. I do not think this quite matches with the Scots' own words, which clearly link the transformation with what we might term now "the Renaissance" and the "early modern print revolution" alongside the Reformation.

unbiased sentiments of the mind."[146] The effect of theology's enthronement as the principal human science "warped" "reasoning and even language ... from their natural course."[147] The irony was that the "speculative dogmas" of the priests had no real content given the limitations of human understanding and experience, yet the theologians demanded absolute adherence to their literally unintelligible notions and punished anyone who challenged the inconceivable.[148] Hume clearly viewed it as his mission to help loosen this fetter. The science of human nature was the key philosophical counterattack, and viable alternative approach, against the distorting effects of theology on the pursuit of truth.

In the *Dialogues*, Cleanthes and Philo discuss the historical relationship between Christianity and philosophy. To Cleanthes, early Christian apologists, inspired by the ancient academic sceptics, declaimed "every principle, derived merely from human research and enquiry" and promoted those rooted in scripture.[149] This was the dominant position until John Locke, the "first Christian" who held that faith was a "species of reason" and religion a "branch of philosophy."[150] By contrast, Philo emphasised how priests had controlled education and prevented "questioning of received opinions."[151] Their power, however, had been "much diminished" because of Europe's increased awareness of the "popular principles of different nations and ages." With non-Christian religions appearing as competing theologies, "our sagacious divines" abandoned dogmatic scepticism and adopted the "language of Stoics, Platonists and Peripatetics."[152] This shift indicated, Philo argued, that priests choose "whichever system best suits ... giving them an ascendant over mankind."[153] There is, if you will, no Christian truth, only the pursuit of power. That power was weakening, however, due to awareness of philosophical diversity which had fundamentally challenging theology's claim to absolute certainty.

---

[146] EPM Appx 4.21.
[147] EPM Appx 4.21.
[148] EHU 11.3.
[149] DNR 1.17.
[150] DNR 1.17.
[151] DNR 1.19.
[152] DNR 1.19.
[153] DNR 1.19.

The Practical Consequences of Hume's Study of Religion

Philo's optimism about the decline of the influence of Christianity is one of several passages where Hume looked forward to an age in which philosophy has regained a position of independence and influence in society.[154] In "Of Miracles," he described how incredulity towards accounts of miracles increases during "enlightened ages," in which educated people understand events previously understood as "prodigies, omens, oracles [and] judgements" instead as the effects of "natural causes."[155] Though the myths of long-established tradition have gained "inviolable sanction and authority" as "received opinions," new supernatural explanations are now dismissed "even by the vulgar."[156] In enlightened ages the seeds of credulity are "sown in a more proper soil," where they do not grow into the superstitions of earlier societies.[157] "Fools industrious in propagating" religious imposture are always with us, but they increasingly act in contexts in which their authority is diminished.[158] Similarly, in "Whether the British Government Inclines More to Absolute Monarchy, or to a Republic' (1741), Hume can be reading as claiming that the "progress of learning and liberty" lead to the rapid decline in the cultural standing of the clergy and their "pretensions and doctrines," with even religion itself "scarcely" able to "support itself in the world."[159] The suggestion here is that ages of greater scientific knowledge will experience less superstitious, fanaticism and, quite possibly, less religion.[160] Some commentators have further drawn out the implications of Hume's argument about the

---

[154] Several instances can be identified of Hume in later life, in conversation or correspondence, expressing his belief that the extent of cultural power of the clergy was being reduced and his wish that this would continue. See Baumstark (2012).

[155] EHU 10.20.

[156] EHU 10.21.

[157] EHU 10.21.

[158] EHU 10.22.

[159] BG 5.

[160] Such a reading has been challenged for taking as Hume's position the voice of an "imagined defender of the notion that the British government leans toward a republic." See Watkins (2019, p. 124 fn. 37). But it tallies with comments elsewhere, such as in the essay "Of National Characters" (1748).

role of the passions.[161] If false religion has its origins in the overwhelming passions of hope and fear, and if those passions are overwhelming because of the danger and unpredictability of human existence, then all improvements in the quality and stability of life will lead to a decline in religious fervour.

Hume ended "Of Miracles" stating his hope that sceptical philosophy might act as a limiting force on the intellectual and social authority of accounts of miracles and intended his argument to be an "everlasting check on all kinds of superstitious delusion."[162] He acknowledged that the "propensity of mankind" to believe tales of the marvellous could never be "extirpated from human nature," but hoped the strength of that propensity could be dampened.[163] Hume clearly viewed loosening the grip of religious authority on society as a long-term project, noting in a passage cut from subsequent editions of the first volume of the *History of England*, that he addressed himself "to a more distant posterity than will ever be reached by any local or temporary theology."[164]

The diminishment of the influence of religion in social life was desirable; Hume did not believe that it would be entirely beneficial if popular religion disappeared. Religion serves no wider positive societal purpose, but it is an inevitable consequence of the human lot and needs to be managed. Superstition "arises naturally and easily from the popular opinions of mankind" and influences the "conduct of our lives and actions" far more than Hume's preferred guide, philosophy, every could.[165] Yet religion is not "absolutely requisite to the well-being of mankind and the existence of society" and usually takes forms that are "frivolous, useless and burdensome."[166] While he did not believe that popular religion could actively make people pious and virtuous, Hume did not recommend that we "disabuse" the multitude of their "prejudices," as this would free them "from one restraint upon their passions" and make vice "more easy and secure."[167] James Harris has described this passage as indicating a degree

---

[161] E.g. Russell (2008).
[162] EHU 10.20.
[163] EHU 10.20.
[164] Hume (1754, p. 8).
[165] T 1.4.7.13.
[166] EPM 3.38.
[167] EHU 11.28.

of "indecision" on Hume's part as to how to manage popular religion; to Ronald Beiner, it is evidence of Hume's belief in the continued utility of civil religion.[168] To my mind, it indicates a fundamental cleavage in Hume's social thought between how he believed the multitude and how he thought people like himself should be treated. The irrational vulgar, ever a potential mob in waiting to attack what they did not understand, must be treated with kid-gloves, and in ways that might require some minimal degree of clerical control, whereas the polite part of mankind needed their freedoms protected from ecclesiastical intrusion.

Throughout his writings, Hume argued that religion, at beast, provided only weak support for morality and, at its worst, actively undermined societies. Philo opined that religion diverts attention away from the "natural motives of justice and humanity," making us judge as meritorious what are actually "frivolous observances," "rapturous ecstasies" and "bigoted credulity."[169] The worst example of such valorisation of antisocial, pointless practices were the "monkish virtues," as discussed in EPM.[170] Hume was even more critical of medieval Catholic piety in the *History of England*, where he accused the Church of forgiving criminality in exchange for "penances, servility to the monks, and an abject and illiberal devotion."[171] Even if religion could align with morals, it could never consistently inform our actions. Hume has Philo explain that religion "acts only by intervals on the temper" and was not as a consistent "principle of action" that informed our "general conduct."[172] "Religious motives … operate only by starts and bounds," and do not become "habitual to the mind."[173] Even the possibility of damnation has little effect on human behaviour, as it is a "remote and uncertain" notion with no purchase on the mind.[174] The habit worshippers do develop, however, is the "habit of dissimulation" in the performance of rites and ceremonies,

---

[168] Harris (2015, p. 231) and Beiner (2010, p. 233). See also Walsh (2020).
[169] DNR 12.17, 12.16.
[170] EPM 9.3.
[171] H 1.71.
[172] DNR 12.17.
[173] DNR 12.14.
[174] DNR 12.13.

with the practice of "fraud and falsehood" in our conduct spreading out to become the "predominant principle of human action."[175]

Like the moral, the "political interests of society" have no inherently positive connection with religion.[176] The key factor here was the existence of a priesthood as a rival to state authority. Part of Hume's analysis involved framing the clergy in social scientific terms, with the inevitable diminution of their standing. They were not a sacred group but a profession that, like any other, was made up of flawed human beings and of very human origin. In "Of Superstition and Enthusiasm," Hume described the priesthood as the "invention" of man's "timorous and abject superstition," and who from their positions of power pretend to act on the behalf of the multitude to their god.[177] The source of their power meant the clerical profession had a vested interest to provoke our natural infirmities and could exploit the multitude to grow their own status, power and wealth or to defeat clerics from rival religious factions. In the anti-clerical footnote in the essay "Of National Characters," Hume noted that the clergy cannot maintain the "degree" and "constancy" of religious sentiment that was their purported professional expertise—this was humanly impossible—and must instead dissimulate.[178] While other professions promote the interests of society when they seek success in their chosen employment, priests can only satisfy their ambition by "promoting ignorance and superstition and implicit faith and pious frauds."[179] The footnote is highly abusive, in a way uncharacteristic of Hume's philosophical writings in general and perhaps is the one publication where he got close to a *philosophe*-level of anti-clerical acrimony—and which, indeed, was favourably quoted by Baron d'Holbach.[180] But the abuse

---

[175] DNR 12.18.

[176] EHU 11.27.

[177] SE 5.

[178] NC 6n2.1. On this footnote see Harris (2015, pp. 244–245) and Susato (2015, pp. 132, 135–136).

[179] NC 6n.2.4.

[180] The subjects of Hume's attack need to be clarified: was the footnote directed solely at Catholic priests (as opposed to Protestant clergy), or all professional divines? Some commentators suggest that Hume wrote the footnote in 1748 having observed priests while serving in Turin as a secretary to his distant relation General James St. Clair. I think this position is unpersuasive. Hume uses "priest" and "clergy" in the footnote, and elsewhere in his writings, as synonyms. When, as in the *Treatise*, Hume wanted to be clear

comes under the cover of the rhetoric of the "science of human nature." The conclusion of his footnote is that "many of the vices of human nature are, by fixed moral causes, inflamed in that profession"—all Hume, the keen-eyed observer of human nature, had done was point out these causes to his readers.[181]

As Hume explained in the *History of England*, the dangers of the priesthood could be limited by a "public establishment of religion" that managed the priests' motivations.[182] The threat posed to civil stability by priesthoods had been brought into sharp relief for Hume by his research for the *History*, and especially his study of the Reformation. Unity of ecclesiastical authority led to persecution, but competition was little better. The existence of rivalrous religious factions did not encourage ostentatious moral and pious behaviour, but the exploitation of the multitude by battling clergies. Seeking victory over their rivals above all else, priesthoods developed their talents for "governing the minds of the people."[183] They encourage "superstition, folly and delusion" amongst their followers, leading to "violent abhorrence" of rival sects, the abandonment of "truth, morals and decency" and the preaching of whatever "best suits the disorderly affections of the human frame."[184]

---

he was talking about *Catholic* priests, he said so. Similarly, many Hume's readers took his criticism as applying all priests—see the discussion of Alexander Gerard in Appendix 2. Other scholars have read it as a deliberate and angry attack on Scotland's clergy in the aftermath of the affair over Hume's failed attempt to be appointed Chair of Ethics and Pneumatical Philosophy at the University of Edinburgh in 1745. Hume found this a bruising affair, having been defeated by the "cabals of the Principal, the bigotry of the clergy, and the credulity of the mob" (see David Hume to Sir James Johnstone, 18 June 1745, *HL* vol. 1 No. 27). Hume would dryly opine in "Of National Characters" that the "uniform character" of priests "in my opinion is, generally speaking, not the most amiable that is to be met with in human society" (see NC 6). The issue is complicated, however, by the presence of a footnote in "Of Superstition and Enthusiasm' in which Hume explicitly distinguishes between priests and clergymen. But the criterion deployed relates to the character of an individual, not the religion they profess, i.e. a priest is anyone with religious authority who is wicked, power-hungry and entirely self-interested, whereas a clergyman is anyone respectable, law-abiding and who seeks to minister to their flocks well.

[181] NC 6n2.9.
[182] H 3:29.1.
[183] H 3:29.5.
[184] H 3:29.4.

Hume's social scientific approach to the problem of managing ecclesiastical authority and its rivalry with civic authority focused on the motivations and character of the clergy as a profession. In *History of England*, Hume argued that the "wise legislator" must actively prevent the "interested diligence" of the clergy.[185] A national church that paid good salaries and dished out honours would nudge the priesthood towards apathy, indolence and erudition. The clergy would be ushered away from seeking total victory in the battle for control of souls, and towards merely preventing "their flock from straying in quest of new pastures."[186] The recommendation of bribing the priesthood into indolence, however, was framed in language that seemed, to Hume's contemporary Christian readers, deliberately designed to offend.[187] In the *Dialogues*, however, Hume let Philo strike a more pessimistic note. It was, Philo claimed, a "certain and infallible maxim" learnt from studying the history of religion that the civil magistrate must limit the "number and authority of priests."[188] They can do this either by managing an established religion or, adopting the "wiser maxim" of allowing many sects, but both policies are "surrounded with inconveniences."[189] The former sets up the national church as a rival for political power, the latter involves the constant management of sects to prevent factional disorder. Priests caused insoluble problems for civil stability that could only be constantly managed, never solved.

The other threat posed to civic stability by religion took the form of the easy descent into fanatical and superstitious excess by the multitude. In "The Sceptic" (1742), Hume's sceptic held that religion must focus on myths not tenets, supported by "popular superstitions and observances," if the goal is to keep the multitude manageable.[190] Popular religion must affect the "senses and imagination."[191] In the ultimately unpublished Preface to the second volume of his *History of England*, Hume claimed that the sensual aids are necessary to "adapt our religion in some degree

---

[185] H 3.29.5.
[186] H 3.29.5.
[187] See also Watkins (2019, p. 83).
[188] DNR 12.21.
[189] DNR 12.21.
[190] Sc 23.
[191] Sc 23.

to human infirmity," given that it was "almost impossible" to prevent the "intrusion of superstition."[192] Hume was recommending that popular religion become detached from theology, which was the cause of controversy and confrontation, and be reframed into its pre-Christian form of consisting solely of rites, ceremonies and traditionary tales.

In this assessment of how to manage the dangers of religious excess, Hume had clearly moved away from his initially positive assessment of the unintended political benefits of religious enthusiasm.[193] In "Of Superstition and Enthusiasm," he had claimed that, due to the sense of independence derived from believing they were inspired, enthusiasts were enemies to "all ecclesiastical power," and a "friend" to "civil liberty."[194] The positive link between enthusiasm and political freedom had loosened in Hume's mind by the time he composed the *History of England*. In the latter he offered an ironical take in which the link between fervour and freedom was emptied of any valorisation of enthusiasm. Fanatical differences of opinion on unimportant religious matters threw the "government into such violent conclusions" and contributed to the civil wars.[195] By contrast, Hume wrote positively about James I and then Archbishop William Laud's reforms of the Church of England.[196] The "pious ceremonies" that Laud encouraged were beneficial because they mollified the "fierce and gloomy spirit of devotion" commonplace amongst the "rude multitude."[197] Laud revived some "primitive institutions" and "popish ceremonies" which gave vulgar minds "some sensible, exterior observances, which might occupy it during its religious exercise."[198] Sensual aids to worship took the mind away from the focus on the "divine and mysterious essence," a notion beyond the "narrow capacities of mankind" and thus a cause of anxiety in the worshipper.[199] By contrast, Laud's "new model of devotion" allowed the vulgar mind to "*relax* itself into the contemplation of pictures, postures, vestments,

---

[192] Quoted in Siebert (1990, pp. 90–91).
[193] Siebert (1990).
[194] SE 9.
[195] H 5:54.45.
[196] H 5:57.62.
[197] H 5:57.62.
[198] H 5:57.62.
[199] H 5:57.62.

buildings" (my italics).[200] A relaxed, rather than an agitated mind, was less likely to cause ructions in a polity.

Aside from the socio-political lessons drawn from the application of the "science of man" to religion, Hume also direct a very clear message to his readers: our happiness as individuals would be improved if we abandoned speculative theology and religious disputation. This was the famous conclusion of the NHR but was reiterated by Philo in the *Dialogues*. No "state of mind" was as "happy as the calm and equable," and that was best achieved by pursuing the path of philosophy.[201] Theology, however, offers only "profound darkness and uncertainty," upsetting the "ordinary frame of the mind" and throwing it into the "utmost confusion."[202] Religious contemplation leads us only to "gloom and melancholy."[203] Hume's recommendation, in the *Treatise* as via Philo in the *Dialogues*, was to choose philosophy as "our guide" and to focus on "common life."[204] This involved being aware that one is battling against the human nature to some degree, for it is "almost impossible for the mind of man to rest … in that narrow circle of objects" that form day to day existence.[205] But we must try. Hume's science of human nature recommended we try to give up on natural theology and religious controversy as much as possible if we know what's good for us.

* * *

So much of Hume's "science of human nature" set the agenda for the discussion of religion in the High Scottish Enlightenment. The dangers of speculative theology, the domineering influence of the passions on religious belief, the very real limits of the reasoning capacities of the multitude, the need to manage the clergy in ways to avoid fanaticism, and many other themes, appear repeatedly in the chapters that follow. What Hume did not do, so prominently, was view religious change in societal contexts, drawing out changes to religion as being in interplay

---

[200] H 5:57.62.
[201] DNR 12.30.
[202] DNR 12.30.
[203] DNR 12.30.
[204] T 1.4.7.13.
[205] T 1.4.7.13.

over the long-term with various other social developments. The principal lenses through which Hume thought about the origins and development of religion were (a) the inherent capabilities of human nature and how they motivated our agitated attempts to comprehend the unknowable and (b) specific historical developments, most importantly Christianity's takeover of philosophy, that explained the undesirable control religion had over modern minds and societies. Hume, then, was not a progressive historian of religious development and we have to turn to other Scots for such accounts. I will actually extend the argument that Hume's treatment of religion did not have a particularly prominent sociological component even in the NHR, that purported ur-text of Scottish Enlightenment "conjectural history," in a subsequent chapter.

References

Ahnert, Thomas. 2019. Philosophy and Theology in the Mid-Eighteenth Century'. In *The History of Scottish Theology: The Early Enlightenment to the Mid-Nineteenth Century*, ed. David Fergusson and Mark Elliott, 56–68. Oxford: Oxford University Press.

Baumstark, Mortiz. 2012. The Empire of Empire and the Death of Religion: A Reconsideration of Hume's Later Political Thought. In *Philosophy and Religion in Enlightenment Britain: New Cast Studies*, ed. Ruth Savage, 231–257. Oxford: Oxford University Press.

Beiner, Ronald. 2010. *Civil Religion: A Dialogue in the History of Political Philosophy*. Cambridge: Cambridge University Press.

Berman, David. 1988. *A History of Atheism in Britain: From Hobbes to Russell*. Abingdon: Routledge.

Box, M.A. 1990. *The Suasive Art of David Hume*. Princeton: Princeton University Press.

Buckle, Stephen. 2004. *Hume's Enlightenment Tract: The Unity and Purpose of An Enquiry Concerning Human Understanding*. Oxford: Oxford University Press.

Costelloe, Timothy M. 2018. *The Imagination in Hume's Philosophy: The Canvas of the Mind*. Edinburgh: Edinburgh University Press.

Demeter, Tamás. 2016. *David Hume and the Culture of Scottish Newtonianism: Methodology and Ideology in Enlightenment Inquiry*. Leiden, NL: Brill.

Fergusson, David. 2019. Hume Amongst the Theologians. In *The History of Scottish Theology. Volume II: The Early Enlightenment to the Late Victorian Era*, ed. David Fergusson and Mark W. Elliott, 301–313. Oxford: Oxford University Press.

Fogelin, Robert J. 2017. *Hume's Presence in the Dialogues Concerning Natural Religion*. Oxford: Oxford University Press.
Fosl, Peter S. 2019. *Hume's Scepticism: Pyrrhonian and Academic*. Edinburgh: Edinburgh University Press.
Gaskin, J.C.A. 1983. Hume's Attenuated Deism. *Archiv für Geschichte der Philosophie* 65: 160–173.
Greig, J. Y. T., ed. 1932. *The Letters of David Hume*, 2 vols. Oxford: Clarendon Press.
Guimarães, Livia. 2009. Skepticism and Religious Belief in *A Treatise of Human Nature*. In *Skepticism in the Modern Age: Building on the Work of Richard Popkin*, ed. Maia Neto, José Raimundo, Gianni Paganini, and John Christian Laursen, 345–364. Leiden, NL: Brill.
Harris, James. 2004. Answering Bayle's Question: Religious Belief in the Moral Philosophy of the Scottish Enlightenment. In *Oxford Studies in Early Modern Philosophy*, vol. 1, ed. Daniel Garber and Steven Nadler, 229–253. Oxford: Oxford University Press.
———. 2005. *Of Liberty and Necessity: The Free Will Debate in Eighteenth-Century British Philosophy*. Oxford: Oxford University Press.
———. 2015. *David Hume: An Intellectual Biography*. Cambridge: Cambridge University Press.
———. 2022. How to Write a History of Philosophy? The Case of Eighteenth-Century Britain. *British Journal for the History of Philosophy* 30 (6): 1013–1032.
Herdt, Jennifer A. 2013. Artificial Lives, Providential History, and the Apparent Limits of Sympathetic Understanding. In *David Hume: Historical Thinker, Historical Writer*, ed. Mark Spencer, 37–59. Philadelphia, PA: Penn State University.
Holden, Thomas. 2010. *Spectres of False Divinity: Hume's Moral Atheism*. Oxford: Oxford University Press.
———. 2020. Religion and the Perversion of Philosophy in Hume's *Enquiry Concerning the Principles of Morals*. In *Reading Hume on the Principles of Morals*, ed. Jacqueline Taylor, 238–254. Oxford: Oxford University Press.
Hume, David. 1754. *The History of Great-Britain, Vol. I, Containing the Reigns of James I and Charles I*. London.
Livingston, Donald W. 1998. *Philosophical Melancholy and Delirium: Hume's Pathology of Philosophy*. Chicago, IL: Chicago University Press.
Merivale, Amyas. 2018. *Hume on Art, Emotion, and Superstition: A Critical Study of the Four Dissertations*. Abingdon: Routledge.
Merrill, Thomas W. 2015. *Hume and Politics of Enlightenment*. Cambridge: Cambridge University Press.
Phillipson, Nicholas T. 2011. *David Hume: The Philosopher as Historian*. London: Penguin.

Pocock, J. G. A. 1999–2015. *Barbarism and Religion*, 6 vols. Cambridge: Cambridge University Press.
Russell, Paul. 1995. *Freedom and Moral Sentiment: Hume's Way of Naturalising Responsibility*. Oxford: Oxford University Press.
———. 2008. *The Riddle of Hume's Treatise*. Oxford: Oxford University Press.
———. 2021. *Recasting Hume and Early Modern Philosophy*. Oxford: Oxford University Press.
Sagar, Paul. 2018. *The Opinion of Mankind: Sociability and the Theory of the State from Hobbes to Smith*. Princeton, NJ: Princeton University Press.
Siebert, Donald T. 1990. *The Moral Animus of David Hume*. London: University of Delaware.
Stewart, M.A. 2022. *Hume's Philosophy in Historical Perspective*. Oxford: Oxford University Press.
Suderman, Jeffrey. 2015. Religion and Philosophy. In *Scottish Philosophy in the Eighteenth Century. Volume I: Morals, Politics, Art, Religion*, ed. Aaron Garrett and James Harris, 196–238. Oxford: Oxford University Press.
Susato, Ryu. 2015. *Hume's Sceptical Enlightenment*. Edinburgh: Edinburgh University Press.
Walsh, Ashley. 2020. *Civil Religion and the Enlightenment in England, 1707–1800*. Woodbridge: The Boydell Press.
Watkins, Margaret. 2019. *The Philosophical Progress of Hume's Essays*. Cambridge: Cambridge University Press.
Wootton, David. 1990. Hume's "Of Miracles": Probability and Irreligion. In *Studies in the Philosophy of the Scottish Enlightenment*, ed. M.A. Stewart, 191–229. Oxford: Oxford University Press.
Yandell, Keith. 1990. *Hume's Inexplicable Mystery: His Views on Religion*. Philadelphia, PA: Temple University Press.
Yoder, Timothy S. 2011. *Hume on God: Irony, Deism and Genuine Theism*. London: Continuum.

Adam Smith on Religious Psychology in Society

Abstract Hume's most sophisticated contemporary interlocutor was his friend Adam Smith (1723–1790). Smith treated religion in a naturalistic fashion, as a subject not framed by theological concepts and biblical frameworks derived from scripture, but as something analysed in terms of psychological, social and historical observations. In both *Theory of Moral Sentiments* (1759) and *The Wealth of Nations* (1776), Smith was in clear dialogue with Hume, part of their wider conversation over human nature and society. Yet Smith's conclusions distinctly differed from his friend, as he saw the "natural principles of religion" as outgrowths of our natural moral sentiments and viewed them as beneficial to morality and society in general. Problems arose when those natural principles were perverted away from being a function of morality.

Keywords Adam Smith · *Wealth of Nations* · *Theory of Moral Sentiments* · "Natural principles of religion" · Religious psychology · Social contexts

'Like his close friend and philosophical interlocutor Hume, Adam Smith (1723–1790) was interested in how the inherent principles of human nature framed the formation and character of religious belief. Smith provided analyses of religious topics in the two published works of his projected four volume science of man.[1] In *Theory of Moral Sentiments* (1759) he explored with empathetic precision the emergence of specific religious beliefs within the context of social interaction, as well as the influence of religion on morality.[2] Smith's account reads as a criticism of Hume's *NHR* of the deleterious effect of religion on morals and society. In *Wealth of Nations* (1776) he responded to Hume's *History of England* on the issue of how civil legislators can manage religion for politically beneficial ends and surveyed the decline of medievalism Catholicism in ways comparable to his famous account of the decline of the feudal barons. The other projected volumes of Smith's science of human nature, however, were destroyed. Similarly, we do not have Smith's lectures on natural theology given while Professor of Moral Philosophy at Glasgow, including what would have been apposite material on "those principles of the human mind upon which religion is founded."[3] But we do find relevant discussion in Smith's "History of Astronomy" and "History of Physics" dissertations, written in the late 1740s but only published posthumously in 1795, containing one of the earliest theories of the emergence and development of theology composed by an enlightened Scot. That said, Smith's analysis of religion in his early essays exhibited a fusion of a Humean "science of man," and traditional philological concerns, especially in terms of the study of cultural transmission. As such, I would suggest we draw a line between the dissertations and Smith's two published works.

Smith's discussions of religion in *TMS* and *WN* were striking in their innovativeness and sophistication. They show Smith to be engaged in a consistent conversation with Hume over the formation of religious belief and the effects of religion and religious institutions on the individual and society. This was the "science of human nature" in action. Setting aside the contested but ultimately insolvable issue of his personal religious opinions, Smith wrote about religious topics in ways that were almost entirely naturalistic and which rearticulated formerly religious concepts in secular ways. Core religious beliefs are not innate to human nature or

---

[1] In this framing of Smith's oeuvre I am following Phillipson's work, esp. (2010). See also Berry (2012).

[2] The literature on Smith's religious views is large, but my interpretation is especially informed by Haakonssen (1981, pp. 74–77), Minowitz (1993), Phillipson (2010), Heydt (2017), Smith (2018) and Sagar (2020).

[3] Stewart (1854–1860, vol. i, p. 18).

learnt from revelation but are consequences of our experience as moral agents in social settings—as Knud Haakonssen put it, for Smith, religion is understood best "primarily [as] a function and continuation of morality," something of human rather than of divine origin and emerging out of social interaction.[4] Part of what Samuel Fleischacker described as Smith's "incessant, almost obsessive refusal to accept anything Hume says as is," Smith declined to view religion in purely negative terms, as an irredeemable but irremovable aspect of human nature.[5]

THE HISTORIES OF PHILOSOPHY AND OF PHYSICS

Smith explored the first religion of humankind and its transformation into philosophy in his "juvenile" essays, the "History of Astronomy" and "History of Physics," most likely penned in the late 1740s.[6] Given that Hume's NHR and Kames' *Principles* were written at roughly the same time, this indicates a common effort to understand long-term religious and theological change, and their relationship to the origin and development of philosophy, amongst Scotland's new generation of philosophers c.1750. Smith's dissertation is notable for its limited interest in the usual concerns of traditional mythography of showing the links between Noahite revelation and subsequent pagan systems of theology, and for its focus on historical change resulting from the interplay between principles of human nature and societal circumstances, and for its claim that philosophy came to replace theology as the principal means for understanding the universe. While unpublished, Smith's discussion of the primordial religion of humankind and religious development contained many of the staple elements of what became the enlightened Scottish discussion of those topics. But like Campbell's *Necessity of Revelation*, Smith's early dissertation contained much carried over much of the methodology from existing philological and mythographical approaches to the topic of religious change.

Smith's dissertations aimed to identify the "principles" which underpin "philosophical enquiries," through examining how philosophers

---

[4] Haakonssen (1981, p. 75).

[5] Fleischacker (2012, p. 282).

[6] For this epithet see Adam Smith to David Hume 16 April 1773, Smith (1795, p. lxxxix).

explained the ordering of the cosmos. He was not interested in whether those enquiries discern the truth or not, but what aspects of human nature and societal context drive them forward. The first attempts of early humanity to develop explanations of the events of the natural world around them took the form of an unsophisticated polytheism. Lacking either the time or ability to consider the "hidden chains of nature," they only paid attention to the "magnificent irregularities" of nature that "overawe[d]" them.[7] Those events which were threatening were responded to with a "reverence that approaches fear," while those events which were "perfectly beautiful and agreeable" were "beheld with love and complacency."[8] The tendency of uncivilised human nature was to ascribe "all the irregular events of nature to the favour or displeasure of intelligent, though invisible beings, to gods, daemons, witches, genii, fairies."[9] Living "before the establishment of law, order and security," the minds of "savage" humans were overwhelmed by "wild nature and passion."[10] Early humans experienced "confusion of thought" trying to understand natural events, before eventually finding a kind of mental stability in ascribing them to the "arbitrary will" of invisible beings.[11] Primitive polytheism emerged from a need to quell mental confusion; this motivate force was not particular to "savages," but was behind all systems of theology. The particular characteristics of primitive polytheism, however, were informed by the precarious circumstances of primordial peoples.

Smith's account of polytheism also bore many similarities with Hume's discussion of the relationship between religion and human nature in the *Treatise* and *EHU*. The anthropomorphic propensity of human nature meant humans "naturally supposed" the natural events "to act in the same manner" as themselves.[12] The imagination sought explanations that assuaged the anxiety caused by the insecurity and dangers of human life and the inexplicability of many natural events. The passions "all justify themselves," meaning that when we feel scared, we believe that there is

---

[7] Smith (1982a, p. 48).
[8] Smith (1982a, p. 48).
[9] Smith (1982a, p. 48).
[10] Smith (1982a, p. 48).
[11] Smith (1982a, p. 112).
[12] Smith (1982a, p. 50).

really something external to us to be scared about.[13] The "uncivilized state" of early humans, that of a dejected state of insecurity, encouraged "cowardice and pusillanimity" and terrified thoughts about the unknown.[14] The state of nature was conducive to superstition: primordial humans were "disposed to believe everything" about inexplicable natural events that could "render them still more the objects of his terror."[15]

Philosophy emerged gradually out of primordial polytheism, Smith held, due to three intertwined societal factors: subsistence security, civic stability and economic advancement leading to the growth of leisure time. When these factors jointly exist in a society, a leisured class of philosophers can emerge who study the order of the natural world and develop better explanations for events previously explained by a form of animism. The philosophers were less motivated by the passions of hope and fear, because in a well-ordered society other hitherto dormant principles of human nature were able to develop—most importantly, that of curiosity. Smith's argument was an implicit extension specifically to the practice of philosophy of the principle established in Hume's "Of the Rise and Progress of the Arts and Sciences" (1742) "from law arises security; from security, curiosity; and from curiosity, knowledge."[16] This has important effects for the abandonment of polytheism: it is "science," developed by philosophers, that "gave birth to the first theism," amongst nations unassisted by revelation.[17]

The first sophisticated religion, then, was consequence of the scientific researches of a philosopher class. Commentators have repeatedly noticed, however, that Smith's analysis here, like Hume's, suggests that natural religion reasoning was a slave to the passions. Smith also places the activity of philosophers in a social as well as a psychological context. As a social group, the philosophers tended to be "those of liberal fortunes," interested in neither trade nor dissipation and "disengaged from the ordinary affairs of life."[18] They were driven by the passion of wonder, the "first

---

[13] Smith (1982a, p. 48).
[14] Smith (1982a, p. 48).
[15] Smith (1982a, p. 48).
[16] RP 14.
[17] Smith (1982a, p. 114).
[18] Smith (1982a, p. 50).

principle which prompts mankind to the study of philosophy."[19] But what drove them forward was the desire for mental calm. While philosophers are delighted by the "regular process of nature," they are "stopped and embarrassed" when existing philosophy fails to explain a new natural phenomena.[20] It is the desire to re-stablish mental tranquillity that leads to renewed attempts to understand the inexplicable: advances in philosophy were driven forward by the desires of philosophers to regain the pleasant sentiments they experienced when they could view the "whole course of the universe" as something "consistent and of a piece."[21]

Sometimes it is argued that the implication of Smith's analysis is that the idea of a natural order designed by a benevolent creator had, per Dennis Rasmussen, "unflattering psychological and sociological explanations" rather than resulting from valid reasoned argument.[22] The need to quell unpleasant feelings of mental confusion motivated the formation of systems of theology and cosmology as much as it did earlier systems of primitive polytheism. This says nothing of the truth or otherwise of such theories, only that the passions behind the emergence of both polytheism and theism were similar. Other commentators, by contrast, read Smith as believing that theism emerged because of the switch to "science," or the investigation of natural causes and effects. Science might still depend on the passions and on our imaginations, but it is motivated by a desire to seek the truth and was no longer motivated the "cowardice and pusillanimity" of primordial polytheism, and thus marked a genuine move closer to learning the actual laws of nature.[23] These two positions do not cancel each other out, and Smith clearly saw the origin of theism as an advance towards the truth, even if he could identify the aspect of our universal human nature that acted as the motive cause, the desire for mental tranquillity.

In Smith's account, the development of philosophical theism was not tied to the political practice of dual religion, consisting of one for the initiated educated elite and one for the ignorant multitude, who could

---

[19] Smith (1982a, p. 51).

[20] Smith (1982a, p. 51).

[21] Smith (1982a, p. 51).

[22] Rasmussen (2019, p. 44).

[23] Fleischacker (2021, §2.9), here explicitly criticising Rasmussen's reading.

not understand the philosophers' advances in knowledge. He did identify the emergence of the practice of dual religion, however, but for reasons of safety not social control. Certain ancient philosophers—Smith refers to the "Italian school" of Pythagoras and his followers—kept their advances hidden from the masses, as to avoid the "fury of the people" and the "imputation of impiety."[24] Their new scientific explanations of the "dreadful phenomena," previously conceived as acts of immaterial beings, were taught to their students under the "seal of the most sacred secrecy."[25] They feared retribution for having taken "from the gods the direction of those [natural] events, which were apprehended to be the most terrible tokens of [the gods'] impeding vengeance."[26] Here, ancient philosophers are not considered as powerful groups within society who learn truths about nature and who also are able manage and inform popular religious belief. Instead, philosophy is a vulnerable practice that requires careful behaviour and secrecy to protect itself from the threat of disturbing the established opinions of the superstitious multitude.

Smith's schematic or conjectural account of religious change based on societal and psychological factors was supplemented by the more traditional appeal to histories of civilisational transmission. Greece and especially its island colonies were the first countries to arrive at a "state of civilized society," and thus to philosophy and, subsequently, theism.[27] While the "great monarchies of Asia and Egypt" established law and order prior to Greece, Smith believed they were despotic societies the "destructive of security and leisure" necessary for the "growth of philosophy"—though this was an explicit conjecture on Smith's part, given the limits of the documentary record.[28] Greek islands, however, were little oases, secure from military threat, and wealthy to boot, and quickly advanced in "civility and improvement."[29] All the "first philosophers" were natives of the Greek islands and colonies. Here, Smith is interested in glossing the successive schools of Greek philosophy, which took its

---

[24] Smith (1982a, p. 56).
[25] Smith (1982a, p. 56).
[26] Smith (1982a, p. 56).
[27] Smith (1982a, p. 51).
[28] Smith (1982a, p. 51). See also Vivenza (2001, p. 19).
[29] Smith (1982a, p. 51).

proper form first with the "school of Socrates" and reached its "most religious" form with the Stoics.[30]

Following Aristotle's *Metaphysics*, Smith (and like Monboddo would do) identified Anaxagoras as the first philosopher to argue that "mind and understanding" were needed to first create the world.[31] The primitive polytheistic view was that immaterial beings acted within an eternally existing world and was reiterated by philosophers prior to Anaxagoras. Within these early philosophy systems, "deity" was one of the "last productions of nature," because they believed whatever was perfect always came last.[32] The shift from an eternal world to one created by a superior mind developed once Anaxagoras and those philosophers who followed realised the "chain which bound all [nature's] parts to one another" and the universe was a "coherent system, governed by general laws, and directed to general ends."[33] Because the universe resembled a machine "produced by human art," thus some Greek philosophers analogised that it was a machine created by superior art.[34] And thus "science gave birth to the first theism that arose among those nations, who were not enlightened by divine revelation."[35] For Smith, as for Monboddo, the idea of a supreme being who created the universe is an idea that only emerges late in the history of mankind. This is one of the few occasions in Smith's writings where he pays lip-service to the relevance of the biblical historical framework.[36] (We have circumstantial evidence that Smith's natural theological lectures did not emphasise the necessity of revelation for understanding the trues of theism, including our moral duties to God).[37]

The issue of the origin and development of religion in relationship to societal context and the extent of philosophy appeared on occasion in Smith's legal lectures and his two published works, though only in passing. He lectured his students at Glasgow that "superstitious fears and

---

[30] Smith (1982a, pp. 53, 116).

[31] Smith (1982a, p. 113). Vivenza (2001, Ch. 1) encourages us to read Smith's discussion as in dialogue with Aristotle's thought more generally.

[32] Smith (1982a, p. 113).

[33] Smith (1982a, p. 113).

[34] Smith (1982a, p. 114).

[35] Smith (1982a, p. 114).

[36] But not the only. Cf. Minowitz (1993, p. 119).

[37] For a summary see Rasmussen (2019, pp. 51–52).

terrors increase" with the "precariousness and uncertainty of the manner of life people are engaged in," with the gods of earlier human societies usually being "local or tutelary" and "supposed to favour only [a] particular people."[38] In a brief but fascinating passage in his "Lectures on Jurisprudence," akin in its psychological insight to the discussion of religious topics in *TMS*, Smith argued that Christianity grew amongst the slave populations of the ancient world because the latter were barred from participating in pagan religion, but found solace for their worldly woes in worshipping the new Christian God from whom they were not barred. Finally, we can note that in both the *TMS* and *WN*, Smith restated his claim from his early essays that early systems of superstition explained the "wonderful appearances" of nature in terms of the "agency of the gods," before systems of philosophy provided more sophisticated explanations.[39]

In the "History of Astronomy," Smith discoursed at length about how the practice of philosophy, astronomy and logic emerged as primordial peoples moved into early civil societies. The dissertation is not a general heuristic outlining the "natural progress of religion," but an attempt to decipher what probably happened between savagery and Anaxagoras and after. Smith's summaries of the theological systems of the rival schools of Plato, Aristotle and the Stoics had a philological precision unlike Smith's later writings or the enlightened Scottish account of religion more generally, Monboddo aside. In these ways, Smith's "juvenile" essays bore more relation to the established genre of histories of ancient philosophy than the more theoretical studies of religion in the second half of the century. But in its lack of interest in biblical history, and its reliance on comprehending human nature within societal contexts, Smith's dissertation also looked forward to the High Scottish Enlightenment's account of religion. It is something of a bridging work.

The Psychology of Religion in the *Theory of Moral Sentiments* (1759)

It is possible to piece together from disparate but thematically related discussions in Smith's *TMS* a theory of the inner origins of commonplace religious notions. Smith was interested in the inherent aspects of human

---
[38] Smith (1982b), 15 February 1763.
[39] WN v.i.f.24.

nature that helped frame religious belief and worship; how they manifested themselves within contexts of social interaction; and how religion affect the inner worlds of socialised individuals. His discussion takes the form of snapshots of the formation of sentiments, rather than a historical account as with his "History of Astronomy" dealing with the progress of religious systems. Nor does Smith's account examine changes to religious belief in terms of changing socio-economic circumstances. And, following Paul Sagar, I am tempted not to read *TMS* as describing the situation of the individual within commercial society in particular, due to lack of textual evidence that this is the social setting Smith had in mind, but any setting of sustained societal interaction.[40] While Smith was more interested in the effect of religion on moral belief and behaviour, the pictures of the psychology of religion presented in *TMS* offered nuanced and completely naturalised accounts of concepts usually treated within the purview of theology.

I read Smith as being uninterested in deciding the question whether the naturalness of our religious beliefs means that their propositional content is true. Smith's primary interest was in the relationship between religion and moral sentiments, and he was ambivalent about whether our natural religious sentiments were the result of design. Smith's language is nearly always that of a dispassionate observer of human nature, describing the intricacies of human psychology without committing himself to the truth of the beliefs developed, though occasionally, to borrow Sagar's nice phrase, he adopts the "rhetorical ornamentation" of an author of nature.[41] The beliefs discussed in *TMS* relate to our moral sentiments emerging in situations of social interaction, though in one overlooked passage Smith reiterates some of the anthropomorphic elements of his discussion in "History of Astronomy". The origin of belief in supernatural power, the foundation of all subsequent religious belief, is something, however, that is presumed in Smith's *TMS* rather than explained.

Smith believed the annals of history recorded the universality of belief in future rewards and punishments, and the origin of this belief in human nature.[42] In the first five editions of *TMS*, he held that this

---

[40] Sagar (2022).

[41] Sagar (2020, p. 1063).

[42] Smith thus plays a limited role in Ahnert (2015), where Smith's unorthodoxy on religious matters is downplayed e.g. p. 142, fn. 4.

indicated how these "original anticipations" coincided with the "doctrines of revelation," as part of a longer passage about the Christian doctrine of atonement.[43] In the sixth and final edition, however, this passage was removed and replaced with the secularly scientific and de-Christianised claim that the belief in future rewards and punishments is present in "every religion and in every superstition that the world has ever beheld."[44] Commentary on the significance of this alteration has varied from viewing it as a deeply personal one about not attacking Hume in language reminiscent of High Flying Churchmen, to emphasising Smith's desire not to offend his Christian mother, altering it only after her death in 1784, to taking it as evidence of his firm and final abandonment of Christianity for Stoicism. One clear implication of such Smith's changed position is that it views Christian doctrine to be just one more instance of a universal human development. Several principles combine to form the common belief in future rewards and punishments: our concern with our future, our anthropomorphic expectation that God will act like us and, a claim that Ferguson would reiterate, our psychological need to believe in a fair and just universe.[45] The idea of future rewards and punishments first results from our natural inclination to want justice to prevail. We "naturally appeal to heaven" when we experience unjust outcomes and believe God will act justly for actions that did not receive appropriate punishment or reward in the temporal world.[46] But we are struck by over overwhelming inferiority and unworthiness when considering the existence of a supreme being. Our resulting terror about our own fates when judged by a perfect being leads in turn to the development of the doctrine of mercy as a salve to our anxieties.

Similarly, Smith examines the motivation behind, and the character of religious confession as rooted in the common human experience of guilt. The sense of having done wrong is a "load upon every mind," and always "accompanied with anxiety and terror" about future repercussions.[47] Humans "naturally" desire to unburden themselves of this psychological weight and seek relief through talking to someone whose

---

[43] TMS 2.2.3.12.
[44] TMS 2.2.3.12.
[45] TMS 3.5.10.
[46] TMS 3.5.10.
[47] TMS 7.3.4.17.

discretion they can rely upon.[48] Smith linked this common human need to the consolidation of the power by Catholic priests. The need to relieve stress through confessional conversation was exploited by "numerous and artful clergy," who asserted themselves as moral judges, confidants of God and capable of influencing God's opinion.[49]

In *TMS* Smith was concerned with understanding how religious belief influenced moral sentiments and behaviour. He made an initial distinction between those religious sentiments that informed moral behaviour and those associated with ritual and piety, and Smith was not particularly interested in the latter. Religious belief can encourage people to "fulfil all the obligations of morality," especially those moral duties that need to be learnt.[50] The most important religious belief was that in future rewards and punishments because it encouraged adherence to moral injunctions that do not benefit us directly. Moreover, we are more likely to trust those we believe act "under an additional tie" beyond social bonds, namely the judgement of God.[51] Smith maintained that public performance of religiosity serves as a social indicator of the probity of the believer and thereby contributes to trust and social cohesion: "sacred regard to general rules" was essential for the endurance of society.[52]

We have to acknowledge, however, the limited extent of Smith's discussion of the formation of religious sentiments in *TMS*. Smith was more interested in detailing those forms of religion which aided morality as the "natural principles of religion."[53] These principles are natural, in Hanley's summary, "insofar as they promote a morality built on natural sentiments."[54] Several commentators have argued that the religious beliefs discussed in *TMS* are built upon the foundations of pre-existing moral sentiments, to the extent that we can describe Smith as authoring a "natural history of religion."[55] We come to believe in future rewards and punishments because our pre-existing moral inclinations—e.g. to see

---

[48] TMS 7.3.4.17.
[49] TMS 7.3.4.17.
[50] TMS 3.5.13.
[51] TMS 3.5.13.
[52] TMS 3.5.2.
[53] TMS 3.5.13.
[54] Hanley (2015, p. 37).
[55] For example, Haakonssen (1981), Hanley (2015) and Sagar (2020).

that virtue is rewarded and vice punished—lead us to form new beliefs that salve the anxieties created when those inclinations are left unsatisfied, such as when evil goes unpunished. Noticeably, Smith does not give an account of the origins the idea of supernatural power, the core notion in early modern explanations of religion, only that we anthropomorphically ascribe human motivations to supernatural beings. We can infer from other passages, though, that religion emerges out of morality. Thus, in a passage present in 1759 but that was excised from the 1790 edition, Smith noted that man has to first "conceive himself as accountable to his fellow creatures, before he can form any idea of the Deity, or of the rules by which that Divine Being will judge of his conduct."[56] This is placed in the context of a child's developing awareness first of the authority of and their obligations to their parents, and from thence to an idea of God as a parent of all humanity. Religion appears as a function and an outgrowth of morality.

For Smith, religious sentiments support morality so long as the religious beliefs and behaviours entailed are moderate. Religious sentiments, however, are susceptible to corruption. Smith's list repeats many of Hume's concerns about the dangers of religion. We can be directed away from true morality by the "factious and party zeal of some worthless cabal," which promotes sectarian bigotry over common decency.[57] Superstitious regard for "frivolous observances" perverts the meaning of true religion by directing our attention away from performing "acts of justice."[58] The comforting but idolatrous idea of a mercenary God makes us believe that our "vain supplications" empower us to "bargain with the deity for fraud, perfidy and violence," which leads to vice being excused.[59] Common to these dangers is that they render religion unsocial and immoral, whereas religion succeeds in its social purpose when it encourages individuals to act from justice and beneficence.

Smith's concern about "false religion" was purely naturalistic, focusing on its social impact and was devoid of content drawn from scripture or a Christian ethos more generally.[60] As a set of sentiments religion "gives

[56] TMS 3.1.3.
[57] TMS 3.5.13.
[58] TMS 3.5.13.
[59] TMS 3.5.13.
[60] TMS 3.6.12.

the greatest authority to the rules of duty" and, similarly, it is "capable of distorting our ideas."[61] "False religious notions" have an unparalleled power to bring about the "gross perversion of our natural [moral] sentiments."[62] As many commentators have noted, Smith can be read as defining "false religion" not in terms of contradiction to scriptural tenets, but as whatever undermines moral behaviour.[63] Smith analysed religion as one societal factor among many that can inform morality, detaching his discussion from any theological content.

Like Hume (and like most authors in this book), Smith was deeply sceptical of the benefits of speculative theology for encouraging morality amongst the multitude. Smith extended this criticism to the practice of philosophy, in ways, as we shall see, similar to Kames and John Gregory. Theology and philosophy can only interest, motivate and persuade the theologian and the philosopher. It was a fact of history, by contrast, that moral laws adhered to the multitude have always been framed as the "commands and laws of the deity."[64] Morality was of "too much importance" to rely upon "philosophical researches" characterised by "slowness and uncertainty."[65] The need to buttress morality with religious injunctions was a truth known from the societies even in their "rudest form."[66] Speculative theology was not the "great business and occupation of our lives," and something had gone wrong if a society's clergy were directing themselves towards such activity at the expense of civic-mindedness.[67] Religion is an aid to morality or the most powerful source of "consolation," not a separate pursuit at odds with common life.[68] The "most

---

[61] TMS 3.6.12.
[62] TMS 3.6.12.
[63] TMS 3.5.13.
[64] TMS 3.5.3.
[65] TMS 3.5.4.
[66] TMS 3.5.4.
[67] TMS 7.2.1.

[68] TMS 7.2.1. In this Smith is characteristic of what Harris sees as the general belief amongst Scottish philosophers, Hume (and Philo) aside, that "the virtuous agent needs to be able to find a place for himself within a larger providential scheme if he is not to be driven to despair by, in Reid's words, 'the calamities to which all are liable'." See Harris (2004, pp. 246–247).

sublime speculation of the contemplative philosopher" means nothing if it led to the "neglect of the smallest active duty."[69]

Similarly, like Hume and Kames, Smith criticised the ascetic life as detrimental to society. Put differently, what was often depicted as the highest form of Christian life while on earth was to be derided as socially useless. Smith scorned those priests who valued the "duties of devotion" as the "sole virtues" just as he chided those obsessed over "sublime contemplation."[70] He mocked those "whining and melancholy moralists, who are perpetually reproaching us with our happiness."[71] Smith drew a contrast here between the "futile mortifications of a monastery" with the achievements of those who have actually contributed to their society. This was all the more galling because the monastic attitude "reserved the celestial regions for monks and friars" and for those who imitated their ascetic lives, but "condemned to the internal all the heroes, all the statesmen and lawgivers, all the poets and philosophers of former ages."[72] A religious position that condemned to hellfire "all the great protectors, instructors, and benefactors of mankind" clearly went against our "natural sense of praiseworthiness."[73] We do not naturally approve the monkish virtues, but we do approve those actions that contributed to the benefit of society at large.

In *WN* Smith expanded on Hume's arguments that philosophy had been corrupted by its subordination to theology, a process which had resulted in the valorisation of life-denying "monkish virtues."[74] The practice of metaphysics, or the study of immaterial substance, a subject upon which we can know very little, expanded at the expense of natural philosophy, or the study of material bodies and upon which observation and experiment can tell us much. Moral philosophy likewise degenerated, polluted by theology.[75] While ancient Greek moral philosophers were dedicated to the "happiness and perfection of human life," modern Christianised philosophy is subservient to the theologians' concern with the

[69] TMS 6.2.3.6.
[70] TMS 7.2.1.
[71] TMS 3.6.9.
[72] TMS 3.2.35.
[73] TMS 3.2.35.
[74] NHR x.
[75] WN v.i.f.28. See also Beiner (2010, p. 247, fn. 53).

"life to come."[76] Christianised philosophy viewed virtue as "inconsistent with any degree of happiness of this life," with salvation earned by "penance and mortification" alone.[77] The subordination of knowledge to Christian theology led to all "branches of philosophy" being "corrupted."[78] Moral philosophy in European universities took the form of a "debased system" focusing on the future rewards and punishments of immortal souls.[79] While fine for ecclesiastics-in-training, these changes to university curricula added "subtlety and sophistry" to the education of gentlemen, focused their attentions on an "ascetic morality" unsuited to their purpose in life and able neither to "improve the understanding" nor "mend the heart."[80] Moral and natural philosophy were corrupted by the introduction of otherworldly Christian tenets.

While speculative and supererogatory theology should be criticised, Smith held positive views about some of the moral benefits of Christianity—at least, perhaps, until his final years. In a passage that was removed from the final edition of *TMS*, Smith emphasised the superiority of Christianity as the religion that best aided worldly happiness and moral behaviour.[81] Given our tendency to develop overwhelming fear about divine rewards and punishments, the mind needs some comforting vision of a post-mortem future. Theistic religions that maintain the doctrine of future rewards and punishments are liable to cause tremendous mental distress if the belief is not coupled with some supra-human mediator between God and man. In Christianity, this intermediary role is played by Christ, and this fact speaks to the superiority of Christianity as a religious system, at least in terms of its ability to assuage our inherent religious fears. The fact that this passage was removed is often taken as evidence of Smith's growing scepticism towards Christianity, and shift towards Stoicism in the final years of his life.[82]

Smith's discussion of the relationship between religion and human nature in *TMS* is similar to his approach in "History of Astronomy" in

[76] WN v.i.f.30.
[77] WN v.i.f.30.
[78] WN v.i.f.30.
[79] WN v.i.f.31.
[80] WN v.i.f.32.
[81] TMS 2.3.13.
[82] E.g. Kennedy (2011).

one respect, and different in two others. The common thread between the two accounts is the continued emphasis on the origin and character of religious sentiments from our anxiety and desire for mental tranquillity. In the case of the leisured philosophers, this is the mental need for our explanatory systems to be comprehensive. In the case of individuals in social contexts, we are driven to comforting notions of divine order and justice prompted by our worldly experiences of misfortune and injustice. In *TMS* Smith offers a deeply humane and naturalised picture of the mental origin and character of certain religion beliefs, in which a threatened and confused humanity struggles with experiences that they cannot easily deal with, and which prompt them to develop comforting beliefs such as divine justice enacted in the hereafter, the utility of confession or belief in the intermediary activity of Christ. What is different in *TMS* compared to "History of Astronomy" is (1) that Smith is not discussing the progress of religious beliefs over time, but the psychological processes that are always at play in their formation in social settings and (2) whereas in "History of Astronomy" the theologies of the philosophers filter down to the multitude, in *TMS* Smith stresses the social utility, in terms of encouraging adherence to morality or encouraging social cohesion, of certain naturally-occurring religious beliefs. Smith claimed the "natural principles of religion" supported moral behaviour and did so regardless of the form of religious belief—polytheistic or theistic. The danger to society is not religion per se, but its corruption into immoderate beliefs and behaviours.

Religious Sects and Social Stability in the *Wealth of Nations*

The focus of Smith's discussion of religious topics in *TMS* was understanding the relationship between religious and moral sentiments. In Book V of *WN*, Smith explored the lessons that legislators needed to learn from examining religion as one interlocking factor amongst many in the science of society. Underpinning this, as with Hume, was Smith's pragmatic assessment that human nature had inherently superstitious tendencies. A legislator was never working with a blank slate when it came to positive law, and this was especially true with religion. If they wished to ensure "public tranquillity," magistrates have to "yield" to the "prejudices" of the multitude over their supposed "happiness in a life to come."[83] The existence of "popular superstition and enthusiasm" were factors that needed to be incorporated into policy decisions, and any attempt at their eradication would likely lead to civil unrest.[84] Smith goes further: "pure and rational religion" is something that "positive law has perhaps never yet established."[85] Smith's discussion here implies two things: (1) the high likelihood that the establishment of a single rational religion on a society-wide basis is not possible because of the enduring, ineradicable superstitiousness of the multitude without some radically new development in the diffusion of philosophical knowledge; and (2) that no existing established Church can be said to maintain a "rational religion."[86]

The central policy questions facing the legislator, then, were those of church-state relations and the management of the clerical profession. Smith's analysis is read productively as being in dialogue with Hume's recommendation for a legislator to create indolent established churches. Smith certainly agreed with Hume's view that the sovereign needed to pay serious attention, in Smith's words, to the thought and activity of the "greater part of the teachers of [established] religion."[87] He stressed that sovereigns in states with established churches were in a difficult situation. National clergies held tremendous power because they could wield "all the terrors of religion" to ensure the loyalty of the populace.[88] Should the prince raise troops against the clergy's political allies, they could not rely upon the loyalty of their own troops, as the clergy could raise threats of damnation. The power wielded by clergy is "superior to every other authority," because the "fears which it suggests conquer all other fears."[89]

Smith rejected Hume's recommendation of encouraging indolence amongst the established clergy on the grounds that this would result in persecution of new religious groups. National churches that owed their position to landed estates, church taxes, state salaries and stipends would be vulnerable to competition with new sects. The latter had no revenues,

[83] WN iv.v.b.40.
[84] WN v.i.g.8.
[85] WN v.i.g.8.
[86] WN v.i.g.8; Minowitz (1993, p. 166).
[87] WN vi.i.g.16.
[88] WN vi.i.g.17.
[89] WN vi.i.g.17.

but established themselves through "exertion," "zeal" and "industry."[90] These qualities meant they could easily attack established clergy as neglectful of their laity. Moreover, established clergies often detached themselves from the people through their erudition and refinement—a point John Gregory would expand on at length. Surgent religious sects, by contrast, were popular with the "common people," not least because of their adoption of an "austere system of morality" which gained them "respect and veneration."[91] Weakened by inactivity, the established clergy become "incapable of making any vigorous defence" of religious orthodoxy and their only option is to call on the state to oppress the new minority religion.[92]

Smith recommended that the legislator ruling over a state with an established church undertake a policy that was the inversion of Hume's suggestion. Rather than bribing the clergy into indolence and erudition, Smith suggested the sovereign manage church livings and benefices in such a way that the clergy held only a "precarious tenure."[93] By encouraging anxiety about future deprivation of living and more desperate hopes for future preferment, the clergy would be rendered both industrious in their ministry and unwilling to challenge state authority. Smith stressed, however, that the sovereign must act with a soft touch, because there was no group within society "so dangerous" and "so perfectly ruinous" as an aggrieved established clergy developing independence of mind.[94] The clergy needed to be kept weak enough that they were concerned only with their religious duties to their flock, but not so weak that they rebelled.

While offering pragmatic suggestions to the problems posed by the existence of an established church to a legislator, Smith also envisioned the abandonment of national churches altogether and the establishment of complete religious freedom. Using arguments that echoed Hume's "Of Superstition and Enthusiasm," Smith depicted state religions as being the religion of whichever political faction had control of a nation at any specific moment. Indeed, established churches were often the creation of political factions calling in the "aid of religion" during conflict, a tool of

---

[90] WN v.i.g.1.
[91] WN v.i.g.11.
[92] WN v.i.g.1.
[93] WN v.i.g.19.
[94] WN v.i.g.19.

war turned into a permanent peacetime institution.[95] Turning the religion of the victorious party into the state religion entrenches a political divide, subordinating the defeated party and religion, but ultimately not removing the underlying problem of conflict between the two.

Ideally, an established church should be dissolved and government should leave the individual "to choose his own priest and his own religion."[96] In *TMS* Smith had already argued for the "greatest mutual forbearance and toleration" of religious difference, and even leniency towards crimes inspired by differing conceptions of religious duty.[97] In *WN* he stressed that state impartiality in the face of religious difference would result in the emergence of a "great multitude of religious sects."[98] In conditions of perfect competition, no sect would rise above the rest. The "interested and active zeal of religious teachers" would be less dangerous given that no one group could dominate. Clergy finding themselves leaders of one sect amongst hundreds would learn "candour and moderation," and abandon all "absurdity, imposture or fanaticism."[99] The causal mechanism at work is the mutual sympathy and respect that equally weak sects would offer each other. Smith was optimistic about the benefits of allowing religious diversity, though he was not about the likelihood of this happening. Sectarian competition would drive all groups towards that "pure and rational religion" that all "wise men have in all ages of the world wished to see established," and which no doubted aligned with the "natural principles of religion" discussed in *TMS*.[100]

In *WN* Smith outlined another cause for optimism that rational religion "might in time probably" be established: the potential for the spread of scientific theism due to improvements in knowledge.[101] Science was the "great antidote" to the "poison of enthusiasm and superstition," and like Hume, Smith seems to have believed he was living in a new age of

---

[95] WN v.i.g.8.

[96] WN v.i.g.8. Reisman (1976, p. 138) notes that all of Smith's proposed solutions for dealing with the problem of ecclesiastical power bear any analogy with liberating commerce. See also Muller (1995, pp. 157–158), Hill (2019, pp. 66–67) and, especially, Anderson (1988).

[97] TMS 3.6.12.

[98] WN v.i.g.8.

[99] WN v.i.g.8.

[100] WN v.i.g.8.

[101] WN vi.g.8.

enlightenment.[102] As Charles Griswold notes, Smith was concerned in *WN* with the "institutional structures that support a free society" and the state and the "middling rank" and above should study science as a means to ward off superstition.[103] Smith hoped that, should the "superior ranks of people" become educated in science, their knowledge would disseminate down to the "inferior ranks."[104] The legislator could speed up this process of scientific education by mandating the study of science and philosophy as a requirement for entry into the professions or any position of public trust. This was not a process of secularisation, but rather of the replacement of superstition and metaphysics-laden theology by natural philosophy in understanding the existence of God and his creation. Moreover, while Smith viewed the testimony of history as suggesting that popular superstition was likely to endure, the power of scientific knowledge, diffused through society, could possibly shepherd in a new age of religious improvement.

Alongside reasons for optimism, recent developments also raised concerns. Smith warned legislators of the need to comprehend religion within the context of growing urbanised commercial societies. Urban populations were more susceptible to religious fanaticism. Again, Smith's empathetic insights are remarkable, as he captures the religious psychology of the alienated, poor solitary individual lost in the large city. Such men "sunk in obscurity" and easily descend into lives of "profligacy and vice."[105] They often find self-respect and social standing by "becoming the member of a small religious sect."[106] The consequences are mixed: sectarian identity encourages "regular and orderly," but also often "disagreeably rigorous and unsocial" behaviour.[107] The legislator can deal with this situation partly by increasing the "frequency and gaiety of public diversions," with the expectation these would "easily dissipate [the] melancholy and gloomy humour" found amongst alienated city-dwellers.[108] In the case of religious sects themselves, Smith looked to

---

[102] WN v.i.g.14.
[103] Griswold (1998, pp. 282–283).
[104] WN v.i.g.14.
[105] WN v.i.g.12.
[106] WN 5.1.g.12.
[107] WN 5.1.g.12.
[108] WN v.i.g.15.

free competition, but in the case of urban misery leading to fanaticism, he looked to a government-led solution of circuses.

The Decline and Fall of Medieval Catholicism

In Book 5 of *WN*, Smith outlined a history of the decline and fall of the Catholic Church that paralleled his more famous story of the decline of medieval feudalism found in Book 3. The former subject was, however, of great importance to Smith and was a key part of his account of the emergence of the modern liberal commercial states in Europe, such that we might speak of post-Catholic as well as post-feudal Europe. The Catholic Church was the "most formidable combination that ever was formed against the authority and security of civil government [and] the liberty, reason and happiness of mankind."[109] Institutional Catholicism was a huge conspiracy in which priests pursued their own private economic and political interests under the guise of furthering religion. The fact it was a monopoly prevented the grossness of its abuses and its superstitions from ever weakening its standing—the exact inversion of Smith's expected consequences of allowing religious diversity and competition. As Paul Sagar has noted, to Smith, "bringing the [Catholic] clergy to heel has been a great achievement of modern European states."[110]

Smith's is a thoroughly un-Protestant account of the Reformation and the decline of the Catholic Church, one in which the "feeble efforts of human reason" plays no role, let alone the heroic efforts of religious heroes.[111] Instead, the development is described as having resulted from the "natural cause of things," which Smith proceeds to explain.[112] The concentration of legal and economic power in the hands of the Church meant that it was "out of all danger from any assault of human reason"—it is only with changes to the economic position of the Church that changes to its power would occur.[113] The decline of the Catholic Church resulted not from the spread of philosophy or rival sects, but

---

[109] WN v.i.g.24.

[110] Sagar (2022, p. 91), though we might quibble with the agent-implying phrase "brought to heel."

[111] WN v.i.g.24.

[112] WN v.i.g.24.

[113] WN v.i.g.24.

the "gradual improvements of arts [and] manufactures"—that is, "the same causes which destroyed the power of the great barons."[114] With the growth of commerce and the availability of luxury goods the clergy, like the barons, shifted their attention away from charity and hospitality and started spending their "revenues upon their own persons."[115] Like the barons, the clergy reduced the number of their retainers and thereby loosened their ties with their communities. Like the barons, they sought to increase their rent revenues by granting leases to tenants on church lands, leading to the latter becoming economic and socially independent of their former masters. Due to the priesthood's pursuit of wealth and luxuries, the ties that bound the "inferior ranks of people" to the clergy were "gradually broken and dissolved."[116] The multitude had been tied to the clergy because they were "fed by them."[117] On top of this relationship of subsistence dependency, the clergy's ability to provide "hospitality and charity" encouraged reverence towards them and a belief in their superstition.[118] Once this material tie between food and superstition was broken, the clergy's sacredness and power amongst the people declined, opening space up for different religious sentiments.

With the Catholic Church increasingly possessing "both less power and less inclination to disturb the state," internal critics began to break away into rival sects.[119] The character and success of the Magisterial Reformers epitomised everything Smith had argued about the psychology of surgent religion and its relationship with politics. Early Protestant preachers acted with "enthusiastic zeal" and were popular with the multitude, who were impressed with their austere manners that differed so markedly from the lax Catholic clergy.[120] The Protestant preachers were less erudite than the established Catholic clergy, but their lack of erudition and return to scripture gave them "some advantage in almost every dispute."[121] Most important was their "coarse and rustic eloquence," which spoke to the

---

[114] WN v.i.g.25.
[115] WN v.i.g.25.
[116] WN v.i.g.25.
[117] WN v.i.g.25.
[118] WN v.i.g.25.
[119] WN v.i.g.28.
[120] WN v.i.g.29.
[121] WN v.i.g.29.

people in a way the Catholic clergy, as a corrupt, complacent, educated elite, no longer could.[122] These developments also took place within an international state system in which alliances or enmity with Rome informed religious alignments. Thus, with the multitude on the side of the new preachers, sovereigns on bad terms with Rome quickly aligned themselves with Protestantism.

Smith methodically dissected two new models of church-state relations appeared in the new Protestant states, revolving around the issue of the "right of conferring ecclesiastical benefices."[123] In the Lutheran/Anglican model the sovereign was the "real head of the church" and controlled clerical appointments. State control of the church was "favourable to peace and good order, and to the submission [of clergy] to the civil sovereign."[124] This model had not resulted in "any tumult or civil commotion," with Smith describing Anglican priests as loyal, cultured, learned, liberal, moderate and polite public servants.[125] The Lutheran/Anglican model was not, however, without its trade-offs. The clergy were "listened to, esteem and respected by their superiors," but were "incapable of defending" their "sober and moderate doctrines against the most ignorant enthusiast."[126] They thereby neglected the multitude, the ultimate source of their "influence and authority."[127] The Calvinist model was the inverse of the Lutheran/Anglican. Parishioners had the right of electing their pastor, and the multitude tended to choose the "most factious and fanatical" preachers.[128] This resulted in "disorder and confusion," in a way that corrupted the "morals both of the clergy and of the people."[129] Clerical competition for preferment within a monopoly church in which the fanatical multitude chose the winner led to increasing fanaticism as preachers outdid each other in vehemence.

Smith argued that these dangers ceased when the "rights of patronage" took over from those of popular election. He thereby provided a

[122] WN v.i.g.29.
[123] WN v.i.g.33.
[124] WN v.i.g.34.
[125] WN v.i.g.34.
[126] WN v.i.g.34.
[127] WN v.i.g.34.
[128] WN v.i.g.36.
[129] WN v.i.g.35.

defence of the 1712 Patronage Act.[130] The Act had reassigned the right of appointing ministers from local landowners and Presbyterian elders, subject to the consent of male heads of households, to lay patrons. It remained one of the most controversial issues within the Church of Scotland and wider Scottish society throughout the eighteenth century.[131] The Calvinist clergy now sought preferment through cultivating qualities that impressed their social superiors, as during Smith's lifetime, patrons were made up principally of wealthy landowners and crown officials.[132] Fears that ministers that were not chosen by the presbyters would be of poor quality, or worse, were misguided due to the small size of Scottish ministers' benefices. Because of their small fortunes and small jurisdictions, Presbyterian clergy were a "learned, decent, independent and respectable set of men" who still minister to their flock with attention, compassion and respect.[133] This defence of patronage positioned Smith fulsomely behind the Moderates within the General Assembly of the Church of Scotland.

Smith had two more important observations on religion stemming from his science of society, that a legislator should take onboard. Firstly, the size of benefices within an established church had direct consequences for where the men of genius in a society end up professionally. In societies where church benefices are small and numerous, such as Scotland's, men of talent seek employment in the universities. In a scenario where clergymen can accumulate benefices and wealth, such as in England, men of genius end up in the church. Echoing Voltaire, Smith held that universities in Catholic countries rarely produce eminent men of letters, as men of genius flock to the Church. The same was true of talented men in England, where university professors of international standing were few and far between. Conversely, in Presbyterian states men of talent sought employment in the universities. Secondly, Smith advised his legislator that they should view the revenue of the church as in direct competition with the revenue of the state. It was a "certain maxim" that the "richer the church, the poorer must necessarily be either the sovereign

---

[130] WN v.i.g.37.
[131] See Sher (2015).
[132] Leathers and Raines (2002).
[133] WN v.i.g.37.

... or the people."[134] Monies accumulated by the church were "diverted to a purpose very different from the defence of the state," the aggrandisement of the church.[135] Smith praised the moderate expenditure of the "very poorly endowed" Church of Scotland, which did nothing to hinder maintenance of "the uniformity of faith, the fervour of devotion, the spirit of order, regularly, and austere morals in the great body of people."[136]

Smith's account depicted the key development in religious history of the past millennia as much in terms of the unintended consequences of socio-economic change as the intended consequence of the actions of priests and reformers. Religious change was understood in terms of the ongoing socio-economic transformation of Europe in conjunction with the all too human motivations and behaviours of Europe's priesthoods. Similarly, the issue of how to manage religion, especially in institutional terms, was viewed as a key question of political economy.[137]

* * *

Smith treated religion in a naturalistic fashion, as a subject not framed by theological concepts and the biblical framework but as something analysed in terms of psychological, social and historical observations. In both his published works, Smith was in clear dialogue with Hume, part of their conversation over human nature and society. Smith's conclusions differed from the views of his friend and principal intellectual interlocutor and contain, as Brendan Long has suggested, a "subtle and very polite rebuttal."[138] Smith saw the "natural principles of religion" as outgrowths of our natural moral sentiments and viewed them as beneficial to morality and society in general. Problems arose when those natural principles were perverted away from being a function of morality, such as when scholastic divinity took over. Similarly, Smith disagreed with Hume over the ideal form of relationship between church and state. While he envisioned a future of immense religious diversity made up of sects in

---

[134] WN v.i.g.41.

[135] WN v.i.g.41.

[136] WN v.i.g.41.

[137] Thus Beiner (2010, p. 241) views Smith as tackling the "central" issue of civil religion, how to manage the rivalry between church and state, in a far more direct way than his friend Hume.

[138] Long (2022).

peaceful and productive competition, Smith viewed the mid-eighteenth-century Church of Scotland as the best form of ecclesiastical arrangement currently available for ensuring social peace.

The fact that Smith saw a positive role for religion, at least as a crutch for morality, should not obscure the purely naturalistic way in which he discussed the subject. I am using "natural" here to mean according to the natural order of things, not to mean secular. What can be lost beneath discussion of whether there is a theological underpinning to Smith's thought, such as whether there is "providential guidance" at work in the processes he describes, is that none of his discussion of the natural principles of religion relied upon concepts drawn from scripture, belief in biblical time or a commitment to Christianity.[139] Smith was interested in the "plan and system which nature has sketched out for our conduct," and nature was to be studied entirely on its own terms.[140]

REFERENCES

Ahnert, Thomas. 2015. *The Moral Culture of the Scottish Enlightenment*. London: Yale University Press.

Anderson, G.M. 1988. Mr. Smith and the Preachers: The Economics of Religion in the *Wealth of Nations*. *Journal of Political Economy* 88: 1066–1088.

Beiner, Ronald. 2010. *Civil Religion: A Dialogue in the History of Political Philosophy*. Cambridge: Cambridge University Press.

Berry, Christopher J. 2012. Adam Smith's "Science of Human Nature." *History of Political Economy* 44: 471–492.

Fleischacker, Samuel. 2012. Sympathy in Hume and Smith: A Contrast, Critique, and Reconstruction. In *Intersubjectivity and Objectivity in Adam Smith and Edmund Husserl: A Collection of Essays*, ed. Christel Fricke and Dagfinn Føllesdal, 273–312. Frankfurt: Ontos Verlag.

———. 2021. *Adam Smith*. Abingdon: Routledge.

Graham, Gordon. 2016. Hume and Smith on Natural Religion. *Philosophy* 91: 345–360.

Griswold, Charles L., Jr. 1998. *Adam Smith and the Virtues of Enlightenment*. Cambridge: Cambridge University Press.

Haakonssen, Knud. 1981. *The Science of a Legislator: The Natural Jurisprudence of David Hume and Adam Smith*. Cambridge: Cambridge University Press.

---

[139] Graham (2016, p. 308).

[140] TMS vii.2.1.43.

Hanley, Ryan Patrick. 2015. Adam Smith on the 'Natural Principles of Religion.' *Journal of Scottish Philosophy* 13: 37–53.

Harris, James. 2004. Answering Bayle's Question: Religious Belief in the Moral Philosophy of the Scottish Enlightenment. In *Oxford Studies in Early Modern Philosophy*, vol. 1, ed. Daniel Garer and Steven Nadler, 229–253. Oxford: Oxford University Press.

Heydt, Colin. 2017. The Problem of Natural Religion in Smith's Moral Thought. *Journal of the History of Ideas* 78: 73–94.

Hill, Lisa. 2019. *Adam Smith's Pragmatic Liberalism: The Science of Welfare*. Cham: Palgrave Macmillan.

Kennedy, Gavin. 2011. The Hidden Adam Smith in His Alleged Theology. *Journal of the History of Economic Thought* 33: 385–402.

Leathers, C., and K. Raines. 2002. The "Protective State" Approach to the "Productive State" in The Wealth of Nations: The Odd Case of Lay Patronage. *Journal of the History of Economic Thought* 24: 427–441.

Long, Brendan. 2022. *Adam Smith and the Invisible Hand of God*. London: Routledge.

Minowitz, Peter. 1993. *Profits, Priests, & Princes: Adam Smith's Emancipation of Economics from Politics and Religion*. Standford, CA: Stanford University Press.

Muller, Jerry Z. 1995. *Adam Smith in His Time and Ours: Designing the Decent Society*. New York, NY: The Free Press.

Phillipson, Nicholas. 2010. *Adam Smith: An Enlightened Life*. London: Penguin.

Rasmussen, Dennis C. 2019. *The Infidel and the Professor: David Hume, Adam Smith, and the Friendship That Shaped Modern Thought*. Princeton, NJ: Princeton University Press.

Reisman, David Alexander. 1976. *Adam Smith's Sociological Economics*. New York, NY: Harper & Row.

Sagar, Paul. 2020. Adam Smith's Genealogy of Religion. *History of European Ideas* 47: 1061–1078.

———. 2022. *Adam Smith Reconsidered: History, Liberty, and the Foundations of Modern Politics*. Princeton, NJ: Princeton University Press.

Sher, Richard B. 2015. *Church and University in the Scottish Enlightenment: The Moderate Literati of Edinburgh*, 2nd ed. Edinburgh: Edinburgh University Press.

Smith, Adam. [1776] 1979. *An Inquiry into the Nature and Causes of the Wealth of Nations*, ed. R.H. Campbell, A.S. Skinner, and W.B. Todd. Indianapolis, IN: Liberty Fund.

———. [1795] 1982a. *Essays on Philosophical Subjects, with Dugald Stewart's Account of Adam Smith*, ed. W.P.D. Wightman, J.C. Bryce, and I.S. Ross. Indianapolis, IN: Liberty Fund.

———.1982b. *Lectures on Jurisprudence*, ed. Ronald L. Meek, D. D. Raphael and Peter Stein. Indianapolis, IN: Liberty Fund.

Smith, Craig. 2018. Adam Smith on Philosophy and Religion. *Ruch Filozoficzny* 73: 23–39.

Stewart, Dugald. 1854–1860. *The Collected Works of Dugald Stewart*, 11 vols., ed. William Hamilton. Edinburgh.

Vivenza, Gloria. 2001. *Adam Smith and the Classics: The Classical Heritage in Adam Smith's Thought*. Oxford: Oxford University Press.

CHAPTER 5

Henry Home, Lord Kames on Mechanistic Human Nature

Abstract In his *Essays on the Principles of Morality and Natural Religion* (1751) and *Sketches of the History of Man* (1774), Henry Home (Lord Kames from 1752) authored two of the most comprehensive and ambitious treatments of religion published during the Scottish Enlightenment. Each work utilised a distinct form of analysis. The *Principles* contained an ahistorical conjectural account of the shift from primitive polytheism to refined monotheism once man had moved into civil society. The *Sketches* accumulated masses of examples from the "history of man" to delineate very specific trajectories of religious change—though, noticeably, without viewing socio-economic development as a significant factor in explaining development. The conclusions Kames drew set him apart from even Moderate Christian theology in mid-eighteenth-century Scotland.

Keywords Lord Kames · Civil society · Primitive polytheism · "History of Man" · Conjectural history · Philosophical theism

In his *Essays on the Principles of Morality and Natural Religion* (1751) and *Sketches of the History of Man* (1774), Henry Home (Lord Kames from 1752) authored two of the most comprehensive and ambitious treatments of religion published during the Scottish Enlightenment.[1] They also reflect two different approaches that are placed under the banner of the "science of human nature." The *Principles*, a treatise-like set of essays on human nature, contained a mechanistic account of how religious belief is formed, in which a number of non-rational, internal senses in human nature responded to exogenous factors. The *Principles* was the first major naturalistic and conjectural discussion of religious development published during the High Scottish Enlightenment, and this fact necessitates we recalibrate any sense of Hume's NHR being the chronological beginning of enlightened Scottish discussions of the progress of religion. The *Sketches*, while utilising much of Kames' earlier work, was a contribution to the "History of Man," and provided taxonomic stadial histories of man's "sense of deity," and systems of theology and idolatry, built on exhaustive historical examples. One key conclusion, however, is that in Kames' *Sketches* the stadial history of religion is not related in any systematic way to socio-economic stadial history, but that religious development has an inner logic of its own. Reading Kames prompts us to question some of our generalisations about the enlightened Scottish discussion of religion.

Kames's *Essays on the Principles of Morality and Natural Religion* (1751)

Kames did not expressly describe the *Principles* as a contribution to the incipient "science of man," but he explicitly linked himself to the project of applying the methods of natural philosophy to the study of human nature. The *Principles* was a "system of morals," based on facts that "arise out of human nature."[2] Kames praised "late inquiries after truth" that had "submitted" the study of moral philosophy "to the slow and more

---

[1] On Kames see, most recently and most fully, Rahmatian (2015, esp. Ch. 4.). See also Lehmann (1971, esp. 270–283), Ross (1972), Grobman (1981), Helo (2001), Harris (2005, Ch. 4), Crowe (2010) and, especially on religion, Mills (2015).

[2] Kames (2005, p. 23).

painful method of experience," as has been "applied to natural philosophy with great success."[3] Without the appeal to "facts and experiments," we develop only "superficial knowledge" and are guided by our imaginations, "own taste and fancy" and the "pleasure of novelty."[4] An empirical study of human nature would lead to a moral philosophy that avoided two major failings Kames viewed as characteristic of the subject: those which "exalt man to the angelic nature" and those that "assign them laws more suitable to brutes than to rational beings."[5] In Baconian and Newtonian language, Kames set out instead to apply the "synthetical method" of deducing the laws of morality from the laws of human nature, a process involving first drawing inferences from accumulated experience of human nature, but then analysing those inferences to draw out the general laws of morality.[6]

In the *Principles* Kames sought to demonstrate that religious beliefs "rest ultimately upon sense and feeling," and not ratiocination.[7] When allowed to function properly, human nature is framed to instinctively develop beliefs about God upon focused experience of the natural world. The "universal conviction" that God exists was found in "all civilized nations," which was evidence that belief in God had some natural foundation, though one that only bore fruit in civil society.[8] Kames placed the earlier internal sense theory of religion, which we can associate with Shaftesbury, Hutcheson and Turnbull, into a conjectural model stressing the deterministic role of the establishment of civilisation. While we have natural religious tendencies, they only function properly in stable social contexts. The trajectory of religious development presented in the *Principles*, however, took the form of a imagined simple progression from "savage" to "civil" society and, resulting from that societal shift, the change of religious beliefs from polytheism to monotheism. This was

[3] Kames (2005, p. 23).
[4] Kames (2005, p. 23).
[5] Kames (2005, p. 23).
[6] Kames (2005, p. 23).
[7] Kames (2005, p. 3). For a useful discussion see McDermid (2018, esp. pp. 57–58).
[8] Kames (2005, p. 214).

unlike the stadial approach, ground in historical facts, that Kames subsequently adopted in his *Historical Law-Tracts* and, when it came to religion, his *Sketches*.[9]

Kames believed that his correct study of human nature provided a superior explanation of the origin of religious ideas to those present in Hume's *Treatise*, *Essays* and *EHU*, that implied by the rationalist natural theology epitomised by the Samuel Clarke's Boyle Lectures and by Locke's arguments set out in Book IV of the *Essay concerning Human Understanding* (1690).[10] Hume viewed commonplace religious beliefs as superstitious errors emerging out of a fear-addled imagination. Kames, by contrast, argued human nature possessed instinctive perceptions and feelings that lead to core religious beliefs, and their instinctiveness demonstrate the naturalness and truth of belief in and worship of God. But Kames was more concerned with rebutting Clarke. The instinctiveness of the processes that led to religious belief were a rebuttal to arguments, found in the latter's Boyle Lectures, for the existence of God that were result of long trains of abstract reasoning.[11] Clarke's "deeply metaphysical reasoning" was not suitable for the multitude and raised the scandal that knowledge of God was left only to "persons of great study and deep thinking."[12] Kames also dismissed Locke's arguments that we can prove God's existence by the argument that "whatever had a beginning must be produced by something else."[13] Locke's argument failed because the alternative suggestion, that humans had existed from eternity, was equally as plausible as the idea of an instance of first creation and was only persuasive to "so consummate a logician as Mr. Locke" because he already possessed an "antecedent conviction of a self-existent intelligent being."[14] Kames aimed to demonstrate that a good God had framed human nature so we instinctively come to knowledge of, and duty to, our creator.

---

[9] On Kames and stadial thinking see Rahmatian (2015, pp. 143–145, 245–249).

[10] Locke (1690, iv.x).

[11] In his *Loose Hints on Education* (1782), Kames described Clarke as one of those "unfeeling men" who denied that God could be the object of the passions. See Kames (1782, p. 232).

[12] Kames (2005, p. 201).

[13] Kames (2005, pp. 202–203) and Locke (1690, iv.x.4).

[14] Kames (2005, p. 202).

Kames thus believed that proofs drawn from a priori reasoning for the existence and attributes of God are inappropriate for "common apprehension," and that all "abstract reasoning upon such a subject, must lead into endless perplexities."[15] Especially amongst those "persons of a peevish and gloomy cast of mind," the pursuit of abstract reasoning when it comes to God inevitably leads to fatalism or atheism.[16] Rather, it is from our experience of the natural world, "a method," by contrast to abstract theology, "entirely suited to our nature," that we derive secure religious beliefs.[17] Our religious notions were not the result of "so weak a principle as reason," but from the combined efforts of a series of affections and intuitive principles.[18] We instinctively perceive causality, order, design and beauty in the world, which leads to the easy acceptance of the cosmological and design arguments for the existence of God. This acceptance in turn triggers our moral sense, and we come to feel awe and gratitude towards the supreme being. These are convictions that we develop "from sense and feeling," and in ways that work "silently and without effort."[19] In a passage added to the second edition published in 1758, Kames refined his description of instinctive processes as those by which "we perceive certain propositions to be true, precisely as by sight we perceive certain things to exist."[20] "Intuitive knowledge," such as that which lead us to belief in a wise, benevolent deity, stood "higher in the scale of conviction" than chains of reasoning, which had greater "chance of error."[21] Befitting a wise creator, the foundations of natural religion were thus built on a more secure footing than reason alone. Human nature is determined to think certain things and we cannot reject these thoughts without doing violence to our very nature.

While he introduced a single "sense of deity" in the *Sketches*, in the *Principles* Kames claimed religious belief and worship were the composite outcome of several principles "wrought into our nature," by which, when they are able to function properly, we "infallibly" come to knowledge

---

[15] Kames (2005, p. 203).
[16] Kames (2005, p. 203).
[17] Kames (2005, p. 204).
[18] Kames (2005, p. 69).
[19] Kames (2005, pp. 3, 215).
[20] Kames (2005, p. 212).
[21] Kames (2005, p. 212).

of God.[22] The two key principles were our internal aesthetic and moral senses, acting in sequence. The aesthetic sense first perceived harmony, order, beauty and design in the natural world. Once we can "relish beauties" of evident design we can "begin to perceive the deity, in the beauty of the operations of nature."[23] Our moral sense instinctively judges the "deliberate intention" behind the operations of nature and quickly attributes to the creator being the attributes of wisdom, benevolence and goodness.[24]

Kames presented human nature as a "complex machine" made up of "so many springs or weights, counteracting and balancing one another," and which only functioned properly in the secure surroundings of civil society.[25] The threatening environment of savage life served to "disorder the balance and derange the whole machine" of human nature.[26] The domination of appetite and passion prevented the individual experiencing the world as anything other a morass of "particular objects" affecting their survival, with our innate ability to perceive "general and complex objects" unable to develop.[27] Man in the first groupings of savages was a "most indigent creature," characterised by "barbarity, roughness and cruelty."[28] Life in insecure and violent surroundings meant early humans were motivated primarily by their "brutish principles of action" and not "according to the whole of [human] nature."[29] "Tyrannised by passion and appetites," they lived in an "instinctive manner, without the intervention of any sort of reasoning or reflection."[30] Moreover, "conscious of nothing but disorder and sensual impulse within," early man projected malevolence onto "every extraordinary event," leading to a polytheism of threatening invisible spirits.[31]

[22] Kames (2005, p. 206).
[23] Kames (2005, p. 207).
[24] Kames (2005, p. 28).
[25] Kames (2005, p. 63).
[26] Kames (2005, p. 63).
[27] Kames (2005, p. 63).
[28] Kames (2005, p. 62).
[29] Kames (2005, p. 41).
[30] Kames (2005, p. 46).
[31] Kames (1751, p. 331). This line was removed from subsequent editions. Cf. Kames (2005, p. 214).

As humans moved from savage to civil society, so their natures went from being disordered to ordered, and so their religious beliefs moved from polytheism to theism. This was a process "directed by immutable laws."[32] As man moves into civil society, the "powers and faculties" of the individual are "improved by education and good culture," and "gradual advances in social intercourse."[33] As society makes "gradual advances in social intercourse" the "dread of evil spirits wears out."[34] It is "to society we owe ... knowledge of the deity," as stability, sufficiency, peace and social interaction allow the religious propensities of human nature to function properly. In civil societies humans were able to look beyond their immediate sense experience and "take in, at one view, the natural and moral world," and from here come to belief in God.[35] Once in civil society, "we need but to open our eyes, to receive impressions of [God] almost from everything we perceive."[36] The perception of the deity was "as distinct and authoritative, as that of external objects" and something that humans were "passive" in receiving.[37] Likewise, we develop "strong and evident feelings" that God is to be worshipped.[38]

Publication of the *Principles* prompted an outcry from the Evangelical or High-Flying Party within the Church of Scotland in summer 1755, though the attempt to censure Kames failed.[39] Though of secondary importance to Kames's denial of free will, his discussions on the foundations of humanity's knowledge of the existence and attributes of God, and his failure to suggest that the immortality of the soul was a belief of

[32] Kames (2005, p. 214).
[33] Kames (2005, p. 214).
[34] Kames (2005, p. 214).
[35] Kames (2005, p. 206).
[36] Kames (2005, p. 207).
[37] Kames (2005, p. 207).
[38] Kames (1751, p. 99). Changed to "cogent principles" in later editions. See Kames (2005, p. 69).
[39] See also Mills (2015), Harris (2005, pp. 97–103) and Ahnert (2015, pp. 96–99, 112–115).

natural origin, were subject to severe criticism.[40] Like Archibald Campbell, Kames was charged by orthodox Presbyterian critics of denying man's ability to learn the tenets of natural religion through the universal means of the light of nature—though unlike Campbell, Kames believed the existence of God was perceived instinctively once we had moved into civil society. Kames' critics rejected his conjectural historical approach, pointing to both scripture and ancient pagan texts as informing us of the true histories of first societies and of the history of idolatry as resulting from fallen human nature. Kames was also guilty of striking omissions: he discussed neither the existence of an immortal soul nor any future rewards or punishments as instinctively developed beliefs. Human nature was only framed, Kames implied, to believe in the existence of God—notions of soul and immortality were not natural.

With help of at least Hugh Blair (1718–1800), Kames penned the anonymous *Objections against the Essays on Morality and Natural Religion Examined* (1756). The work tried to frame Kames' position as more in tune with Calvinist notions of predestination and the *sensus divinitas* than his critics' own views. But the *Objections* could not hide the gulf between Kames' enlightened conjectural theory of religious development, informed by the "science of man," and the strictures of traditional Presbyterianism. When Kames did subsequently refine his argument in the 1758 edition of the *Principles*, it was not in response to clerical pressure but to the arguments of Hume's "Natural History of Religion." Kames abandoned his dichotomous picture of the switch from polytheism to theism and accepted that there were "natural gradations" of religious belief as society progressed.[41] While the first religious beliefs would have been of the existence of malevolent invisible spirits, Kames adopted Hume's view that "tutelary deities" would soon come to be worshipped.[42] Kames rejected, however, that the "deification of heroes" would have happened amongst primordial societies on the grounds that savages do not have any

---

[40] Ahnert (2015, pp. 89, 97) reads Kames as believing that "natural reason was insufficient to demonstrate the existence of a future state," and therefore there was "at least an intellectual affinity" between the "skepticism" of the Moderates on the powers of reason and the necessity of revelation and Kames's position. Still, I find nothing in Kames's thought that suggests that revelation is necessary for understanding immortality or behaving morally.

[41] Kames (2005, p. 217).

[42] Kames (2005, p. 217).

"notions of immortality."[43] Kames' refined picture in the 1758 edition anticipated the more granular stadial history of religious progress he would present in the *Sketches*. This speaks to the growing awareness of the historicity of human nature amongst enlightened Scottish social theorists in the 1750s, something that Kames had contributed to with the *Principles*, but which he refined in response to Hume's NHR.

Overall, the originality and, for what it is worth, chronological priority of Kames's *Principles* within Scottish Enlightenment social theory has been missed. Douglas McDermid views Kames as the "de facto founder of the Scottish common sense realist tradition."[44] This may be true, though it is noticeable that Kames's interest in demonstrating the instinctive quality of religious belief is not replicated in either the published discussions of James Beattie or Thomas Reid on the origins of our religious notions. For our purposes, Kames's *Principles* is more significant because it was the first published conjectural account of the natural development of religion, which set aside the traditional Christian model of the corruption of pristine Noachite theism into idolatry and instead maintained the process of progress from polytheism to theism. Neither scripture nor Christian concepts played a role in Kames's argument; similarly, the other normal tenet of early modern natural religion, the existence of an immortal soul, was quietly rejected as an instinctive belief. But the *Principles* was written with a natural theological aim of explaining how our non-rational religious feelings and intuitions were the legitimate foundations of religious knowledge, as a superior account of the naturalness and truth of belief in and worship of God than those provided by Locke and Clarke, and against the scepticism of Hume.

THE *SKETCHES OF THE HISTORY OF MAN* (1774) AND THE "SENSE OF DEITY"

The discussion of religious topics in Kames's *Sketches of the History of Man* (1774) was the most extensive published by any *literatus* during the Scottish Enlightenment. He dealt not only with the progress of fundamental religious tenets, but also with the origins and development of

---

[43] Kames (2005, p. 216). In a passing comment, Kames later changed his opinion on belief in the immortality of the soul amongst savage peoples in the *Sketches*. See Kames (2007, vol. iii, p. 231).

[44] McDermid (2018, p. 57). See also Fate Norton (1966).

idolatry, of types of religious worship, of tutelary deities, of attitudes towards providence and of views on religious toleration. Whereas the *Principles* was a work of natural theology contained conjectures about religious development based on an account of human nature, as its title indicates, the *Sketches* was a contribution to the "History of Man" constituted of the mass accumulation of historical instances of religious belief and behaviour. Unlike the speculative, schematic analysis of the *Principles*, in the 1770s Kames now attempted to reconcile the existence of universal religious principles with the empirical evidence of religious diversity. His turn towards a more historically-sensitive account of human nature can be pinpointed to composition of his *Historical-Law Tracts* (1758), in the aftermath of the publication of the *Principles*.

Kames prefaced his sketch of the history of religion with an essay on the "Existence of a Deity," in which he restated his position that (a) religion was natural to humans; (b) its naturalness demonstrated the existence of God and (c) the multitude know religion by dint of their internal senses. Kames simplified his account of human nature, claiming it possessed a "sense of deity," that instinctively perceived God.[45] Humanity also possessed "innate" principles that made us believe that we should worship God and that God will punish or reward us for our actions on earth.[46] The existence of these principles were proven by the universality of religious belief and worship and, in turn, the existence of the principles was "complete evidence" that God exists, given that when our senses are "in order" they "never deceive us."[47]

Kames argued he had rebutted several prominent contemporary theories on religion. The view, associated amongst the moderns with Thomas Hobbes, Baruch Spinoza and Bernard Mandeville, that found the origin of religion primarily in fear was rejected as conflating the character of primordial man with man in civil society. Primordial religion emerged from the passions, but the picture changed as improving societal contexts changed which were the dominant passions. Kames also reiterated his criticism in the *Principles* of those philosophers who believed that "perspicuous reasoning" was necessary for believing in the existence of God,

---

[45] Kames (2007, vol. iii, p. 795). Rahmatian (2015, p. 140) holds that there is no "substantial difference in the approaches taken in the *Essays* [i.e. Principles] and in the *Sketches*."

[46] Kames (2007, vol. iii, p. 795).

[47] Kames (2007, vol. iii, p. 796).

on the grounds that the historical record demonstrated that pre-scientific primordial societies believed in God.[48] Finally, he rejected Hume's claim in the NHR that all religions other than philosophical theism should be dismissed as superstition. Religious diversity should be comprehended, instead, in terms of the "progress of men and nations from infancy to maturity," with it being the "plan of providence" that "maturity in the arts" leads to knowledge of true religion.[49] Each stage was necessary in reaching its final endpoint in a heart-felt deistic religion.

Kames on the Improvement of Theology

In his sketch entitled "Progress of Opinions with Respect to Deity," Kames offered a stadial account of the progress of theology "from its dawn in the grossest savages to its approaching maturity amongst enlightened nations."[50] Theology is used by Kames to refer to systems of belief about supernatural power. What is striking about this sketch is that the "order of succession" of theological systems was a linear process propelled forward by its own internal logic.[51] Kames noted that the speed of development differed from nation to nation according to local circumstances.[52] He did not, however, tie improvements in theology to granular socio-economic changes or psychological processes, only to the claim that "improvements in the mental faculties lead by sure steps, though slow, to one God."[53]

Kames maintained that his accumulation of facts of theologies past and present demonstrated a "wonderful uniformity in the progress of religion through all nations" over six stages of religious progress.[54] These ran: (1) primitive polytheism made up of fearful worship of malevolent spirits; (2) humanoid gods, like those of Greco-Roman antiquity; (3) separation of gods into benevolent and malevolent supernatural beings; (4) henotheism, or "one supreme benevolent deity" ruling over inferior

---

[48] Kames (2007, vol. iii, p. 791).
[49] Kames (2007, vol. iii, p. 818).
[50] Kames (2007, vol. iii, p. 813).
[51] Kames (2007, vol. iii, p. 818).
[52] Kames (2007, vol. iii, p. 818).
[53] Kames (2007, vol. iii, p. 811).
[54] Kames (2007, vol. iii, p. 818).

deities both benevolent and malevolent; (5) rivalry between one benevolent and one malevolent god. The end point of this process was (6) the emergence of the "true system of theology."[55] True theology consisted of "gratitude to the Author of our being, veneration to him as the supreme being, absolute resignation to the established laws of his providence, and cheerful performance of every duty."[56] Kames did not believe that Europe had reached this stage yet.[57]

The focus of Kames' attention was setting out some sort of rational order to the mass of evidence of theological diversity in human history. But he did not provide a coherent, consistent explanation of theological improvement. In terms of the gradual appearance of true theism, two processes were important. The "progress of knowledge" inevitability leads over time to the triumph of explanations of the universe under the "general law of cause and effects."[58] Similarly, the "social affections" increasingly prevail in society, leading to a softening of human nature and an increased awareness of the benevolence evidence in nature.[59] The growing influence in society of benevolence, at the expense of the previously dominating passion of fear, completely altered conceptions of the deity, from an angry, vengeful god to one whose prime attribute was benevolence. But alongside these general processes were more localised, stage-specific ones. The shift from the second to third stage of religion resulted from the sustained experience of living under stable government and benevolent leadership, which lead people to believe that gods could be benevolent too. The shift from the third to the fourth stage, by contrast, resulted from the propensity of human nature to attribute good fortune to once cause, and bad fortune to many causes. The shift to the fifth stage of a rival good and evil god resulted from continued improvement in "natural knowledge," which lead to awareness that there is "much less malice and ill-design" in the world "than was imagined."[60]

Kames repeatedly stressed that certain beliefs did not fit easily into his taxonomy of theological progress. The belief in "tutelary deities" emerged

[55] Kames (2007, vol. iii, p. 813).
[56] Kames (2007, vol. iii, p. 864).
[57] Suderman (2015, pp. 224–225).
[58] Kames (2007, vol. iii, p. 813).
[59] Kames (2007, vol. iii, p. 813).
[60] Kames (2007, vol. iii, p. 812).

once a society experienced good fortune, which was not a development "connected with any one [stage] exclusive of the rest."[61] Similarly, all stages of theological development bar that of true theism incorporated "unsound notions concerning the conduct of providence," namely that God would interpose on our behalf.[62] These notions were pretty much universal because the "bias in human nature," our "curiosity about futurity," had an overweening influence at all times.[63] Likewise, Kames emphasised the enduring character of superstition amongst the multitude, even during an "enlightened age."[64] Finally, the succession of theological systems did not always seem to match the development of society and philosophy. Henotheism was the fourth stage of religion yet was found amongst "enlightened savages," whereas the religion of Greco-Romans was characteristic of the second stage.[65] The reader is left with a sense that Kames could not keep all of his materials of the "History of Man" under his control, and counterexamples burst out that contradicted his stadial history of theological progress.

As David Spadafora has noted, "what is missing" from Kames's analysis, especially when compared to earlier avowedly Protestant theorists of religious progress such as Edmund Law and William Worthington, "is any reference to a series of dispensations from God."[66] That said, Kames ended his first sketch on religion by attempting to explain how the history of Christianity fitted into his stadial account. Unlike Robertson's *Sermon* on the same subject, Kames described the appearance of Christ as occurring in unpromising circumstances. Christianity was held back by the strength of pagan superstition, the limited knowledge of natural philosophy and the moral immaturity of Roman society. This explained its quick decline. Early Christianity was adulterated into henotheism (stage 4) and, by the fifth century, into the worship of saints as tutelary deities who care only for "nations, families and even individuals."[67]

---

[61] Kames (2007, vol. iii, p. 814).
[62] Kames (2007, vol. iii, p. 825).
[63] Kames (2007, vol. iii, p. 825).
[64] Kames (2007, vol. iii, p. 824).
[65] Kames (2007, vol. iii, p. 809).
[66] Spadafora (1990, p. 372).
[67] Kames (2007, vol. iii, p. 817).

Compounding the early corruption of Christianity was the "gross ignorance that clouded the Christian world" once the "northern barbarians became masters of Europe."[68] Additional degeneration had occurred with the "absurd" doctrines of the trinity, transubstantiation and worship of saints that formed the "creed of Athanasius."[69] These "unintelligible" doctrines were "purposefully calculated to be a test of slavish submission to the tyrannical authority of a proud and arrogant priest."[70] The "supreme influence of superstition" continued down to even the Magisterial Reformers, with Christianity only in very recent years beginning the real process of purifying itself.[71] When it came to assess Christianity's place in the history of theology, noticeably, Kames switched from his stadial more to a specifically historical one focusing on post-Roman Europe.

On the Character of Religious Worship

Unlike his account of the development of systems of theology, Kames did not apply a stadial approach to his discussion of religious worship. Instead, he judged the various manifestations of man's innate worshipfulness against what Kames viewed as true worship. The essential content of true worship is personal devotion: obeying the dictates of our moral sense and worshipping God. Piety does not consist in external signs of worship, but the possession of correct moral sentiments. The performance of rites and rituals can serve as acts of "cultivation and exercise" which help maintain a "pure heart and a well-disposed mind," while also indicating our religious commitment to our peers.[72] Worship aids sombre self-examination and acts as a bulwark against the deleterious effects of luxury on our sentiments. Religious worship is purified best by "philosophy and sound sense," which contribute most to "warm heart-worship."[73] But public worship was not demanded by God, and legislators should not

---

[68] Kames (2007, vol. iii, p. 817).

[69] Kames (2007, vol. iii, p. 835).

[70] Kames (2007, vol. iii, p. 835).

[71] Kames (2007, vol. iii, p. 832). This suggests a more critical view of the Reformers than he held in earlier life. See Lehmann (1971, p. 278).

[72] Kames (2007, vol. iii, pp. 836, 837).

[73] Kames (2007, vol. iii, p. 844).

mandate it, not least because mandated performance of ritual "cannot reach the heart."[74]

Surveying the "History of Man," however, shows that nearly all systems of worship have been "gross deviations" from God's plan for humanity.[75] Denying that the historical record informed us about the origin of particular erroneous forms of worship, Kames dedicated himself to identifying three commonplace deviations away from true worship and conjectured their root in the malfunctioning of the principles of human nature. These were possible at all stages of theology. The passion of fear was the likely reason behind common practice of "austerities and penances," in the forms of fasting, flagellation, celibacy, repentance, self-mortification and continual prayer, common in savage and Catholic societies alike, as well as the practice of human sacrifice.[76] An equally prominent cause of erroneous worship was the anthropomorphic treatment of God as a "mercenary being" desiring sacrifices and oblations.[77] These practices were characteristic of ancient Hebrew, Greek, Roman and Hindustani religion. A third common deviation was the practice of idolatry, which emerged amongst early humans who were "not at ease without some sort of visible object to fix their attention."[78] Over time the objects themselves become targets of worship. For example, images go from being aids to "animating devotion," to being treated as the "residence" of the deity, to the "image itself" being a deity.[79]

Studying the diverse systems of religious worship across the "History of Man" led Kames to argue for the desirability of rites and ceremonies framed to fit the limited capabilities of the multitude. This involved a finding a middle path between too many and too few aids to worship. The "superfluity of ceremonies" which characterised Roman Catholic worship "quenches devotion, by occupying the mind too much upon externals."[80] Kames held that the "presbyterian form of worship," by contrast, was

[74] Kames (2007, vol. iii, p. 838).
[75] Kames (2007, vol. iii, p. 839).
[76] Kames (2007, vol. iii, p. 839).
[77] Kames (2007, vol. iii, p. 842).
[78] Kames (2007, vol. iii, p. 845).
[79] Kames (2007, vol. iii, p. 859).
[80] Kames (2007, vol. iii, p. 860).

"too naked" and was "proper for philosophers more than for the populace."[81] Recent secessions from the Church of Scotland were the result of the laity's dislike of the Moderate clergy's unanimated preaching style, and their turn to those preachers who "supply the want of ceremonies by loud speaking" and "much external fervour and devotion."[82] Kames here was in agreement with Hume on the need to carefully manage the multitude's worship informed by a realistic expectation of what forms are possible without encouraging enthusiasm or superstition.

Religion and Morality

The last section of Kames' sketch on religion focused on "morality as a branch of religion."[83] Kames here switched genre again, adopting the guise of a moral philosopher rather than a "Historian of Man." He first outlined the correct relationship between religion and morals and then surveyed the principal dangers to good morals posed by bad religion and ended by offering solutions. God has given us the two moral duties of "doing justice" and "loving mercy."[84] If there is a "union of pure religion with sound morality," the personal and social "blessings" are "immense."[85] The union of true piety and morals, however, is rare and the commonplace existence of "impure religion" easily encourages "gross immoralities."[86]

Common to the other enlightened Scots, Kames saw both speculative theology and excessive external worship as dangerous to morality.[87] In terms of the former, if religion consists in "belief of points purely speculative," it has been divorced from the "will of God."[88] Speculative theology involved disputation on metaphysical questions that could never be decided and thus was a cause of controversy and enmity. Kames recommended established churches adopt a "fundamental law" preventing them

---

[81] Kames (2007, vol. iii, p. 860).
[82] Kames (2007, vol. iii, p. 861).
[83] Kames (2007, vol. iii, p. 864).
[84] Kames (2007, vol. iii, p. 865).
[85] Kames (2007, vol. iii, p. 869).
[86] Kames (2007, vol. iii, p. 870).
[87] See also Ahnert (2013, p. 650).
[88] Kames (2007, vol. iii, p. 870).

from loading their creeds with inessential articles.[89] Early religious education for the multitude, likewise, should focus solely on teaching that God loves good, hates evil, is witness to our thoughts and actions which will be surveyed on the "great day of judgement."[90] Anyone with the "penetration and leisure" to pursue speculative theology should do so as a private pursuit only—in their differing was, Hume, Smith and John Gregory would agree.[91]

In terms of external worship, excess rites and ceremonies satiate man's "stock of devotion" and thereby relax the "obligations of morality."[92] Religions get easily corrupted by an addiction to "frivolous observances, by intemperate zeal, [and] by rapturous ecstasies," and the resulting fanaticism is often "set in direct opposition to morality."[93] The fanatic who believes all is ritual maintains that justice, mercy and "heart worship" are insufficient, and makes God's "yoke severe and his burden heavy."[94] Supported by extensive quotation from §14 of Hume's NHR, Kames saw one particularly heinous breakage of the positive relationship between piety and morals in the monkish virtues, underpinned by what Kames termed the "doctrine of supererogation."[95] Yet Kames' position on keeping our internal sentiments pure was the opposite of Hume's recommendation to keep the multitude distracted by meaningless ritual and ceremony. While Kames signalled his agreement with Rousseau on the ridiculousness of mandating external worship, his arguments were of a piece with Adam Smith's in *TMS*.

The "grossest of all deviations" from "sound morality" and "pure religion" is intolerance and persecution, motivated by an impossible goal of religious uniformity.[96] Persecutors are motivated by the "absurd notion" that heretics are God's enemies, with the absurdity often increased by the fact neighbouring sects with near identical beliefs often brutally persecute

---

[89] Kames (2007, vol. iii, p. 871).
[90] Kames (2007, vol. iii, p. 871).
[91] Kames (2007, vol. iii, p. 872).
[92] Kames (2007, vol. iii, p. 878).
[93] Kames (2007, vol. iii, pp. 877, 879).
[94] Kames (2007, vol. iii, p. 884).
[95] Kames (2007, vol. iii, p. 884).
[96] Kames (2007, vol. iii, p. 891). See also Lehmann (1971, p. 281).

each other.[97] Intolerance is exacerbated wherever priesthoods claim themselves to be intermediary figures between laity and a mercenary God, as this gives them the power to pretend that they are the righteous defenders of God against his enemies. Persecution and bribery achieve only dissimulated public shows of belief, Kames held, while the idea that God is pleased by such means was ridiculous. These methods also have the unintended consequence of increasing religious scepticism amongst those who can see these behaviours for the absurdities they really are. The only legitimate form of proselytising is rational debate conducted in polite fashion between the disagreeing parties. Yet any drive for uniformity of religious belief will fail, because while all humans share the same "passions and principles," the "various tones and expressions of these form different characters without end."[98] Indeed, as Jeffrey Suderman notes, Kames suggested that "God delights in the variety of his creation, even in the diversity of man's religious practices."[99]

The most bewildering period of religious persecution was that associated with Christianity. Here, Kames stated, was a "singular phenomenon in the history of man": the opposition between "practice and principle" in the history of Christianity.[100] The message of Christianity should encourage a "spirit of meekness, toleration and brotherly love," but the annals demonstrate that "persecution never raged so furiously in any other religion."[101] Pagan religion has "few traces of persecution" because each nation (a) "valued itself on being the only favourite of its own deity" and (b) had no professional class of ambitious priests rivalrous to magistrates, who desired uniformity and who might develop schisms in pursuit of their own interests.[102] Intolerance raged between Christianity and the established paganism in Rome because the former sought to replace the latter, and the latter, in response, sought to destroy the former. In the process the "meek spirit of the Gospel" had limited effect on the actions of the zealous new converts and "here, the Man got the better

---

[97] Kames (2007, vol. iii, p. 895).
[98] Kames (2007, vol. iii, p. 903).
[99] Suderman (2015, §4).
[100] Kames (2007, vol. iii, p. 900).
[101] Kames (2007, vol. iii, p. 900).
[102] Kames (2007, vol. iii, p. 901).

of the Christian."[103] Persecution *within* Christianity quickly developed because, as votaries of the new religion migrated to pagan Greece, they adopted the Grecian practice of philosophical disputation. The spirit of religion changed from believing in Christ and doing good works into believing the correct things, with different sects disputing what those correct beliefs were. The new "spirit of disputation" meant that "every trifle was made a subject of wrangling; and hence persecution without end."[104] Whereas Hume viewed with distress the loss of philosophy once it had been colonised by Christianity, Kames viewed with the distress the loss of primitive Christianity, understood as a purely moral religion without speculative doctrines, once Christians had adopted the practices of philosophy.

Each stage of the history of Christianity had seen persecution, regardless of whether the persecutors themselves were formerly persecuted. The worst practitioner of religious persecution was the Catholic Church and, like his contemporaries, Kames had stridently critical views of Catholicism. The millennium before the Reformation were the "dark times of Christianity."[105] Catholic theology turned God into a "mercenary being," and this was exploited to make "riches flow into the hands of the clergy."[106] With wealth came "pride, sensuality and profligacy."[107] The Catholic priesthood transformed Christianity into an "easy service" that mainly aided their own accumulation of wealth.[108] They claimed that faith was the essence of religion, and only they could determine if an individual's faith was genuine. They discarded internal devotion and the performance of moral duties from worship and held that practicing external rituals were "sufficient for salvation."[109] They turned God into a being assuaged and affected by the entreaties the clergy made on behalf of the laity. To Kames, "there never was a religion that deviated more from just principles, than that professed by Christians during the dark ages."[110] Catholicism was

---

[103] Kames (2007, vol. iii, p. 901).
[104] Kames (2007, vol. iii, p. 901).
[105] Kames (2007, vol. iii, p. 897).
[106] Kames (2007, vol. iii, p. 897).
[107] Kames (2007, vol. iii, p. 897).
[108] Kames (2007, vol. iii, p. 897).
[109] Kames (2007, vol. iii, p. 897).
[110] Kames (2007, vol. iii, p. 898).

the epitome of all religious error and imposture. No wonder, as Rahmatian notes, that editions of Kames's *Sketches* published in Catholic states in Germany removed this discussion of Christianity, whereas it was included in their Protestant counterparts.[111]

Allegory and Myth as Childish Fictions

Something of Kames's disdain for previous philosophy and theology comes across in his sketch on the "Progress of Reason." He argues that it has not been until very recently that Europe has reached an age of maturity when it comes to reasoning. What is striking is that Kames includes such "moderns" as Hugo Grotius, the Earl of Clarendon and even the Scottish Enlightenment's hero Francis Bacon as exemplifying childish and ridiculous reasoning on religious matters. Kames spends much of the Sketch exposing the failings of past reasoning based on the "imbecility" of the mind during mankind's "nonage;" the error-creating influence of certain inherent propensities of human nature, such as an overriding concern about futurity or a propensity to see mysterious or hidden meanings behind the banal; and the influence of bad education, not least, Kames notes, the overwhelming influence of Aristotle on European thought, especially "scholastic divinity."[112] All these failings are subject to the "correction of the rational faculty; and accordingly, in proportion as human use of reason advances towards maturity" superstition beliefs decline.[113] This reformation has been "exceedingly slow" because the "propensity" to believe in "wonders, prodigies, apparitions, incantations, witchcraft and such stuff … is exceedingly strong."[114]

In terms of our "natural biases" pushing us towards errors in reasoning, Kames dwells on the human mind's propensity to explain things in terms of "mystery and allegory," which he viewed as responsible for much false religious belief.[115] This position informed Kames's dismissal of the practice of mythography as a wholly misguided attempt

---

[111] Rahmatian (2015, pp. 131–132).
[112] Kames (2007, vol. iii, pp. 599, 629).
[113] Kames (2007, vol. iii, p. 617).
[114] Kames (2007, vol. iii, p. 617).
[115] Kames (2007, vol. iii, p. 622).

to find deeper meaning in the religious tales, rites and ceremonies of primitive peoples.[116] To Kames, it was quite simple. Primitive peoples needed rites and ceremonies to remain socially cohesive, not least because such practices are useful for "occupying the vulgar" and it is "of no importance what they be, provided they prevent the mind from wandering."[117] The untutored human mind cannot handle this and must make up myths and allegories to give banal practices greater meaning than they actually possess. The stories developed about them result from our propensity to cloak behaviours or practices we deem important in mystical explanations or fables. Relatedly, Kames examined how the traditional tales of primitive societies were turned into sophisticated allegories by subsequent generations. The Greeks turned the simple fables they inherited into allegories, because their vanity as a civilised people meant they have to dub their ancestors as "profound philosophers" though they were really "mere savages."[118] The "endless attempts to detect mysteries and hidden meanings" in ancient fables betrays the fact that the fables are the ridiculous stories of man in his nonage.[119] Citing Pope as arguing for the profundity of ancient fables, Kames scoffs (with an echo of the opening of Hume's NHR) at the idea that "the farther back we trace the history of man, the more of science and knowledge is found; and consequently that savages are the most learned of all men?"[120] Thomas Blackwell, then, had failed to think like a "scientist of human nature" about the "history of mankind," in not realising how the conditions of primitive peoples affected the forms of religious belief, rite and ceremony they practiced. But, happily, "enlightened reason" is unmasking ancient fables as the "invention of illiterate ages when wonder was the prevailing passions."[121] Here, as clearly as anywhere, was an enlightened Scottish rejection of the pre-existing practice of mythography and an assertion of

---

[116] This was a complete rejection of mythography as an informative discipline relevant to the "history of man": "Let other interpreters of that kind pass: they give me no concern." See Kames (2007, vol. iii, p. 623).

[117] Kames (2007, vol. iii, p. 622).

[118] Kames (2007, vol. iii, p. 623).

[119] Kames (2007, vol. iii, p. 623).

[120] Kames (2007, vol. iii, p. 627).

[121] Kames (2007, vol. iii, p. 628).

the interpretative superiority of the "science of man" tackling the "history of mankind."

Things appear different when the reader turns to another lengthy discussion about religion Kames authored, found in his *Loose Hints on Education* (1781).[122] The work has not been treated as an important item in Kames' oeuvre, not least because it is a guidebook for parents, nurses and tutors and was not a philosophically weighty contribution to the Scottish Enlightenment.[123] However, the *Loose Hints* sees Kames put his understanding of human nature to use in service of educating children; in the process, we get a further sense of how humanity's inherent religiosity is to be guided into benign belief and behaviour. The discussion, in Section VII, on religion built on much of what Kames had already articulated in the *Sketches*, and here, unlike in either *Principles* or *Sketches*, Kames included discussion of the benefits of revealed religion, though written by "another hand" who was not named, and belief in the immortality of the soul in the education of children.[124] The "being of a God and the worship due to him" are "engraved on the mind," and, as such, religion is a "branch of our nature" that needs to be considered when raising children.[125] Kames dismissed Rousseau's argument in *Emile* (1761) that religious education should be staved off until the child was at least fifteen years old.[126] Given humanity's natural religiosity, the duty of the parent was to direct this propensity towards beliefs and behaviours that benefitted the child and their society at large, and which made the notion of a benevolent and human God a "ruling principle of action."[127]

Both natural and revealed religion had a role in teaching children religious notions and worship that will make them happy and virtuous. On a social level, Kames viewed the "impression of the deity" as Britain's last and best hope to "stem the tide of corruption in an opulent and luxurious

---

[122] I use the enlarged second edition published in 1782.

[123] Rahmatian (2015, p. 25) opined that the *Loose Hints* and Kames's *Introduction to the Art of Thinking* (1761) "do not rise beyond comparable literature of their kind at the time."

[124] See also Ross (1972, p. 366), Ahnert (2015, p. 78).

[125] Kames (1782, p. 190).

[126] Kames (1782, pp. 238–239).

[127] Kames (1782, p. 191).

nation."[128] Key was educating them so that they consider "the Deity in the admirable light of a friend and benefactor", which will encourage "serenity of mind and cheerfulness of temper."[129] And this was to be done by casually pointing out God's benevolence as the child experiences the natural world.[130] This avoided the approach that presented God as "severe and unforgiving" and struck fear into the hearts of children, and which produced either "abject superstition" or the "total neglect of religion."[131] Like Joseph Butler and John Gregory, Kames viewed the passions conducive to religious devotion as being highly beneficial and the principal means through which the multitude were religious, but which had been criticised by recent rationalist theologians—Kames again had Samuel Clarke in mind—who were concerned about the dangers of religious enthusiasm. While understandable in an "age of ignorance," in modern terms fear of enthusiasm was getting in the way of the proper cultivation of our religious passions.[132]

Whereas Kames's framing of natural religion in *Loose Hints* was straightforward, according to the anonymous co-writer of the Appendix on Religious Education the meaning of revealed religion was a more complicated issue given that it is "not stamped on the heart, but requires profound reasoning."[133] Misguided engagement with scripture raises the dangers of enthusiasm and superstition and, though not without risk, the best method is usually for parents to stick with the established religion. Christianity was the "most perfect of all" religions, but Kames did not think that "Christianity is the only road to heaven" and he also held that revealed religion had to be subject to the judgements of "reason, the

[128] Kames (1782, p. 199). On Kames's views of "commercial society" see Berry (2013) and Mills (forthcoming). See also Hanley (2011).

[129] Kames (1782, pp. 193, 194).

[130] Kames (1782, pp. 208–213).

[131] Kames (1782, p. 194).

[132] E.g. Kames (1782, p. 232).

[133] Kames (1782, p. 202). Without further evidence, it is unclear what we can infer from the fact Kames asked another author to write guidance on the topic of revealed religion. It might suggest, for example, a deliberate act of putting space between the arguments contained therein and Kames, especially given the striking claim that Christianity was not the only valid religion, and thereby offer some protection should Kames again be on the receiving end of attempts to censure him by more orthodox members of the Church of Scotland. Still, much of the material not written by Kames contained opinions he had expressed elsewhere.

moral sense, and the sense of deity."[134] Sincerity was key, given that most people are raised in the religions of their ancestors and do not have the powers of reason and judgement to make a choice themselves. Participation in "social worship" is praised because it "promotes a sense of God and of the moral obligation among men," but the particular type of worship is not prescribed.[135] Moreover, Kames and his co-writer recommended parents teach religious tolerance, especially when differences between sects are "purely speculative" and pertain nothing to morals.[136] The "oceans of blood" that fill the history of Christianity could have been "entirely prevented by wholesome education ... that difference in opinion is no just cause of discord."[137]

The content of Kames's recommendations on religious education in *Loose Hints* raises the interpretative issue of the differences with the *Principles* and, especially, the *Sketches*. In *Loose Hints*, Kames recommends that parents raise their children to hold a notion of providence that includes acts of direct intervention by God, such as moments when accidents do not lead to severe injury or death and give a child pause for be thankful. Similar, the doctrine of a future state is an "essential branch."[138] He briefly suggests that notions of immortality are opened in the child's mind "through the vale of death" and the "value of iniquity."[139] Later he suggests that learning about Christ's resurrection opens up the possibility of immortality to the "eye of sense."[140] But Kames has little to say about the immortality of the soul and life in the hereafter. Instead, he returns to religious notions developed through learning about natural history, experimental philosophy, and then human nature itself. And the key to moral "uprightness" is not the prospect of future happiness or damnation, but a deeply internalised sense that God is good and is on our side.[141] It is from this "sense of the divine presence" that children will grow into

---

[134] Kames (1782, p. 203).
[135] Kames (1782, p. 238).
[136] Kames (1782, p. 206).
[137] Kames (1782, p. 207).
[138] Kames (1782, p. 213).
[139] Kames (1782, p. 222).
[140] Kames (1782, p. 227).
[141] Kames (1782, p. 235).

pious, virtuous adults.[142] It is noticeable that the reader of *Loose Hints* is encouraged not to be guided on the issue of the afterlife without recourse to the arguments of both "theologians and sceptics," despite the fact the latter have given our ideas of a future life a "discouraging aspect."[143]

Similarly, Article IV of Kames's account of religious education briefly covers the issue of revealed religion. Here, he turns away from direct guidance and towards suggesting that the child is raised to judge for themselves whether Christianity is true or not. This takes the form of a series of questions. And the ultimate standards of truth are the moral effects of Christian doctrine: "does it kindle love to God and man, and established the authority of conscience, and reconcile man to his lot?"[144] If the moral teachings of Christianity align with what the child has already learnt of the benevolent deity, then they can choose to confess their faith in Christianity. Similarly, Article VIII discusses the benefits of prayer for renewing the "impression of God's presence" and establishing "tranquillity of mind on a good foundation."[145] The efficacy of prayer, it is hinted, is an issue of dispute and left up to the individual parent's discretion, and the practice is considered primarily in terms of how it maintains the heart worship Kames had praised in the *Sketches*.[146] The quiet deistic individualism of Kames's position in *Loose Hints*, despite his initial praise of the importance of revealed religion, is evident in his claim that the teachings of scripture had to be subject to the judgements of the individual's "reason, the moral sense, and the sense of deity."[147]

* * *

The implications of Kames's study of religion were to naturalise how to think about religion and to set aside revelation as unimportant to access to true religion. Kames's study of human nature and society led him to a set of arguments about religion that set him apart from even moderate

---

[142] Kames (1782, p. 235).
[143] Kames (1782, p. 213).
[144] Kames (1782, pp. 227–228).
[145] Kames (1782, p. 248).
[146] Kames (1782, p. 248).
[147] Kames (1782, p. 225).

Christian theology in mid-eighteenth-century Scotland. In the *Principles* and Sketches, Kames was clearly an enlightened Deist who rejected so many of the key elements of Christian theology. He did not believe in particular providence, he rejected the existed of free will, his discussion of Christianity lacked any mention of eschatology, he provided no argument for the immortality of the soul and he did not seem to view Christianity as the end point of religious development.[148] Moreover, as Andreas Rahmatian notes, in treating religion as a "socio-anthropological and historical development," Kames turned God and religion into "creatures of man."[149] The implication of his stadial history of religion in the *Sketches* was that the "traditional revealed religions [represented] a lower stage of societal development."[150] It was necessary, in order to reach true conceptualisations of God, was to abandon revelation. While there is a danger here of making Kames more radical than he was—as when Rahmatian describes Kames, despite his clear belief in a benevolent deity, as just as irreligious as Hume, "only more circumspect"—it is clear that the implications of Kames's thought challenged so much of eighteenth-century Scottish Christianity.[151] Difficulties with this reading emerge when we include Kames's discussion of religion in the *Loose Hints*, where Christianity is praised fulsomely. One possible way to explain the difference stances taken on the immortality of the soul and revealed religion being those of issues of genre (educational guidebook) and audience (parents and tutors), while also noting the quietly deistic claim that Christianity is to be judged (and therefore possibly rejected) by the external standard of whether it contributes to encouraging morality.

References

Ahnert, Thomas. 2013. Religion and Morality. In *The Oxford Handbook of British Philosophy in the Eighteenth Century*, ed. James Harris, 638–657. Oxford: Oxford University Press.

———. 2015. *The Moral Culture of the Scottish Enlightenment*. London: Yale University Press.

---

[148] Rahmatian (2015, pp. 131, 135). Cf. Lehmann (1971, p. 274).
[149] Rahmatian (2015, p. 138).
[150] Rahmatian (2015, p. 138).
[151] Rahmatian (2015, p. 51).

Berry, Christopher J. 2013. *The Idea of Commercial Society in the Scottish Enlightenment*. Edinburgh: Edinburgh University Press.

Crowe, Benjamin D. 2010. Religion and the 'Sensitive Branch of Human Nature. *Religious Studies* 46: 251–263.

Fate Norton, David. 1966. From Moral Sense to Common Sense: An Essay on the Development of Scottish Common Sense Philosophy, 1700–1765. PhD Thesis, University of California San Diego.

Grobman, Neil R. 1981. Lord Kames and the Study of Comparative Mythology. *Folklore* 92: 91–103.

Hanley, Ryan Patrick. 2011. Educational Theory and the Social Vision of the Scottish Enlightenment. *Oxford Review of Education* 37: 587–602.

Harris, James. 2005. *Of Liberty and Necessity: The Free Will Debate in Eighteenth-Century British Philosophy*. Oxford: Oxford University Press.

Helo, Ari. 2001. The Historicity of Morality: Necessity and Necessary Agents in the Ethics of Lord Kames. *History of European Ideas* 27: 239–255.

Kames, Lord, Henry Home. 1751. *Essays on the Principles of Morality and Natural Religion*. Edinburgh.

———. 1782. *Loose Hints on Education*. London.

———. 2005 [1751/1778]. *Essays on the Principles of Morality and Natural Religion*, ed. Mary Catherine Moran, 3rd ed. Indianapolis, IN: Liberty Fund.

———. 2007 [1774/1788]. *Sketches of the History of Man*. 3 vols., ed. James Harris. Indianapolis, IN: Liberty Fund.

Lehmann, William C. 1971. *Henry Home, Lord Kames, and the Scottish Enlightenment: A Study in National Character and in the History of Ideas*. The Hague, NL: Martinus Nijhoff.

Locke, John. 1690. *An Essay concerning Humane Understanding*. London.

McDermid, Douglas. 2018. *The Rise and Fall of Scottish Common Sense Realism*. Oxford: Oxford University Press.

Mills, R.J.W. 2015. Lord Kames's Analysis of the Natural Origins of Religion: The *Essays on the Principles of Morality and Natural Religion* (1751). *Historical Research* 89: 751–775.

———. Forthcoming. "Partly social, partly selfish": The Social Evolutionism of Henry Home, Lord Kames. In *The Sociological Heritage of the Scottish Enlightenment*, ed. Tamas Demeter. Edinburgh: Edinburgh University Press.

Rahmatian, Andreas. 2015. *Lord Kames: Legal and Social Theorist*. Edinburgh: Edinburgh University Press.

Ross, Ian Simpson. 1972. *Lord Kames and the Scotland and His Day*. Oxford: Clarendon Press.

Spadafora, David. 1990. *The Idea of Progress in Eighteenth-Century Britain*. London: Yale University Press.

Suderman, Jeffrey. 2015. Religion and Philosophy. In *Scottish Philosophy in the Eighteenth Century. Volume I: Morals, Politics, Art, Religion*, ed. Aaron Garrett and James Harris, 196–238. Oxford: Oxford University Press.

CHAPTER 6

David Hume's "Natural History of Religion" (1757)

Abstract Hume's NHR was the most significant contribution to the Scottish Enlightenment's study of religion, a constant provocation to his contemporaries, and a text of enduring importance. Hume's argument is striking because his naturalistic treatment of religious change was in no way linked to a sense of a providential order. Setting to one side the "minimal theism" known only by a small few since the reformation of letters, Hume charted the development of popular religion as a never-ending cycle between polytheism and theism. This process sprang from the universal properties of human nature, largely without regard to socio-economic and political contexts. But the very existence of this cycle, given that Hume's disingenuous insistence that God existed, was an "enigma" to be pondered by philosophers of human nature.

Keywords David Hume · Natural History of Religion · Religious psychology · Popular religion · Primitive polytheism · "Superstitious atheists"

Hume's "Natural History of Religion," published as one of the *Four Dissertations* (1757), was the most significant contribution to the Scottish Enlightenment's study of religion, a constant provocation to his contemporaries and a text of enduring importance. The dissertation constituted another plank in Hume's application of the "science of man" to natural religion which, as he promised in the Introduction of the *Treatise*, would transform our understanding of the latter subject. Against the somewhat grandiose claims by religious studies researchers about Hume's dissertation initiating the modern study of religion, intellectual historians have identified an extensive set of plausible antecedents to Hume's psychological account of religion such that the dissertation does not appear "remarkably innovative."[1] Some scholars have further downplayed the subversiveness of the NHR by claiming that Hume's arguments were in line with Calvinist orthodoxy.[2] Certainly, many elements of the NHR can be found in earlier works of comparative religion, against which Hume's philology was certainly substandard.[3] Similarly, a number of works shared similar titles, forms of argument and methods, such as John Trenchard's *Natural History of Superstition* (1709) or Fontenelle's *L'origine des fables* (1684). But I think the point can be pushed too far, however, if we fail to comprehend the NHR as part of Hume's "science of man," and treat it instead as an offshoot of the history of idolatry. That is, he was not writing about superstition or fable, but about religion understood in naturalistic terms as a near-universal aspect of our shared human nature. The question here is whether the reader thinks such a generic shift, regardless of the similarity of many of Hume's individual claims in the context of early modern discussions of religion, is a significant moment in the emergence of the secular or naturalistic study of religion.

The NHR was not an original work in the sense that most of its insights about human nature can be found in Hume's previously published works, though they were not supported with ample use of historical examples, principally from pagan antiquity. Still, Hume was clearly engaged in a different exercise to both contemporary Christian mythography and English freethinking, the two usual intellectual contexts into which his work is placed. I would encourage the reader to pay attention to,

---

[1] The most common names in such a list include Hobbes's *Leviathan* (1651), Spinoza's *Tractatus theologico-politicus* (1670) and *Ethics* (1677), Fontenelle's *L'origine des fables* (written in 1684 but published in 1724); Robert Howard's *The History of Religion* (1694); John Toland's *Letters to Serena* (1704); John Trenchard's *The Natural History of Superstition* (1709), and Mandeville's *Fable of the Bees*. See Beauchamp (2007, p. 219), Robertson (2005, pp. 308–316) and Harris (2015, pp. 290–291).

[2] E.g. Stewart (2019, p. 48).

[3] E.g. Levitin (2022, p. 222) and Stewart (2019, p. 48).

borrowing a nice phrase, the "curious, generically novel title" of the NHR.[4] What was fresh, though given Mandeville's contribution not completely new, about Hume's NHR was its entirely naturalistic depiction of the origin and development of religion within human nature. Hume's argumentation is striking because that naturalistic treatment was in no way linked to a sense of a providential order. He did rely upon a distinction between true religion, a "minimal theism," known only by a small few and only since the reformation of letters, and everything else—if anything, this move towards true religion existed entirely separate to the flux and reflux of popular religion between polytheism and monotheism. This meant that the cycle of religious change observable across human history occurred without any regard to truth. The existence of this cycle of religion through various forms of false belief, given that Hume claimed it was clear that God existed, was an "enigma" to be pondered by philosophers of human nature.[5] Hume's NHR provided a fulsome challenge to providentialist accounts of religious progress—such was found in Kames's *Principles*.

Hume's major achievement in the NHR was to provide a sophisticated account of the psychological factors informing the development of religious belief. This was supplemented by three especially provocative arguments: the inevitability of "flux and reflux" between popular idolatry and popular theism; an account of the social and moral superiority of ancient polytheism compared to contemporary popular theism; and the historical conjecture that the first religion of humankind would have been polytheism. These were claims about the psychology of religion grounded in how the passions and the imagination dealt with the difficulties of the human lot. Social, economic and political factors are present in the dissertation, but they are of distinctly secondary importance, especially when contrasted with the theories discussed in subsequent chapters.[6]

---

[4] Levitin (2022, p. 178).

[5] NHR 15.13. I think this reading of the conclusion of the NHR, that the enigma to be explained is not whether religion is true but how to explain the flux and reflux of religious forms given that God exists, is more accurate than which treats Hume as maintain that religion per se was an 'enigma,' e.g. Schmidt (2003, p. 370). Hume believed he had identified the key features of the relationship between human nature and religion. The insuperable problem was how to tally these findings with the existence of God—scepticism was the only plausible response.

[6] But for a reading of the NHR that stresses the importance of socio-historical contexts see Lingier (2022).

The driving force behind religious change was the inner world of the sensuous, passion-addled, ill-thinking multitude faced by an inexplicable natural world and the incessant anxious thoughts it created within them.

The NHR should not be treated straightforwardly as exemplifying enlightened Scottish theories of religion, as there were major differences between Hume's dissertation and the progressivist theories of religion that came after. Importantly, the theorists who wrote after the NHR situated their accounts of religious change in more overtly societal frameworks of improving natural theological knowledge. While rarely doing so explicitly, such progressivist histories of religious change were providing an alternative, less pessimistic trajectory than the one presented in Hume's often humorous but fundamentally bleak dissertation. Similarly, the authors discussed in latter chapters talked about the possibility of arousing human passions in ways that could mitigate the anxiety-creating effects of hope and fear that Hume identified.

Human Nature and the Lack of Universality

The NHR opened with the claim that belief in "invisible, intelligent power" was "very generally diffused," but had never been universal across human history.[7] The lack of universality demonstrated that religion was not an "original instinct or primary impression of nature," but a "secondary" development that resulted from other aspects of human nature.[8] The annals of the "history of man" demonstrated that religious belief has not been universally present nor uniform in character nor the clear object of a natural principle.[9] So while, to pick one of Hume's examples of an "original instinct," parental love has been found in all societies and the "precise determinate object" of the instinct is clear, this is not the case of religious belief. Parents love their children, but there is no fixed object of religious belief.[10] Hume returns to the origin of religious belief at the end of the NHR where he now describes belief in "invisible, intelligent power" as a "universal propensity" of man, but in the

---

[7] N 0.1. See also Cabrera (2001, esp. pp. 75–85, 86–106). Cf. Yandell (1990, pp. 23–25).

[8] N 0.1.

[9] N 0.1.

[10] N 0.1.

form of a "general attendant" and not a "original instinct" of "human nature."[11] NHR articulated a similar position to Hume's earlier claim in "Of National Characters," that "all mankind have a strong propensity to religion," which emphasised that this propensity was felt at "certain times and in certain dispositions."[12] Hume's identification of a propensity to religious belief suggests that commonplace experiences provoke universal aspects of human nature which develop belief in invisible, intelligent power. The questions to be examined in the NHR are what are those experiences and principles of human nature that lead to religious belief.[13] In this, as Alexander Broadie has suggested, the NHR can be seen as a "further step in the programme of the *Treatise*."[14]

Hume thus challenges any confidence in the inherent tools of human nature to reach basic religious truths, as claimed by early modern natural theology—be it orthodox Calvinism, Deist freethinking or recent moral sense philosophy. Such a belief was contradicted by the fundamental lesson of the natural history of religion: humans were not framed to be believers in "true religion." Atheist societies exist, while the differences in conception of supernatural power meant there was no universal consent for the existence of God.[15] Neither fact about the history of mankind would be true if religion was an original instinct. Moreover, religious beliefs are formed due to the influence of various aspects of human nature, but not those of reason or an inherent "sense of deity." Regardless of the society they live in, the multitude only have the intellectual capacity to deify natural events, viewing them as analogous to human acts with human motivations, and respond by attempting to conciliate the supposed

[11] N 15.5.

[12] NC 6n2.1.

[13] We can describe religion as a 'natural' belief, insofar as it is based on the inherent qualities of human nature, but not as an instinctive belief, insofar as it does not result from a single, original principle. Moreover, Hume will go on to argue that we are not actually clear what religious beliefs are and thus they can be classified further, with Donald Livingston, as "virtually natural belief[s]." Livingston (1998, p. 65).

[14] Broadie (2008, p. 187).

[15] By viewing religion as a secondary characteristic of human nature, Hume implied that atheists could exist (as opposed to just being misguided individuals, nominal atheists, who had turned away from their true natures). In this Hume was in line with Bayle and Locke who, against the commonplace arguments of anti-atheist apologetics, held that an individual could be a genuine believer in atheism. See Numao (2013) on Locke and Levitin (2022, Part II) on Bayle.

supernatural power behind those events through prayers and sacrifices. When Hume concedes at the end of the NHR that belief in "invisible, intelligent power" might be a "universal propensity," this just sets up that the deflationary claim that the forms of belief about God created by this propensity, however, are near universally "disfigured" in their representations, when compared to true theism.[16] This "universal propensity" to religion, however, only conjured up beliefs that, echoing either or both Horace and Cicero, seem like "sick men's dreams."[17] Hume has set aside one prominent theistic framework, be it Christian or deistic, that held that human nature was inherently theistic but that the weight of flawed human nature perverts us and redirects us to superstition and idolatry. For Hume, there was no falling away from an innate propensity to true religion, no such thing exists; the declinist view of religion is unpersuasive.

Hume demonstrated that first religion of mankind was polytheism on the combined basis of historical analysis and inferences from the science of human nature. The "clear testimony of history" was that the further we go back in time, the more often polytheism was the dominant religious system. To argue, as Christian mythographers did (or Joseph Butler or Archibald Campbell, for that matter) when talking about the Noahite era, that the very first societies were monotheist was to claim that while men were "ignorant and barbarous" they were theists, but they "fell into error" as their societies progressed in knowledge.[18] Unstated in this claim, but picked up by many of Hume's Christian readers, was Hume's complete rejection of biblical history and the commonplace Christian (and Deist) argument that pristine true religion was corrupted into idolatry under the influence of weak human nature.[19] Further, recent travel accounts of "savage" societies in the non-European world, taken as comparable to primordial humanity, described their religious beliefs as polytheistic. The primacy of polytheism was further supported by Hume's understanding of "savage" man. In language echoing both the *Treatise* and *EPM*, Hume held that primordial man would have been a "barbarous, necessitous animal," overwhelming concerned with safety and

---

[16] NHR 15.5.

[17] NHR 15.5. Cicero, *De natura deorum*, I.16.42; Horace, *Ars poetica*, Stanza 1 Line 9.

[18] NHR 1.3.

[19] See Schmidt (1987).

subsistence, and unable to "admire the regular face of nature."[20] The "first ideas of religion" arouse from the "incessant hopes and fears" about the "various and contrary events of human life."[21] The imagination's anthropomorphic tendencies would fix on visible objects associated with daily life and project imaginary invisible powers that controlled them.

The transition of polytheism into theism was a process driven forward, not by accumulated knowledge or by improved societal stability, but by the internal pressures of weak human nature facing threats to continued existence. Fearing for their futures and seeking some promise of safety, primordial polytheistic societies would identify a tutelary deity amongst their many gods, who they deemed had jurisdiction over their nation. These national deities would receive "newer and more pompous epithets of praise," until the vulgar reached the notion that their god would be best pleased by being praised as omnipotent, omnipresent and the creator of all things.[22] Driving this process forward was the anxious desire to appease or worship their mercenary deity, and certainly not any sense of either some natural theological insight or newly granted access to revelation. The result was a brief but entirely coincidental alignment of popular superstition with "true philosophy." The "doctrine of theism" was embraced on "irrational and superstitious" grounds suitable to the limited "genius and capacity" of the multitude and bore no actual relation to the God of true theism, superficial similarity aside.[23]

Theism left the multitude feeling "uneasy," however, because the idea of an omnipotent, omnipresent creator God was beyond their comprehension. In their anxiety, they created "inferior mediators or subordinate agents" to interpose between humankind and God, and to which they could direct their entreaties. These intermediary beings soon became the "chief objects of devotion," as bodily objects onto which the multitude's passions and imaginations could rest.[24] Theism collapsed into idolatry, but then the process would just begin again, with concern arising anew about whether God felt he was being worshipped properly now that attention had been directed to spiritual mediators. Not even the "utmost

---

[20] NHR 1.6. Compare to THN 3.2.2.17–20 and EPM 3.4.
[21] NHR 2.3.
[22] NHR 6.5.
[23] NHR 6.4.
[24] NHR 8.3.

precaution"[25] could prevent this cycle between theism and idolatry. In effect, the multitude were always "superstitious atheists"[26] in the sense that their religious beliefs were always utterly different to the beliefs of true theism. From the *Treatise* onwards, Hume had indicated that the "science of man" taught that natural theology—the origin of religion in reason, as he put it in the opening of the NHR—had no legitimate grounds in reason nor experience beyond a "minimal theism." In the NHR Hume indicated, likewise, that, with regard to the origin of religion in human nature, it was atheism, not true theism, that was most natural.

While the bulk of the NHR discussed popular religion, Hume also rejected the commonplace apologetic appeal to the agreement of the wise for the existence of God. The god of true religion, understood as "pure spirit, omniscient, omnipotent, and omnipresent," was not known amongst the pagans.[27] Indeed, little of pagan theology deserved the "dignity [of] the name of religion," with many of the supposedly theistic pagans believing in "angels and fairies" and other absurdities. Even Xenophon, one of the few refined thinkers in antiquity, believed that sneezing was an omen. Hume's dismissive mockery of pagan philosophy extended to those Stoic philosophers often pointed to as representatives of an admirable ancient theism in early modern natural theology, from whom many of the leading figures of eighteenth-century Scottish intellectual life took great inspiration.[28] Tim Stuart-Buttle reads this as partly a refutation of Lord Shaftebsury's attempts to articulate a philosophical theism based on the writings of Epictetus and Marcus Aurelius, both of whom Hume names as worshipping angels and fairies.[29] Moreover, like Locke and Pierre Bayle, Hume criticised attempts to flatten down theological differences over the nature of invisible power into an argument that all philosophers believed in God. Diverse attitudes existed over

---

[25] NHR 8.3.

[26] NHR 4.2.

[27] NHR 1.5. See also Harris (2015, p. 292).

[28] See Brooke (2012, pp. 179–180) and Stuart-Buttle (2019, pp. 210–212). See also Robertson (2005, p. 311) and Ahnert (2015, p. 6).

[29] Stuart-Buttle (2019, p. 209). It is beyond the scope of this book, but Hume's NHR warrants an in-depth historical contextualisation, situating the work into the Franco-British debate over the history of religion, though it would primarily involve identifying textual allusions, given that Hume named very few of the authors he was engaging with.

whether such power was "supreme or subordinate," and whether it was singular or "distributed among several."[30] An argument for universal consent of either the multitude or the wise on the existence of a single deity had no empirical basis.

The "Natural Progress" of Religion?

Dugald Stewart famously set out a summary of the enlightened Scots' "theoretical or conjectural history," which he likened to Hume's use of "natural history" in the NHR.[31] The pseudo-explanatory power of this passage has been the bane of Scottish Enlightenment scholarship ever since. Stewart's framing of Hume's dissertation occludes as much as it illuminates. Hume's theory of religious change exhibited a focus on what Stewart termed "gradual steps," and the transition from the "first simple efforts of uncultivated nature, to a state of things so wonderfully artificial and complicated."[32] The shift from the concrete and particular to the general and the abstract is present in the dissertation, but Hume was not charting what Stewart described as the "regular and connected detail of human *improvement*."[33] Hume did examine, per Stewart's model, the "principles of [human] nature," but he did not examine them primarily in relation to the changing "circumstances of their external situation."[34] The Introduction of the NHR stated that the purpose of the dissertation was to identify those primary causes that lead to the secondary effect of man's propensity to form religious beliefs. The reasoning behind Hume's decision to name his study a "natural history" can only be guessed at, especially when he did not use the phrase in the essay itself, but the fact it is more of a study of human nature than a study of social progress is suggestive.[35] We can tell, however, that he described his methods only in terms of undertaking a study into the inherent principles of human nature and how they manifest themselves, and that he was encouraging

---

[30] NHR 4.1.
[31] Stewart (1854–1860, vol. x, p. 34).
[32] Stewart (1854–1860, vol. x, p. 33).
[33] Stewart (1854–1860, vol. x, p. 33). My italics.
[34] Stewart (1854–1860, vol. x, p. 34).
[35] See Beauchamp (2007) for a useful discussion.

his readers to view a purportedly supernatural phenomenon in purely naturalistic terms.

The origin and development of religion are a special case in Hume's theory of how the universal principles of human nature manifests themselves in different contexts. It was un-sociological. In *EHU*, Hume claimed that from the accumulation of historical knowledge, we "discover the constant and universal principles of human nature"—the "regular springs of human action and behaviour."[36] The results of these principles, usually, depend on the character of specific local circumstances, such as the principle of disputativeness presenting in civilised but not barbarous societies. The case of religion in the NHR, however, is unique because the factors informing the manifestation of the religion-creating principles of human nature have not changed significantly. Most humans have lived lives of misery, vulnerability and changeability, have no knowledge of supernatural power, no intellectual capacity to develop such knowledge, and are involuntarily subject to the "regular springs" of their passions and imaginations responding to their lot. The religious beliefs and practices of most of humanity are purely capricious, with no foundation other than the anxious workings of the imagination. Moreover, religious beliefs cannot endure because we do not experience the benefits they are supposed to bring. Humans have no possible sources of knowledge of divine opinion to know whether their forms of worship are working and remain subject to the influence of unfettered hopes and fears. We choose a tutelary God, but we cannot be sure this is the right thing to do; we turn them into an all-powerful God, but we cannot be sure that our entreaties are being heard; we panic and begin to worship intermediaries, but we cannot be sure that our God would prefer to be worshipped directly. We are stuck with the dread of not knowing whether the beliefs and practices we have chosen are the right ones. This means, moreover, that while systems of justice and government can endure if they provide benefits to individuals and societies, one message of the NHR was that religions cannot replicate themselves in the long term—unless, perhaps, they are so light-touch as to be irrelevant to our daily lives, a collection of enjoyable stories to pass the time.

The NHR is primarily based on accumulated examples from antiquity, supplemented by the occasional appeal to facts from recent travel

---

[36] EHU 8.7.

literature. The dissertation contained, as Hume informed his publisher Andrew Millar in June 1755, "a good deal of literature."[37] Hume saw the ancient pagans as our prime source for understanding polytheism, both popular and philosophical. His remarks on the religious behaviour of the "New World," by contrast, are cursory and primarily supplementary. Even when surveying pagan literature, Hume did not demonstrate the erudition and philological interests of eighteenth-century mythographers and treated pagan texts, somewhat straightforwardly, as storehouses of examples. While it can be read as a witty analysis that, by turns, rejects and mocks most contemporary arguments about the naturalness of religion, the NHR can also read like Hume bolted examples from the history of mankind onto the arguments already formed in the *Treatise*, *Essays* and two *Enquiries*.

Hume's use of evidence is indicative of how he was undertaking a "natural history," rather than a work of comparative religion or a "history of idolatry." He identifies particular religious beliefs and practices that reflect a certain stage in the cycle of religious beliefs; he is not identifying them as reflective of an actual historical moment. The traditional Protestant mythographer's account of the history of ancient paganism's replacement by primitive Christianity and subsequent corruption into superstitious Catholicism can be viewed as an example but is not the sum of what Hume is detailing. He has de-historicised his examples and treated them instead as evidence in the composition of a theory about the religious capabilities of human nature. Commentators often note that Hume's philological skills are poor and his erudition distinctly inferior to the practitioners of early modern comparative religion. This is true but is indicative of how uninterested Hume was in their concerns and how "natural historical" facts about human nature were viewed as being easily extractible from particular historical contexts.

If the cycle of popular religion was a never-ending process, Hume's discussion of changes in systems of theology, the preserve of the learned without society, did have a sense of historical specificity. In §1 of the NHR, Hume notes that the "natural progress of human thought" rises from "inferior to superior," from the particular (polytheistic) to the abstract (theistic), as observation and examination of the natural world

---

[37] David Hume to Andrew Millar 12 June 1755, Klibansky and Mossner (1969).

expands.[38] Contemplation of the works of nature can lead to the apprehension of "invisible, intelligent power."[39] We should not read too much into this passage: Hume is using it to defend the argument that polytheism would have been the first religion of the "ignorant multitude" in the first human societies.[40] The fact that popular religion does *not* actually improve in this fashion is one of the main theses articulated in subsequent sections. Instead, the "natural progress" of religion involves the flux and reflux between equally wrong types of popular polytheism and theism. We can also note that the "natural progress" of popular religion is not from a morally inferior to morally superior form of religion, as popular theism causes more social evils than its polytheist counterpart. The former is dogmatic, intolerant and privileges adherence to rites and ceremonies over social morality; the latter is tolerant and does not privilege rites and ceremonies over social morality. This raises the possibility, as Alexander Broadie notes, of a contradiction between Hume's claim in the NHR that popular polytheism is morally superior to popular theism with his claim that philosophical theism is the "true religion" and superior to polytheism. "True religion," understood as "minimal theism," tells us that we can know very little about the existence and attributes of a first cause and leaves the question of how to manage the superstitious tendencies of the multitude as an all-too human problem.[41]

Hume claimed that true religion had only been known in Europe since the "revival of letters," had been the result of recent advances in natural philosophy, and was only understood by philosophers.[42] As David Livingston notes, philosophical theism is not "continuous with [and] a correction of vulgar theism," but a recent development that instead corrects the "philosophical atheism" of a scattered few ancient philosophers.[43] This is a very circumscribed sense of the "natural progress" of theological thought, if it describes a natural progress at all—the whole thrust of Hume's analysis has been that such thinking as leads to "minimal

---

[38] NHR 1.5.
[39] NHR 2.2.
[40] NHR 1.6.
[41] Cf. Broadie (2008, p. 187).
[42] NHR 4.1.
[43] Livingston (1998, p. 65).

theism" is not natural to the mind. Prior to the revival of European philosophy, all religious systems, philosophical and popular alike, have been based primarily on the absurd superstition resulting from the conjunction of the passions, humanity's anthropomorphic tendency and the instability of the human lot. Knowledge of true religion is a modern development, the result of very specific historical causes in the previous three or so centuries. Given that there is no providential teleology at work in Hume's thought, hitting upon true theism could even be described as a historical contingency and certainly the exception to most of human history. Similarly, knowledge of true religion (minimal theism) has no bearing on what the religion of most humans should be to ensure individual and social tranquillity (polytheists).

The real significance of Hume's claim that polytheism was humanity's first religion was that he meant it to be both a claim about chronological primacy and socio-psychological primacy. Many early modern European mythographers were entirely at ease with the claims that in a fictional state of nature without the assistance of revelation, or at post-Flood moments when religious tradition had been lost, humans would naturally tend to be polytheists, usually astrolaters.[44] We have seen this already with Archibald Campbell. Hume's claims about the primacy and psychology of polytheism had a different quality, however, because he set aside scripture as a privileged source and expressed scepticism about the extent of the historical record of primordial societies.[45] The bible was just one historical source amongst many and, given the weight of evidence for the primacy of polytheism, could be dismissed in the same way that accounts of miracles butted up against the accumulated weight of past experience. The first societies did not exist in a post-Flood moment where true religion would have been known via tradition; the start of human history in Hume's mind did not involve Noah and his sons. Whatever his famous nineteenth-century readers, such as Max Müller, might have taken from the NHR, it is this historical claim about the primacy of polytheism, not the anthropological claim of the same fact, which was provocative about Hume's dissertation.[46]

---

[44] See Levitin (2022).

[45] For some helpful discussion see Merivale (2018, §6.1) and Serjeantson (2012).

[46] See also Wheeler-Barclay (2010, pp. 24–25).

What we know of primordial human nature and society tells us that early religion would have been polytheistic. Hume uses the sort of probabilistic reasoning present in "Of Miracles" that the overriding weight of historical evidence holds for the primacy of polytheism and for the implausibility of the Christian (and Deist) account of the primacy of theism. From the perspective of the science of human nature, shorn of attachment to the absolute truth and explanatory relevance of the biblical framework, the primacy of polytheism is a fact about human history and human nature. In general, some Christian historians of religion might stress the providential role of the ancient Hebrews as receivers of God's dispensation before Christ's arrival. More narrowly, the prominent cleric William Warburton's *The Divine Legation of Moses* (1739–1741) had attempted to separate sacred and profane history by demonstrating that the Jews alone did not possess the doctrine of future rewards and punishments, precisely because they had received a special dispensation from God.[47] But Hume's science of man dismisses (a) the supposed deviation of the theist Jews from the rule of the primacy of polytheism as forming "no objection worth regarding", especially given (b) the similarity between "genius and spirit" of the ancient Egyptian, whose ridiculous beliefs Hume has great fun in mocking, and Jewish religion, which is thereby tarred by the implicit comparison as effectively polytheistic despite claims to the contrary.[48] Having dismissed the Jews Hume pays very little attention to this issue, to the occasional consternation of commentators on the NHR who found Hume's disregard to be inexplicable.[49] As John Robertson notes, Hume's "dismissal of the Biblical Hebrews ... did not even bother to name them."[50] The Jews had no special status and were just one counterexample against the overwhelming bulk of evidence to the contrary. Hume did not even pause to consider why they might have been theists,

---

[47] Robertson (2005, pp. 280–283); Stuart-Buttle (2019, p. 209). On the topic more generally see Assmann (1997) and Serjeantson (2012). Byrne suggests that Hume might have had Locke's *The Reasonableness of Christianity* (1695) in view, given the similar assessment that most of mankind were polytheists aside from, for Locke, the Jews and a few philosophical theists. See Byrne (1989, p. 125).

[48] NHR 1.3, 12.7n58.1.

[49] E.g. Webb (1991, p. 147), Malherbe (1995, p. 262). Compare with Merivale (2018).

[50] Robertson (2015, p. 31).

treating them as a chance occurrence, much in the same way that atheistic societies can exist, and unimportant because of the overlap with the polytheistic Egyptians.

The NHR recast many of the explanations of the origins of religious error found in contemporary Christian mythography. The latter explained the origins of idolatry as involving the corruption of an original pristine theism—known, for example, by Noah and his sons—due to the limitations of human nature. Reiterating an argument from "Of Miracles," Hume accepts with the Christian mythographers that historical facts passed down by "oral tradition from eyewitnesses and contemporaries" are "disguised in every successive narration."[51] Stories about the past are corruptible but, Hume claims, knowledge of philosophical truth is not—true theism would retain its "original purity" from generation to generation.[52] This is true whether the arguments for theism were able to convince the "generality of mankind" or were "abstruse" arguments only intelligible to the philosophers.[53] The fact that all known pagans, people and philosophers alike, were polytheists demonstrates that theism was not the first religion of humanity.

Similarly, Hume accepts with the Christian mythographers that many of the pagan gods were deified humans and that the corruption of real history into fable occurred due to the productions of poets, allegorists, painters and sculptors. The deification of men makes sense when existing deities are "so little superior to human creatures."[54] The worship of statutes of past heroes is understandable given the psychological need of the vulgar to worship "sensible representations" of their deities.[55] But he dismissed as psychologically implausible the common mythographic claim that these developments should be understood in the context of an original theism being altered under the influence of postlapsarian human nature. Rather, they are stages in the progress of popular religion emerging out of a simplistic polytheism.

The NHR was also different to most contemporary accounts of religious change, as Hume described popular religion having its own motive

[51] NHR 1.8.
[52] NHR 1.8.
[53] NHR 1.8.
[54] NHR 5.6.
[55] NHR 5.7.

force and logic of development. Commonplace in Christian mythography and freethinking theories of pristine religion's corruption into idolatry and superstition was the argument of religious imposture, usually by priests and princes seeking their own power. Priestcraft and statecraft, however, play a limited role in Hume's psychological explanation of religious change, with popular religion too powerful a social factor to be determined by the whims or self-interest of specific political figures, though they might profit from it. In Hume's vision of popular religion in the NHR, political and priestly elites are barely in charge of rambunctious, irrational and passionate multitudes. This sense of the impotency of the individual against the multitude is a key aspect of the dissertation's pessimism. As we will see, the progressivist histories that followed after Hume often took as their focus systems of theology, not popular religion, and viewed such systems as determinate, at least to some degree, over the beliefs of the multitude.

Hume's sense of the independence and power of popular religion makes the NHR a pessimistic essay. There is little of the optimism about the influence of philosophical or commercial progress found elsewhere in this book or, indeed, in scattered passages in Hume's earlier writings. Socio-economic and cultural improvement have no real influence over the passions of the multitude. They are not moving closer towards true theism and, because of their weak reasoning abilities and susceptibility to their passions, never can. The ostensible improvement of the transition from polytheism to theism does not constitute real improvement because the multitude do not actually understand the theism they briefly maintained, and because they quickly descend into idolatry. The number of believers in genuine theism in the ancient and modern worlds is negligible; those who have seen the light are usually punished as atheists by their uncomprehending peers.

Even Hume's argument for the social and moral benefits of popular polytheism compared to popular theism is impotent. Systems of religion in which the focus is on the performance of idolatrous rituals and ceremonies have two beneficial consequences: ritualistic religion lies comparatively lightly on the inner world of the believer, leading to the limitation of fanaticism, and the focus on ritual also breaks the link between religion and morality, leading to the independence of the latter and potentially the improvement of moral belief and behaviour. The height of theistic piety, however, has tended to involve the "monkish virtues of mortification, penance, humility, and passive suffering," or

6 DAVID HUME'S "NATURAL HISTORY OF RELIGION" (1757)   165

bigoted and intolerant fanaticism amongst the multitude.[56] This speaks to Hume's larger point that monotheisms encourage fanaticism because of the tenet that there is one true God; monotheism legitimises proselytising zealotry and persecution of religious difference.

Hume's discussion in the NHR, however, was not brimming with immediate recommendations for how to deal with its findings, especially if it is read as describing his preference for a light-touch paganism over current dogmatic Christianity. The dissertation can be viewed as Hume's project, informed by academic sceptical philosophy, to expose the baselessness of religion, with commentators attributing to Hume a farsighted project to weaken the intensity of contemporary dogmatism.[57] But the NHR can be also contrasted with Hume's statements, especially in the *History of England*, where he outlines the necessity of the subordination of church to political authority and of the societal benefits of systems of theistic religion. In the NHR compared to his other works, Hume writes as if neither philosophical theist nor wise politician nor moderate priest nor wider societal improvement can control the cycle between popular idolatry and popular theism.

The narrower recommendation of the NHR is that the genuinely philosophically minded should protect themselves from the dangers of the multitude. Hume reiterated his earlier discussion of the dangers that resulted when theistic theology colonised philosophy. This time, however, he was not referring to Christianity, but to all theisms. Pagan mythology was a selection of harmless stories; philosophers existed in a separate sphere, free to pursue the truth, with their disputes having no effect on society. Hume surveyed two millennia of religious controversy to note that the rational group were always branded the heretics.[58] Theistic theology focuses all its attention on an ultimately unknowable God and takes argument beyond the limits of human experience; polytheism sought no such knowledge. Philosophers are forever under threat of potentially fatal accusations of heresy or atheism. The main practical

---

[56] NHR 10.2.

[57] For example, see Foster (1997), Cabrera (2001), Falkenstein (2003, 2009), and Fosl (2019, esp. p. 47, p. 238).

[58] The publication of the *Four Dissertations*, including the NHR, is often read as a riposte to those orthodox Calvinists within the Kirk who had tried to censure Hume and Kames in the mid-1750s. See, for example, Harris (2015, pp. 354–359).

recommendation Hume makes in the NHR is pitched to his philosophical readers concerned about their own happiness. They should withdraw from the chaos of popular religious life. The only temporal betterment that can be relied upon is the internal psychological one of tranquillity experienced by the philosophical reader who abandons the world. Even this can seem like weak medicine: the tranquillity of the philosopher is a fragile and dispiriting one, forever vulnerable to the changing whims of the passionate, irrational vulgar and requiring withdrawal and avoidance.

Many of the Scottish social theorists discussed in the remaining chapters engaged with Hume's dissertation either explicitly or implicitly, with several recurrent themes. Only Adam Ferguson entirely rejected Hume's claim that polytheism was the "natural" religion of mankind; most accepted the primacy of polytheism as an accurate description of the religious beliefs of primordial humans unassisted by revelation. It was the members of the Aberdonian Enlightenment, and less so William Robertson, who were most vocal in reasserting the account of human history found in scripture and therefore the historical (though not psychological) primacy of theism. Similarly, Hume's dissertation had laid the problem of the enduring superstitious nature of popular religion and the real limitations of the passion-ridden multitude into sharp relief. Many of the scientists of human nature writing after 1757 developed proposals, like Hume had done in several of his own writings, for how the multitude could be guided by sensual aids to practise true religion in a pious and tolerant fashion. Many after 1757 also tried to challenge Hume's comment that it was a "riddle, an aenigma, an inexplicably mystery" that human nature was framed to be superstitious given the existence of a supreme being.[59] Hume had demonstrated that religious error was not "dependent on caprice and accident," but sprung from the "essential and universal properties of human nature."[60] The mystery to be explored was what was the meaning of the fact that human nature was framed for superstition and idolatry, if all creation demonstrates the existence of a supreme being and thus that supreme being therefore framed man to be a superstitious idolator. One particularly prominent development in the succeeding decades was the placement of religion into a progressivist context in which beliefs and behaviour improved over time due to the

---

[59] NHR 15.13.
[60] NHR 5.9, 111.

wider societal changes. In a sense, it was Kames, not Hume, who led the way. But as we will see, the Scots disputed the precise character of this development and its relationship to Christianity.

References

Ahnert, Thomas. 2015. *The Moral Culture of the Scottish Enlightenment*. London: Yale University Press.

Assmann, Jan. 1997. *Moses the Egyptian: The Memory of Egypt in Western Monotheism*. Cambridge, MA: Harvard University Press.

Beauchamp, Tom. 2007. Introduction: A History of Two Dissertations. In David Hume, *A Dissertation on the Passions; The Natural History of Religion*, ed. Tom Beauchamp, xi–cxxxii. Oxford: Oxford University Press.

Broadie, Alexander. 2008. *A History of Scottish Philosophy*. Edinburgh: Edinburgh University Press.

Brooke, Cristopher. 2012. *Philosophic Pride: Stoicism and Political Thought from Lipsius to Rousseau*. Princeton, NJ: Princeton University Press.

Byrne, Peter. 1989. *Natural Religion and the Nature of Religion: The Legacy of Deism*. Abingdon: Routledge.

Cabrera, Miguel A. Badia. 2001. *Hume's Reflection on Religion*. Dordrecht: Kluwer.

Falkenstein, Lorne. 2003. Hume's Project in 'The Natural History of Religion.' *Religious Studies* 39: 1–21.

———. 2009. Hume on 'Genuine', 'True' and 'Rational' Religion. *Eighteenth Century Thought* 4: 171–201.

Fosl, Peter S. 2019. *Hume's Scepticism: Pyrrhonian and Academic*. Edinburgh: Edinburgh University Press.

Foster, Stephen Paul. 1997. *Melancholy Duty: the Hume-Gibbon Attack on Christianity*. Dordrecht: Kluwer.

Harris, James. 2015. *David Hume: An Intellectual Biography*. Cambridge: Cambridge University Press.

Klibansky, Raymond, and Ernest C. Mossner. 1969. *New Letters of David Hume*. Oxford: Clarendon Press.

Levitin, Dmitri. 2022. *The Kingdom of Darkness: Bayle, Newton, and the Emancipation of the European Mind from Philosophy*. Cambridge: Cambridge University Press.

Lingier, Hannah. 2022. Religion in Context: History and Policy in Hume's Natural History of Religion. *Journal of Scottish Philosophy* 20: 41–54.

Livingston, Donald W. 1998. *Philosophical Melancholy and Delirium: Hume's Pathology of Philosophy*. Chicago, IL: Chicago University Press.

Malherbe, Michel. 1995. Hume's Natural History of Religion. *Hume Studies* 21: 255–274.

Merivale, Amyas. 2018. *Hume on Art, Emotion, and Superstition: A Critical Study of the Four Dissertations*. Abingdon: Routledge.

Numao, J.K. 2013. Locke on Atheism. *History of Political Thought* 34: 252–272.

Robertson, John. 2005. *The Case for the Enlightenment: Scotland and Naples 1680–1760*. Cambridge: Cambridge University Press.

———. 2015. *The Enlightenment: A Very Short Introduction*. Oxford: Oxford University Press.

Schmidt, Claudia M. 2003. *David Hume: Reason in History*. University Park, PA: Pennsylvania State University Press.

Schmidt, Francis. 1987. Polytheisms: Degeneration or Progress? In *The Inconceivable Polytheism: Studies in Religious Historiography*, ed. Francis Schmidt, 9–60. London: Harwood Academic.

Serjeantson, Richard W. 2012. Hume's Natural History of Religion (1757) and the Demise of Modern Eusebianism. In *The Intellectual Consequences of Religious Heterodoxy 1600–1750*, ed. John Robertson and Sarah Mortimer, 267–295. Leiden: Brill.

Stewart, Dugald. 1854–1860. *The Collected Works of Dugald Stewart*, 11 vols., ed. William Hamilton. Edinburgh.

Stewart, M.A. 2019. Religion and Rational Theology. In *The Cambridge Companion to the Scottish Enlightenment*, 2nd ed., ed. Alexander Broadie and Craig Smith, 33–59. Cambridge: Cambridge University Press.

Stuart-Buttle, Tim. 2019. *From Moral Theology to Moral Philosophy: Cicero and Visions of Humanity from Locke to Hume*. Oxford: Oxford University Press.

Webb, Mark. 1991. The Argument of the Natural History. *Hume Studies* 17: 141–160.

Wheeler-Barclay, Marjorie. 2010. *The Science of Religion in Britain, 1860–1915*. London: University of Virginia Press.

Yandell, Keith. 1990. *Hume's Inexplicable Mystery: His Views on Religion*. Philadelphia, PA: Temple University Press.

CHAPTER 7

William Robertson on Revelation and the Limits of Progress

Abstract Spanning four decades and several different approaches to historical analysis, each of William Robertson's published discussions of religious change contained a different emphasis. The *Situation of the World* (1755) explained the necessity of Christ's mission given the particular societal conditions of the Roman Empire. By contrast, in Robertson's *History of the Reign of Charles V* (1769), Christianity was less powerful as a cause for change. In *History of America* (1777), he utilised sociological methods to analyse "savage" Americans and "semi-civilized" Aztecs and Incas, with his findings mitigating against a naïve sense of a providentially arranged progress of religion. The *Historical Disquisition* (1791), however, reasserted the utility of outlining the "natural progress of false religion," though Robertson saw this as a process of improvement but not perfection.

Keywords William Robertson · Philosophical history · Providence · Necessity of revelation · Natural progress of religion · Paganism

The need to respond to Hume's account of the relationship between religious belief, human nature and society in ways that reasserted the truth of religion is exemplified by the discussion of religious progress found in the historical writings of William Robertson (1721–1793). The following chapter complements the recent analyses of Robertson's avowedly providentialist understanding of religious improvement composed by Thomas Ahnert and Felicity Loughlin.[1] Providing nuanced accounts of Robertson's historical writings when it comes to the role of religion, they have argued that Robertson read the history of paganism and Christianity as demonstrating the inadequacy of man's natural religious propensities and the necessity of revelation in ensuring knowledge of the basics of religious truth. Even in highly developed civilisations, without the assistance of revelation, the height of religious progress would be a *religio duplex* consisting of a popular polytheism and elite theism, but with the latter being shorn of the proper understanding of the immortality of the soul and future rewards and punishments. It was Christ's mission to supply humanity with this knowledge. The "natural," meaning unassisted, progress of religion was not a story of improvement towards perfection. Robertson maintained that true religion was "the offspring of reason, cherished by science and attains to its highest perfection in an age of light and improvement."[2] This statement's apparent kinship with a commonplace enlightened deistic notion of religious improvement, however, needs to be qualified by an understanding of what characterised, for Robertson, an "age of *light*" (my italics).[3]

As Ahnert and Loughlin have suggested, for Robertson, revelation was necessary for knowledge of true religion and unassisted human nature could only develop inferior religious beliefs and moral codes. For Robertson, an "enlightened nation" characterised by scientific improvement, but which had no access to revelation, could never achieve true religion.[4] Assessments that Robertson was the Scottish Enlightenment's "most straightforward 'progress and refinement' thinker" ignore, amongst other things, the role of revelation in his thought.[5] What I want to argue here is that revelation did not serve as a *deux ex machina* that solved the problem of the weakness of human nature. To Robertson, true

---

[1] Ahnert (2010, 2015, esp. pp. 100–103) and Loughlin (2018).

[2] Robertson (1791, p. 313).

[3] Cf. Berry (1997, p. 170).

[4] Robertson (1791, p. 330).

[5] Kontler (2008, p. 209). See, similarly, Nick Phillipson's suggestion that Robertson believed that religion was progressing towards true theism according to a divine plan. See Phillipson (1997). Likewise, see Brown (2009, esp. pp. 308–309).

religion could endure when it existed in conditions of reason, science and social improvement. Knowledge of revelation was powerless against the forces of entrenched superstition, unless also coupled with an improved natural philosophical understanding of the law-bound character of the universe. His "View of the Progress of Society in Europe," that prefaced his *History of the Reign of Charles V* (1769) demonstrated the weakness of revelation in conditions of societal backwardness: it was this that could help explain the quick corruption of early Christianity into Catholic superstition. Robertson's *The History of America* (1777) and *An Historical Disquisition concerning the Knowledge which the Ancients had of India* (1791) both demonstrated the necessity of revelation not only to establish true religion but also to serve as a factor in societal improvement itself. From his *Reign of Charles V* onwards, that is, once Robertson became a sociologically minded "philosophical historian" in the vein of the "science of man," he was stressing the necessity of societal development for the establishment of good religion, always in combination with arguing for the necessity of revelation.[6]

The fact that Robertson was one of the leading figures in the Church of Scotland of his day is key to understanding the significance of his adoption of the characteristic approaches and concerns of enlightened Scottish social theory. This is especially true when he wrote about religion. While he wrote as a believing Christian, Robertson set aside many of the traditional Christian approaches to studying religious diversity. He updated the argument that without access to revelation the natural religion of humankind would be prone to superstition and immorality, but he did so now in framework of societal progress over the long term. Moreover, his approach to historical analysis were characterised by a variety of stadial and narrative approaches to historical explanation, and the adoption of probabilistic evidence and multicausal explanation depending on the extent of the historical record.[7] One consequence of Robertson's approach to writing "philosophical history" was that he treated Christianity as a factor dependent on specific interrelations between other factors for its ultimate success. This informed an apologetic account of the history of religious error as part of a divine plan, but had the concurrent effect of positioning

---

[6] For overviews, see O'Brien (1997, pp. 129–166) and Brown (1997). For a reading of Robertson's pre-sociological *History of Scotland* (1769), see Fearnley-Sander (1990).

[7] See Brown (1997), Kontler (2014), Smitten (2016). On his historical thought, see especially Smitten (2013).

Christianity as one factor amongst many in a naturalistic explanation of religious change.[8]

Robertson is more frequently categorised as an Enlightenment "philosophical historian," than as a practitioner of the "science of human nature."[9] Still, we might observe with Donald Kelley that the "Scottish turn to history in the eighteenth century was undertaken in the shadow of a larger plan … building a science of human nature," with two being in intimate dialogue with each other.[10] Robertson has been described as the "most meticulous and self-conscious" *literatus* when it came to the methodological issues underpinning "philosophical history."[11] That said, Robertson's historical writings lack confident statements about how the application of natural philosophical thinking will lead to improvements in our understanding of human nature and society.[12] He did, however, seek to go beyond the mere narration of facts by providing explanations of those facts, undergirded by an empirically informed conception of human nature. Robertson held, like Hume, that human nature had universal inherent features and knowledge of these informed our historical explanations. How these principles of human nature manifest themselves depend on social context: "the human mind, whenever it is placed in the same situation, will, in ages the most distant, and in countries the most remote, assume the same form, and be distinguished by the same manners."[13] This can be called a tenet of the "comparative method of

---

[8] Several scholars have viewed Robertson's views on providence as a continuation of earlier humanist and Calvinist historians. See, for example, Allan (1993, pp. 207–218). Others, while acknowledging such through-lines, emphasise the qualitative shift in Robertson's thought towards "philosophical history." See, for example, Phillipson (1997).

[9] For an interesting discussion of Robertson's philosophical historical approach contrasted with antiquarian history, see Sebastiani (2014).

[10] Kelley (1998, p. 233).

[11] Berry (1997, p. 61).

[12] Ehrlich (2013) has argued for the strong influence of Newtonian thought on Robertson's historico-religious thought. Smitten (2016, pp. 40–42) offers a more muted account of the influence on Robertson of his tutor Colin Macularin, author of *An Account of Sir Isaac Newton's Philosophical Discoveries* (1748). The positioning of Robertson as significantly Newtonian in his thinking has been criticised as baseless by Ahnert (2015). Kontler (2008, pp. 204–205) is similarly sceptical of any Newtonian influence on Robertson.

[13] Robertson (1769, vol. I, p. 211). Cf. with Poovey (1998, p. 225) who reads Robertson as a theorist of racial difference (like Kames) who thereby undermined the notion of a universal human subject.

scientific history," but it is also the principle at the very root of the enlightened Scottish sense of the historicity of human nature.[14]

ROBERTSON'S NECESSITY OF REVELATION AT THE TIME OF CHRIST'S MISSION

Robertson's first publication was a sermon delivered to the Scottish Society for the Promotion of Christian Knowledge entitled *The Situation of the World at the Time of Christ's Appearance* (1755).[15] This was written prior to Robertson's immersion into "philosophical history" and the sociological analysis characteristic of the High Scottish Enlightenment. The sermon exhibits more confidence about Christianity's determinative influence over the course of European civilisation than can be found in Robertson's later *History of the Reign of Charles IV*. Similarly, the sermon contrasts with the more hesitant attitude, reflecting an author often deeply shocked and troubled by what he learnt about non-European religion amidst the absence of revelation, found in his *History of America* and *Historical Disquisition*. With apologies for stating the obvious, Robertson's sermon was the most overtly Christian of his publications and contains sentiments about the power of Christianity that contrast with his later works of "philosophical history." But it also indicated that Robertson saw the study of history as demonstrating the necessity of revelation.

Robertson was clear that the doctrines of the immortality of the soul and future rewards and punishments were "the chief foundation of virtuous obedience," but only were securely known via revelation.[16] Virtue was not possible amongst societies "who were destitute of the instructions, the promises and assistance of divine revelation."[17] The central thesis of the sermon was that the "light of revelation" was shone on mankind "in proportion as the situation of the world made it *necessary*."[18] What Robertson understands by "necessary" here is key to how we frame the *Sermon*. Robertson's position in *Situation of the World*

---

[14] Broadie (1997, p. 676).

[15] See Kontler (2008), Ehrlich (2013) and Smitten (2016, pp. 101–103).

[16] Robertson (1755, p. 22). Ahnert (2015, pp. 62–63).

[17] Robertson (1755, p. 15).

[18] For a complimentary reading, see Gascoigne (1991, pp. 204–205).

should not be tightly bound to notions of stadial progress, especially if such progress is understood to entail improvement.[19] The urgency behind God's further dispensation of revelation was in response to both the sophistication and the corruption of the Roman world. When commentators argue that Robertson maintained that "with improvement comes an increased understanding of the material and the spiritual world, and only then can God be expected to display more of His being and nature to us," we lose sight of the moral degeneracy, resulting from that "improvement," that prompted God's further revelation.[20]

Robertson holds that there are "general laws" by which God "conducts all his operations," including the phenomena of the natural world, to reach their "final and complete state" in a "gradual and progressive" fashion.[21] But God intervenes when he wishes to bring about an event that could not have been "accomplished by [means] such as are natural."[22] This was the case with the arrival of Christ. The point here is that Roman civilisation had not been the benign force behind the improvement of society, to prepare the world for the "expansion of Christianity and the consequent progress of human societies."[23] Rather, Christ's mission was necessary, as much as propitious, because of the Roman Empire's unification of much of the world and the concurrent moral corruption of its territories. Christ appears at a moment when Roman civilisation had achieved great socio-economic progress but was also suffering great moral corruption because of that progress. Christ's mission was only possible once extensive commerce between societies had been brought about by the Roman Empire. At the same time, Christ's mission was necessary because of the moral degeneration—slavery, luxury, sexual licentiousness and political corruption—that took over the Augustan Empire. God sent his son to save humanity at precisely the moment that mankind most needed saving but also when the social circumstances were most propitious for the mission to succeed.

---

[19] Cf. Spadafora (1990, pp. 374–375), Phillipson (1997, p. 69) and Kontler (2008, pp. 199, 202). On the theory of progressive dispensations in line with social progress, see also Crane (1934).

[20] Kontler (2008, p. 202), somewhat contradicted by his own subsequent discussion of the economic and moral failings of the Roman Empire on pp. 206–209.

[21] Robertson (1755, p. 6).

[22] Robertson (1755, p. 12).

[23] Cf. Sebastiani (2013, p. 96).

For Robertson, the battle between improvement and degeneration is on show too in the modern world. Modern Europe was superior to ancient Rome in its manners, scientific knowledge and military strength. All were "noble instruments in the hand of God, for preparing the world to receive the gospel."[24] Noticeably, in Robertson's sermon, he claimed that the cause behind recent improvements in European civilisation was the growth and social influence of Christianity, and not some wider multi-factor sense of sociological change. Europe and its empires, however, were going through a similar period of moral degeneration as the Roman Empire had experienced. The main aspects of this decline were the same as that of the ancient world: the existence of an immoral slave trade and the increasingly "extravagant demands of luxury and pleasure" at the expense of morals and piety.[25]

Attempts to frame Robertson's *Situation of the World* as a work of enlightened stadial or conjectural history of man's improvement from rudeness to refinement occlude its message. God sent Christ not because man was a new stage of societal improvement that put Rome in a state of readiness for a new stage of religious improvement but because its new stage of societal change had rendered the world a moral morass. Similarly, the sense of Christianity in battle with other societal factors mitigates any sense of Robertson's sermon offering stadial or incremental history of religious improvement. The *Sermon* offers us the first indication that Robertson did not believe that there was a general movement towards true religion based on societal factors without revelation and his sense that religious progress was the result of the direct, if occasional, superintendence of God.[26] Instead, the *Sermon* described an ongoing conflict between Christianity and the degeneracy of man, in which the spread of true religion and good morals, unsurprisingly for the Head of the General Assembly of the Church of Scotland, was dependent upon Christian revelation and not socio-economic progress.

---

[24] Robertson (1755, p. 37).
[25] Robertson (1755, p. 40).
[26] Cf. Kidd (2004, p. 509).

True Religion and the Necessity of Social Progress

Robertson's first venture into "philosophical history," published more than a decade after *Situation of the World*, Robertson set aside his earlier framing of the determining historical influence of Christianity. In his "View of the Progress of Society in Europe," that preface his three-volume *History of the Reign of Charles V*, Robertson went into more depth about the historical role of Christianity in the transformation of European society between the fall of the Roman Empire and the age of the Reformation. The character of Christianity, however, was framed by the state of societal development and the extent of knowledge of the natural world. This led to an account of religious change in Europe where the influence of Christianity was subordinated to secondary causes. Social progress was necessary for true religion, and access to revelation did not serve as a bulwark against superstition while Europe existed in the barbarian, then feudal stage of society.

The quick corruption of primitive Christianity into Catholic superstition was explained as resulting from how the Roman Empire fell, and the societal state of the barbarian peoples that succeeded it. Donald Kelley opines that Robertson "exaggerated the stereotypical Tacitean contrast between furious barbarism and effeminate Romans and the destructive effects of that offshoot of barbarism, feudalism."[27] Notably, Robertson did not view Christianity as a factor in the Empire's fall and only discussed religion when examining what happened to Christianity once it was adopted by the tribes that vanquished the Empire. The latter were warriorlike, nomadic "rude" tribes made up either of hunters or shepherds, "destitute of science … and without leisure," and "strangers to the arts, and industry."[28] The destructive power of the barbarians as they ravaged Europe was so great that by the end of the sixth century, few vestiges of Roman civilisation survived, and "new forms of government, new laws, new manners, new dresses, new languages, and new names of men and countries, were everywhere introduced."[29] The slate was cleaned, with the "effects of the knowledge and civility which the Romans

---

[27] Kelley (1998, p. 237).
[28] Robertson (1769, vol. i, p. 4).
[29] Robertson (1769, vol. i, p. 11).

had spread through Europe" disappearing.[30] The one striking exception to this process of civilisational destruction was the continuation of pagan superstitions in the early Catholic Church, with superstition able to flourish in the anarchic conditions of post-Roman Europe.[31] Robertson agreed with his contemporaries that early Christianity was also quickly corrupted by its fusion with pagan philosophy, leading to the establishment of speculative theology in the place of the simple tenets of Christ's message.[32]

Possession of revealed truth in the form of scripture meant nothing to a society if its religious leaders could not understand that revelation. Europe lived in conditions of "feudal anarchy" from the sixth through to the eleventh centuries. "The human mind neglected, uncultivated, and depressed, sunk into the most profound ignorance."[33] Without the "protection of regular government" and the "certainty of personal security," no "progress in science [nor] refinement in taste, or in manners" was possible.[34] Such was the level of ignorance that the "clergy did not understand the breviary which they were obliged daily to recite; some of them could scarcely read it."[35] Ignorance was compounded by the scarcity of books, the loss of knowledge of how to produce new ones and the widespread inability to read the ones that remained. Europe only began to escape its age of ignorance following the invention of papermaking, which resulted in the "first dawning of letters and improvement in knowledge" at the end of the eleventh century; a similar process happened with the reformation of letters and the invention of printing in the "era of the Reformation."[36]

Christianity on its own was not sufficient to ensure escape from superstition. What is interesting, if Robertson is read as a historian holding that revelation is necessary for people to reach the basics of true religion, is that Christian Europe was not able to escape the influence of feudal disorder on its religious beliefs and practices. Like all other forms

---

[30] Robertson (1769, vol. i, p. 18).
[31] Robertson (1769, vol. i, p. 237).
[32] Ahnert (2015, pp. 80–81).
[33] Robertson (1769, vol. i, p. 19).
[34] Robertson (1769, vol. i, p. 18).
[35] Robertson (1769, vol. i, pp. 18–19).
[36] Robertson (1769, vol. i, p. 236).

of learning, religion "degenerated during those ages of darkness into an illiberal superstition."[37] The clarity of scripture about the precepts of true religion did not prevent the newly converted barbarous nations from fitting Christianity to the pre-existing "spirit of their religious worship."[38] They sought the favour of God through "scrupulous observance of external ceremonies," and believed that religion consisted in "nothing else."[39] The religious beliefs of Europeans at this point, though professedly Christian and with access to revelation, were a "disgrace to reason and humanity."[40]

The establishment of genuine theism required the development of natural theological knowledge. Post-Roman Europeans were ignorant of "the manner in which the Almighty carries on the government of the universe by equal, fixed, and general laws," which contributed to the superstitious belief that whatever affected the "passions or interests" of the individual was also the concern of the deity.[41] Religion in medieval Europe consisted primarily in "believing the legendary history of those saints whose names crowd and disgrace the Romish calendar."[42] These tales encourage men to believe that the "laws of nature might be violated on the most frivolous occasions," and that God was to be seen in "particular and extraordinary acts of power" and not the order evident in nature.[43] With a degree condescension rather than anger, Robertson noted how the modern rites and ceremonies of the Catholic Church were first fixed in this "age of darkness and credulity," and continue still due to the "doctrine of infallibility," despite their evident ridiculousness to the modern mind.[44]

Feudal Christianity did serve as a cause for historical change on several occasions in Robertson's *View*, but as textbook instances of unintended consequences. While the Crusades were a "singular moment in human folly," they inadvertently led to the "first gleams of light which tended

[37] Robertson (1769, vol. i, p. 19).
[38] Robertson (1769, vol. i, p. 19).
[39] Robertson (1769, vol. i, p. 19).
[40] Robertson (1769, vol. i, p. 20).
[41] Robertson (1769, vol. i, p. 51).
[42] Robertson (1769, vol. i, p. 51).
[43] Robertson (1769, vol. i, p. 51).
[44] Robertson (1769, vol. i, p. 237).

to dispel barbarity and ignorance," not least by expanding Christian Europe's knowledge of the east.[45] A similar unintentional consequence was the social benefits derived from canon law. The Christian priests of the Roman Empire were viewed as "objects of superstitious veneration" and were treated with "profound submission and reverence" by the barbarians who conquered the Empire.[46] The clergy exploited this, and established church courts separate to civil legal authority, and proceeded slowly to extend their jurisdiction to cover the bulk of disputes. In this they were aided by the fact that, in an age of darkness, the clergy "alone were accustomed to read, to enquire and to reason."[47] Somewhat contradicting his earlier claims about the slate being cleaned, canon law was built up on the vestiges of ancient jurisprudence and was able to build up a code of laws far more just, uniform and consistent than the "ill-digested jurisprudence" of the civil courts. Eventually, the church courts would inspire the abandonment of the "martial tribunals of the barons."[48] Neither of these examples can be said to be the result of the benign influence of true Christianity on society, but of the unintended consequences of self-interested human action.

The driving forces behind the improvement of European manners were the gradual improvement in science and society's advance towards "more perfect order," but this has only happened very recently.[49] A move away from barbarian superstition required a large degree of science and philosophy, but this was not something that Europe was blessed with until the reformation of letters and the Reformation itself. The volume of European literary endeavours increased from Aquinas onwards but were immediately perverted from the natural course of things. The Europeans "plunged at once into the depths of abstruse and metaphysical inquiry."[50] This was a result of the form of Christianity they inherited. The barbarians had received Christianity from the conquered Romans not as a set of "simple and instructive doctrines," but as teachings meshed up with "vain philosophy" which attempted to explain questions beyond the reach

[45] Robertson (1769, vol. i, p. 27).
[46] Robertson (1769, vol. i, p. 63).
[47] Robertson (1769, vol. i, p. 64).
[48] Robertson (1769, vol. i, p. 64).
[49] Robertson (1769, vol. i, p. 56).
[50] Robertson (1769, vol. i, p. 73).

of the human mind.[51] These "overcurious speculations" were viewed as the "most essential" part of Christianity, rather than accretions that distorted it as a "system of religion."[52] This was compounded by the sources of learning for twelfth-century and thirteenth-century Europeans: the Greeks in the eastern Empire and the Arabians in Spain and North Africa. Both contributed to European theological study being characterised by "speculative refinement," "endless controversy" and a "spirit of metaphysical and frivolous subtlety."[53] When the "spirit of enquiry" returned to Europe from the eleventh century, it was upon this perverted version of Christianity that they directed their attention and "scholastic theology" was the result.[54] Robertson describes the latter as being characterised by an "infinite train of bold disquisitions and subtle distinctions concerning points which are not the object of human reason."[55] The traditional Protestant conclusion drawn by Robertson is that the direction of Christian theology had been altered by its early immersion in pagan philosophy and that it was not until very recently, aided by the technological change in the form of printing and the doctrinal cleansing undertaken during the Reformation, that it had escaped those shackles.

SUPERSTITION'S ROLE IN LIMITING OF PROGRESS: THE *HISTORY OF AMERICA* (1777)

If the "View" suggested that true religion could only be established once there was an appropriate approach to the study of the natural world, in *History of America* (1777) Robertson was provoked by the examples of the Incan and Aztec civilisations into arguing that the unassisted progress of religion led to merely human and inevitably flawed systems of religion and morals regardless of the state of social development. In this latter work Robertson adopted a stadial understanding of society for the first time. In Book IV, Robertson provided a synchronic picture of American religions, based on the accumulation of facts derived from travel literature, as archetypal pre-societal and early societal forms. Despite

---

[51] Robertson (1769, vol. i, pp. 73–74).
[52] Robertson (1769, vol. i, p. 74).
[53] Robertson (1769, vol. i, p. 74).
[54] Robertson (1769, vol. i, p. 74).
[55] Robertson (1769, vol. i, p. 74).

Robertson's well-known gathering of historical information, the bulk of his description of primitive religion was entirely a piece with Hume and Kames, indicating that it was conclusions derived from the "science of man," rather than accumulated historical fact, that underpinned Robertson's views. Far more interesting were his discussions, in Book VII, of the religious development of the semi-civilised societies of Mexico and Peru.[56] Both acted as case-studies in the progress of unassisted religion and forced Robertson to comprehend the role of accident, contingency and "stickiness" in the formation and continuation of systems of irreligion. It is tempting, though Robertson did not make this point, to read his description of the incessant human sacrifice of the polytheist Aztecs as a rebuke to Hume's claim in the NHR that polytheism rarely led to the violence characteristic of monotheism. In helping to spread knowledge of American religion, Robertson seems to have suffered from the "shock of the new," which challenged the secure belief in providence exhibited in the *Sermon* and shifted the sense of a divine plan increasingly towards an article of faith rather than an empirically grounded conclusion.[57] Similarly, as Karen O'Brien notes, Robertson's discussions in Books IV and VII are "morally normative to a degree unusual among Scottish writers," with Robertson clear about the ultimate limits of unassisted human nature to improve.[58]

Robertson might be the most prominent minister amongst the authors of the Scottish "science of human nature," but the tendency of his analysis of the origin and development of religion was to reframe religion in a more naturalistic frame. This comes across in his discussion of the superstitions of the Americans in Book IV of the *History of America*. Robertson viewed the Americans as exemplifying the first stage of humanity as hunters and one whose lack of societal development required explanation. In choosing stadial history as the method for understanding the

---

[56] See also Berry (1997, p. 96).

[57] See Womersley (1986, p. 500). Other readings frame Robertson's account in terms of justifications (or otherwise) for Spanish imperialism. Thus, O'Brien sees Robertson's discussion of the Aztecs and Incas as characterised by a tension "between his desire to prove that these two peoples were, in their superstitious paganism, far less advanced than many historians have supposed, and his sense of their (interrupted) potential for further social evolution." See O'Brien (1997, p. 161).

[58] O'Brien (1997, p. 153). See also pp. 157–158.

"savages" of the Americans, Robertson set aside the traditional Christian approaches. While he reiterated biblical monogeneticism, he denied the utility of pursuing the issue of how the Americas were peopled, a topic which had agitated many biblical historians. There was no historical record upon which such judgements could be made. Similarly, the ongoing effort to identify the vestiges of an original biblical theism in the superstitious practices and beliefs of the Americans, another staple of early modern Christian approaches to new world religion, was a dull and pointless endeavour. Instead, judgements about the Amerindians should stem from travel literature informed by recent works in the natural history of man. The result of this was for Robertson to both position the Amerindians as exemplifying man in his primordial state and as the negation, the opposite, of man in civilised society.[59] It was also to treat them, despite his profession, in a distinctly untraditional manner.

Study of the Americans provided a unique opportunity to "fill up a considerable chasm in the history of the progress of the human species."[60] The method of Robertson's study of American religion in Book IV was not that of narrative history, but of Baconian natural history gathering evidence on the primeval stage of human history. This was built on Robertson's adoption of the Humean claim that human nature assumes the same form, and develops the same manners, when placed in the same situation. Robertson inferred from the accumulation of facts from travel accounts, supported by the identification of correspondences with accounts of ancient primitive peoples, certain general characteristics of religions of primordial societies.[61] "A tribe of savages on the banks of the Danube must nearly resemble one upon the plains washed by the Mississippi."[62] The stress on the universal characteristics of primitive societies meant, in turn, that Robertson had little interest in a granular analysis of the religion of "savage" peoples. Like Kames, he flattened the differences

---

[59] On Robertson's "radical dehumanization" of the Amerindians, see Sebastiani (2013, e.g. p. 95).

[60] Robertson (1777, vol. i, p. 286).

[61] In this Robertson was inspired, like many Scots, by the Jesuit Joseph-Francois Lafitau's *Moeurs des sauvages ameriquains, compares aux moeurs des primiers temps* (1724). On Lafitau's influence on the Enlightenment's study of religion, see Harvey (2008). On Robertson's attempted judiciousness in judging the reliability of travel accounts, see, for example, Berry (1997, pp. 62–63).

[62] Robertson (1777, vol. i, p. 268).

between the many "small independent tribes" under the "denomination of savage," on the grounds that they all shared the same "mode of subsistence."[63] Differences between tribes were superficial and unimportant, Robertson averred, and any study that delineated these differences would involve work of an "immeasurable and tiresome extent."[64] The study of the fables of primordial societies, likewise, was not useful, given they resulted from "childish credulity" and were "altogether unworthy of a place in history."[65] Robertson turned the Amerindians into a prototype of the hunter stage of society and, as Sebastiani puts it, viewed them as a "uniform human type" without cultural or religious differentiation.[66]

Whatever innovations Robertson is supposed to have made with his study of human nature, the bulk of his description of fear-inspired polytheisms of the "savage" American nations was the same as those of his contemporaries. The unique opportunity of understanding primeval human society, offered by the study of America, did not alter the established understanding of primordial religion. On the whole then, he took his lead from established psychological accounts of religion, as might be found in Hume's NHR or Kames' *Principles*. Robertson's researches, however, did lead to two opinions different, though both of which have the status of refinements of the pre-existing account, rather than a conceptual leap. Firstly, Robertson deciphered a separate origins story for the practice of divination, compared to superstition. In systems of superstition, priesthoods pretend to communicate with the gods. The practice of divination, by contrast, was "originally ingrafted on medicine," and was an outgrowth of physicians' claim that they understood the secret workings of nature and were thus able to predict the future.[67] In early religions the physician-diviner was a rival to the priest, as a figure who could use their superior knowledge to convince the credulous of their superior power. The practice of divination became extremely commonplace, with

[63] Robertson (1777, vol. i, pp. 257, 324).

[64] Robertson (1777, vol. i, p. 283). See also Poovey (1998, pp. 225–226).

[65] Robertson (1777, vol. i, p. 385).

[66] Sebastiani (2013, p. 95, and pp. 90–95 more generally). See also Hargraves (2007, pp. 104–105). Compare with Allan's (2013, p. 322) strikingly contrasting assessment that Robertson's portrayal of American tribes was "humane and sympathetic" and based on a universalism that encouraged readers to think of the native Americans as comparable to their own ancestors.

[67] Robertson (1777, vol. i, p. 390).

the consequence that supernatural power was seen to be active within "all the occurrences of life."[68] Secondly, in a passage cited at length by Dugald Stewart, Robertson claimed that belief in the immortality of the soul was found in all tribes, the result of the soul's "secret consciousness of its own dignity," while the idea of God was "profound and abstruse" and reached only after sustained "observation and research."[69] Robertson would make the claim, which he perhaps took from the early volumes of Monboddo's *OPL* and which was also reiterated by Thomas Reid, that belief in an immortal soul was "universal" and "natural" sentiment felt by all peoples, whereas the idea of God required the prior development of language and the conception of abstract ideas.[70]

The claim that one key tenet of true religion was beyond the capabilities of primordial human societies formed a central part of Robertson's criticism of imperial Spain.[71] In his *Sermon*, Robertson wrote confidently of the providential role of the European empires in spreading Christianity. One element of Robertson's version of the "Black Legend" in the *History of America* was, by contrast, his criticism for Spain of its approach to missionary work in the Americas. These efforts failed because, alongside the rapaciousness of the Spaniards and their disdain for both native and slave populations, the Catholic priests did not comprehend the gulf of civilisational development between conquered and conquerors.[72] This was a gulf which meant that core Christian tenets were not intelligible to peoples Robertson believed were without abstract and general ideas. The indigenous populations were baptised into a religion they could not understand, though they could easily participate in Catholic idolatry, given its similarities to their existing polytheistic worship. The "realism" of Robertson's "science of man" underpinned his position that Christianity required a greater level of societal progress before it could take root in the Americas—it was a "long road" to civilisation.[73] But it also

---

[68] Robertson (1777, vol. i, p. 391).

[69] Robertson (1777, vol. i, p. 387).

[70] Robertson (1777, vol. i, p. 387).

[71] Phillipson (1997, p. 66). For an overview of enlightened Scottish thought on Spanish imperialism, see Miller (2018).

[72] Miller (2018, pp. 198–199). As Miller notes, Robertson believed the Spanish had squandered the opportunity to civilise and Christianise the Americas.

[73] See Lucas (2000).

showed the distance between Robertson and earlier Presbyterian orthodoxy, as Robertson did not believe that an innate "light of nature" could discern the existence of God, even if we felt the existence of our immortal souls.[74]

The societal progress Robertson had in mind involved more than simply economic development. In older scholarship on the social theory of the Scottish Enlightenment, Robertson was depicted as proto-historical materialist, yet in his descriptions of early religions there is little evidence of uniformity determined in fixed ways by material conditions.[75] Robertson did claim that the key factor for understanding society was its "mode of subsistence," from which "laws and policy" emerged.[76] But his research on American religions mitigated against the determinism inherent in that view. The Natchez and Bogota tribes were economically undeveloped but practised sophisticated forms of polytheism. Their systems of religion were maintained by educated priesthoods, took place in temples and acted in alliance with political power, and did not fit Robertson's expectations about the fixed link between socio-economic development and religion. The religious systems of these two tribes were "one of the many singular and unaccountable circumstances which occur in the history of human affairs."[77]

The fact that the stadial historian Robertson did not find straightforward evidence of the natural progress from polytheism to theism in his researches in writing *History of America* was further apparent in the discussions of Aztec and Incan religion in Book VII. He viewed the Mexican and Peruvian Empires as two informative case studies in the history of the progress of society, given that they stood "between the rude tribes in the New World and the polished states of the ancient."[78] Both were urban societies living under monarchical rulers concerned with the "maintenance and security" of their subjects.[79] The "empire of laws" had

[74] Ahnert (2010, 2015).

[75] Most prominently Meek (1976, esp. p. 2). Compare with O'Brien's assessment (1997, p. 133) that Robertson was a "somewhat reluctant stadial historian."

[76] Robertson (1777, vol. i, p. 324).

[77] Robertson (1777, vol. i, p. 386).

[78] Robertson (1777, vol. ii, p. 270). I will alternate between Robertson's designation of Mexican and Peruvian, with Aztec and Incan.

[79] Robertson (1777, vol. ii, p. 268).

been established, the useful arts had developed to "some degree of maturity," the ornamental arts had appeared, and the "authority of religion" was acknowledged.[80] However, because they were "totally unacquainted" with metallurgy, husbandry and still used picture writing, they had not "advanced beyond the infancy of civil life" and did not "merit the name of civilized."[81] Their religions were each characterised by a peculiar character, strength and extravagance, which indicated the role of accident and contingency in the progress of religion. In Robertson's *History of America* we find an enlightened Scottish philosophical historian talking through the weaknesses of stadial history and the expected conclusions of the "science of human nature" when it came to the religious other.[82] This is of a piece with Robertson's sense of wonder at how "only [these] two nations in this vast continent … emerged from this rude state, and had many any considerable progress in acquiring the ideas, and adopting the institutions, which belong to polished societies."[83] Moreover, the power of systems of superstition were such that they could wrest societies away from experiencing the expected benefits of socio-economic, legal and political improvement. As Neil Hargraves notes, Robertson resolves the difficulties in explaining the level of Aztec and Incan development, by setting aside stadial notions, and instead appealing to the *deus ex machina* of "national manners."[84]

In the case of Mexico, there was no alignment between level of civilisational and religious development and, likewise, the "stickiness" of the Aztec's religious aberration had prevented the kingdom from developing further.[85] If the historian of man was examining only the Aztec's superstitious worship, "no conclusion [could] be drawn with certainty concerning

---

[80] Robertson (1777, vol. ii, p. 268).

[81] Robertson (1777, vol. ii, pp. 268–269). Dismissing Robertson's professed positioning of the two empires as halfway between savagery and civility, Sebastiani reads him as repeatedly reducing the Mexican and Peruvian kingdoms to the level of savages. See Sebastiani (2013, pp. 96–11). Compare with, for example, Keen (1990, pp. 275–285) for a sense of Robertson's appreciation of what Robertson called "superior progress which the Mexicans had made in refinement and civilization." See Robertson (1777, vol. ii, p. 296). For an overview, see Hargraves (2007).

[82] Roberts (2014, pp. 120–122).

[83] Robertson (1777, vol. i, p. 283).

[84] Hargraves (2007, p. 115).

[85] On 'stickiness' see Berry (2018, *passim*).

the degree of their civilization."[86] On the one hand, it was a "regular system" of rites and ceremonies, in fixed locations and with a professional priesthood. Yet its beliefs were more characteristic of the "rude conceptions of early ages," full of "gloomy and atrocious" sentiments, with humanoid divinities delighting in vengeance and terrifying the Aztec people, and who need to be assuaged by consistent human sacrifice.[87] The reader is left with a strong sense of Robertson's incomprehension at the sheer extent and barbarity of Aztec religion's regime of sacrifice. Such violence prevented "every sentiment of humanity" from developing, leaving the Aztec people vicious to the core.[88]

The barbaric character of Aztec religion was inexplicable given that Mexico was a "well-ordered society."[89] Living in cities, the people were ruled by an elected monarch, with a constitution similar to medieval feudalism. The Mexican economy was built on private property, the "separation of the professions," and a mixed economy, with a legal system based on principles of justice and equity.[90] Mexican religion, by contrast, was a violent, cruel religion based on human sacrifice. Robertson acknowledged the limitations to Aztec societal development. The limited extent of agriculture prevented the peasantry from engaging in other pursuits; there was little commerce between the provinces; and the Mexicans had neither alphabetical language nor money. None of this, however, could explain why the Aztecs were so warlike, motivated by revenge, practised human sacrifice and cannibalism or why their funeral rites included killing the attendants of the deceased.[91]

The Aztec system of religion was "an effect singular in the history of the human species" and its violence left Robertson dumbfounded.[92] Despite being the people "who had made the greatest progress in the arts of policy," the Aztecs were the "most ferocious, and the barbarity of some

---

[86] Robertson (1769, vol. ii, p. 302).

[87] Robertson (1769, vol. ii, p. 302). See also Ahnert (2010, p. 117).

[88] Robertson (1769, vol. ii, p. 303).

[89] Robertson (1769, vol. ii, p. 283). Cf. the assessment in Sebastiani (2013, p. 99) that Robertson viewed Aztec society as similar to neighbouring tribal societies.

[90] Robertson (1769, vol. ii, p. 276).

[91] See also Hargraves (2007, pp. 115–116).

[92] Robertson (1769, vol. ii, p. 303).

of their customs exceeded even those of the savage state."[93] Mexican religion "counterbalanced the influence of policy and arts" to the extent that, despite Mexican society's socio-economic and political progress, their manners "became more fierce."[94] Robertson grasped for explanations for why no parallel progress of religion and civilisation occurred.[95] The fact Aztec society was permanently at war encouraged barbarous religious practices. The constant spectacle of human sacrifice undermined any of expected refinement in humanity resulting from social interaction, growing commerce and political stability. But historical record was too sketchy to decipher the origin of this practice and ultimately it was impossible to determine how "superstition assumed such a dreadful form amongst the Mexicans."[96] The heuristic of stadial history could not help. Here as elsewhere in *History of America*, as Jeffrey Smitten notes, Robertson's "sense of the sheer anomalousness of the New World civilizations" undermined any sense of a "simple hierarchy of civilizations."[97]

The religious system that developed in Peru was more in keeping with the expectations of the natural progress of religion, but the character of Incan religion still had many unique characteristics requiring explanation. The "most singular and striking circumstance" about the Peruvian Empire was the fact, unique in America, that the "whole system of civil policy was founded on religion."[98] The effect was to make the Peruvians' "national character … more gentle than that of any other people in America," and the polar opposite of the Aztecs.[99] Peruvian civil religion revolved around a heliolatry created by its first rulers in the interests of maintaining social stability. The Incan elite ruled by pretending to be demigods and children of the sun, and because of their status as supernatural beings, their authority was "unlimited and absolute."[100] All breaches of the law were treated "insults offered to the deity," meaning that the "number

---

[93] Robertson (1769, vol. ii, p. 303).
[94] Robertson (1769, vol. ii, p. 303).
[95] Noticeably, he did not turn to a theological explanation.
[96] Robertson (1769, vol. ii, p. 303).
[97] Smitten (1985, p. 61).
[98] Robertson (1769, vol. ii, p. 307).
[99] Robertson (1769, vol. ii, p. 307).
[100] Robertson (1769, vol. ii, p. 307).

of offenders" was "extremely small."[101] From this position of immense power, the Incan rulers directed worship towards "contemplating the order and beneficence" of nature, leading a "spirit of superstition" that was mild, undogmatic and moderate.[102] The humaneness of Peruvian religion influenced their approach to war, the opposite of the Aztecs' murderous retribution. The Peruvians sought to "civilize the vanquished, and to diffuse knowledge of their own institutions and arts," an approach that Robertson ascribed to the "genius of their religion."[103] While less of a shock than the Aztec system of superstition, what was significant about the Incan religion was what was unique about it, not how it reflected a stadial heuristic of religious progress.

In *History of America*, Robertson had been interested in the exceptions to the expected religious beliefs and behaviours of the Amerindians. In this, the study of the "natural history of religion" does not serve as a "blueprint" against which a "particular social institution can be diachronically located."[104] While still utilising the language of a providential shift from savage and superstition to civilisation and Christianity, as Jeffrey Smitten has noted, Robertson's history of America is a "story of many failures."[105] The existence of a divine plan behind what he surveyed was a tenet derived from his theological understanding, not something drawn from the study of human history where the weakness of our reason and of our historical understanding prevents us from seeing this plan in full—a departure from his 1755 *Sermon*. Robertson's *History of America* informed its readers that the light of nature, and thus the "science of man" and "philosophical history," will not be able to render the complexities and disjunctures of history intelligible to us, and that what we might derive instead is a sense of the modesty of our ability to understand.[106] I think this is a more persuasive emphasis, the philosophical historian struggling to comprehend the history of mankind utilising the heuristics available to him, than reading the *History of America* as a moral theologian purposefully making the case for the necessity of revelation

---

[101] Robertson (1769, vol. ii, p. 309).

[102] Robertson (1769, vol. ii, p. 309).

[103] Robertson (1769, vol. ii, p. 311).

[104] Cf. Berry (2000, §5).

[105] Smitten (2016, p. 174).

[106] See Smitten (2016, pp. 173–175).

like Archibald Campbell, not least because the latter point, the necessity of revelation, is a second-order claim which the reader has to draw out from a couple of passing mentions of revelation rather than being an argument Robertson stresses.

THE NATURAL PROGRESS OF RELIGION AND THE NECESSITY OF REVELATION

Things are different a decade or so later. In an appendix to his *Historical Disquisition concerning the Knowledge which the Ancients had of India* (1791), Robertson offered an overall theory of the "history and progress of superstition and false religion in every region of the earth," using Hinduism as his main case study.[107] In this work, one of the "core texts" of late eighteenth-century "British Indomania," Robertson returned to a simpler narrative about the direction of religious development and the ultimate importance of revelation.[108] Utilising the explosion of orientalist scholarship in the wake of British imperial expansion from 1757 onwards, Robertson discussed India as an enlightened civilisation, and viewed Hinduism as the end point of the unassisted or natural progress of religion.[109] It is in *Historical Disquisition* that Robertson made his most explicit statement that the height of possible religious development without the assistance of revelation, as indicated by example of Indian Hinduism, was a *religio duplex* in which the piety and morals of the multitude were insecure and prone to corruption. Systems of popular religion do not inevitably improve towards theism in step with wider societal change, leading to increasing tensions between the superstitious people, who were stuck in their ways, and the learned elites, who were improving their religious beliefs and behaviours.[110] Combined, these two points indicated that Christianity was necessary to insure good morals and piety amongst the multitude, and true theistic understanding amongst the philosophical elite.

Robertson was building on the research of East India Company officials who had revolutionised European knowledge of Indian religion

---

[107] Robertson (1791, p. 312).

[108] Trautmann (1997, p. 65).

[109] For helpful discussions, see Young (2000, esp. pp. 92–94) and Brown (2009).

[110] Robertson (1791, pp. 312, 313).

since the 1760s.[111] In the treatises and translations of John Zephaniah Howell (1711–1798), Alexander Dow (1735–1779, Nathaniel Halhed (1751–1830), Charles Wilkins (1749–1836) and William Jones (1746–1796) an influential picture emerged of Hinduism as a reasonable religion bearing many similarities with Christianity, though corrupted, in all too familiar ways, by popular superstition and priestcraft. The British study of Indian religion was focused on tracing an "original religion of reason back to Brahminical philosophy," subsequently corrupted.[112] These accounts presented what they believed was "theological and philosophical core" of Hinduism, reflecting a religion that was "unified, monotheistic, ancient and native to India."[113] These authors contributed to a tendency to focus on the philosophical essence of Indian religion, which determined the "philosophic" approach to European interpretations of Hinduism. Many of these interpreters of Indian religion were religious dissenters and freethinkers, and they were willing to see the crossover between Christianity and Hinduism. Their evangelical critics held that they exhibited a deistic lack of concern for the importance of revelation.

Epitomising the Scottish approach to historical analysis, Robertson, by contrast, was interested in the origin and progress of unassisted religion from primitivism to sophistication over the longué durée—a process that was not unalloyed improvement nor one that reached a benign final form. As such, he rejected the new wave of deistic British orientalists' focus on primitive monotheism's decline into superstition and focus on cunning priestcraft. He did so as a minister, but also an enlightened social theorist. Indeed, Robertson's study of the Brahmic religion epitomised so much about the Scottish study of religion. While across in England and France the debate so often centred on the relative antiquity of the "Hindoo" or "Gentoo" religion and Christianity, Robertson attended to how religious change could be conceived of as a natural pattern and did so in ways that were largely devoid of reference to scripture or revelation.

The end point of religious development of unassisted societies was the creation of an unstable *religio duplex*. Educated elites move towards a form of philosophical theism, as exhibited by the theologies of the Brahmins or the Stoics. The multitude remains mired in systems of superstition

---

[111] Patterson (2021).

[112] Patterson (2021, p. 15).

[113] Patterson (2021, p. 52).

formed in earlier epochs. These systems will endure given the limitations of human nature—theism is impossible for the multitude to comprehend without scripture—though these limitations can be rendered milder if "science and philosophy are diffused" throughout a society.[114] Within limits, such diffusion of unassisted peoples could bring about religious improvement. But, as with Smith, Robertson recommended rulers should only "with timidity" attempt to modify popular religion, for fear of raising the hornets' nest of vulgar fanaticism.[115] A commonplace strategy was the reframing of popular superstitions through "allegorical interpretations," by which popular deities are slowly reconceptualised as descriptions of the powers of nature.[116] New natural theological knowledge could be incorporated into a society's "schools of science," meaning that established beliefs were subject to a "scrutiny to which [they were] formerly exempt."[117]

The evidence of the history of pagan societies was that philosophy, while it can soften popular superstition and establish elite theism, can never fully fathom the truth of religion on its own. The human mind is incapable of forming "an adequate idea of the perfections and operations of the supreme being," meaning that theism amongst the elites, even amongst highly developed societies, remains a mixture of "ignorance and error."[118] Nick Phillipson read this passage as "sailing perilously close to the winds of contemporary freethinking and scepticism," but Robertson is clearly articulating the absolute necessity of revelation.[119] Robertson pointed to the theologies of the Brahmins and Stoics as examples of the maximum height of natural theological knowledge that unassisted philosophy could achieve. Both believed erroneously that in the existence of an *anima mundi*, that God was a "vivifying principle diffuse through the whole creation, a universal soul that animated each part of it." Both also held the erroneous doctrine of the "final re-union of all intelligent creatures to their primaeval source."[120] Knowledge of true religion was

---

[114] Robertson (1791, p. 322).
[115] Robertson (1791, p. 323).
[116] Robertson (1791, p. 323).
[117] Robertson (1791, p. 323).
[118] Robertson (1791, p. 330).
[119] Phillipson (1997, p. 71). Compare with Ahnert (2010, p. 119; 2015, p. 102).
[120] Robertson (1791, pp. 330, 331).

not within the purview of philosophy. Hume would have left it there, but Robertson argued for the need of revelation. It was needed to both (1) teach the tenets upon which true natural theology must be built, in ways that avoided superstition and (2) to teach of our eventual reward and punishment for how we conducted our time on earth, in ways than encouraged morality. Knowledge of this latter outcome had been uncertain in the pagan societies of ancient Greece and Rome, and Hindu Indian, and this uncertainty ensured the doctrine had limited impact on the behaviour of the multitude.

Robertson ended the *Historical Disquisition* by criticising civil theology in which a theistic elite merely managed, rather than tried to improve, the religious beliefs of the superstitious multitude. This might have been a rebuttal of Hume's praise of polytheism in the NHR, but Robertson may have also been legitimising extending British colonial rule given that he believed the Brahmins had abandoned the Indian multitude to religious error. It was the "duty" of philosophers, once they learned the doctrines of theism, to teach the vulgar, even if they knew that the latter were "doomed by their condition to remain in ignorance."[121] But pagan philosopher-priests had instead usually opted for polities of social control which manipulated the people into obedience. Priestcraft, if of a more benign sort, was to blame.[122] Robertson accepted that teaching systems of superstition was an expected error when the philosophers are "destitute of superior guidance," that is, revelation.[123] This was religious imposture—the maintenance of systems of superstition known to be false to ensure political stability—and was further evidence of the inferiority of pagan *religio duplexes* to Christianity. Some commentators have claimed Robertson saw a universal religion shared by pagan and Christian theists alike, and of Robertson's description of contemporary Hinduism as being comparable to contemporary Presbyterianism, but the general gist of the *Historical Disquisition* is a strong sense of the inferiority of paganism.[124]

In arguing in this way, Robertson was not describing the Brahmins as cunning priests who had manipulated their positions to accrue power

---

[121] Robertson (1791, p. 334).

[122] Brown (2009, pp. 307–308).

[123] Robertson (1791, p. 331).

[124] E.g. Trautmann (1997, esp. p. 66), Phillipson (1997), and Brown (2009, pp. 307–309).

and riches to themselves as the expense of the multitude. This was the position of the deistic British orientalists. Robertson's account was far less conspiratorial, viewing the Brahmins as making the wrong choice of how to use the materials available to them, privileging social peace over piety.[125] But from his Christian perspective, Robertson held that without revelation, any efforts on the part of the Brahmins to improve the virtue and piety of the populace were doomed to failure. What was distressing was their decision, despite knowing many of the truths of theistic religion, not to even try to raise the level of enlightenment. This is a criticism of priestly behaviour that focuses on lack of courage and of complacency, not an abundance of cunning. In a way, Robertson was defending priestcraft as the inevitable tactic that had to be employed by the learned to manage, but also help the multitude—what he criticised the Brahmins for doing was for not trying their best to improve the thought and behaviour of their flocks.

* * *

Spanning four decades and a variety of approaches to historical analysis, each of Robertson's published discussions of religious change contained a different emphasis. The *Situation of the World* explained the necessity of Christ's mission, but also power of Christianity itself to alter the trajectory of human history for the better. This sense of providence guiding history is also present in *History of the Reign of Charles V*, but in this work of "philosophical history" Christianity is less powerful as a cause for change in itself and is subordinated to wider historical developments understood as a number of interrelated social, economic, cultural and political factors. Still, Robertson professed a confidence that the history of post-Roman Empire Europe indicated such divine plan. The ability for mere human reason to gain a glimpse of that plan, however, was less apparent in *History of America*, not least because the Spanish had wasted their opportunity to spread Christianity effectively. Here Robertson utilised the sociological methods of the "science of man" in his descriptions of "savage" Americans in Book IV and of the "semi-civilized" Aztecs and Incas in Book VII. His findings mitigated against a naïve sense of a providentially arranged

---

[125] See again Brown (2009, pp. 306–307). Robertson was also, at least implicitly, criticising Hume's recommendation at the end of the NHR for philosophical withdrawal from engaging with popular religion.

progress of religion easily demonstrable by socio-historical study. Robertson's findings indicated that religion did not progress from animistic polytheism to philosophical theism in line with wider societal change, and, as with the case of the Aztecs, could act as a countervailing factor that hindered or even undid other forms of social improvement. The *Historical Disquisition* saw Robertson reassert the utility of outlining the "natural progress of false religion," which drew a very different conclusion to Hume's "Natural History of Religion." Robertson saw this as a process of improvement but not ultimate perfection. The Stoic and Hindu religions indicated, it has been argued, the "natural progress of mankind tended—providentially—towards the truths of Christianity."[126] In a way, this is true. But there was an insurmountable gap between unassisted and true religion, which could only be traversed in developed societies with knowledge of revelation. Without revelation, members of the philosophical elite might come to knowledge of a version of theism, but they would need to use man-made superstitions to enforce moral and pious behaviour amongst the multitude.[127] Christianity was necessary as a moral message intelligible to the multitude, who are otherwise abandoned by the "philosophical theists" of Stoicism and Hinduism's Brahmins and, we might note, also Hume and his intended audience in §15 of the NHR.

References

Ahnert, Thomas. 2010. Fortschrittsgeschichte und Religiöse Aufklärung. William Robertson und die Deutung Außereuropäischer Kulturen. *Geschichte und Gesellschaft*, Special Issue 23: 101–122.
———. 2011. The Moral Education of Mankind: Character and Religious Moderatism in the Sermons of Hugh Blair. In *Character, Self, and Sociability in the Scottish Enlightenment*, ed. Susan Manning and Thomas Ahnert, 67–84. New York: Palgrave Macmillan.
———. 2015. *The Moral Culture of the Scottish Enlightenment*. London: Yale University Press.
Allan, David. 1993. *Virtue, Learning, and the Scottish Enlightenment: Ideas of Scholarship in Early Modern History*. Edinburgh: Edinburgh University Press.

---

[126] Cf. Kidd (1999, p. 51), here echoing Phillipson (1997).
[127] Ahnert (2011, pp. 74–75; 2015, pp. 102–103).

———. 2013. Identity and Innovation: Historiography in the Scottish Enlightenment. In *A Companion to Enlightenment Historiography*, ed. Sophie Bourgault and Robert Sparling, 307–342. Leiden, NL: Brill.
Berry, Christopher J. 1997. *The Social Theory of the Scottish Enlightenment*. Edinburgh: Edinburgh University Press.
———. 2000. Rude Religion: The Psychology of Polytheism in the Scottish Enlightenment. In *The Scottish Enlightenment: Essays in Reinterpretation*, ed. Paul Wood, 315–334. New York: University of Rochester Press.
———. 2018. *Essays on Hume, Smith and the Scottish Enlightenment*. Edinburgh: Edinburgh University Press.
Broadie, Alexander. 1997. *The Scottish Enlightenment: An Anthology*. Edinburgh: Canongate.
Brown, Stewart J., ed. 1997. *William Robertson and the Expansion of Empire*. Cambridge: Cambridge University Press.
———. 2009. William Robertson, Early Orientalism, and the Historical Disquisition on India of 1791. *Scottish Historical Review* 88: 289–312.
Crane, R.S. 1934. Anglican Apologetics and the Idea of Progress, 1699–1745. *Modern Philology* 31: 273–306.
Ehrlich, Joshua. 2013. William Robertson and Scientific Theism. *Modern Intellectual History* 10: 519–542.
Fearnley-Sander, Mary. 1990. Philosophical History and The Scottish Reformation: William Robertson and the Knoxian Tradition. *The Historical Journal* 33: 323–338.
Gascoigne, John. 1991. 'The Wisdom of the Egyptians' and the Secularisation of History in the Age of Newton. In *The Uses of Antiquity: The Scientific Revolution and the Classical Tradition*, ed. Stephen Gaukroger, 171–212. Dordrecht: Springer.
Hargraves, Neil. 2007. Beyond the Savage Character: Mexicans, Peruvians, and the "Imperfectly Civilized" in William Robertson's 'History of America'. In *The Anthropology of the Enlightenment*, ed. Larry Wolff and Marco Cipolloni. Stanford, CA: Stanford University Press.
Harvey, David Allen. 2008. Living Antiquity: Lafitau's *Moeurs des sauvages amériquains* and the Religious Roots of the Enlightenment Science of Man. *Proceedings of the Western Society for French History* 36: 75–92.
Kelley, Donald R. 1998. *Faces of History: Historical Inquiry from Herodotus to Herder*. Yale, CT: Yale University Press.
Keen, Benjamin. 1990. *The Aztec Image in Western Thought*. New Brunswick, NJ: Rutgers University Press.
Kidd, Colin. 1999. *British Identities Before Nationalism: Ethnicity and Nationhood in the Atlantic World 1600–1800*. Cambridge: Cambridge University Press.

———. 2004. Subscription, the Scottish Enlightenment and the Moderate Interpretation of History. *Journal of Ecclesiastical History* 55: 502–519.

Kontler, László. 2008. Time and Progress - Time as Progress: An Enlightened Sermon by William Robertson. In *Given World And Time: Temporalities in Context*, ed. Tyrus Miller, 191–215. Budapest: Central European University.

———. 2014. *Translations, Histories, Enlightenments: William Robertson in Germany, 1760–1795*. London: Palgrave Macmillan.

Loughlin, Felicity. 2018. Religion, Erudition, and Enlightenment: Histories of Paganism in Eighteenth-Century Scotland. PhD thesis, Edinburgh University.

Lucas, Joseph S. 2000. The Course of Empire and the Long Road to Civilization: North American Indians and Scottish Enlightenment Historians. *Explorations in Early American Culture* 4: 166–190.

Meek, Ronald L. 1976. *Social Science and the Ignoble Savage*. Cambridge: Cambridge University Press.

Miller, Nicholas B. 2018. Philosophical History at the Cusp of Globalization: Scottish Enlightenment Reflections on Colonial Spanish America. In *Philosophy of Globalisation*, ed. Concha Roldán, Daniel Brauer, and Johannes Rohbeck, 191–203. Boston, MA: Walter de Gruyter.

O'Brien, Karen. 1997. *Narratives of Enlightenment: Cosmopolitan History from Voltaire to Gibbon*. Cambridge: Cambridge University Press.

Patterson, Jessica. 2021. *Religion, Enlightenment and Empire: British Interpretations of Hinduism in the Eighteenth Century*. Cambridge: Cambridge University Press.

Phillipson, Nicholas. 1997. Providence and Progress: An Introduction to the Historical Thought of William Robertson. In *William Robertson and the Expansion of Empire*, ed. S.J. Brown, 74–91. Cambridge: Cambridge University Press.

Poovey, Mary. 1998. *A History of the Modern Fact: Problems of Knowledge in the Sciences of Wealth and Society*. Chicago, IL: Chicago University Press.

Roberts, Charlotte. 2014. Tracing a Meridian Through the Map of Time: Fact, Conjecture and the Scientific Method in William Robertson's History of America. In *Historical Writing in Britain, 1688-1830: Visions of History*, ed. Ben Dew and Fiona Price, 109–126. Basingstoke: Palgrave Macmillan.

Robertson, William. 1755. *The Situation of the World at the Time of Christ's Appearance, and Its Connexion with the Success of His Religion, Considered*. Edinburgh.

———. 1769. *The History of the Reign of the Emperor Charles V., with a View of the Progress of Society in Europe*, 3 vols. London.

———. 1777. *The History of America*, 2 vols. London.

———. 1791. *An Historical Disquisition Concerning the Knowledge Which the Ancients Had of India*. London.

Sebastiani, Silvia. 2013. *The Scottish Enlightenment: Race, Gender, and the Limits of Progress*, trans. Jeremy Carden. Basingstoke: Palgrave.

———. 2014. What Constituted Historical Evidence of the New World? Closeness and Distance in William Robertson and Francisco Javier Clavijero. *Modern Intellectual History* 11: 677–695.

Smitten, Jeffrey. 1985. Impartiality in Robertson's History of America. *Eighteenth-Century Studies* 19: 56–77.

———. 2013. William Robertson: The Minister as Historian. In *A Companion to Enlightenment Historiography*, ed. Sophie Bourgault and Robert Sparling, 103–131. Leiden: Brill.

———. 2016. *The Life of William Robertson: Minister, Historian and Principal*. Edinburgh: Edinburgh University Press.

Spadafora, David. 1990. *The Idea of Progress in Eighteenth-Century Britain*. London: Yale University Press.

Trautmann, Thomas R. 1997. *Aryans and British India*. London: University of California Press.

Womersley, David. 1986. The Historical Writings of William Robertson. *Journal of the History of Ideas* 47: 497–506.

Young, Brian W. 2000. 'The Lust of Empire and Religious Hate': Christianity, History, and Indian, 1790–1820. In *History, Religion, and Culture: British Intellectual History 1750–1950*, ed. Stefan Collini, Richard Whatmore, and Brian Young, 91–111. Cambridge: Cambridge University Press.

CHAPTER 8

Adam Ferguson, Stoicism and the Individual Alone

Abstract Adam Ferguson's changing views on the relationship between religion, human nature and society contained an increasingly strong deistic or Stoic element. He argued that the religious propensities of human nature direct us towards theistic belief but, equally, that these propensities were easily bent towards superstition. The individual faces a battle to enable the theistic elements of their nature control the character of their religious beliefs. Ferguson also recommended that both individuals and magistrates adopt an ecumenical sense of a universal natural religion. We should be sceptical about the parochial claims to truths of any one form of religion, be aware that all religions originate in the same aspects of human nature and are seeking the same goals and seek religious freedom for all.

Keywords Adam Ferguson · Enlightenment deism · Individual conscience · Religious nativism · Philosophical progress · Religious freedom

William Robertson's study of mankind tempered his early confidence in a humanly observable providential order to history, but confirmed his sense that revelation was necessary for knowing true religion and for teaching a morality most suited to manage frail humankind. We find in Adam

Ferguson, another of the Edinburgh Enlightenment's brightest lights, a very different picture, in which the necessity of revelation is set aside and replaced by the duty of the individual to find out religious truth for themselves. Surveying commentary on Ferguson raises something of a paradox. On the one hand, Adam Ferguson has regularly been treated as a secular theorist of civil society who was largely uninterested in religious topics.[1] On the other hand, scholars will often mention in passing that Ferguson was a student of divinity, under Archibald Campbell at St Andrews, held a position as a chaplain in the Black Watch and was subsequently a church elder, with the implication being that he was more of an orthodox Presbyterian (befitting his supposed outsider status as a Highland Republican critical of commercial society) than Hume or Smith. The extent to which Ferguson's religious thought has been discussed, it has centred on his sense of the providential underpinnings of the universe and man's role within it.[2] Several commentators have argued that Ferguson's theistic beliefs underpinned much of his social thought and that, in the words of one commentator, he embraced the "standard doctrines of eighteenth-century natural theology" combined with a heavy dose of Stoicism.[3] The "study of nature," including the study of human nature, leads us to "true religion."[4] And to study human nature, the moral philosopher should imitate the "natural historian [who] thinks himself obliged to collect facts not to offer conjectures."[5] This study was to be based on "history, observation, experience and recollection."[6]

I want to build on this scholarship by investigating in more detail Ferguson's views on the relationship between religion, human nature, society and history. We can extract a few hints from Ferguson's biography to support the claim that, whatever he was, he was not during

---

[1] For some assessment that Ferguson's thought was characterised by a "deeply ingrained secularism," see Kettler (1965, p. 131) and Merolle (2006, p. xix).

[2] For commentary, see Hill (2006, pp. 44–47) and Smith (2019, p. 119).

[3] Especially Sher (2015, pp. 324–328), Hill (2006), Chen (2008), Heath (2015), Hill (2017), and Heath and Lin (2018).

[4] Ferguson (1996, p. 89). See also Hill (2006, p. 45). On Ferguson as a "scientist of man," see Heath and Merolle (2008, esp. the chapter by Meyer), McDaniel (2013), Vieu (2015), and Berry (2018, Ch. 7). See also the useful discussion in Holt (2016).

[5] Ferguson (1996, p. 8). See also Wood (1990, 1996, pp. 205–206).

[6] Ferguson, Moral Philosophy Lectures, EUL, Dc.1.84.5–6 quoted in Holt (2016, p. 135).

the second half of this life, a Christian. His long-term friend Hugh Cleghorn commented following Ferguson's death in 1816 that the latter's lines intended for his tomb spoke "the language and breathed the sentiments of the Stoic school," and Cleghorn would later recall in 1836 that Ferguson was a "thorough going and confirmed unbeliever."[7] But we can identify the emergence of something other-than-Christian sentiment in Ferguson's published works: thought which is more deistic and stoic. To examine Ferguson's position on religion and human nature, moreover, shows him to be intimately involved in the discussions surveyed in this book and applied his own approach to the science of human nature to the topic of religion. The conclusions derived by Ferguson were that: natural religion was explicable if we search after it using the right methods; external rites and ceremonies were tools to aid us to live virtuous and pious lives, but should be ignored if they contradict our personal sense of religious truth; that revelation was unnecessary and provided no unique source of information about God; and that while the ignorant superstitious multitude will always be with us, we can dampen those idolatrous and fanatical aspects of their character through management of universal passions and the dissemination of natural philosophical education throughout society.[8]

Neither Lisa Hill's bibliography of "sources known or likely to have been consulted by Ferguson" nor Jane Fagg's research on Ferguson's use of the Edinburgh University Library suggest that Ferguson was interested in sacred or ecclesiastical history, works of comparative religion or paganism in general, save for what might be found in works of ancient history or contemporary travel literature.[9] Ferguson would cite the authority of sacred history in his sermon the Black Watch during the Jacobite Rebellion of 1745, but all mentions in his published philosophical writings either quickly glossed over scriptural history or actively distanced his position from revelation.[10] Indeed, as J. G. A. Pocock commented, "what is outstandingly absent" from Ferguson's history of post-Roman Europe in his *Essay on the History of Civil Society* (1767)

---

[7] BL Add MS 39,945 The Diary of William Erksine (1773–1852) f. 34r. I owe this reference to Ian Stewart and Max Skjornberg's edition of new Ferguson correspondence and writings. See Ferguson (2023, p. 231).

[8] In this, my argument complements Bijlsma (2023).

[9] Fagg (2008).

[10] E.g. Ferguson (1996, p. 74). See Arbo (2011) and Chen (2008, esp. p. 173).

is the "independent role of the Christian clergy, secular and regular."[11] The review of Ferguson's *Essay* in Edward Gibbon's journal *Mémoires littéraires de la Grande Bretagne* expressed surprise, as Pocock notes, at how Ferguson did not mention religion at all in his progressive history of civil society.[12] Similar criticisms were made of Ferguson's *History of the Progress and Termination of the Roman Republic* (1783).[13]

The fact that Ferguson was not interested in and chose not to write about the history of Christianity or paganism in any depth is not the same thing as saying he was not interested in the relationship between religion and human nature. Things look a little different if we shift our focus away from Ferguson's *Essay*, which its minimal religious content, and towards the several iterations of his moral philosophy lectures at Edinburgh, especially the third edition of the *Institutes* (1785) and *Principles of Moral and Political Science* (1792).[14] We could go as far as describing a "religious turn" in Ferguson's thought from the 1780s onwards, given the expanded attention he gave to topics raised but primarily glossed in his initial publications.[15] While Ferguson in these texts remains unconcerned with the details of religious history, we do find an author increasingly concerned to understand the inherent propensities of human nature that inform the formation of religious belief, the significance of religious diversity, especially in terms of church-state relations, and how the individual is to seek out the right path in contexts of religious error.[16] Moreover, Ferguson was moving towards a form of enlightened deism underpinned by Stoic natural theology that was appreciably different to orthodox Presbyterianism—the surface-level similarity between his positions and some tenets of Presbyterian orthodoxy stems from the latter itself owing its position on natural reason's powers to know God ultimately from Stoic and Ciceronian sources. Monotheism was the first religion of mankind, both historically speaking and in terms of the natural tendencies of human

---

[11] Pocock (1999–2015, vol. ii, p. 341). See also Lehmann (1930, p. 136).

[12] Pocock (1999–2015, vol. ii, p. 341).

[13] Hill (2017, p. 49).

[14] In moving away from a dominant focus on the *Essay* I have been inspired by Smith (2019).

[15] Cf. Kettler (1965, p. 153) who dismisses the "few injunctions to piety" in the *Principles* as irrelevant, given the more important *Essay* is not interested in religion.

[16] See, similarly, Bijlsma (2023).

nature. Ferguson reasserted the traditional trajectory of monotheism's decline into polytheism, while also using that other traditional proof of early modern anti-atheist apologetics, the universal consent argument for the existence of God. Yet he did so using the language and concepts of enlightened Scottish social theory and Stoic natural theology, not Christianity.

FERGUSON AND THE NATURALNESS OF RELIGION

In the second half of his career as Professor of Moral Philosophy at Edinburgh, Ferguson moved away from a definition of man as *animal rationale* and towards one of man as *animal religiosum*. Certainly, while lecturing students at Edinburgh in 1766, he asserted that "religion is natural" on the basis that human nature is framed to admire, love and obey a supreme being.[17] But in both the early published iterations of his Edinburgh lectures, *Analysis of Pneumatics and Moral Philosophy* (1766), and the more substantial *Institutes of Moral Philosophy* (1769), as well as being implied in the *Essay on the History of Civil Society*, Ferguson was clear that man was differentiated from the animal kingdom "totally and in kind" because of his possession of an "intellectual nature."[18] Ferguson clarified this position subsequently in the *Principles* that the "principal distinction in the description of man," differentiating the species from the rest of creation, was religious belief not reason.[19] Only man has "perception of intelligent power operating in nature," enacts "intercourse with some powers invisible," is aware of a "presence greatly superior to that of his fellow creatures," and builds "temples and places of worship."[20] The "specific excellence of man," compared to the lower animals, was his "power and disposition to perceive, with delight, an intelligent and beneficent author in the system of things around him."[21]

---

[17] Ferguson (1766, p. 27).
[18] Ferguson (1769, p. 118). See also Ferguson (1996, p. 30).
[19] Ferguson (1792, vol. i, p. 163).
[20] Ferguson (1792, vol. i, p. 163).
[21] Ferguson (1792, vol. ii, p. 34). For inadvertently secularising readings of this passage as Ferguson viewing benevolence as being the "specific excellence of man," see Smith (2019, p. 105, 2021, p. 37).

The fact that humans were able to perceive benevolent, wise design in the universe also indicated, Ferguson claimed in the *Principles*, that humanity had "some qualification to participate in [those] godlike principles of beneficence and wisdom."[22] This is Ferguson's version of the *imago dei*. But while we are capable of imitating, to some degree, godlike behaviour, this requires constant cultivation on our part. Religion, understood as the "sentiment of the mind relating to God," is one of those aspects of humanity's "progressive and variable nature."[23] We do not possess knowledge of God as a "blessing already complete," as certain orthodox Calvinist ministers might hold that the light of nature contains.[24] A propensity to theistic belief is "one of the rude materials" with which man is to "exert his talent for art and improvement."[25] The two possible paths here are, on the one hand, that of "extending or improving" our inherent "first materials" and, on the other, "straining them to the model of some favourite prepossession, affection or passion."[26] That is, we either allow our natural propensities to reach their perfection or we pervert them by letting other aspects of our natures get in the way. It is in search of a "model" of religious perfection and a "patron" of our moral beliefs that we "arrive at our best and our highest conceptions of the supreme being."[27] Here, with Ferguson, as with Smith, our best religious notions emerged as justifications and crutches for pre-existing moral notions.[28] Most importantly, it is beneficial "to continually have in view … that we are instruments in the hand

---

[22] Ferguson (1792, vol. ii, p. 34).

[23] Ferguson (1792, vol. i, p. 167).

[24] Ferguson (1792, vol. i, p. 167). Kettler read Ferguson's rejection of innate religious knowledge as evidence of his "disregard of formal Christian principles." See Kettler (1965, p. 172). But here Ferguson is rejecting simplistic innatism, the idea we have fully formed religious notions inbuilt into our natures, a view that it is very hard to find in early modern writings other than in sermons where philosophical subtlety is not relevant. See Mills (2021). Heath and Lin suggest that "Ferguson's perspective" on natural religion "is neither antithetical to nor inconsistent with a continued faith" (2018, p. 107).

[25] Ferguson (1792, vol. i, p. 167). See also (Hill 2017, pp. 176–177) and, more generally, Chen (2008, pp. 176–178).

[26] Ferguson (1792, vol. i, p. 167).

[27] Ferguson (1792, vol. i, p. 167).

[28] Smith (2019, pp. 110–111).

of God for the good of his creatures."[29] As with most other enlightened Scottish theorists of human nature, religion is seen by Ferguson to provide ample support to human happiness, if practised in its correct form.[30]

In the *Principles* Ferguson maintained that several inherent aspects of human nature demonstrated that man is "formed for religion as well as society."[31] We have an innate ability to perceive "universal intelligence in the fabric of the universe," though the accuracy of our understanding improves with improvements in natural philosophical knowledge. The unbidden pangs of "horror and guilt" we experienced when we commit actions we know are wrong demonstrate our awareness of some higher standard of morality.[32] The inherent religiosity of human nature was demonstrated by the universal agreement in the existence of intelligent power, even amongst the primordial peoples of the new world.[33] Ferguson supported his use of the *consensus gentium* argument about supernatural power with an appeal to the key text of early modern religious innatism, Cicero's *De natura deorum*.[34] Akin to Smith's argument in *TMS*, Ferguson also maintained that belief in future rewards and punishments was a "universal belief" stemming from the frustration of man's "instinctive desire" for "distributive justice" here on earth.[35] Aggregated together, all these elements demonstrate that humankind is "fitted to hold communication" with God and to "apprehend his will and to become a willing instrument in promoting the ends of his government."[36] The conduit of communication for apprehending God's will

---

[29] Ferguson (1792, vol. ii, p. 103).

[30] Harris (2004).

[31] Ferguson (1792, vol. ii, p. 175)

[32] Ferguson (1792, vol. ii, p. 175).

[33] Here we see one of the sticking points about how to judge universal consent: to Hume, on the topic of whether humans are inherently religious or not, exceptions in the form of atheist societies reported in travel literature disproved the existence of universal consent; but to Ferguson, like most religious nativists, the exceptions indicated something had gone wrong in that particular society. In passing, we might also note that Hume accepted the significance of atheist exceptions for the issue of humanity's inherent religiosity, but dismissed the exception of the theistic ancient Hebrews for his argument for the primacy of polytheism.

[34] See Mills (2021).

[35] Ferguson (1769, p. 137).

[36] Ferguson (1792, vol. ii, p. 36).

were purely those of natural, not revealed, religion: the propensities of our universal human nature and the findings of our faculty of reason.

To those wishing to find in his works a Christianity that distinguished him from Hume and Smith, it could be said that Ferguson reasserted the orthodox Calvinist belief in the power of the unassisted light of nature to come to the idea of God. (This would also distinguish him from the Moderates, with whom he was close friends, arguing for the necessity of revelation and the limits of natural reason). For Ferguson, the idea was an easily formed notion on which "mankind do not appear to need information" beyond observation of the "system of nature."[37] This was irrespective of whether the mind of the individual was "contracted or enlarged."[38] The existence of God was known by those in the "rudest or most simple state of the human species" as it was in the most civilised.[39] In this Ferguson was an outlier amongst the thinkers of the Scottish Enlightenment, who agreed that the idea of God was either the result of sustained effort by natural philosophers in conditions of societal stability or who believed, such as Ferguson's old divinity tutor Archibald Campbell, the idea of God was unreachable without revelation.[40] And yet it was not to the staple scriptural passages (such as Romans 2:14–15) or the Magisterial Reformers that Ferguson quoted on the issue of man's inherent religiosity but Cicero and Epictetus.[41] And he did not do so in the manner of earlier generations of anti-atheist Christian apologetics, who sought to show that even the pagans believed that religion was natural and therefore true, but because he believed that Cicero and Epictetus were real authorities on human nature.[42]

The issue of whether the idea of God was intelligible to all humankind troubled Ferguson, and he alternated between positions prior to the assessment outlined in the *Principles*. In the first two editions of the *Institutes* (1769, 1773), Ferguson set out the claims that belief in God was

---

[37] Ferguson (1792, vol. i, p. 163).

[38] Ferguson (1792, vol. i, p. 164).

[39] Ferguson (1792, vol. ii, p. 64).

[40] Cf. Ahnert (2015, e.g. p. 2, p. 6, p. 31), where despite being one of the most prominent members of the "Moderate Literati," Ferguson's changing position on the powers of the light of nature, compared to the other Moderates, is not discussed.

[41] Ferguson (1792, vol. ii, p. 359).

[42] For recent arguments for the Stoic underpinning to Ferguson's religious thought, see Bijlsma (2022, 2023).

universal, but that this universality "does not imply any adequate notion" of God.[43] Still, the universality of such belief indicates that it must be "the result of human nature, or the suggestion of circumstances that occur in everyplace and age."[44] The universality of religious belief stems from two tendencies in human nature: our "perception of causes from the appearance of effects" and our perception of "design from the concurrence of means to an end."[45] Our perception of design behind the causes we observe leads us to belief in God: this is not a belief we require argument on, because our "nature has determined that we shall continue to believe" in God.[46] The "final causes" we instinctively perceive in nature is "the language in which the existence of God is revealed to man" and our "interpretation" of this language is "instinctive."[47]

Ferguson's summary of the same topic in the third expanded edition of the *Institutes*, reiterated in the *Principles*, was less confident that the religious propensities of human nature hit upon an adequate notion of God. Rather than belief in God being universal, Ferguson noted the universal tendency to look upon "many operations in nature … as the exertions of mind or spirit, distinct from man."[48] Belief in supernatural power, rather than the specific belief in one supreme being, was now deemed commonplace. Ferguson also introduced a distinction between the ignorant and the knowing: the former conceive of supernatural power in terms of the "little sphere of their own concerns," whereas the latter do so in terms of the "general order of nature" insofar as they observe it.[49] The religious conceptions of "rude minds" are "grovelling," but Ferguson did not believe that primitive peoples were atheists—like John Gregory on scepticism, Ferguson opined that atheism occurred as the "effect of study, and an effort to withstand original feelings."[50] Perception of design in

---

[43] Ferguson (1769, p. 123).
[44] Ferguson (1769, pp. 122, 123). See also Smith (2012, pp. 62–63).
[45] Ferguson (1769, p. 123).
[46] Ferguson (1769, p. 123).
[47] Ferguson (1769, p. 125).
[48] Ferguson (1785, p. 117; cf. Ferguson, 1792, vol. i, pp. 165–166).
[49] Ferguson (1785, p. 118).
[50] Ferguson (1785, p. 119). On Ferguson's views on the dangers of book learning, see Smith (2006), to which we can add the threat of losing one's natural religious sentiments, the source of ultimate human happiness.

nature was still "instinctive" and design was evidence in "every material to which our knowledge extends."[51] As we will see below, Ferguson explained in the *Principles* that it is in our power to develop correct religious notions, but it required effort and usually the direction from the "learned" versed in the study of natural philosophy.[52]

FERGUSON ON THE LINK BETWEEN RELIGION, HAPPINESS AND SOCIETY

Alongside the extent of humanity's powers to come to notions of God, Ferguson was also concerned with the social role of religion and what the correct relationship should be between religious authority, political power and the individual conscience. In line with his enlightened colleagues (including Hume of the *History of England*, though not the NHR), Ferguson argued that the "institutions of religion" are to be found in "every well ordered community."[53] Religion encourages our adherence to our moral duty in two ways: (1) by making us "love wisdom and beneficence" and making us love "our situations and [our] duties"; (2) by the prospect of future reward and punishment, which acted as the most powerful incentive to moral behaviour in the here and now, though, as we shall see, Ferguson was sceptical about how secure the argument for the immortality of the soul was.[54] Still, we can be said to be "possessed of religion," as well as of "virtue and happiness," when we are "employed for the good of [God's] creatures."[55]

Correct religious sentiment and action are the source of the greatest happiness. In the *Institutes*, Ferguson stated that the enlightened mind able to understand God's providence as displayed in nature experienced the "most pleasant" affection possible.[56] In the second edition of the *Institutes*, he clarified this claim. The "foundation of happiness" was

---

[51] Ferguson (1785, p. 91).

[52] Ferguson (1792, vol. I, p. 166); Heath and Lin (2018, pp. 108–109), who also note that in his later manuscript essays, Ferguson moved further away from his initial position that our instinctively developed religious notions aligned with accurate notions of God.

[53] Ferguson (1792, vol. ii, p. 175).

[54] Ferguson (1769, p. 236). See also Heath and Lin (2018, pp. 111–112).

[55] Ferguson (1792, vol. ii, p. 103–104).

[56] Ferguson (1769, p. 154).

"benevolent affection," with such affection directed directly towards God as the "supreme" source of happiness. This is an affection requiring wisdom and an "extensive and just understanding" and will lead, amongst other things, to "piety."[57] This built on the claim in the first edition of the *Institutes* that one of the principal ways to bring about our happiness and our improvement is to "have continually in view ... that we are instruments in the hand of God for the good of his creatures" and that whatever our station in life, we have been placed there by God.[58] This realisation is the "highest point to which moral science conducts the mind of man."[59]

The fact that Ferguson believed we can only become possessed of religion, virtue and happiness through our own diligent activity speaks to the individualist strain to his discussion. As will be developed momentarily, Ferguson believed that the path to religion is not to be found in unthinking adherence to the teachings of revelation or established rites and ceremonies, but in the vigorous activity of the self-willed individual, exhibiting through action the virtuous character that is wise, courageous, temperate and benevolent. People with such characters are most likely to be able to recognise the "providence and moral government of God" and "settle religion ... on its best foundations of integrity and goodness."[60] The individual can never abandon responsibility for their own beliefs and actions: we must pay heed, above all else, to our own consciences—or what Ferguson termed, in figurative language, as the "lamp of God in the soul of man."[61] Our instinctive sense of right and wrong is a "species of compulsory law," but it is one, Ferguson argued, that is applied "by every person only to himself."[62] We alone are responsible for our actions, and we must be sceptical about local religious circumstances lest we let a "temporary vogue in the world" distort our attempts to maintain a "just and manly virtue."[63] Elsewhere, Ferguson would hold that one of the ramparts against the consolidation of superstition was for individual men

---

[57] Ferguson (1773, p. 151).
[58] Ferguson (1769, p. 169).
[59] Ferguson (1792, vol. i, p. 313). See also Heath and Lin (2018, p. 120).
[60] Ferguson (1792, vol. ii, pp. 45–46).
[61] Ferguson (1792, vol. i, p. 183). Hill (2006, pp. 79–80).
[62] Ferguson (1773, p. 215). See also Ferguson (1792, vol. ii, p. 104).
[63] Ferguson (1792, vol. ii, p. 320).

to employ the "watchfulness, penetration and courage" they did in the "management of common affairs" to their superstitious beliefs, as they would quickly see the absurdities they really were.[64]

The topic of the individual in relation to their society raises one of Ferguson's principal concerns: the relationship between the individual's religion and that of their society's. Each culture's religious rites and observances are "retained as mere arbitrary signs or expressions of the affection" to God that "religion or good manners require."[65] The individual should perform these as long as they do not encourage cruel behaviour, as in the cases of human sacrifice or religious persecution—these two are based on the false notion that God is "jealous, vindictive and cruel."[66] The individual must counteract these practices as a "corruption of religion itself."[67] The criterion of truth however is not *sola scriptura* or the Church, but the individual's own thought-out sense of the natural order of the universe.

The distinction between a universal natural religion and the useful but ultimately indifferent aspects of particular local religions is a key theme in Ferguson's thought. From the mid-1760s, he maintained a distinction between the "fixed" and universal expression of religion and the "arbitrary expressions" of particular religions resulting from the local circumstances of specific cultures and traditions.[68] The essence of religion was not found in Christian scripture but in those "actions which concur" with God's design for "promoting the good of his creatures."[69] Christianity has no special status in Ferguson's account of the duties of religion. All we are "charged" with doing by God is "choosing what is good, and of doing what is right."[70] Ferguson frames the "different ceremonies and institutional observances" found in "different ages and countries" as containing no inherent worth in themselves, but though they can serve, when properly arranged, to support individual action and

---

[64] Ferguson (1996, p. 89).

[65] Ferguson (1792, vol. ii, p. 154).

[66] Ferguson (1792, vol. ii, p. 154).

[67] Ferguson (1792, vol. ii, p. 154).

[68] Ferguson (1766, p. 27).

[69] Ferguson (1766, p. 27).

[70] Ferguson (1766, p. 27).

social cohesion.[71] The "history of mankind" demonstrates that the "sentiments of devotion" have been associated with "external rites of any description," the implication being that the rites and ceremonies we find are merely parochial in their content and can serve to distort the natural sentiments of religion beneath.[72] Viewing the subject from the sociologist's perspective, Ferguson avers that religious rites and ceremonies are to be understood as the means by which the "thoughts and affections of men are made known," and which reflect the societies in which they appear.[73] Ferguson stresses that differences in "rites of devotion or worship" admit not a variety of "sentiment but of the external performance."[74] The criterion of judgement of other societies' religious practices is not whether they align with our own—there is no single correct set of rites and ceremonies—but whether they have a "cruel or pernicious tendency."[75] Ferguson is not a relativist. There are standards by which we judge systems of religion—namely, do they encourage immorality or prevent it. But there is no single correct set of rites and ceremonies, as they are merely aids of human creation to support the perfection of our natural religious sentiments.

Problems occur when we confuse our parochial customs, emerging out of a specific historical moment, as a universally applicable system of religion. From this error arises religious dogmatism, intolerance and persecution. The two dangers here are "false notions of religion" and "systems of bigotry and intolerance" as two overlapping "ways of thinking" that "corrupt whole nations at once."[76] The former involves relying upon the authority of God to justify "frivolous or cruel" practices, whereas the latter refers to "persecution" on the basis of indifferent "matters of faith and worship."[77] The essence of religion is virtuous behaviour in imitation of God; locally specific rites and practices serve as aids to

---

[71] Ferguson (1766, p. 27).

[72] Ferguson (1792, vol. i, pp. 145–46).

[73] Ferguson (1792, vol. i, p. 146).

[74] Ferguson (1792, vol. ii, p. 143). See also (vol. i, p. 223) and Smith (2019, pp. 52–60).

[75] Ferguson (1792, vol. i, p. 146).

[76] Ferguson (1792, vol. ii, p. 100). The role of superstition in corrupting both individual and society is not prominent in existent literature on Ferguson's views on corruption, e.g. Fleischacker (2018).

[77] Ferguson (1792, vol. ii, p. 100).

religion but do not constitute true religion itself. Danger arises when the "arbitrary signs of devotion are supposed essential to religion" and any "deviations from established practice" are attacked.[78] There is an equality of all religions here where worship is intended to "acknowledge and to adore the intelligence power and moral government of God," and to dogmatically persecute others' religious worship is the equivalent of an Englishman persecuting a Frenchman for speaking French.[79]

The threat of religious corruption is also great because the influence of religion on moral conduct means it serves as an "aid [to] the magistracy" and, conversely, religion acts as the "final effect in regulating" politics.[80] Ferguson classifies the belief of those with political power that they are "armed with the sanction of religion" as a form of superstition, defined as "the abuse of religion."[81] It has led to "very fatal effects" in a list that bears similarities with Hume, Smith and Kames: "misapplication of moral esteem," switching from genuinely virtuous behaviour to whatever superstition is preferred by the magistrate; "substitution of frivolous rites for moral duties"; the "cruel animosities of party" and a "false apprehension of sanctity in any acts of injustice … proceed[ing] from a supposed religious zeal."[82]

Sitting uneasily alongside his description in the *Principles* of the "fatal" dangers of magistrates believing they had the gods on their side was Ferguson's praise of the alignment of political and religious power in early Rome. Taking his lead from Machiavelli's account of civil religion in the *Discourses on Livy* (1532), Ferguson believed that Rome profited from a particularly harmonious alignment of religion and civic virtue, which they owed to the benign management of popular religion by Numa.[83] Key to the success of republican religion were the lack of distinction between political and religious authority, and the complete alignment of the interests of religion and state. With "no distinction of clergy and laity," the authority of "priest was often united with that of statesman" in ways that

---

[78] Ferguson (1792, vol. ii, p. 143). See also Hill (2006, p. 45 fn. 246).

[79] Ferguson (1792, vol. ii, p. 143).

[80] Ferguson (1792, vol. ii, p. 175); Ferguson (1783, p. 10).

[81] Ferguson (1769, p. 237).

[82] Ferguson (1769, pp. 237–238).

[83] Ferguson (1783, vol. i, p. 11). See also p. 272. On Ferguson and Machiavelli, see Pocock (2005, pp. 399–417).

made religion "subservient to the purposes of state."[84] Ferguson viewed Roman statesmen as able to manipulate the populace "to a degree that has not been equalled by mankind in any other instance."[85] The "extreme superstition" of ancient Italy became an effective "principle of public order and of public duty" that "superseded the use of penal or compulsory laws."[86] Upon such foundations in which "every citizen revered in the sacred rite of his country," Ferguson claimed following Machiavelli, the "seed of Roman greatness was laid."[87] Rivalry between priests and military leaders in early societies might lead to beneficial circumstances as when the druids brought the "rudiments of civil government" to Britain, but equally likely could lead "despotism and absolute slavery."[88] Ferguson seems to have praised early Roman civil religion on the grounds that it encouraged virtuous behaviour, even it was based manipulating on "extreme superstition."

His praise of Roman religion was another instance of Ferguson's repeated act of contrasting ancient republicans thinking about the commonwealth and moderns concerned with the individual.[89] I do not think, however, that Ferguson pointed to the Roman Republic as an exemplary society, but as a striking one that illustrated so many aspects of the relationship between religion, society and politics that interested the "scientists of human nature." Amongst the moderns, Ferguson argued that the ideal relationship between state and religion was the practice of near complete religious freedom—the age of all-encompassing civil religion had passed. In his *Principles*, in place of state involvement in religion, Ferguson argues for a tolerant and universalistic understanding of religious difference. We should not be threatened by nor persecute different "rites of devotion or worship" as these reflect not a variety of "sentiment but of the external performance."[90] Ferguson thus stresses the fundamental equality and equivalency of all religions where worship is meant

---

[84] Ferguson (1783, vol. i, p. 10).

[85] Ferguson (1783, vol. i, p. 10).

[86] Ferguson (1783, vol. i, p. 229).

[87] Ferguson (1783, vol. i, p. 10).

[88] Ferguson (1996, p. 103).

[89] Kidd (2018, p. 111).

[90] Ferguson (1792, vol. ii, p. 143). For an early hint of this sentiment, see Ferguson (1996, p. 187).

to acknowledge and worship a wise, benevolent God. Moreover, religious persecution has no religious warrant, and brings only negative effects.

It should be clear by now that Ferguson did not believe in the necessity of revelation and did not attribute to Christianity any special status. Purportedly revealed religion did not offer anything additional to our knowledge of morals and religion. Ferguson was explicit about setting aside revealed religion in the Preface of the *Principles* and did so on the grounds that "natural religion and reason" were the "foundation of every superstructure whether in morality or religion" and had to be treated separately to scripture.[91] Knowledge derived from books other than reason and nature could help improve our understanding of existing truths, but never superseded them. Moreover, our knowledge of nature must be the "test of every subsequent institution that is offered as coming from him": natural not revealed religion was the ultimate source of truth.[92] Again, Ferguson's enlightened deism shines through.

We see more of the distinctly unchristian quality of Ferguson's later religious thought in his exploratory discussion of the immortality of the soul in the *Principles*. In the *Institutes*, he had argued that the desire for immortality was instinctual and thus it was "generally supposed" that the soul was immortal.[93] In the subsequent *Principles*, Ferguson maintained, while noting his arguments took place in the "regions of conjecture," the possibility of our soul's immortality.[94] But the inconclusive nature of humanity's knowledge and reasoning about our purportedly immaterial, immortal souls suggested it was the "will of Providence" that man "attend to his present task and not suffer himself to be diverted from it by prospects of futurity."[95] We can "contribute nothing" to solving the question of the what happens after death, which leaves our task while on earth to live as fulsomely virtuous lives as possible according to standards

---

[91] Ferguson (1792, vol. i, p. vii). See also Hill (2006, p. 45, 2017, p. 49).

[92] Ferguson (1792, vol. i, p. viii).

[93] Ferguson (1769, p. 135). See also Heath and Lin (2018, pp. 114–115).

[94] Ferguson (1792, vol i, p. 317).

[95] Ferguson (1792, vol. i, p. 318).

of virtue that we have deciphered by ourselves.[96] This leads to a proto-Weberian sentiment: it is the very uncertainty about our souls that makes us virtuously act in the here and now.[97]

THE PRIMACY OF THEISM AND THE POWER OF SUPERSTITION

In the *Principles*, Ferguson also intervened in the debate over the origin and development of religion, and was clearly arguing for the primary of theism. Ferguson had included brief mention of this theme in his lectures from the mid-1760s. The first edition of the *Institutes* quickly summarised polytheism as consisting of "many gods having their different attributes and separate provinces in nature," which resulted from ancient theistic nations combining their gods rather than reconcile their experience of other gods to their theism.[98] As with other topics surveyed in this chapter, Ferguson expanded and clarified this discussion in subsequent publications, most significantly, the *Principles*.

Ferguson boldly averred that the first religion of humankind was theistic, both historically and psychologically. He went entirely against the grain of Scottish Enlightenment thinking which had maintained, as Chris Berry phrases it, "that it is as certain a conclusion as it is possible to get that the religion of savages will naturally be polytheistic."[99] No primordial people "originally conceive[d] more than one God."[100] The easy apprehension of God was a divine "gift," with evident design a "lesson … obvious to every beholder."[101] This was not an argument based on an original revelation from God but from a deduction from the natural world, based on Ferguson's belief that the design of nature was evident. The "most ignorant" would notice design in their daily lives as powerfully as the "learned may read" about it now.[102] Ferguson acknowledged that early societies would also explain "alarming occasions" by appeal to

---

[96] Ferguson (1792, vol. i, p. 318).
[97] Heath and Lin (2018, p. 115).
[98] Ferguson (1769, p. 127).
[99] Berry (2000, §5).
[100] Ferguson (1792, vol. i, p. 169).
[101] Ferguson (1792, vol. i, p. 166).
[102] Ferguson (1792, vol. i, p. 165).

supernatural power, but the dominant cause of religious belief was "beneficent design in nature."[103] Ferguson gave the example of the "exquisite construction and obvious design" found in the "fabric of animal organs," which would have been noticed by the earliest hunters in an experience more common than that of unusual natural events.[104] Implicit in Ferguson's argument is the view that human nature is framed to instinctively attribute design to a single designer.

Ferguson maintained that theism declined into polytheism and not vice versa. While this bore parallels with the argument of traditional accounts of the origin of idolatry, Ferguson was using the language of enlightened Scottish "science of man" and positioned his claims outside the limits of biblical history. Indeed, Ferguson's primary explanation for the appearance of polytheism after theism was a historical argument critiquing Hume's NHR. Hume's claim that the historical record demonstrated that all early societies were polytheistic, Ferguson contended, wrongly "collated together" independent small theistic societies into larger polytheistic lumps.[105] Proponents of the primacy of polytheism had inverted the chronology when they argued societies selected a tutelary deity from amongst a plethora of gods. Each nation had its own god first, and the plethora only appeared when national gods joined with others. The key historical moment was when these small theistic societies began interacting with other similar societies. If relations between societies were peaceful, the religious practices of each society were respected without being viewed as a challenge to the other's theism. But if relations between the societies were violent, the god of the two societies were viewed as "rival powers," leading to "continual war under the banners of their respective gods" and, with this, the first sense that many gods existed and were in competition.[106]

The development of polytheistic and superstitious attitudes was explained by several factors inherent in human nature. In the identification of several of these, Ferguson was a good Humean. The psychology of religious error is to be found in the experience of the "vehement

---

[103] Ferguson (1792, vol. i, p. 165).
[104] Ferguson (1792, vol. i, pp. 164–165).
[105] Ferguson (1792, vol. i, p. 169).
[106] Ferguson (1792, vol. i, p. 169).

emotions," especially those of "repugnance or horror."[107] When the mind is "strongly affected" by an impression or an association, we tend to view this intensity as "equivalent to strong conviction of reality in its object."[108] Thus in subjects that are "of great concern," such as religion, we are "rash in forming our notions" and then "tenacious of the errors or mistakes" that we have made.[109] Our "strong passions" serve to close our minds off to rational argument, and we treat alternative opinions and behaviours as "so many acts of profaneness."[110] This is especially true of the "brutish and depraved," who easily degenerate into religious error; the "wise and happy," by contrast, try to expand their knowledge of the supreme being, but still can succumb to pedantry and virulent disagreement about purely speculative matters.[111] Ferguson repeated the standard observation that the "bulk of mankind" were too foolish and indolent to "pursue a serious chain of observation and thought" without error entering their reasoning about God.[112] Alongside these claims about the origin of superstition in the weakness of human nature, Ferguson also, like Kames in the *Sketches*, explained the development of polytheism as a result of the "diversity of character in the multitude of men."[113]

The picture in the *Principles* was slightly more optimistic about the possibilities of managing superstition than was found in Ferguson's *Essay*. In the latter work, he briefly explored how, while the first religion of humankind was theism, most religions, and not just "rude nations alone," were systems of superstition.[114] Ferguson saw a vast uniformity of superstitions across societies, constituted of the "similar weaknesses and absurdities" and derive from a "common source, a perplexed apprehension of invisible agents" over events mankind cannot predict.[115] When the human mind is perplexed by "strange and uncommon situations," it

[107] Ferguson (1792, vol. i, p. 145).
[108] Ferguson (1792, vol. i, p. 145).
[109] Ferguson (1792, vol. i, p. 145).
[110] Ferguson (1792, vol. i, p. 145).
[111] Ferguson (1792, vol. i, p. 167).
[112] Ferguson (1792, vol. i, p. 168).
[113] Ferguson (1792, vol. i, p. 168).
[114] Ferguson (1996, p. 89).
[115] Ferguson (1996, p. 89). See also Smith (2019, p. 63).

loses its courage and resorts to divination and other irrational practices.[116] Nor was superstition reduced by socio-economic or political improvement. The "childish imbecility" of superstition was not undermined by even the "highest measures of civilization," as evidenced by the example of the Greco-Romans.[117] Here, as elsewhere, there is no sense of linear progress from polytheism to theism on the grounds of stadial societal change.

In both the *Essay* and, in more depth, the *Principles*, Ferguson discoursed further on the possibility of reducing the extent and effects of superstitious religious belief amongst the multitude. Such change could not be brought about the "effects of mere reason" but had to be dealt with in pragmatic ways informed by knowledge of human nature.[118] "Wild systems of enthusiasm or superstition" are usually only supplanted by equally wild systems of the opposing doctrine.[119] In their religious beliefs, "ordinary men" are motivated by the combination of the "horrors they feel" and their "habits of thinking"; to be changed in their beliefs requires the "impulse of an opposite doctrine, urged with similar passions."[120] Ferguson did, however, see means of improving this predicament. Again, in the *Essay*, and in more depth in the *Principles*, Ferguson explained how the substitution of a "wise providence operating by physical causes, in place of phantoms that terrify or amuse the ignorant" was a principal means by which societies improved their religious sentiments.[121] The improvement and dissemination of natural philosophical knowledge, suitably packaged for weaker minds in a reassuring message about the benignity laws of the universe, would help reduce superstition. Superstition is the "fear of harm and disorder from invisible powers"; the more knowledge of nature we have, the more our conceptions of God improve, the more we realised our superstitious fears are

---

[116] Ferguson (1996, p. 89).

[117] Ferguson (1996, p. 89).

[118] Ferguson (1792, vol. i, p. 305).

[119] Ferguson (1792, vol. i, p. 306).

[120] Ferguson (1792, vol. i, p. 305).

[121] Ferguson (1996, p. 90). The implication of this passage (pp. 89–90) is that the proper "study of nature" was not pursued by the Greeks or Romans, but has only been practised in recent times.

ungrounded.[122] Knowledge of the orderliness of the natural world help "extricate" the mind from its "superstitious conceptions and habits."[123] Ferguson argued, in a manner similar to John Gregory's recommendation for encouraging devotion, that the problem of managing popular superstition involved the encouragement of the positive religious passions, such as gratitude, at the expense of the negative ones, such as fear—these could be taught as the appropriately felt responses to God's creation. This was a purely naturalistic assessment of how to manage the superstitious tendencies of human nature.

* * *

The above reading of Ferguson's views on the relationship between religion, human nature and society indicates a strong deistic or, if you prefer, Stoic element to his thought. The picture of the religious propensities of human nature is one of the naturalness of theistic belief, but also that theism's equally natural corruption into superstition. The battle is one of enabling the appropriate elements of human nature control the character of religious belief. Success would involve abandoning any sense of the parochial truth of one particular form of religion, accepting that all religions originate in the same aspects of human nature and are seeking the same truths, and allowing for religious freedom. Somewhat contradictorily, benefit would be gained by magistrates seeking to encourage the positive or natural passions that encourage imitation of God at the expense of the negative or perverted ones that encourage only superstition. Aside from a more ecumenical sense of a universal natural religion, Ferguson also recommended the dissemination of natural philosophical knowledge throughout society as a means of directing minds towards the God of nature. A tension, therefore, existed in Ferguson's religious thought between his arguments directed towards individuals independently seeking to know and follow their consciences and his arguments directed towards magistrates managing popular religion to more the multitude towards better religious opinions and worship.

---

[122] Ferguson (1792, vol. i, p. 304).
[123] Ferguson (1792, vol. i, p. 305).

References

Ahnert, Thomas. 2015. *The Moral Culture of the Scottish Enlightenment*. London: Yale University Press.

Arbo, Matthew B. 2011. Adam Ferguson's Sermon in the Ersh Language: A Word from 2 Samuel on Martial Responsibility and Political Order. *Political Theology* 12: 894–909.

Berry, Christopher J. 2000. Rude Religion: The Psychology of Polytheism in the Scottish Enlightenment. In *The Scottish Enlightenment: Essays in Reinterpretation*, ed. Paul Wood, 315–334. New York: University of Rochester Press.

———. 2018. *Essays on Hume, Smith, and the Scottish Enlightenment*. Edinburgh: Edinburgh University Press.

Bijlsma, Rudmer. 2022. Of Savages and Stoics: Converging Moral and Political Ideas in the Conjectural Histories of Rousseau and Ferguson. *Philosophy & Social Criticism* 48: 209–244.

———. 2023. Adam Ferguson on True Religion, Science, and Moral Progress. *History of European Ideas*. Published online 11 April 2023. Accessed 11 June 2023. DOI: https://doi.org/10.1080/01916599.2023.2190748.

Chen, Jeng-guo S. 2008. Providence and Progress: The Religious Dimension in Ferguson's Discussion of Civil Society. In *Adam Ferguson: History, Progress and Human Nature*, ed. Eugene Heath and Vincenzo Merolle, 171–186. London: Routledge.

Fagg, Jane B. 2008. Ferguson's Use of the Edinburgh University Library: 1764–1806. In *Adam Ferguson: History, Progress and Human Nature*, 39–55. London: Routledge.

Ferguson, Adam. 1766. *Analysis of Pneumatics and Moral Philosophy*. Edinburgh: A. Kincaid & J. Bell.

———. 1769. *Institutes of Moral Philosophy*. Edinburgh: A. Kincaid & J. Bell.

———. 1773. *Institutes of Moral Philosophy*, 2nd ed. Edinburgh: A. Kincaid & J. Bell.

———. 1783. *The History of the Progress and Termination of the Roman Republic*, 3 vols. London: Jones & Co.

———. 1785. *Institutes of Moral Philosophy*, 3rd ed. Edinburgh: A. Kincaid & J. Bell.

———. 1792. *The Principles of Moral and Political Science*. 2 vols. Edinburgh: A. Kincaid & J. Bell.

———. 1996. *An Essay on the History of Civil Society*, ed. Fania Oz-Salzberger. Cambridge: Cambridge University Press.

———. 2006. Introductory Essay. In Ferguson, Adam, *The Manuscripts of Adam Ferguson*, ed. Vincenzo Merolle, with Robin Dix and Eugene Heath, xi–xlv. London: Pickering.

———. 2023. *Adam Ferguson's Later Writings*, ed. Ian Stewart and Max Skjönsberg. Edinburgh: Edinburgh University Press.

Fleischaker, Samuel. 2018. 'Dismembering the Human Character': Adam Ferguson's Conception of Corruption. *Social Philosophy and Policy* 35: 54–72.

Harris, James. 2004. Answering Bayle's Question: Religious Belief in the Moral Philosophy of the Scottish Enlightenment. In *Oxford Studies in Early Modern Philosophy*, vol. 1, ed. Daniel Garber and Steven Nadler, 229–253. Oxford: Oxford University Press.

Heath, Eugene, and Vincenzo Merolle, ed. 2008. *Adam Ferguson: History, Progress and Human Nature*. London: Routledge, 2008.

Heath, Eugene. 2015. In the Garden of God: Religion and Vigour in the Frame of Ferguson's Thought. *Journal of Scottish Philosophy* 13: 55–74.

Heath, Eugene, and Zisai Lin. 2018. The Kingdom of Freedom in the Garden of God: Ferguson's Postulates of Moral Action. *Journal of Scottish Philosophy* 16: 105–123.

Hill, Jack A. 2017. *Adam Ferguson and Ethical Integrity: The Man and His Prescriptions for the Moral Life*. London: Lexington Books.

Hill, Lisa. 2006. *The Passionate Society: The Social, Political and Moral Thought of Adam Ferguson*. Dordrecht: Springer.

Holt, Randall Joseph. 2016. Reasoning with Savages: The Anthropological Imagination of the Scottish Enlightenment. PhD Thesis, University of California Los Angeles.

Kettler, David. 1965. *Adam Ferguson: His Social and Political Thought*. Columbus, OH: Ohio State University Press.

Kidd, Colin. 2018. The Scottish Enlightenment and the Matter of Troy. *Journal of the British Academy* 6: 97–130.

Lehmann, William C. 1930. *Adam Ferguson and the Beginnings of Modern Sociology*. New York, NY: Columbia University Press.

McDaniel, Iain. 2013. *Adam Ferguson in the Scottish Enlightenment: The Roman Past and Europe's Future*. Cambridge, MA: Harvard University Press.

Merolle, Vincenzo. 2006. Introductory Essay. In Ferguson, Adam, *The Manuscripts of Adam Ferguson*, ed. Vincenzo Merolle, with Robin Dix and Eugene Heath, xi–xlv. London: Pickering.

Mills, R. J. W. 2021. *The Religious Innatism Debate in Early Modern Britain: Intellectual Change Beyond Locke*. Basingstoke: Palgrave Macmillan.

Pocock, J. G. A. 1999–2015. *Barbarism and Religion*. 6 vols. Cambridge: Cambridge University Press.

Sher, Richard B. 2015. *Church and University in the Scottish Enlightenment: The Moderate Literati of Edinburgh*, 2nd ed. Edinburgh: Edinburgh University Press.

Smith, Craig. 2006. Adam Ferguson and the Danger of Books. *Journal of Scottish Philosophy* 4: 93–109.

———. 2012. Adam Ferguson and Ethnocentrism in the Science of Man. *History of the Human Sciences* 26: 52–67.

———. 2019. *Adam Ferguson and the Idea of Civil Society: Moral Science in the Scottish Enlightenment*. Edinburgh: Edinburgh University Press.

———. 2021. Self-Interest in the Thought of Adam Ferguson. In *A Genealogy of Self-Interest in Economics*, ed. Susumu Egashire et al., 31–46. Singapore: Springer.

Vieu,. 2015. L'homme introuvable: Fondements et limites du discours anthropologique chez Adam Ferguson. *Archives de philosophie* 78: 631–648.

Wood, Paul B. 1990. The Natural History of Man in the Scottish Enlightenment. *History of Science* 18: 89–123.

———. 1996. The Science of Man. In *Cultures of Natural History*, ed. Nicholas Jardin, J. A. Secord and Emma C. Spary, 197–210. Cambridge: Cambridge University Press.

CHAPTER 9

George Campbell on Miracles and the Weakness of Hume's "Science of Man"

Abstract George Campbell's *Dissertation on Miracles* (1762) contained the first volley of the Aberdeen Enlightenment's challenge to Hume's writings on religion. Campbell's criticisms of Hume's approach to judging testimonial evidence raised larger questions about the credibility of Hume's "science of man." With a view to demonstrating Christianity's unique truth, Campbell's arguments included a focus on local events that challenged the generalisations of Hume's 'Of Miracles'. Hume's sociological sense of the religious passions of barbaric peoples came up against Campbell's scriptural and historical account of a purported specific moment in time. Campbell averred that revealed religion could be defended by applying findings derived from the study of "human nature" and the "history of mankind."

Keywords George Campbell · David Hume · Aberdeen Enlightenment · "Science of man" · Miracles · Testimonial evidence

The following three chapters survey the contributions of several members of the Aberdeen Philosophical Society (1758–1773), the intellectual centre of the Aberdeen Enlightenment, who responded to the challenge posed to established Christian understandings of the relationship between religion, human nature and society by Hume's "science of man."[1] The Society was praised by Dugald Stewart for "awakening and directing that spirit of philosophical research" which became the "Scottish school of philosophy."[2] It would be possible to bring together scattered passages in the published writings of Thomas Reid and James Beattie, as well as their fellow Aberdonian, though not Society member, James Oswald, on the origin of religious beliefs. But such a discussion would remain piecemeal, indicative of how "common sense philosophy," especially in the hands of Reid, did not seek to articulate in print a new theory of religious nativism. Rather, it is to the works of James Dunbar, John Gregory and George Campbell that we turn, and in which we find a variety of discussions of the relationship between religion and human nature, and not all in the form of progressive histories of religious development.[3] This is not least because, while the Society brought together the lights of the Aberdeen Enlightenment in a fecund intellectual atmosphere, there was never a unity of theme, genre and arguments. What did unify those works which emerged out of the Society's studied engagement with Hume's philosophical writings, however, was a goal to defend the truth of theism in general, and Christianity in particular, against the subversive implications of Hume's thought.

The leading figures of the Aberdeen Enlightenment claimed both that human knowledge was built on testimony, and that testimony was a reliable source of evidence due to several "common sense" principles. They were provoked, in part, by Hume's "Of Miracles," discussing in depth those features of Hume's essay that focused on the inherent tendencies and principles of human nature and belief in witness testimony. I will, following Suderman, take Campbell's theory of testimonial evidence, found in his *Dissertation on Miracles* (1762), as being the definitive statement of the Aberdonian School, emerging out of the activities of

---

[1] For a useful overview, see Wood (2006) and, for more detail, Ulman (1990).

[2] Stewart (1854–1860, vol. x p. 254).

[3] My focus on the natural origins of religion means I will not examine those Aberdonian publications that defend the historical truth of Christianity, such as Alexander Gerard's *Dissertations on Subjects Relating to the Genius and the Evidences of Christianity* (1766). But for some discussion of Gerard, see Appendix 2.

the Philosophical Society and articulating the position on miracles reaffirmed by its members, as well as being the most frequently published.[4] The *Dissertation* moreover, contained the "first salvoes" of the Aberdeen Enlightenment's challenge to Hume's writings on religion.[5] This is with due acknowledgement of the near identification of Campbell and Thomas Reid's position on the subject, as articulated in the latter's logic lectures of 1763 and subsequently appearing in his *Essays on the Intellectual Powers of Man* (1785).[6] Campbell's discussion is significant for a second reason, especially relevant to the theme of this book, for his criticisms of Hume's approach to judging testimony raised larger questions about the credibility of Hume's "science of man." With a view to demonstrating Christianity's unique truth, Campbell's arguments included a focus on local events that challenged the generalisations of Hume's 'Of Miracles'. Repeatedly in *Dissertation on Miracles*, Hume's sociological sense of the religious passions of barbaric peoples came up against Campbell's scriptural and historical account of a purported specific moment in time.[7]

Campbell averred that revealed religion could be defended by applying findings derived from the study of "human nature" and the "history of mankind."[8] Campbell, like Hume, claimed he reasoned from the "knowledge that experience affords us of human nature" and of the universal "motives by which men are influenced in their conduct."[9] Hume's version of the same science had failed to comprehend the true nature of testimonial evidence. Campbell would repeatedly describe Hume as an "infidel" who believed that Christians were "fools."[10] He also repeatedly jibed that

---

[4] Suderman (2001, esp. p. 108, p. 28 and on its publishing success p. 3). On Campbell's *Dissertation*, see also Walzer (2003, esp. Ch. 11). For a reading of Campbell's *The Philosophy of Rhetoric* (1776) as teaching trainee ministers how to use rhetoric to support revealed religion, see Manolescu (2007).

[5] Stewart (2022, p. 37).

[6] Suderman (2001 p. 171). For a useful overview of the arguments against Hume put together by the Common Sense school, see Falkenstein (2014).

[7] This aspect of Campbell's *Dissertation* has been largely overlooked, e.g. Golden (1996) and Pitson (2006) and in the literature summarising the debate on miracles (from Hume and Campbell onwards) more generally.

[8] Campbell (1762, e.g. pp. 121, 146 and especially p. 281).

[9] Campbell (1762, p. 121).

[10] Campbell (1762, p. 242). In this, Campbell was characteristic of the greater degree of hostility found amongst the luminaries of the Aberdeen Enlightenment towards Hume's insinuating manner of arguing on religious topics, compared to that of the Edinburgh

Hume was more of an "orator," concerned more with pleasing prose and snide remarks than being a serious theorist of human nature—at least when it came to religion.[11] Hume's account, according to Campbell, is rooted in "metaphysical refinements" and "oratorical declamation," which allowed him to opine so inaccurately on the role of miracles in establishing systems of religion—and Campbell surely intended to accuse Hume of the same sort of criticisms Hume had made of theologians.[12] Overall, however, Campbell engaged with Hume's treatment of religion as an insightful if misguided contribution to their shared pursuit of the "science of man," and one which could be rebutted by using many of the same methods. Often this took the form of exposing how Hume had failed to sufficiently examine either human nature or the specific events of Christ's miracles.

We do not accept testimonial evidence on the basis of whether it aligns with our accumulated experience, Campbell reasoned. Rather, our "faith in testimony" is "prior to experience," and is based on "some original grounds of belief, beyond which our researches cannot proceed."[13] Testimony has a "natural and original influence on belief" that is "antecedent to experience."[14] As Campbell put it in a passage directed against Hume's 'Of Miracles' in his *Philosophy of Rhetoric* (1776), we respond to testimony in the exact opposite way to that which Hume described: we give an "unlimited assent" to testimony, unless there are clear reasons not to, and do so on the basis of an "original principle in our nature."[15] The reliability of testimony was aided by the inherent inclination of human nature to tell the truth. Together, Campbell concluded in the final sentences of the *Dissertation*, these beliefs form part of the "common sense of mankind," that set of pre-rational beliefs we instinctively form and cannot doubt.[16]

---

variant. One possible reason for this is that Campbell, Gregory and Beattie were not on personal terms with Hume.

[11] The idea that Hume's antipathy to religion got in the way of the proper study of human nature was shared by Campbell's Aberdonian colleague Alexander Gerard. See Suderman (2001, p. 108 fn. 190).

[12] Campbell (1762, p. 138).

[13] Campbell (1762, p. 16).

[14] Campbell (1762, p. 14).

[15] Campbell (1776, vol. ii, p. 149).

[16] Campbell (1762, p. 288).

Campbell rejected Hume's claim that the mind's "bias to the marvellous" undermined the credibility of miracle testimony.[17] Campbell did not deny that human nature had this bias, only that Hume had misconstrued its effects. If it were true that we should reject any evidence that clashed with our established knowledge, then it was impossible that there could be any "progress of philosophy and letters."[18] Hume's account of how we judge testimonial claims in "Of Miracles" failed in generally to provide a persuasive account of how new knowledge is formed and, more powerfully, to explain how we judged the testimonial accounts that first formed the basis of our concept of a specific law of nature.

Hume had, likewise, misconstrued the influence of the "prejudices of education" and pre-existing "religious affection" on whether we trust miracle testimony.[19] Campbell agreed with Hume that religious passion informs our judgement, but Hume's argument failed because he did not see that such passion "may just as readily obstruct as promote our faith in a religious miracle."[20] We easily accept evidence that supports what we already believe, and we easily reject evidence that challenges us. We can be confident of the reliability of miracle testimony in those instances where the miracle related confuted the pre-existing beliefs of the reporter. As such, there is the "greatest disparity" between accounts of miracles performed in favour of established religions and those performed in contradiction to opinions generally received.[21] The fact that Christianity spread "in defiance of all the religious zeal and prejudices of the times" and canvassed amongst those of a "temper of mind the most unfavourable to conviction" reflects the truth of its miracles.[22]

Campbell rejected Hume's insinuations about early belief in Christ's miracles being rooted in fanaticism and imposture, but he did so by pointing to "facts" about scripture with which Hume would not have concurred. In doing so, Campbell gave a different account of Christ and the apostles' motivations and actions compared to that implied at the end of Hume's "Of Miracles." It was implausible that a new religion could

---

[17] Campbell (1762, p. 81).
[18] Campbell (1762, p. 82).
[19] Campbell (1762, p. 86).
[20] Campbell (1762, p. 84).
[21] Campbell (1762, p. 87).
[22] Campbell (1762, pp. 105, 107).

have been established merely because of the "address and eloquence" or the "appearances of uncommon sanctity, and rapturous fervours of devotion" of a few fishermen.[23] The apostles were not "animated by passion like enthusiasts" nor did they work on the "passions of their readers," and instead were neutral, indeed sceptical, observers.[24] Even if hypothetically some of them were enthusiasts who, in Hume's words, imagine they see "what has no reality," this could not explain why other observers testified to the same miracles.[25] On the issue of religious imposture, Campbell accepts it as a "fact" that "ignorant zealots" have lied to the multitude in an effect to control them.[26] But he rejected as implausible the idea that the apostles would have acted as "false witnesses concerning God" and be the "wilful corrupters of the religion of their country" out of motivation to aid a cause they did not believe in.[27] Hume's claim that religious impostures fake miracle testimony to secure the social standing of being God's prophet made no sense, Campbell claimed, when applied to the apostles. They were humble men from humble backgrounds who faced "insurmountable difficulties and distresses" because of their religion, who were conscious of their own sinfulness and yet persevered in their beliefs in spite of "infamy and torture."[28]

Campbell made his own assessment about miracles derived from a study of the "history of mankind," one that rebutted Hume's deployment of historical examples. Hume claimed two things Campbell dismissed: that all peoples have accepted absurd miracle stories and that all new religions have been established through the use of pretended miracles. Campbell's response was to draw a distinction between miracles supporting pre-existing religions and miracles converting people to a new religion. It is true that miracles "wrought in support of the received superstition" build on pre-existing "popular prejudices," but the historical record did not demonstrate the truth of Hume's claim that miracles are always used to establish new "systems of religion."[29] The annals of

[23] Campbell (1762, p. 105).
[24] Campbell (1762, p. 110).
[25] Campbell (1762, p. 112 quoting from EHU 10.17).
[26] Campbell (1762, p. 115).
[27] Campbell (1762, p. 118).
[28] Campbell (1762, p. 119).
[29] Campbell (1762, p. 124).

history contained only Judaism and Christianity as religions "attended in their first publication with the evidence of miracles."[30] Muhammad disdained miracles while Greco-Roman paganism did not contain much miracle testimony, and the myths recounted by the poets came centuries after the purported events. Pagan mythology also, Campbell claimed, was written to entertain rather than record accurately the events described and was clearly allegorical.

The examples of the establishment of Christianity and Islam demonstrated the falsity of Hume's claim that new religions were always attended to with miracles. In the case of Islam, seventh-century Arabia was precisely the sort of setting in which religious imposture would flourish, and yet Muhammed expressly denied he could perform miracles. Muhammed had a "practical knowledge of mankind" which informed him that fraudulent miracles could not convince prejudiced individuals and that "pious frauds" were too dangerous a method given the possibility of detection.[31] In terms of the Jewish context for Christ's miracles, "every physical, every moral motive" existed for the Jews to maintain their religion and reject miracle testimony that went against their own religion.[32] They lived according to a civil theology that engaged their "patriotism," their pride was "inflamed" by their status as God's chosen people, they lived "under one spiritual head" and celebrated "in one temple," their forms of worship were numerous, lengthy and "flattered their senses."[33] The gospel, by contrast, Campbell claimed, was motivated by a "spirit of humility, and moderation, and charity, and universality."[34] Campbell overturned Hume's analysis that miracles establishing new religions easily spread amongst credulous primitive peoples by demonstrating that in the case of both Christianity and Islam, the exact opposite case was true. Christianity was established by miracle testimony in circumstances entirely unconducive, whereas Islam was established without the aid of miracles despite appearing in societal circumstances entirely conducive to religious imposture.

[30] Campbell (1762, p. 125).
[31] Campbell (1762, p. 139).
[32] Campbell (1762, p. 140).
[33] Campbell (1762, p. 141).
[34] Campbell (1762, p. 141).

Campbell used Humean reasoning to deflect the argument that the evident impostures taking place in the primitive church immediately after the "times of the apostles" undermined the truth of Christ's miracles.[35] Both the "history of mankind" and "our own experience" teach that reports of miraculous events are quickly followed by new reports of new miracles.[36] Miracles that were "well attested" would encourage pretenders to "propagate innumerable false reports," not least because the "presumption against miracles from uncommonness must be greatly diminished" amongst those who witnessed Christ and the apostle's true miracles.[37] Campbell accepted Hume's claim that zealots in favour of the new religion would use miracles "as the most effectual expedient for accomplishing their end."[38] Hume had missed the key historical facts, however: miracles, according to Campbell, did not occur prior to the "publication of the gospel," reports of miracles were only effective because of actual miracles occurring, and both actual miracles and the effectiveness of miracle reports ceased soon afterwards.[39]

Campbell also focused on the contradiction between Hume's account of the Pentateuch at the end of "Of Miracles" and the thesis of Hume's NHR. In the former, Hume described the Pentateuch as composed by a primitive people writing about an even earlier primitive people. The existence of a primordial theistic society contradicted Hume's account in NHR that polytheism was the first religion of primitive humankind, that theism was the result of improvements in philosophy and science, and that it was inconceivable that man knew true theism was "ignorant and barbarous" but forgot it as they grew in learning.[40] Campbell accepted Hume's reasoning in the NHR about the quality of primordial religion, but only when applied to unassisted peoples and pointed out that Hume had failed to explain the exception of the early Jews, who were theists. This should be taken as evidence of the truth of their religion: they alone were theists in the primordial past, whereas the rule is that barbarous peoples are polytheists. The fact that the barbarous Israelites were theists

---

[35] Campbell (1762, p. 143).
[36] Campbell (1762, p. 146).
[37] Campbell (1762, p. 145).
[38] Campbell (1762, p. 145).
[39] Campbell (1762, p. 148).
[40] Campbell (1762, pp. 264–265 citing NHR 1.3).

is evidence that they were the recipients of revelation or transmission of revelation via tradition.

Hume had only partially addressed this issue in the NHR, but in a way that demonstrates the chasm between his fully naturalistic "science of man" and Campbell's Christian version. Hume included a footnote stating the example of the ancient Hebrews was no evidence against his general claim that polytheism came first. This footnote treats the Hebrews as one society amongst many, that is, as one fact in the history of mankind to be judged amongst many, many other examples pointing to the primacy of polytheism. Hume could do this, evidently, because he did not believe that the ancient Hebrews were the recipients of revelation and could point to their existence as an historical accident. There are different ways of reading Hume's footnote, but one way is to take it as evidence of the generalising effect of the "science of human nature": its sociological assessments tended towards drawing conclusions about what was generally true, leading to exceptions being treated as historical accidents or exceptional occurrences not worthy to incorporate into the science. Obviously, this involved treating the Christian religion as an exception to the rule, but the phrasing of Hume's footnote is not that of someone who believed the Hebrews had received revelation, but rather that of a theorist of religious development who did not believe that the theistic Israelites mattered as evidence for his account.

In an additional lengthy footnote added to the second edition of the *Dissertation* (1766), Campbell strengthened his assertion that the first religion of humankind was theism and was the result of revelation, rather than a polytheism resulting from the inherent propensities of human nature in conditions of violence and scarcity. "Collateral evidence" can be amassed to demonstrate that the "ancients owed [the doctrine of a creator God] to a tradition handed down from the earliest ages," which their own absurd theologies could not fully erase.[41] Campbell's retort to Hume's NHR utilised some of the methods of mythography and the history of idolatry, and reiterated the claims of (though did he not cite) his namesake Archibald Campbell's *Necessity of Revelation*. The widespread adoption of the division of the days of the year into weeks is an arbitrary choice than can only be explained by the transmission of "some tradition … which has been older than the dispersion of mankind into different

---

[41] Campbell (1766, pp. 210–211).

regions," namely that of the Israelites.[42] Those pagan philosophers and poets who expressed theistic views did not owe their judgements to philosophical advances, but to the continuation of enduring tradition—not least because Campbell could find point to theistic writers long before Hume's examples of theistic pagans, Ovid and Cicero. Campbell also listed examples of societies viewed by the ancient Greeks as barbarians—the Parthians, Medes, and Persians—who were "genuine theists."[43] But in partial agreement with "Mr. Hume's hypothesis," that theism is the result of "the utmost improvement of the mind in ratiocination and science," the existence of these theist societies was explicable only by their religions being "derived originally from revelation, preserved by tradition."[44] Polytheism dominated the ancient world partly because tradition gets corrupted due to migrations, mixtures of peoples, revolutions in governments or was "corrupted and disfigured" by reliance upon oral transmission.[45]

The fact that theism was the result of revelation, subsequently transmitted by tradition, clarifies our understanding of Campbell's conceptions of common sense principles. They did not include belief in the existence of God or of future rewards and punishments for our immaterial, immortal souls. Across his writings, Campbell writes of the conscience as teaching us many moral imperatives and these could either be viewed as (a) granted providentially and (b) as having religious consequences, such as the compelling of religious belief being understood instinctively as an immoral act. While these beliefs were related to a religious understanding of human nature—thus the universal pangs of conscience demonstrated their origin in a providential framing of man—they did not extend to foundational religious tenets. Common Sense philosophy in neither Campbell nor Reid nor Beattie took the form of reasserting religious innatism, or the doctrine that foundational religious notions are instinctively and pre-rationally or pre-experientially known. These were to be known by revelation alone. But once truths only known via revelation and tradition went out into the world, George Campbell, like his namesake Archibald, believed that natural theology could be safely built

---

[42] Campbell (1762, p. 269, 1766, p. 209).
[43] Campbell (1766, p. 211).
[44] Campbell (1766, p. 211).
[45] Campbell (1762, p. 271, 1766, p. 213).

on these truths in ways that secured our knowledge of the existence and attributes of God.

To return to our main theme, Campbell criticised Hume's approach to the study of religion as being insufficiently informed by the facts of the "history of mankind," including those of sacred history, and insufficiently subtle about the qualities of human nature. Such inattention leaves us in danger of reaching a high "pitch of incredulity."[46] "Laziness" underpins the sort of generalised dismissal of miracle accounts as being the practice of primitive peoples, as we fail to undertake the "irksome task of considering things in detail."[47] This complacency is "unworthy [of] a philosopher."[48] Campbell was not claiming that sacred history should trump the "science of human nature." Indeed, much of his argument was predicated precisely on the sort of experientially based analysis that underpinned Hume's essay, but it was combined with a knowledge of the specific local history of Judaism, Christianity and Islam. Hume was not a religious historian nor were his essays characterised by erudition. This laid him open to the charge that Campbell made: that Hume could not back up his arguments with facts as we have them. (Hume might have replied that Campbell's "facts" were no such thing.) Campbell brought to bear a level of knowledge that Hume either did not have or did not utilise in his essay and criticised Hume for failing to consult all necessary authorities, imprecision in his relation of facts and lack of sophistication in his textual reading. But he also treated the exceptionality of the ancient Hebrews as evidence of the truth of revelation, rather than as an exception that did not undermine a general pattern. Campbell believed his application of a more informed "science of man" helped to demonstrate the truth of Christ's miracles and therefore the truth of Christianity.

References

Campbell, George. 1762. *A Dissertation on Miracles*. Edinburgh: A. Kincaid & J. Bell.

———. 1766. *A Dissertation on Miracles*, 2nd ed. Edinburgh: A. Kincaid & J. Bell.

———. 1776. *The Philosophy of Rhetoric*. Edinburgh: A. Kincaid & J. Bell.

---

[46] Campbell (1762, p. 149).
[47] Campbell (1762, p. 149).
[48] Campbell (1762, p. 149).

Falkenstein, Lorne. 2014. Hume and the Contemporary 'Common Sense' Critique of Hume. In *The Oxford Handbook of Hume*, ed. Paul Russell, 729–752. Oxford: Oxford University Press.

Golden, James L. 1996. The Hume, Campbell and Whately Debate on Miracles: A Representative Anecdote of British Theories of Argument. *Revue internationale de philosophie* 50: 265–295.

Manolescu, Beth Innocenti. 2007. Religious Reasons for Campbell's View of Emotional Appeals in *Philosophy of Rhetoric*. *Rhetoric Society Quarterly* 37: 159–180.

Pitson, Tony. 2006. George Campbell's Critique of Hume on Testimony. *Journal of Scottish Philosophy* 4: 1–15.

Stewart, M. A. 2022. *Hume's Philosophy in Historical Perspective*. Oxford: Oxford University Press.

Stewart, D. 1854–1860. *The Collected Works of Dugald Stewart*, 11 vols, ed. William Hamilton. Edinburgh.

Suderman, Jeffrey. 2001. *Orthodoxy and Enlightenment: George Campbell: In the Eighteenth Century*. London: McGill-Queen's University Press.

Ulman, H. L. 1990. *The Minutes of the Aberdeen Philosophical Society 1758–1773*. Aberdeen: Aberdeen University Press.

Walzer, Arthur E. 2003. *George Campbell: Rhetoric in the Age of Enlightenment*. Albany, NY: State University of New York Press.

Wood, P. B. 2006. Aberdeen Philosophical Society [Wise Club] (act. 1758–1773), *Oxford Dictionary of National Biography* [https://doi.org/10.1093/ref:odnb/95092, accessed on 11 January 2024]

CHAPTER 10

John Gregory on Human Nature, Happiness and Religious Devotion

Abstract In his *A Comparative View of the State and Faculties of Man* (1765), John Gregory set out a well-observed account of the alternative effects of religious devotion and scepticism on happiness of humankind. Our natural religious propensities direct us to comforting devotional beliefs in the face of life's difficulties; failing to pay attention to these aspects of our nature would make most of us unhappy. The opposite of devotion was scepticism, which was deleterious to the happiness of all aside from philosophers. Gregory criticised speculative theology on the same grounds. He was clearly in critical dialogue with Hume's philosophical writings on religion within a shared framework of the "science of human nature," but also contained a implied critique of the Moderates within the Church of Scotland.

Keywords John Gregory · Aberdeen enlightenment · Moderate party · Religious devotion · Sceptical philosophy · Speculative theology

The contribution of the physician John Gregory to the enlightened Scottish discussion of religion was found in his *A Comparative View of the State and Faculties of Man, With Those of the Animal World* (1765).[1] This work was a thematically-disparate collection of discourses loosely united by a common focus on rendering "human life more comfortable and happy," part of Gregory's Baconian sense that the role of science was, as he put it in his *Observations on the Duties and Offices of a Physician* (1770) furthering "public utility, or what contributes to the convenience and happiness of life."[2] Gregory pursued this goal by examining the workings of human nature, divided into the study of the body and of the mind. The latter study has "peculiar difficulties" that have meant "enquiries into human nature ... have been prosecuted with little care and less success."[3] Beneath the immense variety of belief and behaviour, however, there are laws of human nature "as fixed and invariable as those of the material system"; "human nature consists of the same principles every where."[4] Quietly but firmly, Gregory argued for the benefits of lay engagement with religious subjects, which had developed "since the laity have asserted their right of enquiry into these subjects" during the Reformation and accompanying reformation of letters.[5] Lay participants in the study of human nature and the natural world had greatly promoted the "interests of real religion" and, through their engagement with lay writing, made the clergy a "more learned, a more useful and a more respectable body of men."[6]

It was in the guise of a lay writer and practitioner of the science of human nature that Gregory discussed, in the fifth essay of the *Comparative View*, the "sense of religion" as one of the unique features of human nature that "made life more happy and comfortable."[7] Informed by his professional experience as a physician helping the sick, dying and

---

[1] For a biography of Gregory see McCullough (1998a, pp. 15–171). See also McCullough (1998b) and Haakonssen (1997, Ch. 2).

[2] Gregory (1767, p. xv, 1770, pp. 126–27). See also the summary in McCullough (1998a, pp. 149–58).

[3] Gregory (1767, p. 4).

[4] Gregory (1767, pp. 5, 95).

[5] Gregory (1770, pp. 181–82).

[6] Gregory (1770, pp. 181–82).

[7] Gregory (1767, pp. 64, 194).

bereaved, Gregory held that religion served as a source of comfort and consolation for the travails of life and needed to be encouraged and protected. The enlightened scientists of man should concern themselves with how to manage our religious tendencies of human nature in ways that maximises the psychologically beneficial consequences of devotion and piety, while avoiding the pitfalls of bigotry and zealotry. The benefits people gain from religious solace was the best argument against the spread of sceptical philosophy, which brought about debilitating and depressing effects on the majority of minds incapable of handling its view of man's place in the universe. In other words, Gregory was warning Hume and Hume's readers that Hume's philosophical writings on religion would increase the sum total of unhappiness in the world, and they would do so because they did not really understand the true relationship between religion and human nature or, as Gregory implied, did not care about the destructive effects of their philosophy on the benighted.

Gregory wrote from a position of medical expertise to contribute to the Scottish Enlightenment's general "science of human nature." While the Preface to subsequent editions of the *Comparative View* framed his discussions within the context of the natural progress of society, Gregory wrote primarily as a physician inspired by the potential gains for human happiness that could be expected from the application of Baconian natural philosophy to the study of medicine and human nature more generally, and of scientists of human nature incorporating both the study of the human body and the mind.[8] As part of this, Gregory applied his scientific understanding of human nature to make a series of claims about the inherent character, utility and best means of managing the passion of religious devotion.

Though he professionally linked to the medical branch of the Scottish "science of man," Gregory clearly wrote in dialogue with Hume's writings on religious topics and contributed to the Scots' shared concerns over whether religion was natural, what social and political role it played

---

[8] E.g. Gregory (1767, p. 5). Gregory added a hastily composed preface to subsequent editions of the *Comparative View*, partly in response to public comment that the work's contents lacked a common theme. Here Gregory positioned his essays as investigations emerging out of recent "consideration of mankind in the progressive stages of society" and attempts of "uniting together the peculiar advantages of these several stages" (1767, p. xv). Despite this, notions of man as a progressive being or of progress through stages of society have no prominent role in the collection.

and how it should be managed by ecclesiastical and political institutions. Gregory adopted much of Hume's understanding of human nature, but utilised it in ways that pushed back against Hume's conclusions on religious topics. While Gregory was a practising Christian, befitting his professional standing, he wrote as a secular observer on the influence of religion on temporal happiness and did not draw natural theological conclusions from his observations, e.g. that the consoling power of religious devotion demonstrated the truth of those beliefs. He did, however, mean to chastise those theologians in the Church of Scotland more concerned with participating in the literary life of enlightened polite society for their failure to properly understand and tend to the multitude. The findings of the "science of man," however, would help them rectify their mistakes.

Speculative Theology and Effective Affective Preaching

Gregory's *Comparative View* emerged out of five discourses he gave to the Aberdeen Philosophical Society between 1758 and 1763.[9] Like most philosophical publications associated with the Society, Gregory engaged seriously with Hume's thought but also attempted to nullify the perceived threats of Humean scepticism—which, in Gregory's case, was that accepting what Hume argued was likely to make us unhappy. Through observation, the scientist of human nature could learn the best ways to direct this propensity to make us happy. Gregory's repeated observations of human nature taught that man was inherently religious and that appropriate religious belief had many beneficial effects on our well-being. Like Smith's *TMS*, Gregory stressed the singular importance of those "soothing and comfortable" notions that assuaged the anxious human mind faced by the challenges of existence—worldly suffering, the death of loved ones, our own mortality.[10] Religion was not the cause of human misery and terror, as Hume had suggested in the NHR (and which Philo would do with greater force in the *Dialogues*), but the best means for

---

[9] For a more detailed discussion of the historical context of Gregory's *Comparative View* see Mills (2020a).

[10] Gregory (1767, p. 194).

alleviating some of the pain arising from the unceasing challenges of our existence while on earth.

Christianity made people happier because it provided them with the reassuring belief in a providentially arranged universe ruled over by a benevolent deity, in which suffering had a purpose and life did not end with bodily death. Gregory recommended that everyone should make religion a "permanent object" in their lives, so it could "support the mind" when the inescapable traumas of life inevitably took their toll.[11] He had stressed the therapeutic and psychological benefits of religion in his medical lectures at Edinburgh, telling students that faith "alone can support the soul in the most complicated distresses."[12] Religion encourages the patient to "enjoy life with cheerfulness, and to resign it with dignity," and was more likely to console a sick or dying patient than anything the physician themselves could say.[13] Gregory was of the same mind as his close friend and philosophical ally James Beattie, who argued in the Postscript added to the second edition of the *Essay on Truth* (1771), that individuals who sought to curtail religious belief were "traitors to human kind" and "murders of the human soul."[14] Beattie was referring to Hume, and, in private correspondence at least, Gregory agreed with this assessment. To Gregory, part of what Hume got wrong in dismissing the consoling benefits of belief in providence, was framing this belief as the result of abstract reasoning, rather than stemming from an intuitive principle lodged in human nature and available to everyone, not just the subtle reasoner.

Gregory also argued that religion provided necessary support for morals, especially amongst the multitude, providing that theologians were able to manage the passions. Religion provided an additional motivating factor for encouraging moral behaviour and had an influence on human nature, and especially that of the vulgar, which was not matched by either

---

[11] Gregory (1767, p. 235).

[12] Gregory (1770, p. 63).

[13] Gregory (1770, p. 63). Kames reiterated similar arguments in his *Loose Hints*, see Kames (1782, p. 242).

[14] Beattie (1771, p. 528). I do not agree with interpretations, such as McCullough (1998a) and Haakonssen (1997 p. 50), that distance Gregory from Beattie's vehemence. Gregory caught some flak for his well-known friendship with Beattie, but he not only sincerely believed but also actively encouraged his friend in both his arguments and his manner of arguing. See Mills (2020a) and (2020b).

man's faculty of reason or innate moral sense. We are constantly challenged by our passions and constantly being tempted by the allurements of pleasure. The appeal to reasoned arguments to live a virtuous and pious life fails, especially amongst the multitude, given our inherent tendency to superstition and the often-domineering influence of our imaginations. It is only religion, and specifically the prospect of future rewards and judgements in an afterlife, that has enough affective power to control our imaginations and passions and direct them towards moral behaviour. Taught that God can be conciliated, and that virtue and piety are to be rewarded, we are all more likely to behave morally. The weakness of the Humean position was that it positioned the influence of the passions on popular religion as utterly ungovernable, whereas Gregory, like Smith, Kames and Ferguson, believed that our passions could be redirected in beneficial ways.

The benefits of religion were especially vital for individuals living in commercial societies. The challenges to religion posed by urban living prompted Smith, Ferguson and Stewart to suggest pragmatic solutions. Gregory's position, however, was more characteristic of that vehement dislike of commercial society exhibited by Kames and Monboddo. To Gregory, individuals in commercial societies were in the "most unhappy state" of all in human history, and the purported advances of modern society had led men to leave the "plain road of nature."[15] They were sickly, greedy, sexually deviant, immoral and apathetic when it came to religious devotion. Progress had not yielded greater happiness, but anxiety, social division and misery. With the Moderates within the Church of Scotland probably in mind, Gregory complained that religion was increasingly being recategorized under the banner of manners, leading to a form of secularisation in which only religious sentiments in tune with contemporary notions of politeness were deemed acceptable. Gregory's proposed solution to religious listlessness was to take inspiration from the worship, though not the beliefs, of earlier societies. He was especially praising of the ancient Scots detailed in James Macpherson's *Ossian* writings and Hugh Blair's *Critical Dissertation on the Poems of Ossian* (1763).[16] The ancient Scots were devout, passionate believers and modern man should imitate the heartfelt character of their religion;

---

[15] Gregory (1767, pp. xi, x).

[16] Blair's *Dissertation* is discussed below in Appendix 1.

inspired by his great admiration of Rousseau's writings, Gregory argued his contemporaries had much to learn from their "primitive" ancestors.

Polite society, however, was fearful of religious devotion, which had the knock-on effect of encouraging immortality and unhappiness amongst the multitude. The fear of destabilising fanaticism had gone too far, Gregory claimed, because polite society was now hostile towards any strong religious sentiment, regardless of its beneficial effects. He accepted that the benign link between religion, human nature and happiness could be perverted, and did not defend fanaticism. But Gregory did argue that it was the height of naivety about human nature to think that if publicly professed superstition and enthusiasm were the subject of public censure by cultural and religious elites, they would go away, as opposed to reappearing via different avenues in different forms. Gregory was deliberately provoking his readers: their complacently critical views on popular religious devotion had detrimental effects on the happiness of the multitude and increased the likelihood of outbreaks of religious fanaticism. In effect, it was they, the self-anointed, not the ineradicably superstitious tendencies of the benighted multitude, that were the problem.

As with the other *literati*, Gregory believed that a realistic assessment of the needs and capabilities of the multitude entailed specific forms of religious institution, belief and worship. Religion cannot be detached "entirely from superstition" given the limits of human nature and the immense significance of the subject."[17] This was not an "enigma," per §15 of Hume's *NHR*, however: to Gregory, the multitude were "made to act, not to reason."[18] To direct the vulgar towards the right path, it was necessary to enshrine religion in a particular form of "public establishment."[19] The issue, for Gregory, was how to make sure the clergy of an established church did their jobs well. So while he was concerned about the clergy, it was not in terms of reducing the social or political power of the clergy by encouraging indolence (Hume), poverty (Smith) or peaceful competition (also Smith), but by redirecting the focus of their activities back onto their flocks and encouraging them to develop a real understanding of human nature. The "science of man" taught that religious instability was to be reduced by focusing on the passions of laity,

---

[17] Gregory (1767, p. 198).

[18] Gregory (1767, p. 236).

[19] Gregory (1767, p. 198).

not the power dynamic between sovereign and priesthood. An established church should avoid the "accidental circumstances" that lead to superstition flourishing, which Gregory seems to have meant the stressing of adherence to doctrines rooted in speculative metaphysics (e.g. the doctrine of the trinity).[20] Instead, the focus of the Church should steer clear of theological controversy and direct their energies to encouraging the healthy practice of the multitude's inherent religious devotion in ways that were both personally and socially beneficial.

The other major hindrance to benign religious devotion, then, was the continuing prominence of speculative theology, exacerbated by the misguided motivations of contemporary clergymen.[21] Unlike Hume, Gregory saw the rise of abstract and metaphysical theology coming at the expense of practical divinity, rather than to the detriment of philosophy. Still, speculative theology tended neither to "enlarge the understanding, sweeten the temper [nor] mend the heart."[22] A Humean understanding of human nature underpinned Gregory's criticism. Speculative theology pushed individuals beyond the power of their reason and the extent of their experience. This could only leave them in a state of confusion and embarrassment, often resulting in gloomy severity. When faced with unintelligible, unanswerable questions that seem to pertain to the vital issues of the future of one's soul, confused individuals easily fall into the comforting embrace of religious enthusiasm. Moreover, as speculative theology was without empirical foundation and as there was no agreed upon criterion of truth, it was always likely to occasion disagreement. The "habit of frequent reasoning and disputing" had the knock-on effects of reducing reverence for religion and increasing social disharmony.[23]

Whereas Hume had argued that Christian theology had colonised the social space formerly taken up by philosophy, Gregory claimed that the rise of speculative theology to cultural dominance had a more recent origin. Writing as a bad-tempered critic of contemporary polite society, Gregory claimed that the clerical profession had stopped tending to their flocks and instead tended to their own vanity as members of a cultural

---

[20] Gregory (1767, p. 199).
[21] See also Haakonssen (1997, pp. 83–85).
[22] Gregory (1767, p. 218).
[23] Gregory (1767, p. 214).

elite. At first blush, Gregory's position bore some similarity with the criticism of the Moderate Party within the Church of Scotland associated with the Popular Party and epitomised by John Witherspoon's satire *Ecclesiastical Characteristics* (1753).[24] The Moderates who came to prominence in the 1750s were known for their conspicuous adherence to politeness and esteem for scientific and literary achievements, which prompted the accusation that they had abandoned their pastoral duties and their concern for salvation of the benighted. What Smith would claim was true of the Catholic Church, Gregory believed was true of the Church of Scotland: talented men entered the church to pursue literary endeavours that publicised their genius. Rather than being moral and religious leaders, the clergy became obsessed with literary fame and financial reward. Pastoral duties were disdained as mere practical arts, aided by snobbery towards the devotional tendencies of the multitude. Abdicating their responsibility for tending to the souls of their flocks had an unintended (if entirely explicable) consequence: confining "themselves to a tract," rather than becoming effective preachers, the clergy left the duty of religious guidance of ignored multitude to those of the "wildest fanaticism."[25] The ironic consequence, for Gregory, of the Moderates' turn away from religious dogmatism and towards politeness, avoidance of doctrine, focus on moral preaching and celebration of philosophical and scientific attainment was that it encouraged the very thing it was aimed to stop.[26] The focus on moral culture at the expense of religious devotion would also fail because it ignored an inherent quality of human nature that, while the Moderates might wished to have suppressed it, could not be eradicated, and would manifest itself in other, often unpredictable ways.

Gregory's correspondence with Beattie from the mid-1760s to his death in 1773 indicates that Gregory disdained the airs and graces, but especially what Gregory viewed as the moral complacency, of the Moderate elite.[27] His criticism of their preaching, and solution to their disregard of the needs of the people, did not align him, however, with the Popular Party in the Church of Scotland. Not a minister himself, Gregory's argument was not a doctrinal one, but it did imply that theologians

---

[24] On Witherspoon see Mailer (2017, esp. pp. 1–100).

[25] Gregory (1767, p. 229).

[26] For popular pushback against Moderatism see, for example, Brekke (2010).

[27] See Mills (2015, 2020a, 2020b).

should take instruction from scientists of man. The failures of Scotland's clerical elite were not to be undone by a return to orthodox Presbyterian doctrine or changes to the patronage law. His solution was an alternative path to enlightenment: Scotland's ministers must refocus on their duties to their flock by becoming practitioners and imbibing the findings of the "science of human nature." Certainly, speculative theology should be separated from empirical natural theology and should be stopped from treating scripture as a source of philosophical propositions. Scripture should be "viewed at a distance" and as objects of "silent and religious veneration," rather than a source of propositions for abstract theological reasoning.[28] But more relevant for the moment, the clergy should refine their skills in affective preaching and ministering by becoming keen, precise and sympathetic observers of human nature, imitating the relationship provided by the physician to their parent.

The key to becoming effective affective preachers was to first become a kind of priestly scientist of human nature. This involved two steps. Firstly, the clergy needed to focus on the practical duties of their job: "assiduous and accurate observation" followed by the "proper application of such observation" to the religious needs of their flock.[29] They had to accumulate, through repeated experience of "life itself," an "intimate knowledge of the human heart."[30] This knowledge was to be combined with a "devotional spirit united to good sense and a cheerful temper."[31] The priest needed to learn about the "artful association of ideas" that informed the influence of vice on the imagination, effectively becoming a student of a Humean science of man, though for radically different ends.[32] The priest needed to know the different internal and external factors that informed an individual's unique religious beliefs. Only practical divinity cultivated in this way can lead to "universal charity," "love of mankind" and a "cheerfulness [during] the darkest hours of human life."[33]

---

[28] Gregory (1767, p. 212).

[29] Gregory (1767, p. 222).

[30] Gregory (1767, p. 222).

[31] Gregory (1767, p. 233).

[32] Gregory (1767, p. 222). The influence of Hume on Gregory's understanding of human nature is argued for by McCullough (1998a, 1998b).

[33] Gregory (1767, pp. 233–34).

Secondly, in terms of preaching, the priest needed to realise that the "general defect" of current sermons "intended to reform mankind" was that they sought to persuade the head not the heart.[34] The informed observer of human nature knows that the sinner understands their actions are wrong but acts anyway. They will only properly face the "deformity" of their actions if a minister can speak to them in a lively and arresting way, by appealing to their passions and self-interest rather than to abstract argument.[35] The effective preacher did not adopt a stance of intellectual superiority, but sought to be a kind-hearted student of human nature, equipped with a "lively and well-regulated imagination," and able to communicate affectingly to the multitude.[36] Again, to do this, the clerical profession needed to become proficient in the science of human nature—to understand why people develop the religious beliefs that they do, and what purposes those beliefs serve them—and apply this knowledge when tending to their flock.

Anti-Scepticism

From without the Church, the other major threat to the benign relationship between religion and happiness was the growing prominence of sceptical philosophy. In his correspondence in the years immediately preceding his death, Gregory complained bitterly about the failure of Scotland's cultural and religious elite to respond to the spread of scepticism with due seriousness. Blithely unaware of the dangers Hume's writings posed, Gregory believed the Edinburgh religious and academic elite treated Hume as a good man and a friend of mankind. Gregory warned his students at Edinburgh that sceptical philosophy had ceased to be the "gloomy entertainment of a few recluse men" and had infected wider society.[37] Despite his evident horror at its newfound popularity, Gregory's published discussion of the appeal of sceptical philosophy was striking in its empathetic nuance. The character of the philosophical sceptic was, in some respects, admiringly drawn. And Gregory's advice

---

[34] Gregory (1767, p. 223).
[35] Gregory (1767, p. 224).
[36] Gregory (1767, p. 225).
[37] Gregory (1770, p. 61).

was couched in the language of paternalism: the mental tranquillity of his readers was threatened if they engaged with scepticism.

Gregory's aetiology of scepticism bore parallels with his aetiology of religious fanaticism. We can be seduced by the sceptic's claim that we gain no knowledge of the truth when we put our minds to work on intellectual tasks that we have neither the reasoning ability nor the experience to comprehend. Our terrifying awareness of the limitations of human nature can lead to the delusional comfort of believing our God talks directly to us, in the case of the enthusiast, but also the "gloomy and forlorn" sense that knowledge is not possible, in the case of the sceptic.[38] These dangers are especially real when, as with the practice of speculative theology, we combine metaphysical and practical reasoning together. Threatened by their sense of their inability to comprehend their place in the universe, the soon-to-be sceptic throws out both legitimate empirical and illegitimate abstract forms of human reasoning as equally useless.

For most people, the adoption of scepticism results in several consequences that undermine their happiness. The newly-minted sceptic, overwhelmed by irresolution, fails to recall that the "business of life is only a conjectural art" in which we learn through activity alone.[39] (Just as Gregory was critical of speculative theology, so he was critical of sceptical philosophy, on the grounds that it took us away from quotidian living and the proper limits of human nature.) The sceptic is liable to neglect their "devotional spirit," and they will fall into a "melancholy temper."[40] The "suspense of judgement" on religious matters leads to "fatal effects" for our souls, as the sceptic disregards how our worldly actions effect their lives in the hereafter.[41] Not everyone, however, is affected by scepticism in the same way. Gregory drew a distinction between the philosophical sceptic and those engaging with scepticism, but who were not of a philosophical temperament. The philosophical sceptic—it is impossible not to think that Gregory had Hume in mind—does not suffer from a "bad understanding or a bad heart," but they do have a "want of imagination

---

[38] Gregory (1767, p. 83).
[39] Gregory (1767, p. 83).
[40] Gregory (1767, pp. 215, 235).
[41] Gregory (1767, p. 205).

and sensibility of heart."[42] Philosophical sceptics lack emotional sensitivity. Their affections are not aroused by matters of life and death, and the meaning of existence: they can persuade themselves of the aimlessness of the universe and yet "appear easy and contented."[43]

The sceptical philosopher was a rare and distinct sort of person, and most people cannot handle suspension of judgement on the great matters of the human lot. Most people become distracted and despairing if they contemplate issues, such as the finality of death, for long. Similarly, they find comfort in religion when faced with forms of earthly suffering that are otherwise sources of despair. The sceptic can say nothing to alleviate the suffering of the parent who has lost their child.[44] The arguments of scepticism do not phase the cooly rationally, unfeeling philosopher; to nearly every one else, to truly believe them would be a cause of tremendous misery. People can only deal with the "pressures and afflictions" of life with "cheerfulness and dignity," if supported by faith. The sceptical philosopher should "consider the situation of the rest of mankind," who may wish to be happy and need religion to be so, and stop promulgating their ideas to a wider audience.[45]

The other sort of sceptic—the ones without philosophical temperaments—were also dangers to society. Like Smith's empathetic portraits of how humans act when confronted with psychological challenges, Gregory offers an intricate and compassionate picture of the psychology of the flailing individual both threatened and persuaded by sceptical philosophy. The unphilosophical sceptic—that is, the individual who still possesses some feeling—tends to proselytise their scepticism to others. This might be out of a vain desire to gain admirers, but Gregory viewed it as more likely that the sceptic was trying to escape the "disagreeable feeling" of being "alone in the midst of society" while in possession of their upsetting thoughts about the pointlessness of life.[46] To escape this mental anguish, they attempt to convert others—misery loves company. While

---

[42] Gregory (1767, p. 201).

[43] Gregory (1767, p. 204).

[44] As mentioned previously, it seems highly likely that, when arguing this point, Gregory had in mind the passage from Hume's *EHU* where Hume noted that someone being tortured would be angered by supposedly comforting messages about the providential order of the universe. See EHU 8.34.

[45] Gregory (1767, p. 210).

[46] Gregory (1767, p. 207).

they pretend they act from a praiseworthy desire to spread wisdom, they are really seeking to re-establish their mental quietude through developing companionship. But what they actually achieve is only the dragging down of others to their own level of immiseration. Gregory was concerned about sceptical philosophy as a form of social contagion spreading misery, especially amongst youthful minds who do not know better.

* * *

In *Comparative View*, Gregory set out a well-observed psychological account of the alternative effects of religious devotion and religious scepticism on happiness of the vast majority of humankind. Our natural religious propensities direct us to comforting beliefs in the face of life's difficulties and failing to pay attention to this aspect of our nature would make most of us unhappy. Gregory's discussion of religious devotion and practical divinity was shot through with the rhetoric of affection, love, tenderness of heart and antagonism to speculative theology. The opposite of devotion was scepticism, which was deleterious to the happiness of all but those cool, calm individuals whose natural religious tendencies were not much in earnest in the first place.

Gregory's discussion was clearly in dialogue with Hume's philosophical writings on religion within a shared framework of the "science of human nature." A Bacon-inspired scientific approach produced naturalistic account of devotion and scepticism; the motivation behind this pursuit was to improve temporal happiness. The clergy could get better at helping their flock achieve some solace and manage potentially unruly religious passions by abandoning speculative theology, adopting the methods of the "science of man" and remembering their role was as caregiver not status-seeker. Gregory did not choose to say that scepticism was wrong, only that it would make you unhappy; he did not choose to say that religion was true, only that it will help you endure the unavoidable suffering of a human life. The sceptical philosopher should limit their audience to others of their kind, and not try to remove the crutch of religion from the bulk of humankind. Gregory agreed with Hume's recommendation in §15 of NHR that sceptically minded philosophers should withdraw from society, but Gregory believed this would be for society's benefit, the happiness of the many being threatened by the philosopher, more than that of the sceptic, threatened by the uncomprehending angry multitude.

Gregory's argument reads like a direct rebuke of Hume's arguments about manging popular religion, which damned anyone unlucky enough not to be born a philosopher to unhappiness and ignorance and saw the best way of managing their unruly passions was by cynically encouraging "superstitious atheism." It was also a challenge to his contemporaries amongst the Moderates. Ever the caregiver, Gregory did not want to abandon the multitude to lives of misery and superstition. Happily, when organised by priests inspired by the "science of man"—indeed by a version of that science heavily indebted to Hume—popular religion could be managed in ways that helped both the multitude and society at large. While Gregory clearly saw belief in God's benevolence and justice, and prospect of future reward as key, his emphasis was more on clerical conduct than specific doctrines. Gregory also posed a different solution to the issue of popular religion than that proposed by Hume in his *History of England*. Established churches needed to encourage religious devotion within moderate limits, aided by ministers who were sympathetic observers of human nature and thus able to direct the multitude's passions and imagination to beneficial ends. In understanding that to get humans to act we have to appeal to their passions, Gregory would build this argument on Humean grounds—the need for affective religious guidance was a position he would share with many of his contemporaries. But the rebuttal of Hume was combined with an underlying sense that contemporary, we might say enlightened, theologians had made some false steps in their disdain of religious affection and praise for abstract philosophy. A good physician and scientist of human nature, Gregory recommended solutions to alleviate the symptoms of a multitude made unhappy by modern, polite commercial society's dislike of religious devotion; his arguments implied a critique both of Hume and his supporters amongst the Moderates in the Church of Scotland.

References

Beattie, James. 1771. *An Essay on the Nature of Truth*, second edition. Edinburgh.

Brekke, Luke. 2010. Heretics in the Pulpit, Inquisitors in the Pews: The Long Reformation and the Scottish Enlightenment. *Eighteenth-Century Studies* 44: 79–98.

Gregory, John. 1767. *A Comparative View of the Faculties of Man with Those of the Animal World*, fourth edition. London.

———. 1770. *Observations on the Duties and Offices of a Physician*. London.
Haakonssen, Lisbeth. 1997. *Medicine and Morals in the Enlightenment: John Gregory, Thomas Percival, and Benjamin Rush*. Amsterdam: Rodopi.
Kames, Lord, Henry Home. 1782. *Loose Hints on Education*. London.
Mailer, Gideon. 2017. *John Witherspoon's American Revolution*. Chapel Hill, NC: University of North Carolina Press.
McCullough, Laurence B. 1998a. *John Gregory and the Invention of Professional Medical Ethics and the Profession of Medicine*. Dordrecht: Springer.
———. 1998b. *John Gregory's Writings on Medical Ethics and Philosophy of Medicine*. Dordrecht: Springer.
Mills, R.J.W. 2015. The Reception of 'That Bigoted Silly Fellow' James Beattie's *Essay on Truth* in Britain 1770–1830. *History of European Ideas* 41: 1049–1079.
———. 2020a. Religion, Scepticism and John Gregory's Therapeutic Science of Human Nature. *History of European Ideas* 46:916–333.
———. 2020b. James Beattie, Jean-Jacques Rousseau and the Character of Common Sense Philosophy. *History of European Ideas* 46:793–810.
Stewart, Dugald. 1854–60. *The Collected Works of Dugald Stewart*, 11 vols. Ed. William Hamilton. Edinburgh.

CHAPTER 11

James Dunbar on Climate and Civil Religion

Abstract We find a characteristically Aberdonian emphasis on the historical truth and necessity of Christianity in James Dunbar's *Essays on the History of Mankind in Rude and Cultivated Ages* (1780). The *Essays* are further evidence of the generic variety of the contributions of the Aberdeen Enlightenment, but also the Aberdonian's shared aim of defending and explaining Christianity's place within the findings of the new "science of human nature" and "history of mankind." Dunbar took the influence of climate to be highly determinate of what form of religion developed in a specific society, but held that Christianity alone had a moral message capable of rising all societies up to the level of true religion.

Keywords James Dunbar · Climate · "History of Mankind" · Necessity of revelation · Civil religion · Aberdeen Enlightenment

We find a characteristically Aberdonian emphasis on the historical truth and necessity of Christianity in James Dunbar's *Essays on the History of Mankind in Rude and Cultivated Ages* (1780). Dunbar was first a Professor of Moral Philosophy at King's College Aberdeen before being appointed a regent there in 1766. He was part of the second generation of scientists of human nature, whose social theory refined and supplemented the arguments of the generation of Hume, Kames, Smith and, in

Dunbar's case, especially Robertson.[1] The *Essays* are neatly summarised by Sebastiani as containing an "attempt to write a comparative, progressive, and stadial history of man in society, following the example of the Edinburgh literati, but integrating it with the Christian universalism of the Aberdeen intellectual milieu."[2] As such, the *Essays* are further evidence of the generic variety of the contributions of the Aberdeen Enlightenment, but also their shared aim of defending and explaining Christianity's place within the findings of the new "science of human nature" and "history of mankind."

The principal thematic context for Dunbar's views of the relationship between religion and human nature was his contribution to the Enlightenment debate of the comparative influence of "moral causes" and "physical causes" on man and society. The former referred to influences rooted in behaviours and institutions that resulted from human action; the latter referred to elements exogenous to human nature and society, such as environmental factors. Dunbar is often seen as significant within this debate because of his discussion on the influence of climate. For our concerns, Dunbar argued climate as a major influence on the origin and character of non-Christian religions, in interplay with other factors such as the extent of scientific knowledge and political systems. The findings of the "history of mankind" informed an argument for Christianity's truth, because it was unique amongst world religions for its universal and (at least initially) non-political character. These characteristics demonstrated Christianity did not originate as a tool of policy of "oriental" despots in hot climates, a unique characteristic and one that was evidence of its truth.

Climate had a determining role in the formation and character of religious beliefs, both directly and indirectly. Most directly, warm climates create abundances of food, which in turn enables the leisure necessary for the thinking part of mankind to develop theological systems. The first coherent "religious sentiments and opinions" appeared in the luxurious climates of Chaldea, India and Egypt.[3] Natural produce abounded, and subsistence was secure. For Dunbar, as it would be for Monboddo, it

---

[1] On Dunbar see Berry (2018, Chs. 2, 3 and especially 4). I should note that Berry rejects my more deterministic reading of Dunbar's views on influence of climate on religion set out in this chapter.

[2] Sebastiani (2013, p. 104).

[3] Dunbar (1780, p. 223).

was climate and not the division of labour, that allowed for the creation of the leisure necessary for religious notions to develop. The peoples of the "more productive regions of Asia and Africa" initiated the first "philosophic age" of humanity.[4] "Fertile and luxuriant countries" act as the first "nursery of refinement," though they can only establish the sciences, not advance them.[5] The leisure enabled by the abundance of nature leads to an awakening of curiosity towards all aspects of human life and the natural world. With leisure, mankind can move beyond the "demands of animal nature" and the full scene of life "opens to the intellectual eye."[6] It is with leisure that mankind begins to ask the big questions of human existence, though the resulting views on the "economy of invisible powers" and the means to "render the divinity propitious" were many and varied.[7]

Climate also had an indirect but equally significant role in the formation of religion via its influence on the establishment of political authority. Societies in warm climates tended to be despotic, and the emergent religions were rendered subservient to the needs of tyrannical rulers. The first religions of humankind were formed by a perverted alliance of philosophy, theology and policy, in which philosophy was subordinated to alliances of priests and princes. The pact was "instrumental … in consecrating absurdity and giving consistency to error," in which "religious imposture" was used to control the people.[8] The results were religions made up of "abject superstition," "wildest fanaticism" and "sublime theology," deployed by princes and priests, to "allure and fascinate the crowd," in the interests of keeping them under control.[9] The first religions appeared in those countries "first enlightened by science," yet took a form that "disgraced reason and humanity" because they were quickly subordinated to political power.[10] The sciences which emerged out of this alliance were those superstitious practices of augury, divination and "wretched literature" full of mysteries.[11] Influenced by its political role of

---

[4] Dunbar (1780, p. 229).
[5] Dunbar (1780, p. 228).
[6] Dunbar (1780, p. 228).
[7] Dunbar (1780, p. 229).
[8] Dunbar (1780, pp. 225–226).
[9] Dunbar (1780, pp. 224–225).
[10] Dunbar (1780, pp. 223–224).
[11] Dunbar (1780, p. 226).

ensuring the "credulity and superstition of mankind," the study of nature descended into "judicial astrology."[12] The "religious passions" aroused by these early religions tend to ferment the "greatest violence" and produce the "most astonishing effects."[13]

These countries on the "torrid zone" "propagated" their superstitious systems "over various and distant regions."[14] Here, religions were transmitted via the imperial expansion of the major early civilisations of Chaldea, India and Egypt. Dunbar's sense of the transmission of "cultural heritage" from these civilisations to the rest of the world has been described as a form of the "stadial history of man in society."[15] But it is just as resonant with those histories of the transmission of religion found in the productions of the *Academie des sciences* or in Smith's "Essay on Astronomy," which is to say, not of the progressive histories of society that I have been arguing are so characteristic of the Scottish Enlightenment. The sense of nations as "cultural units" developing and influencing others speaks more to the established traditions of mythography and the history of idolatry than they did to the "science of human nature."

Warm or luxurious climates both gave birth to the first systems of religion and enabled their quick prince and priest-led perversion into superstition. It is in cold climates, as environments of less abundance, that the arts, sciences, philosophy, and therefore religion take "root and flourish," developing into a more "mature form" than the first polytheisms.[16] Once religions are established in cold climates, they did not coagulate into systems of civil superstition, but rather progress towards growing natural philosophical knowledge about nature. Peoples in luxuriant climates "want of the chief incentives to action," whereas those in colder climates need to understand the world to survive in it.[17] The climatic influence on the potential for the "extension and cultivation of the liberal arts," including theology, marked a "fundamental and *fixed* distinction between the communities of mankind in the lower and higher

---

[12] Dunbar (1780, p. 226).
[13] Dunbar (1780, p. 224).
[14] Dunbar (1780, p. 233).
[15] E.g. Sebastiani (2013, p. 104).
[16] Dunbar (1780, p. 230).
[17] Dunbar (1780, p. 230).

latitudes."[18] While Dunbar's assessment of the role of climate left space for the moral causes to override its influence, on the issue of issue of intellectual (including theological) refinement, his position can be described as straightforwardly deterministic.[19]

This position informed Dunbar's other major conclusion about religion that he drew from the "history of mankind": all religions were demonstrably political creations apart from Christianity. Systems of superstition, universally, had acted as "guardian[s] of public manners" and as a "useful auxiliary to legislative power."[20] Realising this helped the student of human nature comprehend why the "ancient codes" of so many religions were filled with "striking examples of credulity and fanaticism."[21] These religious were actually "monuments of human sagacity," not least because they often served to prevent the "most wretched debasement," "religious fanaticism."[22] As such, systems of superstition could often be deployed, with judicious management by rulers, in ways that contributed to human "felicity" and avoided the more extreme practices of unfettered religious passion.[23] Political utility explained their otherwise absurd beliefs and rites. Every religion beside Christianity was the all too human creation of conniving priests and princes, but Christianity was a universal religion "adapted to all climates and governments."[24] Importantly, Christian teaching broke the near universal relationship between political authority and religion because it "leaves the details of policy" to rulers.[25] While to Hume this separation led to the creation of rivalrous ecclesiastical power, to Dunbar it demonstrated that Christianity was meant to exist only in the world of piety and morals, not politics—and that there were only human, not religious, reasons should the Church gain political power.

* * *

---

[18] Dunbar (1780, p. 232). My italics.
[19] Cf. Berry (2013, pp. 81–82).
[20] Dunbar (1780, p. 354).
[21] Dunbar (1780, p. 355).
[22] Dunbar (1780, p. 355).
[23] Dunbar (1780, p. 355).
[24] Dunbar (1780, p. 355). Note here, again, the implication that climate has a determining influence on the form of religion that can emerge.
[25] Dunbar (1780, p. 355).

Viewed together, the luminaries of the Aberdeen Enlightenment who practiced the "science of human nature," sought to reject the subversive implications of that science when applied to the subject of revealed religion. In the case of the Professor of Divinity at Marischal College, Aberdeen, Alexander Gerard this involved a reiteration of the traditional arguments of early modern histories of idolatry and anti-atheist apologetics. But the bulk of authors covered in this section were committed to the naturalistic study of human nature and the applicability of the origin and development of religion from primitive polytheism to philosophical (if flawed) theism in contexts of unassisted human nature and societal improvement but combined with a firm belief in the truth of biblical history. Indeed, the sorts of argument found in Hume's NHR were often redeployed as demonstrating the truth of the Christian religion, as the latter was viewed to have developed in very different ways compared to the "natural" progress of religion.

References

Berry, Christopher J. 2013. *The Idea of Commercial Society in the Scottish Enlightenment*. Edinburgh: Edinburgh University Press.

———. 2018. *Essays on Hume, Smith, and the Scottish Enlightenment*. Edinburgh: Edinburgh University Press.

Dunbar, James. 1780. *Essays on the History of Mankind in Rude and Cultivated Ages*. London.

Sebastiani, Silva. 2013. *The Scottish Enlightenment: Race, Gender, and the Limits of Progress*, trans. Jeremy Carden. Basingstoke: Palgrave.

CHAPTER 12

James Burnett, Lord Monboddo on Egyptian Daemons

Abstract The peculiar characteristics of Lord Monboddo's discussion of religion help clarify what is distinct and about the Scottish Enlightenment's approach to the subject. Found in the latter volumes of his *Origin and Progress of Language* (1773–1792) and especially his *Antient Metaphysics* (1779–1799), Monboddo's approach to religion was an untimely fusion of conjectural history, natural history inspired by Buffon, Christian theology including belief in intermediate supernatural beings, Platonic and Aristotelian philosophy, credulous acceptance of ancient history and travel literature and personal research projects on "savage" individuals. By the time Monboddo addressed the issue of religion in depth, his thought had been overtaken by both Egyptomania and a belief in the necessity of daemonic intervention to bring about key steps in human development.

Keywords Lord Monboddo · "History of Man" · Ancient Egypt · Daemon-kings · Religious development · Materialist philosophy

The final chapters of this book examine two of the Scottish Enlightenment's least studied and most unusual thinkers on religious topics, Monboddo and Hutton, before using Dugald Stewart as a bookend for our survey of the discussion of the High Scottish Enlightenment's exploration of religion and human nature. Monboddo and Hutton are like chalk and cheese: the former believed that, prior to Christ's mission, all religious history had been one long story of decline since pure theism of ancient Egypt; the latter exhibited an optimistic belief that philosophy was wresting control from superstition and would soon lead mankind into the promised land of pure natural religion. Readers more interested in the most sophisticated of Enlightenment philosophy might find both Monboddo and Hutton underwhelming, but they play important roles. Monboddo provides a useful counterpoint to my identification of a more naturalistic and innovative study of religion during the High Scottish Enlightenment, while Hutton took a usually strong deist stance compared to his Scottish contemporaries. While utilising many of the concepts of the Scottish "science of man" and study of the "history of mankind," Monboddo was clearly interested in questions of civilisational transmission and the antiquity of human history in ways that the other authors in this book were not. Hutton, by contrast, can be seen as articulating an almost millenarian sense of the power of philosophy to undo superstition.

The peculiar characteristics of James Burnett, Lord Monboddo's discussion of the origin and development of religion help clarify what is distinct and socially scientific about the Scottish Enlightenment's approach to religion.[1] Found in the latter volumes of his *Origin and Progress of Language* (6 vols., 1773–1792; hereafter *OPL*) and especially his *Antient Metaphysics* (6 vols., 1779–1799; hereafter *AM*), Monboddo's approach to religion involved a unique combination of conjectural history, natural history inspired by Buffon, Christian theology including belief in intermediate supernatural beings, Platonic and Aristotelian philosophy, credulous acceptance of ancient history and travel literature and personal research projects on "savage" individuals. These discussions formed what Monboddo called his studies in the "History of Man," framed by an account of the diversity and historicity of the human species.[2] By the time Monboddo addressed the issue of religion in depth, his thought had been overtaken by both Egyptomania and a belief in the necessity of daemonic intervention to bring about key steps in human development. These idiosyncratic elements were intermixed with the explanatory concepts and methods that characterised enlightened

---

[1] For a biography, see Cloyd (1972). For a very useful overview of Monboddo's historical thought, see Bottin (2015).

[2] On this theme see, variously, Wokler (1988), Sebastiani (2013, esp. pp. 82–85) and (2022), and Mills (2021b).

Scottish social theory. I will dwell a little longer on Monboddo's approach than is normal in literature on enlightened Scottish social theory precisely because of its almost uncanny quality.

While he used similar methods and was interested in similar conceptions of human nature as his contemporaries, Monboddo's main discussion of religious development was characterised by an Egyptomania wholly out of step with the mainstream Scottish Enlightenment.[3] He placed his stadial history of religious development in the specific location and time of the first epochs of ancient Egyptian civilisation, replacing biblical chronology with Egyptian chronology derived from Herodotus. God had chosen the Egyptian civilisation and religion to prepare the world for Christianity, with Egyptian priests as recipients of revelation from their daemon-kings, intermediary spiritual beings who knew the will of God. With this support, religion in Egypt took the form of a *religio duplex* in which the elite priest class knew true theism but ministered a polytheism framed for popular consumption. As God intended, Monboddo claimed, Egyptian religion spread out to conquer the world, taking hold in ancient Greece, India and China. But it was downhill from there. Monboddo developed his own Egyptian version of the corruption theory of the mythographers. Once Egyptian civilisation collapsed, the story of humanity had been one of vice, disease, war and future apocalyptic collapse. The mistake made was jettisoning the Egyptian model of living, which was in tune with nature and God's will for man. The human species itself was in danger and, Monboddo intoned, could only be saved by adopting Egyptian practices of diet, dress, houting, exercise, politics, philosophy and religion. Everything about Egypt, Monboddo believed, was the best social arrangement found in the annals of human history. This was partly due to its merging of religious and political authority. Egypt had been given two providential roles in the course of human history. Initially it was given the "gift of science and philosophy," with which to aid the worldwide development of civilisation in preparation for the coming of Christ.[4] Notably, when Monboddo thought about humanity's future salvation, this did not involve a return to primitive

---

[3] See in more depth Mills (2021a).

[4] Monboddo (1779–1799, vol. iii p. vi).

Christianity but to habits and beliefs of ancient Egyptian civilisation. In the late eighteenth-century, the record of Egypt was to serve as a model to religiously and culturally corrupted Europeans, to be imitated in a providential act of saving humanity from itself.

Monboddo's Curious "History of Man"

Monboddo's Egyptomania took hold of his worldview by the 1780s, but the duality of his approach—both modern and anti-modern—was evident from the first volumes of *OPL*. Provoked by what he saw as the irreligious materialism of Locke's empiricism, Buffon's natural history and Hume's scepticism, Monboddo wished to resurrect the understanding of human nature found in pagan philosophy. Modern philosophers had abandoned what Monboddo viewed as the ancient Greek understanding (recategorised from the 1780s onwards by Monboddo as ancient Egyptian) of immaterial spirits inhabiting the universe. This was a major philosophical error, and one with disastrous consequences that Monboddo believed was playing out across the Christian world. Returning to the pagans would demonstrate that religion was the "great tamer and civilizer of men," which enabled society to exist and would be sorely missed should modern philosophy succeed in fully gutting it of its core doctrines on immateriality.[5] But in wishing to demonstrate that the pagans understood human nature and society better than moderns, Monboddo repackaged their philosophy with the concepts and methods of his contemporaries.

Unlike any of the other authors discussed in this book, who all believed, one way or another, in the progress of religious understanding, Monboddo argued that we needed to return to the theology of the ancients. It was necessary to re-learn the "purest theology" from the ancients and to re-found both the "great truths of natural religion" and some of the "fundamental doctrines of Christianity" upon the ancient understanding of immaterial spirit or "mind."[6] Monboddo understood "mind" to be reason, vitality and the principle producing motion in the universe. It acted constantly. The consequence for Monboddo's religious thought was that he developed a concept of the great chain of being,

[5] Monboddo (1779–1799, vol. iv p. 95).
[6] Monboddo (1779–1799, vol. i p. xxxi).

with various gradations of mind at work in the world, including intelligences that existed between those of man and God. Ancient philosophy's concept of "mind" schooled Newtonian empiricists that reason was not sufficient for understanding man and the universe. Humans are not self-reliant and require the "counsel and assistance of superior powers" to guide them.[7] This was more than an argument for the necessity of revelation, however, as Monboddo outlined the historical role of Egyptian daemons in securing the first civilisation of humankind.

Monboddo claimed that the return to pagan models of civilisation and philosophy were conclusions emerging from the study of the "History of Man." This form of investigation did not have the "history of any particular nation" as its subject, but that of the "whole species."[8] We discover "the nature of man from fact and experience," and need to approach this study "in the same manner as we collect the history of any other animal."[9] Monboddo imbibed the emphasis of "science of human nature" on observation and experiment, but he views its modern thinkers associated with it—Locke, Hume, Buffon and Newton, for example—as being materialists who denied the existence of active supernatural power in the world. Despite his evident engagement with contemporary studies of human nature, and his evident admiration for Rousseau's anthropological commentary, Monboddo framed his approach as following that of Aristotle's *Historia animalium*.[10] Imitating Aristotle's examination of man's body, "affections and dispositions," will teach us "what sort of animal we ourselves are."[11] Aristotle's thought was spliced with Platonic, then Egyptian, doctrines on immaterial spirits and only this combination would allow for the writing of an accurate natural history of humankind.

In this regard, Monboddo was one of the most forthcoming of the Scottish Enlightenment thinkers when it came to outlining his methods. The study of man involved: general conclusions induced from the accumulation of individual historical facts; the subsequent deduction of claims based on earlier inductions; and appeals to arguments from authorities deemed trustworthy. There is a cantankerous, oppositional quality to

---

[7] Monboddo (1779–1799, vol. ii p. 301).

[8] Monboddo (1779–1799, vol. iii p. 2).

[9] Monboddo (1773–1792, vol. i p. 144, p. 445); Monboddo (1779–1799, III: ii–iii).

[10] On Monboddo and Rousseau see Wood (1990 esp. pp. 105–106, 120–21).

[11] Monboddo (1779–1799, vol. iv p. 81).

Monboddo's articulation of his methods—he was, as Chris Berry put it, "wilfully perverse" in his approach.[12] Most illustrative of this is Monboddo's explanation of his methods when it came to testimonial evidence. He gleamed "facts as I find them," holding that "if the author is credible," he believed them regardless of what they claimed.[13] Testimony was credible if the witness possessed expertise and was of good character, and if their claims tallied with the accounts of other credible witnesses and did not contain anything that was "by the nature of things, impossible to be true."[14] Monboddo's application of these rules was anything but strict, with Monboddo seemingly believing the most outlandish claims precisely because they were outlandish. As might be expected from a man who believed in daemons, kraken and men with tails, Monboddo was exceedingly generous when assessing whether his sources against the criterion of what was "possible" in nature. Monboddo viewed his approach as a uniquely able to reach genuine insights in the "History of Man," and complained of the "spirit of incredulity" exhibited by his contemporaries towards ancient history and travel literature.[15]

Monboddo might have been a crank, but he was someone utterly immersed in the intellectual, philosophical and legal life of late eighteenth-century Scotland. What is fascinating about Monboddo's approach to studying the "History of Man" is that he was applying, as Silvia Sebastiani has shown, ways of thinking about evidence that were informed by his profession duties as a judge in the Court of Session.[16] When possible, he interrogated individuals who had direct experience of the phenomena he was interested in, and testimonial evidence from these interviews found their way into his published work. He took testimonial evidence made under oath by a respectable member of society very seriously and offered to arrange publication of signed affidavits supporting his more outlandish "facts."[17] Monboddo also was more proactive than his contemporaries in his accumulation of information about the non-European peoples. He developed a network of contacts,

---

[12] Berry (2012, p. 126).
[13] Monboddo (1779–1799, vol. ii p. 132).
[14] Monboddo (1779–1799, vol. ii p. 133).
[15] Monboddo (1779–1799, vol. iii p. 251).
[16] Sebastiani (2022).
[17] E.g. Monboddo (1773–1792, vol. i. p. 262).

principally imperial officials and East Indian Company men, who sent him information directly. Most proactively, Monboddo undertook a series of research projects on "wild" children, using both "mine own eyes" and research assistants.[18] Monboddo's personal study of "savage" individuals taught him that unsocialised humans were atheists, which was evidence that man's "intellectual capabilities" had to develop in society first before religious belief was possible.[19] Only Marie-Angélique Leblanc, the "Wild Girl of Champagne," had religious beliefs, showing that religion was adventitious and only possible in the "first state of civil society."[20]

Similarly characteristic of how Monboddo was one step removed from mainstream Scottish Enlightenment thought, his analysis of religious change incorporated evidence, themes and arguments that rarely appear in the work of other authors. Indeed, Monboddo incorporated many of those approaches to the study of religion, outlined in the Introduction, that characterised the study of idolatry and mythology by pre-Enlightenment historians of religion. Monboddo was very much interested in the issue of cultural transmission, an approach more commonly found in Christian histories of idolatry, though we saw versions in Smith's "History of Astronomy" and Dunbar's *Essays*. He claimed that the religion of the Egyptians reached Europe "by the Phoenicians by sea, and the Pelasgi by land" and that Orpheus the mystagogue, and bearer of Egyptian wisdom, was the "first civilizer of men" in Europe.[21] Monboddo was, like Sir William Jones but not like the enlightened Scots, interested in the practice of aligning gods from different traditions, claiming that the Buddha was clearly a "successor" to the Egyptian ruler-god Osiris in India.[22] Similarly, he was interested in the question of which civilisation was the most ancient and the father of other civilisations. By the final decades of his life, Monboddo believed it was a "fact" that

---

[18] Monboddo (1779–1799, vol. vi pp. 164–65).

[19] Monboddo (1779–1799, vol. vi pp. 164–65).

[20] Monboddo (1779–1799, vol. vi p. 165). For relevant discussion, see Edwards (2021).

[21] Monboddo (1773–1792, vol. i p. 260, p. 445) and Monboddo (1779–1799, vol. i p. xxxi).

[22] Monboddo (1779–1799, vol. iv pp. 309–10).

Chaldean, Babylonian, Chinese, Indian, Greek and even Peruvian civilisations stemmed from an original Egyptian one.[23] One noticeable fact about Monboddo's practice of these forms of research into the history of religion is that he was explicitly engaging with debates going on in England and France amongst antiquarians, philologists, historians of linguistics and mythographers, in a way that firmly distinguished him from his Scottish contemporaries.

Monboddo's Two Accounts of Religion

It is a challenge to piece together a coherent account of Monboddo's belief that religion developed "in the process of time."[24] Partly this is because Monboddo was constantly re-drafting the material that eventually formed the contents of *OPL* and *AM*, which often took the form of discrete and frequently contradictory chapters.[25] Relatedly, Monboddo was declining into decrepitude as he finished the final volumes of *OPL* and especially *AM*, which was evident in the deterioration of his arguments and an increasingly bizarre system of cross-references. Reflecting of his practice of authoring separate essays on similar topics that then were brought together in his published work, in *AM* Monboddo provided both a progressive history of how religions change from savage to civil society and one tying the emergence of religion very firmly to ancient Egypt.

Much of Monboddo's progressive history of religious change was in line with the commonplace theory as found in Smith, Kames, Hume, Robertson, Ferguson and Hutton. An unsophisticated polytheism, informed by anthropomorphic thinking aroused by conditions of scarcity and violence, gradually transformed into a theism inspired by study of the natural world, at least amongst society's priests and philosophers. This

---

[23] Monboddo (1773–1792, vol. i pp. 464–65, vol. ii p. 438). For some useful discussion, see also Trautmann (1997, pp. 80–84).

[24] Monboddo (1779–1799, vol. iv p. 151, p. 367).

[25] If they could convince themselves that it would be worthwhile to work on Monboddo in such depth, a historian could write a really rich study of how Monboddo approached reading, accumilating evidence, note-taking, essay-drafting and composing manuscripts, given the sheer extent of the Monboddo archives at the National Library of Scotland.

process was a consequence of the move into civil society, and developments in civility and the arts and sciences. Two emphases distinguished Monboddo's position a little from this general picture. Inspired by his belief that humans were the same creatures as apes, Monboddo stressed the sheer length of time that passed before the human species developed even the rudiments of thinking. Relatedly, Monboddo was very clear in his delineation of the prior states of mental development, it was necessary for mankind to achieve before they could even begin to comprehend the notion of supernatural power. Language must develop first, then thinking in terms of abstract and general ideas. The "idea of cause and effect," fundamental to even the most basic of primordial polytheisms and so blithely assumed in so many of his contemporaries' theories of religious change, was not an instinctively nor easily achieved idea.[26] The emergence of the notion of immaterial substance, a further step in the development of religious notions, required "great effort" by the "human intellect," given that it required "abstracting from body all its qualities of shape and figure, of solidity and resistance, and even of parts."[27] The notion of immaterial substance required sustained introspection, and the gradual process of "knowing ourselves."[28] It was first achieved, Monboddo claimed, like the "juvenile" Smith, following Aristotle's *Metaphysics*, by the Greek philosopher Anaxagoras. Religion, in this version of Monboddo's theory of religious change, was the result of sustained mental effort, first by primordial and then socialised humans, and eventually by philosophers. This was a theory of religious improvement comparable to the standard enlightened Scottish position.

The second version of Monboddo's theory of religious development was the near-inverse of the first. Monboddo claimed that religious first emerged in a specific location, ancient Egypt, and took the form of a pristine theism that was developed under the guidance of God-sent daemon-kings. His argument here incorporated both diffusionist elements, i.e. that Egyptian religion spread out across the world, and declinist elements, i.e. that ancient Egyptian theism descended into corrupt polytheism until the arrival of Christ. Already in the first volume of *OPL*, Monboddo had claimed that not only did all elements of civilisation come "originally

[26] Monboddo (1779–1799, vol. iii p. 10, vol. iv pp. 64–68).
[27] Monboddo (1779–1799, vol. iv p. 369).
[28] Monboddo (1779–1799, vol. iv p. 100).

from Egypt," but so did the "race of man" itself.[29] The oldest society on historical record, at some point Egyptians moved from the nomadic life to "living by agriculture in cities," with the concomitant development of the rule of law and growth of the arts and sciences.[30] Given that constitutive parts of civilisation—language, civil society, religion, philosophy—were the fruits of sustained activity of many years, only Egyptian civilisation was of sufficient age to account for their emergence.

Some elements of Monboddo's analysis of why ancient Egypt played this world-historical role were informed by standard enlightened Scottish notions of the shift from primitive to civil society. Egypt was the "first country of religion" because it was the first "regular polity."[31] The primitive beliefs of pre-social humans did not warrant the name "religion." The shift to a "well regulated society" was "absolutely necessary" for introducing actual religion "among men."[32] Only in secure polities did a division of labour emerge in which theology could be studied by privileged groups. Whereas his enlightened contemporaries would leave this as a theoretical point, Monboddo sought to identify in history the nation to form the first highly developed civil society. It was clearly Egypt, for reasons Monboddo explained in depth. Egypt benefitted from the outstanding fertility of the Nile delta, and the resulting prosperity enabled the emergence of a caste system headed by a caste of hereditary, leisured priest-philosophers "set apart for the duties of religion, and the cultivation of sciences."[33] Egyptian agriculture was so fecund that no commerce with other nations was required, and thus Egypt escaped the degenerative influence of the influx of luxury goods. Similarly, the size of Egypt's population meant, Monboddo claimed, that wealth was spread out evenly, and the country avoided an elite of very wealthy individuals.

Where Monboddo parted company with his enlightened contemporaries was his belief that the development of Egyptian civilisation was directed by daemons. Once his Egyptomania had taken hold in the final volumes of *OPL* and *AM*, Monboddo claimed that Egypt was the cradle

---

[29] Monboddo (1773–1792, vol. i p. 445).
[30] Monboddo (1779–1799, vol. iii p. iv).
[31] Monboddo (1779–1799, vol. iv p. 373).
[32] Monboddo (1779–1799, vol. iv p. 367).
[33] Monboddo (1779–1799, vol. iii p. iv).

of religion and civilisation because Egypt's first monarchs were daemon-kings, actual "intermediaries betwixt Gods and men."[34] Monboddo did not mean, as Robertson had argued of the Incan rulers' claims to be divine or as was one of the staple explanations in mythographical works examining ancient pagan religion, that the Egyptian kings pretended to be daemons as the best means to get the multitude to do their bidding. He meant that they were daemons. Commentators have conjectured on how Monboddo came to believe in the 1780s and 1790s in the reality of intermediary beings.[35] Whatever might be made of his experiences of visions during bouts of illness, Monboddo's belief in the great chain of being made reports of daemons in ancient Egypt entirely plausible in his worldview. So did travel literature and ancient histories: he found corroborating evidence in accounts of Chinese and Peruvian religious traditions, as well in the reports of ancient authors including Herodotus, Diodorus Siculus and Plutarch. Moreover, Monboddo claimed that the existence of intermediary beings between man and God was also the "doctrine of our scripture as well as of philosophy."[36] Monboddo's credulity when it came to ancient sources, including scripture, and reports in travel literature meant that the existence of intermediary beings was actually a "fact" derived from studying the "History of Mankind."

The appeal to daemonic guidance was a sort of "god of the gaps" argument. The equivalent to an early twenty-first century believer that aliens built the pyramids, the antiquity and development of ancient Egyptian civilisation was incomprehensible to Monboddo without an appeal to some extraordinary series of events. Daemonic intervention in *AM* served a similar purpose in Monboddo's account for religion as it did for his explanation of the origin of language in the final volumes of the *OPL*. In both cases, Monboddo became convinced that the first major leaps from pre-social to social human nature required divine intervention. He abandoned his earlier linguistic polygeneticism, and came to maintain that there was "one language of which all the others on earth are derivates."[37] There were other linguistic monogeneticists publishing the late eighteenth century, but most held that it was impossible to identify

---

[34] Monboddo (1779–1799, vol. iv p. 159).

[35] E.g. Cloyd (1972).

[36] Monboddo (1773–1792, vol. v p. 115).

[37] Monboddo (1779–1799, vol. iv p. 337).

which language was the first given our historical records do not go back to primordial man. Monboddo, by contrast, declared the originator to be Egypt and be explained this arguments by appealing to supernatural intervention.[38] There is an unresolved tension in Monboddo's position: Egypt benefitted from the "intervention of the daemon kings" in first developing language, but Egypt was also the only society of sufficient antiquity in which language could develop.[39] The same tension is present in Monboddo's account on the emergence of religion between the direct intervention of superior intelligences and his belief in the incremental improvement through sustained interaction and effort.[40]

In a sense, Monboddo had contributed his own version of the necessity of revelation argument that we have seen as so prominent amongst the avowedly Christian participants in the Scottish science of human nature. But Monboddo was a distinctly unorthodox Christian and his view on when revelation was disseminated and by who differed entirely with biblical history. The daemon-kings established a *religio duplex* in which a philosopher-priest caste was gradually educated into a "genuine system of theism."[41] Those who became the educated elite in Egypt were the recipients of an admittedly esoteric but ultimately true theism, revealed by supernatural beings on earth. When the era of daemon-kings came to an end, Egypt was left with the arts, sciences and knowledge of philosophy that allowed them to develop the "most perfect system of natural religion that ever was among men."[42] As with Archibald Campbell, Monboddo held that natural religion was built on tenets that were only known via revelation. The Egyptian elite were taught the doctrines of the existence of a supreme creator being; the immortality of an immaterial soul; the great chain of being; and the doctrine of the trinity. It did not include the doctrine of future rewards and punishments, nor those of universal humanism, that is, love of humankind, or of charity. It was Christ's role, subsequently, to divulge these.

The inclusion of the trinity, as one of the revealed tenets of true religion, stands out given that this doctrine was one of the principal targets

---

[38] See also Cloyd (1972, p. 161, p. 168).

[39] Monboddo (1779–1799, vol. iv p. 357).

[40] E.g. (1779–1799 vol. iv, comparing pp. 158–160 and pp. 378–80).

[41] Monboddo (1773–1792, vol. v p. 115).

[42] Monboddo (1779–1799, vol. iv p. 165).

of heterodox Protestantism and freethinking. For Monboddo, it was not a truth "above reason," but played a key role in his understanding of man as microcosm of the universe. The human soul was itself a trinity, constituted by intellectual, animal and vegetable minds. Analogising from our own souls, we infer God to be constituted of being, intelligence and vitality. Noticeably here, the Christian doctrine of the trinity was viewed by Monboddo as one local instance of a core doctrine of an original revealed theism, and one which could be found in other religious traditions across the world. While the trinity was often seen as a mystery held on faith or, as in the case of Kames, a priestly accretion forcing the supplication of reason to blind adherence to the whims of a Catholic hierarchy, to Monboddo it was a truth known to all philosophical and religious traditions and entirely necessary for properly understanding the role of mind in the universe, though revealed to the Egyptians first by their demonic overlords.

In *AM*, Monboddo came to argue that the "Egyptian polity" was the "most perfect of any that ever existed," not least because it provided the best model for the relationship between political and religious authority.[43] Rule first by the daemonic representatives of God on earth, and then by humans living amongst sacred animals, meant Egypt was the "most religions of all nations."[44] The Egyptians "lived with their Gods" and knew the supreme being's will via oracles who provided direct communication with God.[45] The Egyptian theocracy combined a secret theism maintained by a priest-philosopher caste and a popular polytheism suitable to the weakness of the multitude. This arrangement was at the core of the success of Egypt as a polity, along the priest-philosopher caste having the leisure and initial guidance to develop their knowledge of true religion. This caste managed a popular religion framed to inculcate piety, morality and adherence to political authority. The people are "only conversant" with material objects and hence they needed to be directed by "signs and symbols, rites and ceremonies" that appealed to their senses and passions.[46] Monboddo marvelled at accounts of Egyptian "pomps and processes … wonderfully attended by the people," as well as the rule

---

[43] Monboddo (1779–1799, vol. iv p. 213).
[44] Monboddo (1779–1799, vol. iv p. 157).
[45] Monboddo (1779–1799, vol. iv p. 168).
[46] Monboddo (1779–1799, vol. iv p. 172, vol. iv pp. 382–83).

that sacred animals played in keeping the reality of supernatural power in mind for the multitude.[47] The Egyptian people thus knew, and did, what was expected of them. All the errors and terrors of subsequent religions, such as the practices of human sacrifice or persecution of heretics, did not appear in Egypt because of the perfectly pitched quality of its popular religion, and were the result, instead, of a fall away from the methods of this most exemplary society.

Monboddo's views on Egyptian civilisational primacy and superiority, and the role of daemons in both, are clearly only tangentially part of the "science of human nature." It is true that many of arguments were comparable to those of his enlightened Scottish contemporaries. He concluded, like Robertson and Dunbar had done, that only Christianity had the moral message to ensure piety and morality amongst the multitude once the Egyptian model had come apart. But the uniqueness of his position is clear when Monboddo discusses the global transmission of Egyptian religious wisdom, as part of his framing of Egypt as the cradle of civilisation. Egyptian religion spread eastwards and westwards. But without the powerful influence of daemonic rulers, Egyptian religion was corrupted in transmission by the accretion of the new practices of hero-worship and animal sacrifice. The ancient Egyptians had worshipped heroes, Monboddo claimed, as symbolic representations of the attributes of the supreme being. The Greco-Romans, however, worshipped heroes as actual deities—a change which marked the moment when popular religion degenerated into pure idolatry. Monboddo's arguments here were a highly idiosyncratic iteration of the declinist staples of much early modern scholarship on the history of idolatry.

Like Robertson's *Sermon*, Monboddo argued that Christianity arrived just when it was most needed. And, like Dunbar and Robertson, and to an extent Kames, Monboddo viewed Christianity, considered as a system of moral and religious teachings, was an improvement on earlier Egyptian religion due to its superior ability to motivate the multitude through beliefs rather than evidence of divine rule. Following the corruption into ignorant idolatry of Greco-Roman religion, the "happiness of man" required a "better popular religion."[48] Concurrently, the improvements of pagan moral philosophy had spread throughout the multitude,

---

[47] Monboddo (1779–1799, vol. iv p. 166).

[48] Monboddo (1779–1799, vol. iv p. 385).

who would be receptive to Christianity as the "most philosophical religion."[49] The Christian religion combined a philosophical understanding of the "established order of nature and the system of the universe" with the doctrines of love, charity and future rewards and punishments that appealed to the multitude.[50] Monboddo agreed with Robertson that Christianity brought the doctrine of future rewards and punishments into the world, and that this perfected religion insofar as it could fully motivate the multitude. Yet he still predicted that the world was approaching to a cataclysmic collapse, leaving open the option of a second attempt to imitate the perfections of the Egyptian polity.

* * *

Monboddo's "History of Man" was peculiar, not least on religious topics—his writings were characterised, as one contemporary reviewer put it, "the most ludicrous eccentricities of an enthusiastic mind … delivered with all the solemnity of learned discovery, and all the dogmatism of magisterial assertion."[51] Monboddo's discussion of religious change utilised a veritable hodgepodge of methods: conjectural history, philology, mythography, empirical research projects, avowedly credulous use of ancient authorities and appeals to supernatural intervention. He believed the Egyptian chronology over the scripture, yet he positioned his studies in the "History of Mankind" as demonstrating the truth and necessity of Christian moral teachings. His history of the emergence of the notion of supernatural power was entirely contradicted by his account of the establishment of a *prisca theologia* by daemon-rulers in ancient Egypt. In the vein of early modern histories of idolatry and not the "science of human nature," Monboddo traced the transmission of Egyptian religious wisdom out into the rest of the world and viewed the subsequent emergence of religious error in declinist terms uncharacteristic of his enlightened contemporaries. Monboddo was both involved in and criticised the Scottish Enlightenment's conversation over human nature. His account of religion shared family resemblances with both mythography and the "science of human nature." Ultimately, the contribution of Monboddo to our subject is paradoxical and I am loathe to position him

---

[49] Monboddo (1779–1799, vol. iv p. 386).
[50] Monboddo (1779–1799, vol. iv p. 396).
[51] Anon. (1796, p. 18).

straightforwardly as a participant in the Scottish Enlightenment.[52] His accounts of religion, however, do help clarify what was distinct amongst those more straightforwardly enlightened of his contemporaries.

References

Anon. 1796. Article III: Lord Monboddo's Antient Metaphysics. Vol. IV. *The British Critic* 7:11–18.

Berry, Christopher J. 2012. *The Idea of Commercial Society in the Scottish Enlightenment*. Edinburgh: Edinburgh University Press.

Bottin, Francesco. 2015. The Scottish Enlightenment and "Philosophical History". In *Models of the History of Philosophy*, Vol. III: The Second Enlightenment and the Kantian Age, eds. Gregorio Piaia and Giovanni Santinello, 383–472. Dordrecht, NL: Springer.

Cloyd, E.L. 1972. *James Burnett: Lord Monboddo* Oxford: Clarendon Press.

Edwards, Pamela. 2021. From the State of Nature to the Natural State: Transforming the Foundations of Science and Civil Progress in Eighteenth-Century British Political Thought. In *The State of Nature: Histories of an Idea. Volume 6: Histories of European Political and Constitutional Thought*, ed. Mark Somos and Anne Peters, 303–33. Leiden: Brill.

Mills, R.J.W. 2021a. Egyptomania and religion in James Burnett, Lord Monboddo's History of Man'. *History of European ideas* 47:119–139.

———. 2021b. The 'Almost Wilfully Perverse' Lord Monboddo and the Scottish Enlightenment's Science of Human Nature. In *The Scottish Enlightenment: Human Nature, Social Theory and Moral Philosophy*, eds. R. J. W. Mills and Craig Smith, 49–70. Edinburgh: Edinburgh University Press.

Monboddo, Lord, James Burnett. 1773–1792. *The Origin and Progress of Language*. 6 vols. Edinburgh.

———. 1779–1799. *Antient Metaphysics*. 6 vols. Edinburgh.

Sebastiani, Silva. 2013. *The Scottish Enlightenment: Race, Gender, and the Limits of Progress*. Trans. Jeremy Carden. Basingstoke: Palgrave.

———. 2022. Monboddo's 'Ugly Tail': The Question of Evidence in Enlightenment Sciences of Man. *History of European Ideas* 48:45–65.

Trautmann, Thomas R. 1997. *Aryans and British India*. London: University of California Press.

Wokler, Robert. 1988. Apes and Races in the Scottish Enlightenment: Monboddo and Kames on the Nature of Man. In *Philosophy and Science in the Scottish Enlightenment*, ed. Peter Jones, 145–68. Edinburgh: Donald.

Wood, Paul B. 1990. The Natural History of Man in the Scottish Enlightenment. *History of Science* 18:89–123.

---

[52] Compare Mills (2021b) and Sebastiani (2022).

CHAPTER 13

The Radicalism of James Hutton

Abstract James Hutton's three-volume *Principles of Knowledge and the Progress of Reason* (1794) was one of the last works of the High Scottish Enlightenment. Hutton maintained an optimistic deism and a belief in the forthcoming triumph of philosophy. The *Progress* contained a radical theory of religious improvement that positioned philosophers as the pioneers and purveyors of truth and dismissed theology and theologians as sources of ignorance and error. The extent to which philosophers were free to develop their intellectual faculties and accumulate knowledge about the world framed the extent to which all society develops its understanding of true religion. In this Hutton had more in common with revolutionary French theories of religious development that he did his Scottish contemporaries.

Keywords James Hutton · David Hume · Philosophical improvement · Enlightenment deism · Superstition · Philosopher-rulers

Contemporaneous to Monboddo's account was another of the Scottish Enlightenment's forgotten theories of religious change, that found in the last volume of James Hutton's (1726–1797) three-volume *Principles of*

© The Author(s), under exclusive license to Springer Nature Switzerland AG 2023
R. J. W. Mills, *Religion and the Science of Human Nature in the Scottish Enlightenment*, https://doi.org/10.1007/978-3-031-49031-6_13

Knowledge and the Progress of Reason (1794).[1] Like his friend Monboddo, Hutton's position set him apart from the enlightened mainstream, though for opposing reasons. As one of the last works of the High Scottish Enlightenment, the *Progress* also brings us full circle with its imitation of Hume's stated goal in the *Treatise* of ascertaining "the principles upon which our reasoning must be founded in every science," including theology.[2] But while Hume alternated between optimism and pessimism over any decline in the social power of priests and theology, Hutton maintained an optimistic deism and belief in the forthcoming triumph of philosophy. The *Progress* contained a radical theory of religious improvement that positioned philosophers as the pioneers and purveyors of truth and dismissed theology and theologians as sources of ignorance and error. The extent to which philosophers were free to develop their intellectual faculties and accumulate knowledge about the world framed the extent to which a society develops its understanding of true religion. What philosophers ultimately learnt was that it was the "benevolent intention of the first cause" to guide humankind towards action conducive to their individual happiness and pious behaviour towards their god.[3] And it was philosophers, rather than theologians, who were to act as our guides.

The end point of religious progress, for Hutton, was the replacement of theologians with philosophers. The boldness of Hutton's deism did not go unnoticed amongst his contemporaries. Monboddo had written to John Hope in April 1779 that Hutton had "no historical faith at all" and was dismissive of ancient religious traditions.[4] Samuel Taylor Coleridge, hoping to find the *Principles* to be the atheistic treatise its was reported to be, found Hutton to be a "profoundly pious Deist."[5] Hutton's lengthy work has not been given much status by historians of the Scottish Enlightenment who, understandably, have been far more interested in his contribution to geology. Hutton's *Theory of the Earth* (1795) was a major advancement in European scientific understanding. By contrast,

---

[1] For an overview see Jones (1984).

[2] Hutton (1794, vol. i, p. x). On Hutton's geology see Dean (1992) and for his contemporary influence see the useful if bad-tempered Şengör (2020). For Hutton's views on history see also Şengör (2001).

[3] Hutton (1794, vol. i, p. xxxii).

[4] Knight (1900, p. 107).

[5] Samuel Taylor Coleridge to John Thelwall, 22 June 1796, Coleridge (1895, vol. i, p. 167).

the *Principles*' small print run of only 250 suggested limited contemporary interest. Moreover, as Coleridge wrote on the title page of his copy, Hutton's work "loses itself in its own enormous house, in the wilderness of the multitudinous chambers and passages."[6] Adam Ferguson would opine that Hutton's writing style was "obscure, unintelligible, and dry."[7] Examining Hutton's *Principles*, however, helps us reach a more fully rounded understanding of his deism—one that looks forward to a new age of philosopher-led societies, rather than one examining the origins of the earth without recourse to scripture. Hutton's deism contributes to the sense that while the "science of human nature" practised during the High Scottish Enlightenment should be viewed as contributing to a religious Enlightenment in Scotland, it cannot be straightforwardly described as medium for Christian Enlightenment. Moreover, Hutton was a firm believer in religious progress, holding for a more linear trajectory towards the triumph of philosophy than any other author of the period.

Philosophers and the Science of Religion

Religion was a subtopic within Hutton's larger study of the "proper end of science and the means of happiness."[8] The study of religion had the "object" of discovering the "will of God, so far as relates to the conduct of mankind," an object which must treated "scientifically" and therefore "necessarily requires philosophy" (and never "theology," a term which Hutton did not use).[9] This goal meant that "religion and philosophy" were "commutable," and that "to study religion is to study philosophy."[10] This involved setting aside superstition and using only the methods of observation and experience, to draw out the general laws of nature and then working out the proper application of those laws. The result was learning that "man acts according to the will of God when he

---

[6] Coleridge (1969, vol. xii, part 2, p. 1204).

[7] Ferguson (2023, p. 188). Ferguson also claimed that Hutton read few, if any, books other than works of travel literature.

[8] Hutton (1794, vol. i, title page).

[9] Hutton (1794, vol. iii, pp. 629, 633).

[10] Hutton (1794, vol. iii, p. 629).

makes himself happy, in the progress of his wisdom, and in pursuing the rules of virtue with a philosophic patience."[11]

Hutton wrote confidently of how modern philosophy had advanced our religious knowledge, though his argument is hard to follow. The first cause and design arguments required thinking that involved "proof or principle," of the sort that had only been properly understood in recent years.[12] The first cause argument was "unique" because the "proposition and its contrary are both inconceivable." Because the human mind cannot "conceive an event to happen without a cause," it struggles to understand that the "first cause is no event, but has been always, and will be without end."[13] We cannot reject the proof on the grounds that we have no knowledge of the first cause, as we have no knowledge of the opposite conclusion of infinity either. We can, however, infer that the first cause is "absolute, self-existing, efficient and final."[14] More importantly, we can infer the existence of God from the "beauty, order, wisdom and design" evident in the universe, demonstrated by recent advancements in natural philosophy.[15]

Just as with progress in natural religion, Hutton argued that only recently had philosophy come to understand true morality, in the form of providential utilitarianism. The science of human nature taught that God framed us to be happy if we fulfil our natures and unhappy if we do not. Virtue is whatever make us happy, and vice is what makes us unhappy. This was a deistic version of morality. God does not judge our actions, and we do not undertaken actions to please God. Pain and misery are not signs of divine punishment but are indicators that we are acting in opposition to our nature. True philosophy understands that "vicious" behaviour is really foolish behaviour, resulting from "want of wisdom sufficient to avoid evil," with "evil" a descriptor of purely human origin for whatever causes unhappiness.[16] The philosopher knows that there is "no absolute evil in the constitution of things."[17]

---

[11] Hutton (1794, vol. iii, p. 630).
[12] Hutton (1794, vol. iii, pp. 651, 656).
[13] Hutton (1794, vol. iii, p. 134).
[14] Hutton (1794, vol. iii, p. 136).
[15] Hutton (1794, vol. iii, pp. 651, 656).
[16] Hutton (1794, vol. iii, p. 633).
[17] Hutton (1794, vol. iii, p. 623).

Hutton claimed that religious knowledge was learnt by philosophy alone, holding that philosophy and superstition are "diametrically opposite to each other."[18] Hutton, however, defined "superstition" in a way different to his contemporaries' definition of fear-driven erroneous belief about supernatural power. Rather, "superstition" referred to all unthinking practices of submitting to authority, including religious authority. These included receiving "maxims by faith," "trusting to the veracity of an informing mind" and believing claims based on "authority which has not been examined."[19] Hutton's unsubtle insinuation was that these were all aspects of priestly teaching to the laity. True religious knowledge was to be gained by philosophers independently pursuing their own lines of inquiry. Philosophers would learn about God by "reading his word," but the book they were reading was the book of nature and not the book of scripture.[20] It was also a task that they alone could undertake, for the will of God had not been communicated in the "language of men," by which Hutton meant the language of common sense, but in that of philosophy.[21]

Hutton's homologation of religion and philosophy leads him to justify a benign form of *religio duplex*. "True worship of the deity" consists in the "proper culture of the mind," and such culturation occurs best when "man is taught philosophy."[22] "Mankind in general" does not "consist of theoretical philosophers," and thus knowledge of true religion will always be beyond them.[23] Piety and "civic virtue" can be encouraged amongst the multitude, however, if philosophers develop "practical" policies that get the people to behave according the principles of a true religion they cannot understand.[24] Recent improvements in natural philosophy must be rendered intelligible to the vulgar and philosophers must replace priests as moral educators of the laity.[25] If "philosophy properly conducts the

---

[18] Hutton (1794, vol. iii, p. 621).
[19] Hutton (1794, vol. iii, p. 286; vol. ii, p. 621).
[20] Hutton (1794, vol. ii, p. 113).
[21] Hutton (1794, vol. ii, p. 113).
[22] Hutton (1794, vol. iii, p. 634).
[23] Hutton (1794, vol. iii, p. 626).
[24] Hutton (1794, vol. iii, p. 622).
[25] Hutton (1794, vol. iii, p. 626).

faith of mankind," there will follow "nothing but the happiest effects."[26] This included a replacement of civil theology with civil philosophy, in which the "power and administration of the state was conjoined to wisdom and philosophy."[27]

Only those with "enlightened views of science" were capable of genuine piety, because only they could see the evidence of benevolent design in the world.[28] Philosophers, however, should take responsibility to encourage piety amongst the laity. Hutton defined piety as a "frame of mind" of holding God in the "highest esteem."[29] Nearly all systems of religion had promulgated ridiculous notions of piety, in which worshippers sought to appease or solicit favour from a vengeful deity. But it was sheer impiety to believe that God was influenced by such behaviour or that we should act out of self-interest when worshipping. Philosophy, by contrast, taught that God was a wise and benevolent being who inspires love and veneration. One of the tasks for philosophers was to communicate this religious knowledge as accessibly as possible to the multitude. Hutton envisioned the not-too-distant future as being one in which philosophers regulated religions principle and practice and worship would be "freed from all absurdity" and would "strictly conform to nature," rather than being framed, as in systems of civil theology, to manipulate the multitude in the interests of priest and prince.[30] Quaintly, Hutton believed that philosopher-educators would be motivated by nothing more than their love of wisdom and would be dedicated in their task to raise the consciousness of wider society, a new caste of pious, virtuous individuals to bring true religion where superstitious priests have failed.

Hutton set out a strident deism uncharacteristic of the High Scottish Enlightenment, going beyond even the deistic tones of Kames's discussion of religion. To Hutton, philosophers alone teach religion to the multitude. Revealed religion has no positive role, though it still can be useful in helping to package up complicated ideas in forms intelligible to the generality of humankind. The will of God is learnt by

---

[26] Hutton (1794, vol. iii, p. 627).
[27] Hutton (1794, vol. iii, p. 635).
[28] Hutton (1794, vol. iii, p. 645).
[29] Hutton (1794, vol. iii, p. 642).
[30] Hutton (1794, vol. iii, p. 618).

"studying nature or the constitution of things," and not by any "supernatural knowledge of the divine will."[31] While "common sense" thinking in a society tended to accept the "received religion" as the "only true religion," religious knowledge is found only in the knowledge of "intellectual and material systems," by which Hutton meant our understanding of human nature and natural philosophy, and is understood by man "in proportion only as he perfects his philosophy."[32] Hutton did not reject revelation entirely, but stressed that the "purity of a received religion" was to be judged by philosophers, according to the standards of natural philosophy, and not vice versa.[33] If the theological and moral content of revelation fails the test of philosophical scrutiny, then it is either faked or corrupted. If it has been corrupted, and Hutton seemed to think most revealed religion was corrupted, philosophy was the "only means" by which it could be corrected.[34] Hutton's bold overall conclusion was that "no other system" bar philosophy informs us of the "will of God," and that the gradual spread of philosophy will lead to the end of religious diversity and shared awareness of the one true religion.

HUTTON ON THE NATURAL PROGRESS OF RELIGION

Hutton charted the progress of religion from primitive polytheism via civil theology through to civil philosophy. His account differs from the others discussed in this book by the sheer explanatory weight given to the power of philosophy. The philosopher is clearly the hero of human history and the human agent who will bring to a close the process of removing priestly authority from religion, that began, somewhat unintentionally, with the Reformation. Hutton opened his progressive history with an account of religion in the "savage state" as an unsophisticated polytheism that restated the commonplaces of enlightened Scottish theories of religion.[35] This primordial polytheism, characterised by instinctive anthropomorphic judgements about natural events, developed into a formalised polytheism, characterised by specific beliefs about specific spirits. This occurred with

---

[31] Hutton (1794, vol. iii, p. 637).

[32] Hutton (1794, vol. iii, p. 637).

[33] Hutton (1794, vol. iii, p. 651).

[34] Hutton (1794, vol. iii, p. 652).

[35] Hutton (1794, vol. iii, p. 617).

the shift from savagery to barbarism, or the stage of the first "established order and government among men," in which "more enlarged or general views of nature" were now possible, though this did not prevent absurd rituals and violent sacrifice.[36]

Further progress towards religious truth occurs when science and philosophy are "properly pursued."[37] Framing this progress as the gradual and ongoing achievement of philosophers, Hutton was more interested in discussing the fetters on philosophical inquiry, which prevent progress. One group of limitations related to existing systems of superstition. It is the inevitable consequence of the pursuit of knowledge that the gains of philosophy exist in an admixture with pre-existing superstitious beliefs. Improvement is never pure, and philosophers are always battling with the backward elements in contemporary thought. Similarly, the "national religion," which Hutton means the superstitious religion of the multitude, is always at odds with the "religion of the learned," leading to antagonism between the two groups, and a constant source of threat to the latter.[38] The antagonism between the religion of the multitude and of the learn has been a "source of irreligion," resulting in Pyrrhonian scepticism on the one hand and superstitious bigotry on the other.[39] In terms of the former, the "corrupt" quality of popular religion encourages atheism, because "men of loose morals" use it as an excuse to doubt everything "without evidence or examination."[40] In terms of the latter, philosophers are under constant threat of being persecuted by bigots who mistake the philosophers' pursuit of the truth as atheism or irreligion.[41]

Philosophers were fettered in their pursuit of the truth by priesthoods and by would-be philosophers. Priesthoods created an unholy alliance with political authority to create civil theologies that perverted the course

[36] Hutton (1794, vol. iii, p. 662).

[37] Hutton (1794, vol. iii, p. 619).

[38] Hutton (1794, vol. iii, p. 634). It is perhaps significant that several of the more heterodox thinkers amongst the Scottish Enlightenment—in this case Hume, Smith, Hutton and Kames—all worried about mob violence towards the learned, in a way that the more orthodox did not. This fear informed their understanding of the origin of dual religions, with an emphasis on the protective quality of much esoteric and exoteric religion.

[39] Hutton (1794, vol. iii, p. 634).

[40] Hutton (1794, vol. iii, p. 622).

[41] Hutton (1794, vol. iii, p. 621).

of human history. Priests had appeared almost concurrently with the emergence of man's belief he could influence the gods. Through the "arts of divination" and access to "pretend revelation," "crafty" priests "ingrafted" onto the "natural superstition of mankind" additional "artificial superstition," which served to subordinate the people to the priests.[42] Priests did so in partnership with political rulers who believe it to be wise "civil policy" to utilise "superstition for the purpose of imposing obedience to social laws."[43] The tragedy of this development was that morality was conflated with the dictates of false religion, and both were limited to obedience to political authority. When the superstitious control the "reigns of government," they extend a "despotic empire over the mind of man."[44] The damaging effects of systems of superstition are manifold but fundamentally they serve to turn the individual—"by nature innocent" and "ignorant of vice"—into a vicious, violent and terrible creature.[45]

Aside from the alliance of priest and prince, philosophers were also prevented from securing control of religion by the presence within society of a "third order of men" who jostled for authority with them. This group sat between the multitude and the philosophers, being men who cannot philosophise properly and yet assume the "right of forming principles" based on their own admixtures of superstition and philosophy.[46] They pit themselves as rivals to philosophers, and desire political power and social standing. Their combination of intelligence and mercenary desires mean they are capable of aggravating "among the rest of mankind ... the greatest zeal and bigotry in their persuasions and the utmost violence and atrocity in their persuasions."[47] Hutton does not clarify the social or professional identity of this group but, as we will see, it matches his subsequent description of Catholic theologians.

---

[42] Hutton (1794, vol. iii, p. 618).
[43] Hutton (1794, vol. iii, p. 618).
[44] Hutton (1794, vol. iii, p. 627).
[45] Hutton (1794, vol. iii, p. 628).
[46] Hutton (1794, vol. iii, p. 636).
[47] Hutton (1794, vol. iii, p. 637).

The Alignment of "Christianity" and Philosophy

Hutton ended his discussion of the relationship between philosophy and religion by offering a broad overview of the Judaeo-Christian tradition, much like Kames' provided in his *Sketches*. And, like Kames, Hutton reached the conclusion that Christianity, or at least a specific vision of Christianity, is in line with true philosophy. The discussion subjected "our religion" to the test of philosophical scrutiny, a necessary step since unthinking adherence to received tradition turns us into a "brute animal" repeating worship we have been "trained to perform."[48] Hutton claimed that Christianity passed the test of philosophy, but his version of the religion was stripped of its supernatural content and left philosophy, not scripture, as the ultimate source of truth. Moreover, the motive force behind religious improvement in recent centuries was not a return to primitive Christianity, but that of freely pursued philosophy. Hutton heavily implied both the inadequacy of revelation-based religions, not least because they were not able to replicate themselves due to the superstitious qualities of human nature, and the complete independence and superiority of modern philosophy from past systems of religion.

Both Judaism and Christianity were quickly corrupted by the influence of priestcraft. The ancient Hebrew faith was a cruel, superstitious and idolatrous national religion until it was transformed according to the "light of science" and "philosophical principle."[49] Hutton does not expand upon this claim—as to whether, say, Moses was a philosopher or the recipient of revelation containing philosophical truths—but did stress that the Hebrews were the first to acknowledge theism. The Hebrew's "reformed" religion maintained that God made man "after his own image," and that man's purpose was acting virtuously and avoiding vice.[50] As reported in scripture itself, Hebraic theism was quickly overwhelmed by "false opinions, unwarrantable rights, and … improper worship."[51] The same process of philosophy's advance and retreat occurred with the emergence of Christianity. This was a "true religion" of "gratitude, love and harmony," built on the "rational principles of human nature," required "no metaphysical reasoning" and was "adapted to the common

---

[48] Hutton (1794, vol. iii, p. 660).
[49] Hutton (1794, vol. iii, p. 663).
[50] Hutton (1794, vol. iii, p. 664).
[51] Hutton (1794, vol. iii, p. 664).

understanding of mankind."[52] Here, Christ is a moral philosopher. The purity of early Christianity was short lived, and it was corrupted by the rise of barbarism, the establishment of a priestly "hierarchy" and the decline of the standing of philosophy.[53] It is clear that the Catholic priesthood were examples of Hutton's "third order of men," assuming over early Christianity "authority and power noways falling to their share."[54] This priesthood brought bigotry, ignorance and superstition, and it was testament to the "beauty of the pure religion" that theism survived despite the best efforts of Catholic clerics.[55]

The core factor driving forward the corruption of Christianity was the priests' practice of developing "speculative opinions" on theological topics, without the philosophical knowhow to do so properly.[56] Yet because the speculative approach could not answer the major questions of theology, priests resorted to the disastrous step of explaining away what they did not understand by appeals to "miracle and mystery."[57] This made them the "greatest enemies of mankind," because the introduction of mystery perverted religion away from its true grounding in philosophy.[58] The record of priestly rule had been of utter catastrophe, and resulted in the emergence of atheism and irreligion. Things had only improved since the Reformation, as philosophers began recapturing some control of religion, but the process of further liberating philosophy must continue. The boldly deistic conclusion that Hutton drew from his sketch of Judaeo-Christian history was that philosophers "alone must judge" in religious matters as they are the only ones "capable of making a reformation" to towards true religion. Humankind "should be distinguished" into "two sorts:" philosophers and everyone else.[59] Again, somewhat naively, philosophers would not cut their religion with bigotry,

---

[52] Hutton (1794, vol. iii, p. 665).
[53] Hutton (1794, vol. iii, p. 666).
[54] Hutton (1794, vol. iii, p. 669).
[55] Hutton (1794, vol. iii, p. 667).
[56] Hutton (1794, vol. iii, p. 667).
[57] Hutton (1794, vol. iii, p. 668).
[58] Hutton (1794, vol. iii, p. 668).
[59] Hutton (1794, vol. iii, p. 702).

intolerance, superstition, supernatural explanation and appeals to either revelation or mercenary self-interest. Hutton's philosophers, in terms of their entirely pure and virtuous motivations, have an almost superhuman, indeed, *messianic*, quality about them.

* * *

Hutton's account of religious progress is strikingly confident in the world-historical role of philosophy and philosophers to liberate humankind from superstition, and its correlate attacks on theology and (Catholic) theologians. In the *Progress of Reason*, Hutton discusses an ongoing battle for authority between superstition and philosophy in which the heroic philosophers, presumably including men like Hutton, were finally gaining the upper hand. In this, Hutton was treading in Hume's footsteps in wishing for a wholesale transformation of the standing of philosophy. But unlike Hume, Hutton believed this was happening, rather than being a distant goal. And, unlike Hume, Hutton believed that philosophy taught something more extensive than a minimal theism, and that this knowledge meant they should take control of religion as a social institution. Hutton did not position his argument explicitly as anti-Christian, but the implications of his account are clear. Philosophers should not rely upon authority and should subordinate scripture to their judgement, whereas theologians are implied to be proponents of superstition. Christ taught the basics of morality and nothing more and certainly did not die to save humankind.

Scholarship on Hutton's religious thought is bedevilled, like that on many of the figures in this book, by the unanswerable question of what he *really* believed. A few scholars have suggested that Hutton used the techniques of esoteric writing to avoid charges of outright atheism. This is often based on the internal contradictions of both Hutton's *Theory* and *Principles*, where his arguments are seen as directly undermining any belief in a divine order to nature.[60] But what is not in doubt is that Hutton was not a traditional Christian by any means. Moreover, in the *Principles*, he moved further towards explicit deism. Hutton is known to have abandoned a preface written in 1785 to initial publication of the *Theory of the Earth* (1788), in which he asserted the absolute independence and superiority of natural philosophy over revelation for

---

[60] E.g. Şengör (2001, esp. pp. 20–22).

understanding the natural world.[61] He had been encouraged to tone down his arguments by his friend William Robertson, who drafted a milder preface more palatable to Scotland's clergy. But if in 1785 Hutton would claim that natural philosophy was of "equal authority with that of revelation," by 1794 he was arguing more explicitly that revelation had to be judged by philosophy.[62] By the criteria set by his earlier preface, Hutton's *Principles* was "impious."[63] He now did not hide the deistic implications of arguments beneath anything but the thinnest veneer of Christian orthodoxy, even if he avoided the direct provocations of Hume. His account of the progress of religion is characterised by an optimism and linearity not found amongst the other authors of the High Scottish Enlightenment. As such, our sense of Hutton's deism must not only include his setting aside of biblical chronology but also his progressive history of religious change resulting from the gradual emergence of philosophy at the expense of superstition and theology, climaxing with the hoped-for cultural rule of philosophers over the rest of mankind.

REFERENCES

Coleridge, Samuel Taylor. 1895. *Letters of Samuel Taylor Coleridge*, ed. Ernest Hartley Coleridge, 2 vols. New York.

———. 1969. *The Collected Works of Samuel Taylor Coleridge. Volume 12: Marginalia. Part 2: From Camden to Hutton*. Princeton, NJ: Princeton University Press.

Dean, Dennis R. 1992. *James Hutton and the History of Geology*. Ithaca, NY: Cornell University Press.

Ferguson, Adam. 2023. Minutes of the Life and Character of Joseph Black. In *Adam Ferguson's Later Writings*, ed. Ian Stewart and Max Skjönsberg, 173–189. Edinburgh: Edinburgh University Press.

Hutton, James. 1794. *Principles of Knowledge and the Progress of Reason*, 3 vols. Edinburgh.

Jones, Peter. 1984. An Outline of the Philosophy of James Hutton. In *Philosophers of the Scottish Enlightenment*, ed. Vincent Hope. Edinburgh: Edinburgh University Press.

---

[61] Reproduced in Dean (1992, pp. 19–21) with William Robertson's suggested alternative text at pp. 22–23.

[62] Dean (1992, p. 20).

[63] Dean (1992, p. 20).

Knight, William. 1900. *Lord Monboddo and Some of His Contemporaries*. London: John Murray.

Şengör, A.M.C. 2001. Is the Present the Key to the Past or Is the Past the Key to the Present? James Hutton and Adam Smith Versus Abraham Gottlob Werner and Karl Max in Interpreting History. *Geological Society of America: Special Papers* 355: 1–52.

———. 2020. Revising the Revisions: James Hutton's Reputation Among Geologists in the Late Eighteenth and Nineteenth Centuries. *Geological Society of America Memoirs* 16. https://doi.org/10.1130/MWR216 [Accessed on 21 December 2022].

CHAPTER 14

Dugald Stewart, Religion and the End of the "Science of Human Nature"

Abstract Our final study examines one of early nineteenth-century Europe's foremost moral philosophers, Dugald Stewart (1753–1828), who sort to defend the legacy of Scottish Enlightenment philosophy. In his writings on religious topics, Stewart aimed to defuse the irreligious elements of Hume's analysis by showing how study of religious diversity and development confirmed the existence of God. Stewart accepted the standard emphasis on the primacy of polytheism, and the role of civil society, philosophy and education in bringing about religious development. He put this common picture to natural theological use and brushed off the disconcerting inferences about the naturalness of religion raised by Hume. In doing so, Stewart repeatedly aligned himself with the late seventeenth and early eighteenth-century English tradition of natural theology.

Keywords Dugald Stewart · David Hume · Religious innatism · Natural theology · Religious diversity · Primitive polytheism

Our final authorial study examines one of early nineteenth-century Europe's foremost moral philosophers, Dugald Stewart (1753–1828), who took on the role on defending the legacy of Scottish Enlightenment philosophy.[1] His framing of that legacy still informs current scholarship, including a definition of conjectural history that has constrained interpretations of the Scots' religious theory. Stewart's account of religious change and diversity can be taken as his attempt to provide an authoritative interpretation on the discussion of his enlightened predecessors. Stewart's attempts in the *Philosophy of the Active and Moral Powers of Man* (1828) to answer the "historical question" "concerning the priority of monotheism or of polytheism" epitomised the approach of the Scottish "science of human nature."[2] The question was not to be adjudicated on the basis of available traditionary accounts about the first societies, but on the basis of inferences drawn from an understanding of primitive man drawn from the findings of the enlightened study of human nature. Stewart aimed to defuse the irreligious elements of Hume's analysis by showing how the study of this question actually helped confirm the existence of God. Stewart accepted the standard enlightened Scottish account of the primacy of polytheism, and the role of civil society, philosophy and education in bringing about religious development. He put this common picture to natural theological use and brushed off the possible disconcerting inferences about the naturalness of religion raised by Hume's account. In doing so, Stewart repeatedly aligned himself with the late seventeenth and early eighteenth-century English tradition of natural theology. The final significant contribution to the application of the "science of human nature" to religion thus reiterated the common arguments of anti-atheist apologetic that preceded the Scottish Enlightenment.

Stewart's return to the staple proofs of early modern natural theology is an anticlimactic end to our survey of the enlightened Scottish discussion of religion. His motivation was a strong sense of profound threats to the social order, from the "inundation of sceptical [and] atheistical publications" crossing over from Revolutionary France to those Scottish divines who wished to "set at nought the evidences of natural religion" because they believed this defended the necessity of Revelation.[3] The

---

[1] On Stewart see Macintyre (2003) and, especially, Bow (2022). I am grateful to Dr Bow for letting me read his book in manuscript. See also Bow (2018).

[2] Stewart (1854–1860, vol. vii, p. 77).

[3] Stewart (1854–1860, vol. vi, p. 112).

past century had been marked by the twin evils of triumphant sceptical philosophy and a "credulity so extraordinary" that the numbers of "visionaries and imposters" was at a level higher than any since the "revival of letters," nothing less than a threatened end of Enlightenment itself.[4] In walking the "steady course of inquiry between implicit credulity and unlimited scepticism" in the *Active and Moral Powers*, Stewart would argue for the truths of natural religion on the basis of a re-assertion of the arguments from universal consent.[5]

The principal philosophical challenge, however, came not from French atheists but from David Hume. In his earlier *Elements of the Philosophy of the Human Mind* (1792), Stewart had claimed that Hume's procedure of weakening the "authority" of religious belief by emphasising the "endless variety of forms" was an "employment unsuitable to the dignity of philosophy."[6] In *Active and Moral Powers*, Stewart substantiated his criticism of Hume's interpretation of the meaning of religious diversity. He politely set aside his former tutor Adam Ferguson's critique of Hume in Ferguson's *Moral and Political Science*, on the grounds it was unpersuasive to argue for the primacy of monotheism. While accepting Hume's arguments for the priority of polytheism, Stewart criticised how Hume had analysed religious diversity and argued instead that beneath superficial difference was the universal belief in God.

Stewart's account of our ability to develop religious belief stressed the role of curiosity, a more benign principle than fear. Knowledge of the existence of God was not an "intuitive truth" nor an "immediate object of human perception," but a "natural and spontaneous growth of man's intellectual and moral constitution."[7] Humanity's natural curiosity about the world and futurity would gradually lead to "contemplation of the infinite perfections of the deity," should the individual choose and able to make "proper use" of their faculties.[8] The idea of God "forces itself irresistibly" onto any "serious and reflecting mind," but

---

[4] Stewart (1854–1860, vol. ii, p. 321).

[5] Stewart (1854–1860, vol. ii, pp. 70–71).

[6] Stewart (1854–1860, vol. ii, p. 321) referring to NHR 115. For a deeper dive into Stewart's engagement with Ferguson and Hume see Mills (2018).

[7] Stewart (1854–1860, vol. vi, p. 46, vol. vii, p. 92 and vol. ii, p. 158).

[8] Stewart (1854–1860, vol. vii, p. 191, 91).

does not do so on the minds of the "thoughtless and inconsiderate."[9] Echoing Smith's "History of Astronomy" essay, which he edited, Stewart claimed the motive force behind improvement of religious notions was human nature's "principle of curiosity," which made people "inquire more anxiously about distant and singular phenomena."[10]

In the *Elements*, and uniquely for the enlightened Scots discussed in this book, Stewart explained the different origins of "genuine religion" and superstition in a pedagogical rather than progressive context. What type of religious belief an individual developed depended on whether they were educated under the "regulation of an enlightened understanding" or the "influences of prejudices and a diseased imagination."[11] Humans are apt to see a "constancy of conjunction" between events in close proximity but which have no actual connection, rendering life a "series of absurd terrors."[12] The liveliness of these notions act as proof to the young mind that what they represent is real. A teacher or parent must prevent these notions from becoming "steady and habitual" by guarding the child from representations of "spectres and demons, and invisible scenes of horror."[13] The young should only be given images which inspire "just and elevated notions" of the order of nature.[14]

In *Active and Moral Powers*, Stewart shifted the context of religious development to one of long durée historical change. What was different about Stewart's analysis was his stress that the priority of polytheism and the existence of religious diversity were not challenges to theism. To Stewart, Ferguson had argued against all historical and ethnological evidence when he claimed polytheism emerged as a corruption of an initial theism. Stewart accepted, instead, Hume's claim in the NHR that polytheism was the religion of those living in the "infancy of reason and experience," and that theism was "slow result" of improvements in philosophy.[15] The "historical question" of the first religion of mankind was answered by the "prevalence of polytheism" in the ancient world.

---

[9] Stewart (1854–1860, vol. vii, p. 90, 91).
[10] Stewart (1854–1860, vol. ii, p. 188).
[11] Stewart (1854–1860, vol. ii, p. 158).
[12] Stewart (1854–1860, vol. ii, p. 310).
[13] Stewart (1854–1860, vol. ii, p. 157).
[14] Stewart (1854–1860, vol. ii, p. 158, vol. vii, p. 322).
[15] Stewart (1854–1860, vol. vii, p. 79, 78).

The unchristian implications of Stewart's position—that he was rejecting the status of the Bible as a source that took precedence over all others for understanding the history of humankind—were left unstated. When revelation did enter into Stewart's account, it was as a force driving latter polytheistic peoples towards theism.

Stewart was not concerned by the argument in the NHR for the historical primacy of polytheism, but he was concerned by Hume's insinuations that no positive relationship existed between human nature and religion. The priority of polytheism did not justify the "suggestions of scepticism."[16] Hume's identification of the first religion of mankind, but his analysis of the meaning of this was wrongheaded. For Stewart, Hume drew a series of questionable distinctions that undermined the arguments that (a) religion was natural and that this naturalness was proof of its truth and (b) humanity was moving towards improved religious notions under the influence of philosophy. Hume had distinguished between popular theism and true theism; between the henotheism of the pagan philosopher and true theism; and held a rigorist definition of true religion as consisting only in minimal theism. Stewart rejected these distinctions, restated the providentialist naturalist's view on man's inherent religiosity and claimed that religious diversity did not undermine the arguments from the *consensus gentium* and *consensus sapientium*. As we will see, he did so primarily by loosening Hume's definition of "religion." Stewart also rejected Hume's argument that the move from polytheism to theism was the primarily the result of the workings of passions of hope and fear.

Humanity was progressing towards religious enlightenment on a trajectory set by providence but achieved via the practice of philosophical inquiry. The progress from polytheism to theism was the "slow result" of the expansion and improvement of "philosophical views of the universe." The "mind of the uncultivated savage" and that of the "enlightened citizen" were the same: the difference was the context in which individuals lived.[17] Knowledge of the existence of a deity was "entirely the result of observation and experiment" and developed only after lengthy periods of investigation undertaken by philosophers with leisure time living in stable societies.[18] Praising the achievements of recent natural philosophy,

---

[16] Stewart (1854–1860, vol. vii, p. 89).

[17] Stewart (1854–1860, vol. vii, p. 75, 321).

[18] Stewart (1854–1860, vol. vii, p. 12).

Stewart celebrated how "new light is continually breaking in upon us from every quarter."[19] Briefly and weakly, Stewart also suggested that religious progress was aided by the "light of divine revelation." The "idolatrous tendency of the uninformed understanding" was rectified by the dissemination of revelation.[20]

The alignment of these two competing trajectories—gradual philosophical progress and moments of divine revelation—sat uneasily in Stewart's account. Unlike Archibald Campbell or William Robertson, Stewart did not stress the importance of revelation for granting knowledge of key doctrines that would be otherwise unknown. He claimed that revelation was as uninformative on the question of the immortality of the soul and its future rewards and punishments as reason. Stewart mentioned in passing that revelation could provide reassuring messages on the question of why evil exists, before his own exploration of the issue. Similarly brief was his claim that revelation was an important factor in bringing early polytheists towards the light of theism. The briefness of all these claims in what was essentially a university textbook suggests Stewart included them for the sake of keeping up appearances.

Stewart also clearly demarcated religious progress from socio-economic progress. Whatever the recent achievements of natural philosophy, the move into urban, commercial societies encouraged irreligion. Stewart's line here was different to Smith's fear about religious fanaticism or Gregory's stress on the baleful influence of luxury. For Stewart, people living in cities become obsessed with "artificial habits" which directed their attention from the "beautiful and sublime spectacle of the universe" necessary to develop "love and admiration [for] the deity."[21] The proportion by which a people "recede from the simplicity of natural occupations and pursuits" and "acquired the superinduced habits either of commercial drudgery or of fashionable life," the more they develop a "total insensibility to all religious and moral impressions." Atheism was the "genuine offspring" of life in cities, and only to be found in "populous and commercial and artificial societies of men."[22]

---

[19] Stewart (1854–1860, vol. vii, p. 214).
[20] Stewart (1854–1860, vol. vii, p. 79).
[21] Stewart (1854–1860, vol. vii, p. 76).
[22] Stewart (1854–1860, vol. vii, p. 92, 76).

Part of Stewart's message to his young charges under threat of the secularising character of urban living and the allures of sceptical philosophy was that religion was natural and beneficial to humankind. The bulk of Stewart's discussion of the significance of religious diversity involved reasserting two traditional arguments of Christian anti-atheist apologetics. He defended the proof from the *consensus sapientium*, which held that if all philosophers believed something to be true, it was likely to true. Stewart rejected Hume's two arguments against the agreement of the pagans in the NHR that: (1) supposed ancient theists held beliefs not "worthy of the honourable denomination of theism" and (2) the belief the ancient poets were theists was the "fancy and conceit of [Christian] critics and commentators."[23] Hume's definition of true theism was too narrow: ancient pagans were henotheists, not polytheists. They might believe in "subordinate ministers," but more importantly they maintained the "unity of the deity." Stewart cited the heathen worthies—Cicero, Seneca and Plutarch—who had been amongst the staple authorities for early modern religious innatism.[24]

Stewart also defended the proof from the *consensus gentium*: the universal consent of mankind that God existed was an argument for the existence of that God. This involved a quiet elision of all forms of religious belief. Stewart initially argued that belief in immaterial power was found "universally among mankind in any stage of society."[25] It was thus a "fact" that religion had "some foundation in the general principles of our nature," one which did not take the form of innate religious ideas or an internal sense of religion but a "universal prejudice" that natural philosophy has subsequently demonstrated to be justified.[26] The existence of a common origin of religion rooted in our common nature was not disproved by the reality of religious diversity. Notably, though Stewart accepted Hume's argument about the priority of polytheism, he now argued that belief in the "existence of the deity" was supported by the "universal consent of all ages and nations."[27] He quietly shifted from maintaining that belief in immaterial power—which might take the form

---

[23] NHR 34, 36.
[24] Stewart (1854–1860, vol. vii, p. 80).
[25] Stewart (1854–1860), vol. vii, p. 87).
[26] Stewart (1854–1860), vol. vii, p. 87).
[27] Stewart (1854–1860), vol. vii, p. 84).

of one or many gods—was natural to human nature to claiming that there existed a universal belief in single immaterial power, or God.

Stewart's elision was exactly the kind of capacious categorisation that Hume rejected as baseless. In §IV of NHR Hume accepted that immaterial power was "almost universal," but this belief had nothing to do with, and could not be used as a proof of the naturalness of true religion. Stewart adopted the opposite position: universal consent in the existence of immaterial power was proof that religion was natural to man, and that its naturalness demonstrated its truth. As with the proof from the *consensus sapientium*, Stewart supported his claims about universal consent of all peoples with the staple quotations of pagan worthies found in early modern Christian religious innatism.[28] Further, Stewart made a similar argument about the naturalness of belief in a "future state," decipherable beneath the various "accessory articles" of the many religions of the world.[29]

Stewart directed his re-statements of the proofs from consent of all peoples and of the wise against "Mr Hume himself, the most sceptical of all writers." He rejected Hume's claim that it was an "inexplicable mystery" that nearly all religion took the form of religious error, which had severed the connection between commonality and truth. Stewart believed his argument was conclusive. Belief in God was common amongst all peoples and all the wise. This dual universality was, Stewart stated, the "highest evidence by which any truth can possibly be supported."[30] Characteristic of the traditional quality of Stewart's argument, he cited Aristotle's argument in the *Topics* as an authority. To Aristotle, and to Stewart, whatever the vulgar and the philosopher agree upon has the "highest probability, and approaches near to demonstration" and it was "ridiculous arrogance" to deny the truth of the common belief.[31]

Hume had argued that it was an unpersuasive argument to point to the "sick men's dreams" that made up the history of religion as evidence of the naturalness of true religion.[32] Stewart's response was to turn this

[28] Stewart (1854–1860, vol. vii, pp. 85–86).

[29] Stewart (1854–1860, vol. vii, p. 206).

[30] Stewart (1854–1860, vol. vii, p. 87).

[31] Aristotle I.8; Stewart (1854–1860, vol. vii, p. 85).

[32] NHR 115; Stewart (1854–1860, vol. ii, p. 319).

argument on its head: only the innate propensity to believe in immaterial power could explain how humankind had held such perverse religions notions. Most religions were indeed made up of "absurd tenets and extravagant ceremonies," but their absurdity served as evidence that belief in immaterial power was "irresistible."[33] Similarly, in his earlier *Elements*, Stewart argued that the "more strange the contradictions, and the more ludicrous the ceremonies the stronger is our evidence that religion has a foundation in the nature of man," because if religion was not natural to us we could not believe such absurdities.[34]

While he built on the enlightened Scottish account of religious change, Stewart's restatement of the proofs from the *consensus gentium* and *sapientium* set him apart from most of his predecessors. He was the leading pedagogical figure of his time and was clearly presenting a comforting set of apologetic arguments for his intended audience of young students and readers. In this he argued for the progressive improvement of natural theology, from polytheism to theism, adopted the enlightened Scots' abandonment of the biblical framework for the one of gradual improvement and paid only lip-service to the necessity of revelation. At the same time, Stewart reiterated the traditional universal consent arguments of early modern apologetics in an attempt to diffuse the dangers of a Humean "science of man," though he clad his arguments in the language of that science. In a sense, then, Stewart marks the end point of the innovative and exploratory quality of the Scottish Enlightenment's discussion of religion.

As we have seen, Stewart's depiction of providential naturalism, in which the human species is framed for gradual religious progress, was a commonplace attitude amongst the *literati*. Stewart was confident in the religious improvement and perfectibility of human nature, and this underpinned his dismissal of Hume's discussion of religion. Equipped with the universal consent proofs, the enlightened study of religious change did not lead to sceptical conclusions about the truth of religion, but actively confirmed the belief that theism is the end point of human development. Yet Stewart clearly got to this point by adopting a capacious definition of religion, characteristic of early modern apologetics, that viewed all religious belief as evidence of a providentially arranged natural tendency.

---

[33] Stewart (1854–1860, vol. vii, p. 89).
[34] Stewart (1854–1860, vol. ii, p. 320).

REFERENCES

Bow, Charles Bradford. 2018. Dugald Stewart and the Legacy of Common Sense in the Scottish Enlightenment. In *Common Sense in the Scottish Enlightenment*, ed. Charles Bradford Bow, 200–220. Oxford: Oxford University Press.

———. 2022. *Dugald Stewart's Empire of the Mind: Moral Education in the Late Scottish Enlightenment*. Oxford: Oxford University Press.

MacIntyre, Gordon. 2003. *Dugald Stewart: The Pride and Ornament of Scotland*. Brighton: Sussex Academic Press.

Mills, R. J. W. 2018. The "Historical Question" at the End of the Scottish Enlightenment: Dugald Stewart on the Natural Origin of Religion, Universal Consent, and Religious Diversity. *Intellectual History Review* 28: 529–554.

Stewart, Dugald. 1854–1860. *The Collected Works of Dugald Stewart*, vol. 11, ed. William Hamilton. Edinburgh

CHAPTER 15

Conclusion

Abstract The Scottish Enlightenment's science of human nature had the quality of an ongoing conversation by a group of thinkers debating the same themes and issues, dealing with similar concerns, with frequently overlapping arguments, but each with their own distinct position. The Scots explored: the dangers of powerful priests, the wayward paths speculative theology took believers down, the ineradicability of popular superstition and its potential to spill over into fanaticism, the failures of contemporary rationalist preaching, issues of church-state relations and religious tolerance, and how to comprehend knowledge of other major civilisations. They were also motivated by a sense of recent progress in our understanding of natural theology, resulting from the reformation of letters and the achievements of recent natural philosophy.

Keywords Scottish Enlightenment · "Science of man" · "History of man" · Popular superstition · Philosophical progress · David Hume

Scottish social thought, including the application of social theory to religion, declined dramatically in the nineteenth century.[1] This has been attributed in part to the decline of the Moderate Party within the Kirk, and with it the appeal to the "empirical approach to religious apology."[2] The moral philosophers of nineteenth-century Scotland were not concerned to the same degree with the relationship between religion, human nature and society, especially in terms of progress, and redirected their attention to the defence of theism based on the arguments of natural theology. This included, taking the characteristic case of Thomas Chalmers' *Natural Theology* (1836), reasserting the staples of pre-Enlightenment anti-atheist apologetics, the "innate and a prior [i.e. a priori] character to some of the notions and feelings of natural theism" and the "declinist" explanation of religious diversity that our innate theism is never "wholly obliterate[d]" under the "barbarous theology" of polytheism but can be discerned in all religions.[3]

The theorists I have covered did not establish a Scottish school of social theory that endured into the following century. Hume's discussion on religion retained standing and we can find ample evidence of the sustained influence of the NHR on a variety of theorists across a variety of disciplines across the Western world and beyond through to present-day interest amongst evolutionary psychologists in the dissertation. Occasionally, as in the case of Auguste Comte's engagement with Adam Smith's "History of Astronomy," other enlightened Scots influenced subsequent thinkers on religious change.[4] But French and especially German theories of religion took over by the early nineteenth century. Looking back in 1858 on the previous century, the Waynflete Professor of Metaphysical Philosophy at Oxford Henry Longueville Mansel observed that the view that humanity was in a "constant state of religious progress" and that we can study the "religions of antiquity as successive steps in the education of mankind" had been a "favour with various schools of modern

---

[1] Brewer (2014). For overviews defending the insights and significance of nineteenth-century Scottish philosophy, see Broadie (2008, Ch. 10), Graham (2022) and Fyfe and Kidd (2023).

[2] Suderman (2015, §6).

[3] Chalmers (1836, vol. I, p. 333).

[4] Iacono (1994, p. 677).

philosophy."[5] For exemplars, Mansel turned to Comte and Hegel, and elsewhere to Strauss and Feuerbach, and not to Kames and Hume.[6] But, the appeal of Hume's NHR aside, it is not upon the enduring significance of the enlightened Scottish study of religion that the contribution of this book rests, but rather the significance of the subject within wider Scottish Enlightenment social theory.

The Scottish Enlightenment's science of human nature had the quality of an ongoing conversation or research project by a group of thinkers debating the same themes and issues, raising the same concerns, with frequently overlapping arguments, but each with their own distinct position. The Scots were motivated by the religious issues of their age: the dangers of powerful priests, the wayward paths speculative theology took believers down, the presence of popular superstition and its potential to spill over into fanaticism, the failures of contemporary rationalist preaching, issues of church-state relations and religious tolerance, and how to comprehend knowledge of other major civilisations. They were also motivated by a sense of Protestant Western Europe's superiority in religious wisdom in the second half of the eighteenth century, resulting from the reformation of letters and the achievements of recent natural philosophy, though this was qualified by a sense of the continuing dangers of popular superstition. The enlightened Scottish study of the relationship between religion and human nature was not driven on by controversy over narrow theological doctrines, though such controversies form part of the context of certain contributions (Campbell's *Necessity of Revelation*, Kames's *Principles*).[7]

This research behind this book started off as an attempt to understand the Scottish Enlightenment's treatment of the origin and development of religion in a holistic fashion, and thus move away from Hume- and Smith-centred histories. Many of the Scottish Enlightenment's lesser and lesser-known lights have been given space alongside Hume and Smith. But the attempt to decentre Hume has just meant the project has taken

---

[5] Mansel (1858, pp. 419–420).

[6] Mansel (1858, pp. 419–424).

[7] See also Kidd (2004).

a longer route to get to a familiar location.[8] When it comes to discussion the relationship between religion, human nature and society, all roads lead to or at least make a substantial detour past Hume. As in the case of the discussion of religion, as with other topics, it was Hume, to borrow John Robertson's words, who "initiated Enlightenment in Scotland."[9] As Dugald Stewart put it, Hume's *Treatise* "contributed, either directly or indirectly, more than any other single work to the subsequent progress of the Philosophy of the Human Mind," including, we would add, its religious capabilities.[10] Hume's writings on religious topics set much of the agenda of the Scottish discussion of the inherent religious propensities of human nature, and much of what I have covered can be read as an ongoing conversation with Hume's texts. This conclusion stands firmly against the assessment that eighteenth-century Scottish thinkers participating in the "philosophy of religion .... sought to minimise [Hume's] impact and played down his significance" and were "complacent" in their insubstantial engagement with Hume's thought.[11] While the enlightened Scots regularly sought to rebut Hume's more radical conclusions, they just as commonly found much of his account of the relationship between religion and human nature important and persuasive. As such, the enlightened Scottish discussion of religion did not take the form of dogmatic controversy against Hume—James Beattie's best attempts in the *Essay on Truth* (1770) aside—but did include efforts to remould Hume's findings in ways that defended religion's moral and political role. The work with the most explicitly combative language towards Hume, Campbell's *Dissertation on Miracles*, was actually praised by its target for its "civil and obliging manner" in rebutting Hume.[12] Indeed, we can view much of the Aberdeen Enlightenment's contribution to this survey—as found in Gregory, Campbell, Dunbar and Gerard—as taking the form of concerted attempts to demonstrate that the "science of man" could support rather than undermine Christianity.

---

[8] For some scepticism about a Hume-centric reading of eighteenth-century British philosophy, see Harris (2022).

[9] Robertson (2005, p. 381).

[10] Stewart (1854–1860, vol. 1, p. 431).

[11] Stewart (2019, p. 33).

[12] See Harris (2015, p. 300).

The focus on responding to Hume is indicative of the somewhat internal and insular character of the enlightened Scottish conversation over the "science of man," as opposed to any engagement to larger religious debate or to ongoing changes in mythography or the history of idolatry. The preceding discussions, on the whole, exist in a separate genre to the history or idolatry or comparative religion, and this separateness needs to be incorporated into our understanding of eighteenth-century European approaches to understanding religion.[13] After Archibald Campbell and Turnbull, the common topics of the Scots' discussion of religion were ones either set by or heavily influenced by Hume's writing and should be seen as common participants in a "science of human nature" that became more historically-minded from the 1750s onwards. The extent of engagement with Hume's "science of man" differed from author to author, as did the thematic focus of that engagement. More importantly, our survey has also shown that what was controversial about Hume's discussion about religion was not its attack on speculative theology, the argument for the primacy of polytheism (depending on how this was related to biblical history) or that human nature was inherently superstitious. Nearly all the enlightened Scots after Hume agreed. What they debated was the significance of these arguments relative to the overall truth of religion in general and Christianity in particular, the role of biblical history, the providential direction (or otherwise) of religious development, the character of institutionalised religion and the management of ineradicable popular superstition.

The Scots were interested in naturalised accounts of religious change that embedded the history of religious belief and worship within the history of societal development. But they did not agree on the trajectory of or the factors directing that change. And they did not, as a group, hold for a linear progression from primitive polytheism to sophisticated theism nor uniformly hold for religious progress being rigidly tied to socio-economic, philosophical or political progress. Kames did not much engage in socio-economic contextualisation in either his *Principles* or *Sketches*—indeed, the stadial history of religion in the latter existed separate to societal change. Hume's NHR was more interested in the enduring psychology of the multitude, rather than wider societal changes, while the move towards "true religion" (minimal theism) was the specific

---

[13] Cf. Levitin (2022).

result of the accumulation of natural philosophical knowledge following the revival of European letters.[14] Robertson's discussions of the Aztecs and Incas in his *History of America* positioned superstition as both a sticky institution unaffected by and often an active fetter on socio-economic improvement.[15] Monboddo situated his account at a specific historical point and with very specific circumstances, not least, the existence of daemons. Hutton viewed philosophers as heroic figures driving forward man to his ultimate perfection. Dunbar saw climate as determining the possible development of religion.

The Scots dealt with the contradictions between the expected "natural progress of religion," derived from the universal principles of human nature, and the actual history of religion. Attempts to identify the natural processes underpinning religious change would always fail if they tried to be anything other than heuristics, but they would nonetheless be worthwhile. Alexander Gerard captured something of the problem in his *A Sermon, Preached before the Society in Scotland for Propagating Christian Knowledge* (1792), directed partly against Hume's NHR. We find "unevenness and breaks in the most regular processes of nature."[16] Religious change, be it corruption or improvement, must always be "sometimes progressive, sometimes interrupted, and sometimes retrograde; sometimes accelerated, and sometimes checked or retarded, by a variety of causes."[17] The tension between the "natural" and "actual" progress of religion left the conclusions of the "science of man" vulnerable to arguments from scholars grounded in the detail, as we see in George Campbell's criticism of Hume's discussion of miracles.

One topic where all the Scots did agree—Ferguson's religious innatism notwithstanding—was that there were very real limits to religious progress due to the capacities of the multitude.[18] The bulk of mankind could not participate fully in the progress of knowledge: a real cleavage existed

---

[14] So here disagreeing with the 'sociological' reading of the NHR in Berry (2000, §4).

[15] On the Scottish views of the enduring quality, or stickiness, of decrepit or actively detrimental social institutions, see Berry (2018, *passim*).

[16] Gerard (1792, p. 48).

[17] Gerard (1792, p. 49).

[18] Cf. Sebastiani (2013). On the idea of 'popular religion' becoming a category of analysis during the Enlightenment, see Frijhoff (2006, pp. 201–204).

between the educated and the multitude. It is true to say that the religion of all humans changed as a result of the shift from savage to civil society, and that there is a progress from primitive animism to polytheistic superstitions due to changing societal contexts. The "rude religion" of primordial man living in conditions of scarcity, instability and violence is, necessarily, different to the polytheism of the Roman Republic or the pseudo-theism of Catholicism. But improvements in the state of civilisation, or in the religious knowledge of priests or philosophers, do not alter the fact that the multitude are always superstitious. Here are two key conclusions of the Scottish science of man: religious belief and worship change with societal changes, but also the capabilities of unchanging human nature meant that such change did not include "improvement" away from popular superstition. This point can get lost beneath glosses that the Scots believed that the "natural progress" of religion was just one of many progressivist histories of human behaviours and institutions: not all "progress" is even, not everyone participates or participates to the same degree, and "progress" is not always "improvement."[19]

Aside from Hume's pessimism in the NHR (elsewhere he struck a different note), the enlightened Scots offered pragmatic solutions to the issue of popular religion, though widespread popular enlightenment through the dramatic expansion of education was not on the table.[20] To Kames, Robertson, Monboddo, Dunbar and Smith until 1790, it explained the genius of Christianity (or a desacralised version of Christianity), as a religion fitted to satisfy both the rational and passionate aspects of humankind. For Turnbull and Ferguson, popular superstition was evidence of humanity's inherent weakness. But they also, with Gregory and Stewart, saw the need to reform preaching and pedagogy in ways that better spoke to the people's superstitious tendencies. Smith wrote pragmatically of the magistrates who need to accommodate the demands of the populace. The wholly unpragmatic Hutton thought philosophers should take over the management of vulgar minds, though he did not say how. Gregory wanted the clergy to become scientists of man. Robertson criticised the Brahmins for abandoning their flocks by manipulating, and not elevating, their religious passions. None but Hume

---

[19] Cf. Emerson (1984) and, to a degree, Berry (2000, esp. §5), though I am in complete agreement with the argument that the shift from savage to civil society involves a complete shift in the character of religious belief.

[20] For comparisons with France see Vyverberg (1958).

wished to abandon the multitude to their fate, a callous position rebuked by Gregory, but which demonstrated Hume's wholly pessimistic view about the sheer power of popular superstition against which, Hume maintained in the NHR at least, little could be done. All agreed that religions would inevitably take a *religio duplex* form of a popular religion managing the limitations of the multitude and a philosophical religion practised by the philosophical elite. The notion of *religio duplex* or twofold religion has often been depicted as a radical theory adopted by freethinking initiates as a means to protect themselves in hostile superstitious societies, as a topic of interest for Orientalist scholarship studying Eastern religions or reflecting an enduring esoteric tradition in Western thought.[21] For the Scots, it was an empirical fact derived from the "science of human nature," true of contemporary Christendom as of anywhere else, rather than a historical fact about a specific region or religion.

This fact required thoughtful responses. While the multitude were not likely to be raised up to the echelons of philosophical theists, they could be protected from the abuses of priests. The Scots' "science of man" contributed to their discussion of the professional status and activities of priesthoods. All maintained that for a millennium Christendom was under the yoke of a Catholic Church defined by ignorance, intolerance, corruption, venality and moral and religious perversion. They differed over the primary cause of the turn away from Catholic superstition, be it the revival of letters in what we might call the Renaissance, the Reformation, the Church's wasteful consumption or a combination of these factors. And they differed over the question of how to manage the clerical profession within a polity.[22] The solutions differed—encouraging indolence (Hume), enforcing poverty (Smith), breaking up the church into powerless factions (Smith again), retraining priests as empathetic "scientists of human nature" (Gregory, Stewart), ensuring the philosophers not the theologians ruled (Hutton)—but all were informed by an understanding of priesthoods as a professional group, made up of humans with human frailties, and which will always appear in civil societies. The Scots were all, also, critical of speculative theology, as useless at best and dangerous at worst. The Scots did not engage in theological disputes, then, only out

---

[21] For example, see the analyses in Harrison (1990), Apps (2010), Assmann (2014), Melzer (2014) and Patterson (2021).

[22] Cf. Suderman's (2015) claim that the "Scottish advocates of Enlightenment seldom questioned the need of an established church."

of a desire to avoid controversy but because they believed that theology was characterised by abstract and metaphysical thinking. The focus was on happy and moral living in the here and now, as well as the cultivation of practical morality and piety.[23]

The question of whether the Scottish study of religion involved the secularisation of the study of religion can easily get bogged down in questions of definition, but their approach to study religious change differed in innovative and profound ways to the established practices of mythography and the history of idolatry.[24] These differences include: (a) the abandonment of the detailed study of cultural and religious transmission (with the exception of Monboddo, Dunbar briefly and Smith in his juvenile essays), where single figures transmit religions from one society to another or bodies of knowledge shift from one society to another, towards the notion of religion as a human institution that is formed to a large extent by its development in a societal context; (b) the abandonment of tracing the heathen gods back to identifiable historical original moments of corruption, though retaining an interest in whether the gods were allegorical representations of nature if this tells us something important about the workings of human nature; (c) the abandonment of avowedly Christian conceptions of human nature and their application to accounts of the origins of idolatry that focus on the failings of sinful man, but instead shifting focus to endogenous (e.g. an internal religious sense) and exogenous (e.g. climate) factors informing how human nature manifests itself; and (d) the abandonment of the motivation of studying paganism to better understand the historical character of Christianity, though the study of paganism could underpin notions of Christianity's truth (as in the case of Robertson). While the Scots inherited some of the components of earlier studies of religion, what distinguished their accounts was their naturalistic and progressive character, and the change in the subject of their studies.[25]

---

[23] The focus on temporal well-being is *the* definite characteristic of the Enlightenment for John Robertson (2005) and Ritchie Robertson (2020). On the practical morality point, see Ahnert (2015).

[24] For an account of the Edinburgh Enlightenment as being secular in character, see Jacob (2019, Ch. 5). For a discussion of the secularisation question in terms of Scottish religious thought, see Mills Daniel (2020).

[25] See Manuel (1959), Manuel (1983) and Levitin (2022) for accounts showing the links between the High Enlightenment and earlier approaches to studying religion.

While the "science of human nature" and the "history of mankind" were different approaches to the established genres studying religious change, the enlightened Scots all claimed their discussions demonstrated the truth of religion and, sometimes, of the Christian religion in particular. In the case of Hume, his proclamations about Christianity can be read as an act of philosophical lying undertaken to protect him from persecution, but he retained a "minimal theism" that set him apart from the atheistic *philosophes*. I think that the same can be said of similar passages in Kames, Smith, Hutton and Stewart: that they said the acceptable thing about Christianity to ensure peace and quiet. From the opposite perspective, several of the enlightened Scots, notably Robertson, Dunbar and Monboddo, held that Christianity had the world-historical role of bringing about the end of exploitative *religio duplexes* and the establishment of genuine moral and pious behaviour amongst the multitude. They, like Ferguson and Gregory, stressed the potential benefits to popular religion that would derive through the informed management of commonplace passions. Alongside these judgements, however, were criticisms of contemporary Christianity informed by the "science of human nature," such as the sustained censure of speculative theology, failed missionary efforts that did not consider the extent of societal development in non-European nations or the need to appeal in benign ways to the passions of the multitude.

Scholarship on the emergence of new approaches to religion in early modern Europe often stresses that they resulted from, to quote one commentator, a "deepening crisis [in] Europe's dominant ideological matrix."[26] One scholar has described the cumulative researches of the Académie des inscriptions studying paganism using naturalistic methods as "inevitably corrosive to religious orthodoxy."[27] If the more religious Scots felt themselves disorientated and distressed by their studies of religion, they did not show it—apart from, perhaps, Robertson at various points in his *History of America* and *Historical Disquisition*, where the belief in providence was detached from historical evidence and was firmly an article of faith.[28] The application of the "science of man" and the "history of mankind" to religion did not inevitably serve as a dissolvent

[26] Apps (2010, p. xiv). See also Stroumsa (2010) and Hunt, Jacob & Mijnhardt (2010).
[27] Matytsin (2022).
[28] Smitten (2013) and (2017).

of Christian faith for many enlightened Scots, though it seems to have done so for Hume, Kames, Smith, Ferguson and Hutton. Turnbull, the two Campbells, Robertson, Gregory, Dunbar, Monboddo and perhaps also Stewart did not end up viewing Christianity as one parochial religion amongst many. Rather, their enlightened understandings of human nature confirmed to them that Christianity was the one universal religion and the sole religion whose message both chimed with scientific truth and contained the necessary moral content to appeal to all humans. Hume and Hutton aside, the enlightened Scottish study of religion was not characterised by an active subversiveness or radicalism of the sort that informed much of the Enlightenment's more (in)famous writing about religious change. This is possibly a consequence of the developmental level at which most of the Scots' theories were pitched, such that, unlike in the Académie des inscriptions in Paris, they did not go into the similarities between, say, particular Christian and particular pagan miracles or stories.[29] That said, I do think that a sizeable minority of the authors discussed here articulated deistic accounts of religion and that we mischaracterise the Scottish Enlightenment's discussion of religion if we emphasise continuity with Calvinist tradition and stress a sense of the discussion occurring primarily within an enlightened party in the Church of Scotland.[30] From the perspective of the application of the "science of human nature" to the science of man, the claim that "the Enlightenment in Scotland was a fundamentally Christian Enlightenment" seems misplaced.[31]

On religious matters at least, most enlightened Scots were members of the moderate rather than radical enlightenment insofar as they wished to reduce religious fanaticism but did not wish to overturn the religio-political order. Hume worked for the secularisation of society, but viewed

[29] Matytsin (2022).

[30] Cf. Suderman (2015), which claims that the "sociological study of man" involved the "recognition that God's true plan of salvation required the social perfection of his virtue" (§6). This reads very much like the unwarranted coating of all the practitioners of the 'science of man' with Calvinist doctrine—is it true for either Hume or Smith? It may not be true for Kames, Ferguson or Hutton for that matter.

[31] Suderman (2015, §6). See more cautious description of the Scottish Enlightenment as a 'religious Enlightenment' in Ahnert (2015, pp. 1–2), though as mentioned above, I think this glosses over the key cleavage, between avowedly Christian and quietly deistic positions, identified in the preceding chapters, as well as directing attention away from the epicentre of the enlightened Scottish 'science of man', Hume.

this a long-term development and, depending which text you read, not even a likely one. Hutton wished to replace theology with philosophy but viewed this as replacing one inept ruling caste with a superior one. The division that does stand out from the preceding study is that between the Christian believers and the "philosophical theists." The heterodox, irreligious or unchristian practitioners of the "science of human nature" could share with their orthodox Christian colleagues the belief that religion developed in certain identifiable ways due to certain identifiable factors. Gregory, Robertson and George Campbell could agree with Hume on a lot. The orthodox practitioners of the "science of human nature," however, would theorise religious change in terms of the natural religious development of unassisted human nature and would continue to maintain that the Judaeo-Christian history was correct (Archibald Campbell, Robertson, George Campbell). The heterodox or irreligious practitioners, by contrast, either ignored the issue of biblical history (as in the case of Kames and the juvenile Smith), dismissed the relevance of the bible (as in the very different cases of Hume and Monboddo) or wrote about it in ways that suggested they were protecting themselves (as in the cases of Hutton and Stewart).

Reading several enlightened progressive histories of religion successively raises in the reader a strong sense of the unsatisfying quality of heuristic accounts not rooted in the kind of philological erudition that characterised the following century's "science of religion." Clearly, the "science of human nature" and the "history of mankind" had immense explanatory potential for understanding how humans and societies functioned. But without an established means of referencing, and with no fixed rule existing for the meaning of exceptions, any general claim made could be rebutted. Arguments could read like a series of assertions and counter-assertions. Hume claimed that primordial human societies would have been atheistic; Ferguson rebuked Hume for getting the chronology the wrong way round. Hume claimed that priests imposed themselves on gullible people; Shaw rebuked Hume for getting the chain of events the wrong way round. The reading of, presumably, the same works of ancient history and travel literature lead to the conclusions that the existence of God is both universally believed and not universally believed. Rarely is the evidence supplied to back up what are either conjectures or purported generalisations about the "history of mankind." Kames is the main outlier here, with his *Sketches* providing exhaustive examples for his claims, though what is striking about Kames's disparate investigations contained within his sketch on religion is the fact that they do not and cannot align with each other.

The most comprehensive account of the European Enlightenment's attempts to provide naturalistic explanations of the origin and development of religion remains Frank Manuel's classic study, *The Eighteenth Century Confronts the Gods* (1959), even if he caricatures what came before the Enlightenment. But apart from Hume's NHR, the Scots play very little role in Manuel's work. A striking difference appears between the character of the Scots' study of religion and the myriad works Manuel surveys, namely, that whereas Manuel's authors were principally concerned with understanding the origins and nature of paganism, the Scots of this volume were interested in understanding the origins and character of religion. The latter is a naturalistic, even neutral, category, defined as one subject amongst many in the study of human nature, whereas the former is defined in opposition to the Abrahamic religions. Many of the concerns of Manuel's subjects were not replicated by the Scots—allegorical interpretations of the pagan gods, the character of religious imposture or detailed accounts of euhemerism. One of the Enlightenment's legacies, according to Manuel, was its "embryonic" sense that the "character of the gods was determined by socio-economic systems," but as we have seen, the Scots, usually attributed with such stadial thinking, did not apply it to religious change in any sustained or profound sense.[32] The "science of human nature" did, however, provide an approach to religion that lead the enlightened Scots to accounts of religious change rooted in accumulations of evidence about human nature and the practice of providing conjectural histories or heuristics of religious change. To possess more accurate pictures of both the Scottish Enlightenment and history of the science of religion, we need to incorporate the enlightened Scots' study of the origin and progress of religion.

References

Ahnert, Thomas. 2015. *The Moral Culture of the Scottish Enlightenment*. London: Yale University Press.

Apps, Urs. 2010. *The Birth of Orientalism*. Philadelphia, PA: University of Pennsylvania Press.

---

[32] Manuel (1959, p. 311).

Assmann, Jan. 2014. *Religio Duplex: How the Enlightened Reinvented Egyptian Religion*. Cambridge: Polity Press.

Berry, Christopher J. 2000. Rude Religion: The Psychology of Polytheism in the Scottish Enlightenment. In *The Scottish Enlightenment: Essays in Reinterpretation*, ed. Paul Wood, 315–334. New York: University of Rochester Press.

Berry, Christopher J. 2018. *Essays on Hume, Smith and the Scottish Enlightenment*. Edinburgh: Edinburgh University Press.

Brewer, John. 2014. The Scottish Enlightenment and Scottish Social Thought c. 1725–1915. In *The Palgrave Handbook of Sociology in Britain*, eds. J. Holmwood and J. Scott, 3–29. Basingstoke: Palgrave Macmillan.

Broadie, Alexander. 2008. *A History of Scottish Philosophy*. Edinburgh: Edinburgh University Press.

Chalmers, Thomas. 1836. *The Works of Thomas Chalmers*, 25 vols. Glasgow.

Emerson, Roger L. 1984. Conjectural History and Scottish Philosophers. *Historical Papers/Communications Historiques* 19: 63–90.

Frijhoff, Willem. 2006. Popular Religion. In *The Cambridge History of Christianity. Vol. VII: Enlightenment, Reawakening and Revolution 1660–1815*, ed. S. J. Brown and T. Tackett, 185–207. Cambridge: Cambridge University Press.

Fyfe, Aileen, and Colin Kidd, eds. 2023. *Beyond the Enlightenment: Scottish Intellectual Life, 1790–1917*. Edinburgh: Edinburgh University Press.

Gerard, Alexander. 1792. *A Sermon, Preached before the Society in Scotland for Propagating Christian Knowledge; At Their Anniversary Meeting in the High Church of Edinburgh*. Edinburgh.

Graham, Gordon. 2022. *Scottish Philosophy After the Enlightenment: Essays in Pursuit of a Tradition*. Edinburgh: Edinburgh University Press.

Harris, James. 2015. *David Hume: An Intellectual Biography*. Cambridge: Cambridge University Press.

———. 2022. How to Write a History of Philosophy? The Case of Eighteenth-Century Britain. *British Journal for the History of Philosophy*. https://doi.org/10.1080/09608788.2022.2116695. Accessed on 19 December 2022.

Harrison, Peter. 1990. *'Religion' and the Religions in the English Enlightenment*. Cambridge: Cambridge University Press.

Hunt, Lynn, Jacob, Margaret & Mijnhardt, Wijnand. 2010. *The Book That Changed Europe: Picart and Bernard's Religious Ceremonies of the World*. London: Belknap.

Iacono, Alfonso M. 1994. The American Indians and the Ancients of Europe: The Idea of Comparison and the Construction of Historical Time in the 18th Century. In *European Images of the Americas and the Classical Tradition, 2 parts*, ed. Wolfgang Haase and Reinhold Meyer, 658–691. New York: De Gruyter.

Jacob, Margaret. 2019. *The Secular Enlightenment*. Princeton, NJ: Princeton University Press.
Kidd, Colin. 2004. Subscription, the Scottish Enlightenment and the Moderate Interpretation of History. *Journal of Ecclesiastical History* 55: 502–519.
Levitin, Dmitri. 2022. *The Kingdom of Darkness: Bayle, Newton, and the Emancipation of the European Mind from Philosophy*. Cambridge: Cambridge University Press.
Mansel, Henry. 1858. *The Limits of Religious Thought Examined in Eight Lectures*. Oxford.
Manuel, Frank E. 1959. *The Eighteenth Century Confronts the Gods*. London: Harvard University Press.
———. 1983. *The Changing of the Gods*. London: Brown University Press.
Matytsin, A. 2022. Enlightenment and Erudition: Writing Cultural History at the Académie des inscriptions. *Modern Intellectual History* 19: 323–348.
Melzer, Arthur. 2014. *Philosophy Between the Lines: The Lost History of Esoteric Writing*. Chicago: University of Chicago Press.
Mills Daniel, Dafydd. 2020. *Ethical Rationalism and Secularisation in the British Enlightenment: Conscience and the Age of Reason*. Basingstoke: Palgrave Macmillan.
Patterson, Jessica. 2021. *Religion, Enlightenment and Empire: British Interpretations of Hinduism in the Eighteenth Century*. Cambridge: Cambridge University Press.
Robertson, John. 2005. *The Case for the Enlightenment: Scotland and Naples 1680–1760*. Cambridge: Cambridge University Press.
Robertson, Ritchie. 2020. *The Enlightenment: The Pursuit of Happiness, 1680–1790*. London: Penguin.
Sebastiani, Silvia. 2013. *The Scottish Enlightenment: Race, Gender, and the Limits of Progress*. Trans. Jeremy Carden. Basingstoke: Palgrave.
Smitten, Jeffrey. 2013. William Robertson: The Minister as Historian. In *A Companion to Enlightenment Historiography*, ed. Sophie Bourgault and Robert Sparling, 103–131. Leiden: Brill.
———. 2017. *The Life of William Robertson: Minister, Historian and Principal*. Edinburgh: Edinburgh University Press.
Stewart, Dugald. 1854–1860. *The Collected Works of Dugald Stewart*, 11 vols. Ed. William Hamilton. Edinburgh.
Stewart, M.A. 2019. Religion and Rational Theology. In *The Cambridge Companion to the Scottish Enlightenment*, 2nd ed., ed. Alexander Broadie and Craig Smith, 33–59. Cambridge: Cambridge University Press.
Stroumsa, Guy. 2010. *A New Science: The Discovery of Religion in the Age of Reason*. London: Harvard University Press.

Suderman, Jeffrey. 2015. Religion and Philosophy. In *Scottish Philosophy in the Eighteenth Century. Volume I: Morals, Politics, Art, Religion*, ed. Aaron Garrett and James Harris, 196–238. Oxford: Oxford University Press.

Vyverberg, Henry. 1958. *Historical Pessimism in the French Enlightenment*. Harvard, MA: Harvard University Press.

Appendix 1: Two and a Half 'Four Stage' Theories of Religion

While Frank Manuel viewed stadial histories of religion as one of key legacies of the European Enlightenment's study of paganism, such theories are not to be found in Scotland, one of the two purported homes, alongside France, of the four-stage theory of society.[1] One conclusion drawn from the preceding study is that the enlightened Scots did not produce stadial histories of religion rigidly tied to socio-economic development and definitely not to any, strictly interpreted, four stages theory. Another conclusion is that there was often a major difference in theories of religious change between those Scots who were practising ministers and those who were not, with the former stressing the necessity of revelation and more likely to reject any simple alignment of religious to societal or philosophical improvement. In this appendix, I want to point to two examples of explicitly four-stage theories of religious development

---

[1] Manuel (1959). Obviously, we must allow for the deployment of "four-stage theory" in historiography as a shorthand for more complex theories and as a synonym for theories of change that stressed economic factors. See Berry (2013, esp. pp. 39–40) and Salber Phillips (2000, pp. 171–189) and Berry (2000) with specific regard to religion. But it is easy to be misled about just how uncharacteristic and unimportant the four stages theory was most literati when discussing the central questions of the science of man, and especially when discussing the origin and progress of religion. This is illustrated by the fact that Meek (1976) is a case study in the mythology of doctrine as described in Skinner (1969). The point here might be simply that "four stages theory" is a placeholder for far more complicated historical theory—and clearly, many scholars use it in this non-strict sense—but it inevitably leads to distortion and mischaracterisation.

© The Editor(s) (if applicable) and The Author(s), under exclusive license to Springer Nature Switzerland AG 2023
R. J. W. Mills, *Religion and the Science of Human Nature in the Scottish Enlightenment*, https://doi.org/10.1007/978-3-031-49031-6

coming from students of the Scottish Enlightenment, William Falconer and George Gregory, rather than the Scots themselves. Their reductionist theories indicate, I think, how the complicated social theory of the enlightened Scots was parsed and simplified by students who extracted what they took as its essential features and deployed them in different in contexts.

We search in vain for amongst the Scots for a four-stage theory of religion. How could it be otherwise? The explanatory variety and sophistication of argument we have surveyed in this book reflect how the enlightened Scots never contemplated reduced their explanations to something as blunt as a four stages model of societal progress. We have seen that Smith did not apply a rigidly stadial model to his discussion of religious psychology and religious change.[2] Kames's explicit use of the four stages theory appeared in his *Historical-Law Tracts*, and was not the trajectory described in the "Sketch" on religion in 1774. The other best-known proponent of a four stages theory was John Millar (1735–1801), but he was not interested in religious topics—at least, in *The Origin of the Distinction of Ranks* (1771).[3] Another explicit mention of the "four stages" taxonomy appears in Blair's *Critical Dissertation on the Poems of Ossian* (1763), though here stadial theory hits up against conclusions drawn from the accumulated evidence of the history of mankind and specific local circumstances. Blair, having briefly restated (though without attribution) the four stages Smith proposed in his Edinburgh lectures, took the Gaelic society described by Ossian as one in the barbarian stage of society, in which "hunting was the chief employment of men, and the principal method of their procuring subsistence."[4]

The rigidity of a four stages theory repeatedly, however, comes apart in Blair's analysis. He both holds that humans "never bear such resembling features, as they do in the beginnings of society," i.e. that barbarian societies are characterised by uniformity, yet also that "barbarity ... is a very equivocal term [and] admits of many different forms and degrees."[5] Ossian's mythology took the form of "departed spirits" in "airy forms,"

---

[2] For an enjoyably iconoclastic account of how Smith was neither a conjectural nor four stages historian see Sagar (2022, pp. 10–53).

[3] On Millar see Miller (2017).

[4] Blair (1763, p. 17).

[5] Blair (1763, p. 13).

as was consonant with the "notions of every rude [i.e. barbarian] age."[6] The characteristic belief of "those times" was that supernatural beings were "material, and consequently, vulnerable" to worldly events.[7] Yet Blair also describes the supernatural beings described in Ossian as the "mythology of human nature ... the popular belief in all ages and countries and under all forms of religion."[8] The myths in Ossian both reflected the "peculiar ideas of northern nations" *and* the "general current of a superstitious imagination in all countries."[9] Into this mix is added historical specificity. Blair notes the "total absence of religious ideas" in Ossian, with Blair using "religious" here to mean theistic beliefs managed by a priesthood.[10] He accepted Macpherson's explanation that Ossian lived in between the era of the druids and the initial establishment of Christianity, i.e. at a specific historical moment with particular, indeed unique, characteristics. We should observe, however, that Blair was writing not as a "scientist of human nature," but as a theorist of belles-lettres. His discussion of Ossian's mythology emphasises that the absence of mention of a "supreme being," while Blair accepted Macpherson's explanation as to why, "must be held a considerable disadvantage to the poetry."[11]

Our first example of a non-Scottish Briton applying an explicitly four-stage model to understanding religion was Irish-born, Liverpool-educated and London-based jobbing man of letters George Gregory's reasonably well-received *Essays, Historical and Moral* (1785; second edition, 1788). His brief discussion of the stadial development of religion demonstrated how the theoretical model could be incorporated into sacred history without much conceptual difficulty. In his essay entitled "Of the Progress of Manners and Society" Gregory narrated a four-stage theory of human development from the state of nature through to commercial society. Gregory's stages ran: (1) savage society; (2) the state of war, later described as the state of hunters, (3) a state of fixed property, later described as the pastoral state and (4) a state jointly characterised by agriculture and commerce. Each was held to have "uniformity in manners"

---

[6] Blair (1763, p. 34).
[7] Blair (1763, p. 39).
[8] Blair (1763, p. 38).
[9] Blair (1763, p. 39).
[10] Blair (1763, p. 20).
[11] Blair (1763, p. 40).

which "enables us to mark with precision the progress of civilization" until they reached the fourth stage.[12] At this point, nations developed unique characteristics which meant that the stadial model can be set aside: civil history begins with agriculture.

According to Gregory's stadial model, the trajectory of religious progress went from violent fearful polytheism of pre-social humanity to a milder, less fanatical polytheism of the first commercial societies. While his account of the character of religion demonstrated the clear influence of the enlightened Scots, especially Robertson's History of America, Gregory adopted a series of simple causal relationships between core religious belief and societal stage. In the state of nature and the state of war, the overwhelming passion of fear, due to the insecurity of life, leads to polytheisms made up of "cruel and capricious" gods.[13] The shift to the state of fixed property and security of subsistence saw the establishment of fixed systems of religion, not least as a policy to established social stability in response to the earlier state of war. The shift to societies characterised by "agriculture, commerce, and established laws" saw the emergence of a "milder and more ingenious species of superstition," and the growing neglect of religion itself.[14] The rule of law led to notions of equity and right that, in turn, changed notions of the gods into more peaceable, moderate figures. All this was religious change, but hardly religious improvement towards theism and, rather, demonstrated the necessity of revealed religion for knowledge of the existence of God, the immortality of the soul and our future rewards and punishment in a life hereafter.

Gregory maintained that his account described the progress of society from the generations immediately after Noah through to the first ancient agricultural and commercial societies of Egypt and Greece. He combined this stadial model with a lengthier disquisition on the psychological origins of false religion entitled "Remarks on the History of Superstition,' which served to justify why Christianity was not subverted by a theory of religion which started with a fear-ridden polytheism in savage society. Here Gregory expanded on how the original pristine monotheism in the first human societies would have been corrupted by the human tendency

---

[12] Gregory (1785, p. 44).
[13] Gregory (1785, p. 64).
[14] Gregory (1785, pp. 36, 75).

to develop theological beliefs on the false basis of the fear- and ignorance-driven anthropomorphic analogy. Once knowledge of the "primitive tradition of Noah" had been lost, only "rude notions of religion" can be found amongst the earliest societies.[15] Wishing to demonstrate the truth and necessity of revelation, Gregory spliced together both the model of religious degeneration and religious progress, the latter happening after the act of forgetting the Noahite inheritance had finished. In doing so, he argued that the stadial history of religion that could be discerned from the "history of mankind" in no way undermined and, rather, demonstrated the truth of Christianity.

Our second example is the Chester-born, Edinburgh- and Leiden-educated, and Bath-based physician William Falconer in his *Remarks on the Influence of Climate* (1781). I have discussed elsewhere the full range of Falconer's application of the "science of human nature" to religion, but here want to emphasise that the *Remarks* linked the development of religion to clearly delineated socio-economic stages.[16] Each of the four stages had a characteristic set of religious beliefs and worship practices, with religious improvement occurring in contexts of socio-economic development within temperate climates. Inspired especially by Montesquieu's embryonic taxonomy of societies in the *Spirit of the Laws* (1748), but clearly immersed in the writings of the Scottish Enlightenment, Falconer developed an optimistic message about religious development that positioned England at the height of improvement. The study of religious diversity evident in past and present societies was arranged into a comforting trajectory of development that positioned late eighteenth-century England as, effectively, God's chosen nation on earth.

The final book of the *Remarks* included Falconer arranging facts about religion according to a four-stage model of societal change—savage, pastoral, agricultural and commercial. The different "way[s] of life" were defined especially by their "different occupations and modes of living."[17] Falconer did not address why a people moved from one stage to the next, and instead identified the essential characteristics of their society. He was aware that, given the "diverse degrees of improvement" found in the history of mankind, the heuristic he was using involved a major

---

[15] Gregory (1785, p. 16).

[16] For discussion see Mills (2018).

[17] Falconer (1781, p. 257).

simplification of human diversity and history.[18] Falconer's identification of religious characteristics of each stage of society took the form of a necessary causal relationship: religion was natural to human nature, but its precise manifestations were directly informed by socio-economic circumstance.

We can briefly summarise the main claims of Falconer's causal account. The first two stages of society were nomadic, precarious and dominated by violence. They, therefore, had gods of a "warlike kind" and worship that intended to either placate angry deities or secure their providential support in future conflict.[19] Nomadic living meant "no temples, no rites, no ceremonies," leaving "savage" nations with little "attachment" to religion other than when the gods were called upon prior to war.[20] Idolatry did not exist as nomadic peoples were "compelled often to make the most rapid migrations."[21] By contrast, the fixity of agricultural society led to the building of temples and the establishment of priesthoods. The reliance on agricultural production meant peoples worshipped "agricultural deities."[22] Agricultural peoples were devout and pious, partly because priesthoods and princes used religion as a political instrument to secure social stability. The emergence of commercial society brought many benefits for religious attitudes: the constant interaction with the rest of the world necessary for trade made people more sociable, polite, sympathetic to others, less prejudiced and more tolerant and curious about other religions. The emergence of commercial society in a moderate climate resulted, so Falconer argued, in the moderate, tolerant, rational Christianity of late eighteenth-century England.

Clearly, the Scots had at their disposal a sense of different sorts of society informing different sorts of religious belief and practice. But the sort of reductive account (societal type A leads to religious type B) of how socio-economic stages determined the character of religion, maintained by Gregory and Falconer, was rarely key to the enlightened Scottish project. Nor, indeed, did it serve much purpose for Blair, who was open

---

[18] Falconer (1781, p. 257).
[19] Falconer (1781, p. 315).
[20] Falconer (1781, p. 321).
[21] Falconer (1781, p. 351).
[22] Falconer (1781, p. 395).

to the complexity of societal characterisation. Similarly, there is no discussion in Falconer and Gregory's accounts of the progress of theology, the role of philosophy or the necessity of *religio duplex* arrangements. Gregory and Falconer's observations were on a societal level, a form of proto-historical materialism, and they maintained a simple and simplistic causal relationship between societal stage and character of religion. Both were clearly synthesising the findings from their reading of the Enlightenment's literature on religious change and through this process, they lost the complexity, nuance and occasional messiness of the enlightened Scots' study of religion. It is arguable that we have lost the same in our treatment of enlightened Scottish discussions of religious development when we have relied upon the umbrella concept of four stages history.

References to Works Cited

Berry, Christopher J. 2000. Rude Religion: The Psychology of Polytheism in the Scottish Enlightenment. In *The Scottish Enlightenment: Essays in Reinterpretation*, ed. Paul Wood, 315–334. New York: University of Rochester Press.

———. 2013. *The Idea of Commercial Society in the Scottish Enlightenment*. Edinburgh: Edinburgh University Press.

Blair, Hugh. 1763. *Critical Dissertation on the Poems of Ossian, The Son of Fingal*. London.

Falconer, William. 1781. *Remarks on the Influence of Climate*. London.

Gregory, George. 1785. *Essays, Historical and Moral*. London.

Manuel, Frank E. 1959. *The Eighteenth Century Confronts the Gods*. London: Harvard University Press.

Meek, Ronald L. 1976. *Social Science and the Ignoble Savage*. Cambridge: Cambridge University Press.

Miller, Nicholas B. 2017. *John Millar and the Scottish Enlightenment. Family Life and World History*. Oxford: Voltaire Foundation.

Mills, R.J.W. 2018. William Falconer's *Remarks on the Influence of Climate* (1781) and the Study of Religion in Enlightenment England. *Intellectual History Review* 28: 293–315.

Sagar, Paul. 2022. *Adam Smith Reconsidered: History, Liberty, and the Foundations of Modern Politics*. Princeton, NJ: Princeton University Press.

Salber Phillips, Mark. 2000. *Society and Sentiment: Genres of Historical Writing in Britain, 1740–1820*. Princeton, NJ: Princeton University Press.

Skinner, Quentin. 1969. Meaning and Understanding in the History of Ideas. *History and Theory* 8: 3–53.

Appendix 2: Alexander Gerard and the Inadequacies of Progressive Histories of Religion

It was entirely possible for a participant in the High Scottish Enlightenment to reject the very premises of recent progressivist studies of the relationship between religion, human nature and society. In his *Essay on Genius* (1774), another product of the fecund intellectual atmosphere of the Aberdeen Philosophical Society, and Professor of Divinity at Marischal College, Alexander Gerard positioned himself as a participant in the "science of human nature."[23] We turn here, instead, to Gerard's lesser-known theological writings, which demonstrate his familiarity with the productions of that science relative to religion, and include critical engagement with Hume's NHR and a more praising assessment of Kames's "Sketches" on theology. I want to briefly discuss Gerard's contribution because it indicates how an academic theologian responded to the challenges posed by Hume's "science of man." Like his Aberdonian colleague George Campbell, Gerard claimed that Hume's NHR failed to account for the historical reality of the history of religion. But unlike Campbell, Gerard reiterated the traditional arguments of anti-atheist apologetics, Christianity histories of idolatry and the reliability of biblical history as sufficient to rebut Hume.

Gerard addressed the question whether recent theories of religious psychology and religious change undermined the truth of Christianity in a sermon given to the Society in Scotland for Propagating Christian

[23] Gerard (1774, p. 2).

Knowledge, in Edinburgh in June 1791.[24] Gerard argued that the "whole history of religion" demonstrates that we can distinguish between true religions that are corrupted over time and false religions that progress towards truth, though he paid little real attention to the latter.[25] The three "universally and invariably true religions" on biblical record—the primeval religion of mankind, the Jewish, and the Christian—all degenerated over time.[26] Recent theories of religious improvement over time had to be placed back into biblical context to be understood properly. As with George Gregory, in Gerard we find how the potentially subversive character of progressive histories of religion was blunted by the claim that theistic religions fitted a separate pattern befitting their establishment via direct revelation rather than the accumulation of human knowledge and practice. Indeed, the question of the subversiveness of progressive histories of religion vis-à-vis Christianity focused on whether the former were seen to develop in the immediate aftermath of some early point following the Flood (per, say, Gregory) or were conceived of as entirely distinct views of the history of humanity (per, as Gerard emphasised, Hume's NHR).

Gerard did not employ any sustained psychological or societal explanation for the historical developments he outlined, beyond the claim that human nature is flawed and inherently superstitious. The simplistic animism characteristic of primordial peoples resulted from living in pre-social conditions. The deification of dead heroes resulted following the "establishment of civil society and the successive inventions of arts," with the criteria for deification loosening over time to the point that even trivial successes lead to the creation of gods.[27] The superstitious character of human nature "soon demanded statues of the gods," and eventually those statues were worshipped rather than the gods themselves. The "most detestable form of paganism" was the worship of animals and inanimate objects, a practice which emerged as the ancient Egyptians forgot the symbolic meaning of the hieroglyphs and began to worship the symbols instead.[28] The Israelites knew of true religion but, during

---

[24] Gerard (1792).
[25] Gerard (1792, p. 4).
[26] Gerard (1792, p. 4).
[27] Gerard (1792, p. 10).
[28] Gerard (1792, p. 13).

their Babylonian captivity, got obsessed their neighbours' gods, fixated on ceremonies instead of moral codes and also intermixed their religion with the "learning and philosophy of the east."[29]

False religions are eminently improvable because they have such base origins. As contrivances of ignorant and superstitious men, false religions "must be always capable of amendment."[30] What drives the improvement of false religions forward is the extent to which man's "understandings are improved, cultivated and enlightened."[31] All false religions improve by the "diffusion of knowledge."[32] Gerard posited that the end point of such refinement is the realisation by the wise that false religion cannot be rendered true. They determine to abandon it: "every false religion destroys itself" eventually, under the weight of its own absurdity.[33] This is not a movement that ends up with true religion, but with an abandonment of polytheism and the search for a replacement, at least amongst the philosophers and theologians within a society. This leads to dual religions of irrational theisms developed by philosophers struggling without the aid of revelation and an ineradicable popular polytheism based on ignorance.

The trajectories of true religions (degeneration) and false religions (flawed improvement) were two separate developments, discerned from reading the history of religion. From this vantage point, Gerard dismissed Hume's argument in the NHR with a simple reiteration of the truth of biblical history. Hume had argued, Gerard summarised, that the historical record and our understanding of human nature demonstrated that savage man could not have come to an understanding of theism through the use of his reasoning. But to get to this point, Hume had dismissed as irrelevant the example of the ancient Hebrews and the Old Testament in his description of the near universality of primeval polytheism. This was "doubtless prudent," Gerard ironically intoned, as the inclusion of the "most ancient" history in the world would have undone all of Hume's argument.[34] Gerard could agree with Hume that primeval man did not discover religion by "force of reason," though he could not

---

[29] Gerard (1792, p. 21).
[30] Gerard (1792, p. 51).
[31] Gerard (1792, p. 52).
[32] Gerard (1792, p. 53).
[33] Gerard (1792, p. 52).
[34] Gerard (1792, pp. 5–6).

have disagreed with Hume more when Gerard claimed the learned of religion because they were "taught by God."[35] As with Archibald Campbell, George Campbell, and William Robertson, Gerard held that revelation was both the original "mode of conveying" true religion but also the "sole foundation" of some of primeval man's theological principles.[36] *Pace* Hume, we know, Gerard averred, from the "oldest of histories, that in the remotest antiquity a more perfect religion, the acknowledgement and worship of the One God, did prevail."[37] Similarly, the Mosaical religion took the form of a true theism, was learnt via revelation not reason and was subsequently corrupted under the weight of human failing.

In a backhanded sort of way, however, Gerard agreed with Hume that all religion was flux between theism and polytheism, though Gerard took this as evidence for the weakness of human nature and the necessity of revelation. The infidels, presumably as much the radicals of the French Revolution as Hume himself, sought to "banish Christianity from the world," but they failed to properly understand the role of human nature in the formation of religion. To destroy Christianity would only leave a religion-shaped whole in the soul of man. Both the "constitution of man" and the "whole history of mankind" demonstrated that atheism will never take the place of religion, and that without access to revelation, any attempt in forging a new natural religion will break against the rocks of popular superstition.[38] But any new theism, regardless or even because of its basis on reasonable natural religion, will "degenerate[s] into polytheism and idolatry," because this is what theisms do, they degenerate.[39] Even amongst primeval humanity, despite being "fortified by a memorial of all other things being created by [God]," did this process occur.[40] The idolatry of the Israelites was purged, but just as quickly their religion "degenerated anew."[41] The Magisterial Reformers moved just as quickly from relying upon scripture alone to relying upon their vain human judgement, and soon created very human and therefore very flawed systems of

---

[35] Gerard (1792, p. 6).
[36] Gerard (1792, p. 6).
[37] Gerard (1792, p. 15).
[38] Gerard (1792, p. 54).
[39] Gerard (1792, p. 55).
[40] Gerard (1792, p. 55).
[41] Gerard (1792, p. 56).

doctrine. Any attempt to "explode revelation is in fact a project to bring the world back to the worship of stocks and stones," not that revelation seemed to serve, for Gerard, as a particularly strong bulwark against the weakness of human nature.[42]

Unlike false religions, however, Christianity had an ever-present escape route, Gerard told his SSPCK audience: the return to scripture, which provides us with the means of "rectifying the grossest misconceptions."[43] The history of mankind taught that we must seek the truth in scripture in an honest and diligent manner, with all due awareness of our inherent fallibility and the consequent necessity to "give ready indulgence to the opinions of others."[44] Speculative theology should be discontinued, as a source of contention and difference between believers, and religious tolerance encouraged. The history of religion demonstrated that the "free and sober exercise" of reason had considerable benefits, though it jointly demonstrated the "utility and importance of revelation."[45] In the flux and reflux of religious belief, the only stable and reliable thing is scripture, and it is something that we, as individuals, must turn to and interpret.

A similarly traditional reiteration of the anti-atheist universal consent argument for the existence of God appeared in Gerard's posthumously published *Compendious View of the Evidences of Natural and Revealed Religion* (1828), based on his divinity lectures at Marischal College in the late eighteenth century, Gerard confidently declared that one proof for the existence of God was the argument from the "general consent of mankind."[46] The *Compendious View* was a work in the "science of theology," described by Gerard as a science covering all branches of knowledge that served to demonstrate and illuminate the truth of Christianity. This included but was more extensive than the "science of human nature," and thus takes us a little beyond the intended confines of this survey. Gerard's explication of the *universal consent* argument was comparatively extensive, but contained pretty much all the commonplaces of this staple of seventeenth-century natural theology and apologetic works. Beneath the evidence of religious diversity, it is "absolutely certain

---

[42] Gerard (1792, p. 56).
[43] Gerard (1792, p. 59).
[44] Gerard (1792, p. 59).
[45] Gerard (1792, pp. 53–54).
[46] Gerard (1828, p. 78).

that almost all nations, in all ages, have had some God, and some sort of religious worship."[47] The being of God is a "primary opinion" as there are no other universally held opinions from which it could have been derived.[48] Similarly, it is a belief "remote from all the suggestions of the senses," and must owe its origins to something other than experience and reflection.[49] Such universality must result from either revelation or from "our very nature," or both.[50] We know that it is a true belief not simply because it is universally held, but because it is "a principle of such a nature, that, except it were true, mankind could not possibly have consented in believing it."[51]

Exceptions to common consent do not amount to much, nor do the explanations of the origin of religion spread by religion's critics. Travel accounts of atheist societies were composed by superficial observers of society and have been proven to be wrong; those atheist societies which do exist are rare exceptions that "have no force" against the proof.[52] (Evidently, Hume's use of this argument to reject the relevance of Hebrew theism did not deter its apologetic use). Likewise, professed atheists are "too few to hinder the consent of mankind from being reckoned general."[53] The claim that belief in God originates in the "fears of men" merely mistakes the effects of that belief for its cause, and, if the claim were true, would more properly lead to belief in a world of "evil spirits."[54] No "historical evidence" exists for the irreligious claim that belief in God was the "artifice of politicians, for keeping the bulk of mankind in awe" or that the belief resulted from some manmade tradition.[55] Like Dugald Stewart, Gerard held that the objection resulting from the variety of beliefs about God was to be dismissed, because if it were true it merely shows that while humans "agree in nothing else," they

---

[47] Gerard (1828, pp. 78–79).
[48] Gerard (1828, p. 80).
[49] Gerard (1828, p. 80).
[50] Gerard (1828, p. 82).
[51] Gerard (1828, p. 82).
[52] Gerard (1828, p. 79).
[53] Gerard (1828, p. 79).
[54] Gerard (1828, p. 82).
[55] Gerard (1828, p. 81).

do agree in the existence of God.[56] False opinions about the particular attributes of God result from the "weakness of our reason, the suggestions of our senses, and our vicious passions."[57]

While Gerard's arguments rehashed the staples of early modern Protestant natural theology, he was not oblivious to the key works of the Scottish Enlightenment's discussion of the religious propensities of human nature. He cited Hume's NHR as exhibiting how critics of the universal consent argument could not provide plausible alternative explanations for the sheer extent of religious belief. Similarly, Gerard cited approvingly Kames's essay on the "Existence of the Deity" in *Sketches*, where Kames argued for the existence of an innate "sense of deity" demonstrated by the near universality of religious belief. But what is unusual about Gerard, aside from his limited interest in the issue of the progress of (false) religion and its relationship to societal factors, is his situating his argument in the traditions of Protestant anti-atheist apologetics. Thus, alongside Kames, Gerard's sources are the earlier natural theological works of the Boyle Lecturers Francis Gastrell and John Leng, as well as seventeenth-century luminaries Hugo Grotius, Gilbert Burnet and Francis Turretin. Gerard's use of these figures as authorities could be explained, as I have suggested was the case with Dugald Stewart, by appealing to the nature of these texts and its audience—young minds at Aberdeen receiving moral and religious instruction. But while we might be sceptical about the complete sincerity of Stewart's arguments on religious matters, Gerard remained convinced in the *consensus gentium* argument for the existence of God and saw nothing in the theories of the origin and progress of religion of the previous half century that undermined his conviction. In this, and in his argument for the overriding significance of biblical history to understanding the "history of mankind" and the "history of religion," Gerard is characteristic of that branch of the High Scottish Enlightenment which held for the necessity of revelation, though, equally, not a participant, at least on religious topics, in the "science of man."

---

[56] Gerard (1828, p. 83).
[57] Gerard (1828, p. 83).

REFERENCES TO WORKS CITED

Gerard, Alexander. 1774. *An Essay on Genius*. London.

———. 1792. *A Sermon, Preached before the Society in Scotland for Propagating Christian Knowledge; At Their Anniversary Meeting in the High Church of Edinburgh*. Edinburgh.

———. 1828. *Compendious View of the Evidences of Natural and Revealed Religion*, ed. W. Gerard. London.

Index

A
Aberdeen Philosophical Society, 223, 238, 321
Allegory, 140
Americas, the, 182, 184
Anaxagoras, 98, 99, 265
Anthropomorphism, 67
Apologetics, anti-atheist, 153, 203, 256, 293, 298, 321, 327
   consensus gentium, 293, 327
   consensus sapientium, 293
Aristotelianism, 258
Asceticism, 77, 105
Atheism, 125, 156, 165, 207, 280, 283, 284, 292, 324
Augustine, Saint, 6
Aztec empire, 180, 181, 185–189, 194, 195, 302

B
Bayle, Pierre, 9, 47, 156
Beattie, James, 129, 224, 232, 239, 243, 300
Biblical history, 6, 17, 99, 154, 216, 256, 268, 301, 308, 321, 323, 327
Blackwell, Thomas, 10–12, 17, 141
Blair, Hugh, 128, 240, 314, 315, 318
Bogota tribe, 185
Brahmins, 191–195, 303
Brosses, Charles de, 15
Buffon, 17, 258, 260, 261
Butler, Joseph, 19, 26, 27, 143, 154

C
Calvinism, 153
Campbell, Archibald, 3, 12, 14, 16, 38, 45–51, 93, 128, 154, 161, 190, 200, 206, 224–233, 268, 292, 299–301, 307, 308, 324
Campbell, George, 14, 224, 232, 302, 308, 321, 324
Catholic Church/Catholicism, 12, 13, 92, 112, 113, 139, 159, 177, 178, 243, 283, 303, 304
Chalmers, Thomas, 298
Christianity

history of Christianity, 133, 138, 139, 144, 202
primitive Christianity, 77, 139, 159, 176, 260, 282
relationship with 'science of human nature', 17, 74, 84, 231, 233, 237, 252, 261, 270, 275
relationship with societal development, 171, 176, 187, 301, 306
Church of England, 86
Church of Scotland, 18, 46, 64, 115–117, 127, 136, 171, 175, 238, 240, 243, 249, 307
church-state relationship, 108, 114, 202, 299
Cicero, 6, 154, 205, 206, 232, 293
Clarke, Samuel, 19, 124, 129, 143
Cleghorn, Hugh, 201
Clerical profession, 83, 242, 245, 304
management of, 108
Climate, 5, 252–255, 302, 305, 317, 318
Colonialism, 193
Commercial society, 100, 200, 240, 249, 315, 318
Comte, Auguste, 298, 299
Condorcet, 15
Conjectural history, 11, 88, 175, 258, 271, 288
Conscience, 26, 145, 208, 209, 219, 232
Curiosity, role in religious development, 289

D
Daemons, 12, 69, 261, 262, 266, 267, 270, 302
Deism, 45, 47, 202, 214, 274, 275, 278, 284, 285
Divination, 183, 218, 253
Dual religion, 96, 97, 323

Dunbar, James, 14, 16, 224, 251, 252, 254, 255, 263, 270, 300, 302, 303, 306, 307
Dupuis, Charles-François, 15

E
Egypt, 252, 254, 258–260, 264–271, 316
Enthusiasm, 64, 68, 73, 86, 136, 143, 241, 242
Europe, 8, 79, 112, 116, 132, 140, 160, 175–180, 263, 287, 299, 306

F
Falconer, William, 314, 317–319
Fanaticism, 68, 73, 74, 80, 87, 111, 112, 114, 137, 164, 165, 192, 227, 241, 246, 292, 299, 307
Ferguson, Adam, 9, 14, 20, 101, 166, 200–219, 240, 264, 275, 289, 290, 302, 303, 306–308
Feudalism, 112, 187
Freethinking/'English Deism', 12, 13, 150, 153, 164, 269, 304

G
Geddes, Alexander, 10
Geddes, James, 9
Gregory, George, 314, 315, 322
Gregory, John, 14, 70, 104, 109, 137, 143, 207, 219, 224, 236–243, 245–249, 300, 303, 304, 306–308, 315–319

H
Happiness, 69, 87, 106, 144, 166, 205, 208, 209, 237, 238, 240, 241, 245, 246, 248, 274

Herodotus, 259, 267
Hinduism, 190, 191, 193, 195
History of idolatry, 7, 44, 49, 51, 128, 150, 159, 231, 254, 256, 263, 270, 271, 301, 305, 321
'History of mankind', 3, 4, 8, 17, 18, 29, 51, 53, 98, 141, 142, 153, 159, 189, 211, 225, 228, 230, 231, 233, 252, 255, 258, 267, 271, 306, 308, 314, 317, 325, 327
Hobbes, Thomas, 17, 19–21, 27, 61, 130, 150
Hutcheson, Francis, 19, 23–26, 28, 43, 45, 60, 123
Hutton, James, 14–16, 18, 257, 258, 264, 273–285, 302–304, 306–308
Hyde, Thomas, 17

I
Idolatry, 5, 7–9, 13, 28, 44, 45, 64, 122, 129, 130, 135, 151, 154–156, 163–166, 184, 216, 263, 270, 301, 305, 318, 324
Incan Empire, 180, 185, 186, 188, 189, 267
India, 190, 252, 254, 259, 263
Islam, 229, 233

J
Judaism, 229, 233, 282
  ancient Hebrews, 233

K
Kames, Lord, Henry Home, 2, 7, 9, 11, 13–18, 28, 29, 52, 53, 60, 61, 93, 104, 105, 122–146, 151, 167, 181–183, 212, 217, 240, 251, 264, 269, 270, 278, 282, 299, 301, 303, 306–308, 314, 321, 327

L
Locke, John, 19, 21–23, 26, 28, 47, 79, 124, 129, 156, 260, 261
Luxury, 113, 134, 174, 266

M
Machiavelli, Niccolò, 212, 213
Macpherson, James, 240, 315
Mandeville, Bernard, 19, 27, 28, 130, 150, 151
Mansel, Henry Longueville, 298, 299
Minimal theism, 14, 58, 59, 151, 156, 160, 161, 284, 291, 301, 306
Miracles, 5, 52, 72–75, 80, 81, 161, 225–230, 233, 302, 307
Mode of subsistence, 183, 185
Monboddo, Lord, James Burnett, 12, 14, 18, 98, 99, 184, 240, 252, 257–271, 273, 274, 302, 303, 306–308
'Monkish virtues'. *See* Asceticism
Montesquieu, 17, 317
Moral causes, 252, 255
  distinguished from physical causes, 252
Myth, 11, 12, 80, 85, 141, 229, 315
Mythography, 6, 9, 50, 93, 140, 141, 150, 163, 164, 231, 254, 271, 301, 305

N
Natchez tribe, 185
Natural philosophy, 3, 11, 38–42, 46–48, 51, 66, 105, 106, 111, 122, 123, 133, 160, 208, 237,

276, 277, 279, 284, 285, 291–293, 299
Bacon, Francis, 39, 40, 237
Influence on 'science of human nature', 3, 38, 40, 276
Newton, Isaac, 39, 40, 51
Natural religion, 1, 2, 12, 16, 22, 23, 46, 48, 49, 51, 52, 58, 61, 70, 95, 125, 128, 129, 143, 150, 171, 201, 210, 219, 258, 268, 276, 289, 324
Natural theology, 19, 29, 46, 47, 52, 59, 61, 62, 75, 87, 92, 124, 130, 153, 156, 193, 202, 203, 232, 244, 288, 295, 298, 325, 327
and the ultimate ends of the 'science of man', 18, 61, 62, 92, 156, 295

O
Oswald, James, 224

P
Paganism, 7–9, 12, 13, 15–17, 49, 78, 138, 159, 165, 170, 193, 201, 202, 229, 305, 306, 309, 313
Passions, 4, 24, 25, 27, 28, 39, 63, 65–68, 71, 72, 74, 81, 87, 94–96, 124, 126, 130, 132, 135, 143, 151, 152, 155, 158, 161, 164, 201, 219, 225, 227, 237, 239–241, 245, 248, 249, 255, 269, 291, 303, 306, 316
'Philosophical History', 4, 171–173, 176, 189, 194
Philosophy, 3, 12, 25, 40–42, 45, 48, 49, 51, 52, 58, 59, 61, 62, 66, 70, 75–81, 87, 88, 93, 95–99, 104–106, 111, 112, 122, 123, 133, 139, 140, 144, 153, 156, 161, 165, 177, 179, 180, 192, 193, 202, 230, 232, 237, 242, 245–249, 253, 254, 258–261, 266, 268, 270, 274–285, 288–291, 293, 308, 319
corruption by theology/Christianity, 134, 283
Platonism, 258, 261
Political power, 85, 185, 208, 212, 241, 253, 255, 281
Polytheism, 5, 8, 27, 45, 78, 94–96, 123, 126–129, 131, 151, 154, 155, 159–166, 170, 181, 183, 185, 193, 195, 203, 215–218, 230–232, 254, 256, 259, 264, 265, 269, 279, 288–291, 293, 295, 298, 301, 303, 316, 323, 324
Popular religion, 22, 77, 78, 81, 82, 85, 86, 151, 156, 159, 160, 163, 164, 166, 190, 192, 212, 219, 240, 249, 269, 270, 280, 303, 304, 306
Presbyterianism, 45–47, 128, 193
Priestcraft, 15, 28, 45, 50, 164, 191, 193, 194, 282
Protestantism, 114, 269
Providence, 16, 41, 130, 132, 144, 146, 181, 194, 208, 239, 291, 306

R
Reason, 2, 5, 8, 21, 22, 24, 25, 28, 41, 42, 44–48, 50, 51, 53, 58, 59, 64, 71, 73, 97, 111, 125, 130, 135, 144, 153, 156, 170, 171, 189, 194, 202, 203, 206, 214, 225, 226, 240, 242, 255, 260, 261, 266, 269, 274, 292, 324, 325
Religio duplex. *See* Dual religion
Religion

and the focus of the 'science of human nature', 3, 6, 8, 10, 45, 50, 51, 87, 92, 154, 201, 288, 317
and the improvement of knowledge, 27
definition of, 6, 291, 295
diversity, 5, 9, 16, 22, 28, 110, 112, 116, 130, 131, 171, 202, 279, 289–291, 293, 298, 317, 325
origin of, 17, 20, 22, 26, 58, 156, 293, 326
relationship between human nature, 2
relationship with philosophy, 75
'Religious Enlightenment', 14, 275, 291
Religious innatism, 22, 205, 232, 293, 294, 302
innate ideas, 22
innate propensity to religion, 153
Religious toleration, 69, 130
Revealed religion, 5, 26, 40, 42, 45–47, 58, 59, 71, 142, 143, 145, 146, 214, 225, 256, 278, 279, 316
necessity of revelation, 71, 214
relationship with 'science of human nature', 256
'Revival of Letters', the, 78, 160, 289, 304
Rites and ceremonies, 17, 82, 135, 137, 141, 160, 178, 187, 201, 209, 211
Roman Republic, the, 213, 303

S
Savage society, 315, 316
Scepticism, 18, 71, 79, 106, 129, 138, 161, 207, 238, 245–248, 260, 280

'Science of human nature'/'Science of man'
different approaches, 306
naturalisation of study of religion, 6
relationship to earlier theories of religion, 5, 18
role of 'Facts and experiments', 123
Scottish Enlightenment, 1–3, 5, 10, 13, 14, 18, 28, 29, 38, 50, 88, 122, 129, 140, 142, 149, 157, 170, 185, 206, 215, 237, 254, 257–259, 261, 263, 271–274, 287, 288, 295, 299, 307, 309, 314, 317, 327
Contrast with French Enlightenment, 15
'High Scottish Enlightenment', 2, 9, 28, 87, 122, 274
Secularisation, 111, 305, 307
Shaftesbury, Third Earl of, Anthony Ashley Cooper, 19, 23–26, 28, 43, 45, 60, 123
Slavery, 174
Smith, Adam, 2, 9, 13, 14, 19, 27–29, 91–117, 137, 192, 200, 204–206, 212, 238, 240, 241, 243, 247, 251, 254, 263–265, 290, 292, 298, 299, 303, 304, 306–308, 314
Soul, 6, 42, 49, 59, 61, 64, 65, 85, 106, 128, 129, 184, 185, 192, 214, 215, 232, 239, 242, 243, 246, 268, 269, 324
belief in, 142, 184
existence of, 70
immortality of, 46, 52, 65, 127, 142, 144, 146, 170, 173, 184, 208, 214, 292, 316
Spanish Empire, 194
Speculative theology, 7, 71, 76, 87, 104, 136, 137, 177, 242, 244,

246, 248, 299, 301, 304, 306, 325
Stadial history, 7, 13, 50, 122, 133, 181, 186, 188, 252, 259
  of religion, 122, 129, 146, 301, 317
Stewart, Dugald, 3, 13, 14, 18, 29, 157, 184, 224, 240, 257, 287–295, 300, 303, 304, 306–308, 326, 327
Stoicism, 101, 106, 195, 200
Superstition, 62, 68, 69, 71, 78, 80, 81, 95, 99, 111–113, 131, 133, 136, 140, 143, 150, 154, 155, 161, 164, 166, 171, 176, 177, 179, 181, 183, 186, 189, 191–193, 195, 209, 212, 217–219, 240–242, 249, 254, 255, 258, 275, 277, 280, 281, 283–285, 290, 299, 301–304, 324

T

Theism/monotheism, 5, 8, 12, 15, 26–28, 45, 46, 50, 51, 75, 78, 96–98, 110, 123, 127–129, 131–133, 151, 154–156, 160–166, 170, 178, 182, 185, 190–193, 195, 202, 203, 215–219, 224, 230–232, 256, 258, 259, 264, 265, 268, 269, 282, 283, 289–293, 295, 298, 301, 316, 323, 324, 326
The Reformation, 84, 112, 139, 151, 176, 177, 179, 180, 236, 279, 283, 299, 304

Tradition, 12, 22, 46, 47, 51, 61, 80, 161, 163, 231, 232, 282, 288, 304, 307, 326
  traditionary religion, 86
Transmission, 47, 92, 231, 232, 254, 263, 270, 271
  civilisational, 97, 258
  religious, 305
Turnbull, George, 3, 12, 38–47, 50, 51, 123, 301, 303, 307

U

Universal consent, argument from, 289
  and belief in an immortal soul, 184
  and belief in future rewards and punishments, 205
  and belief in God, 289

V

Virtue, 27, 41, 75, 103, 105, 106, 137, 164, 173, 194, 209, 212, 215, 240, 276
Vossius, G.J., 17

W

Worship, 7, 25, 43, 44, 49, 59, 63, 64, 86, 124, 125, 129–131, 133–137, 139, 142, 144, 145, 155, 158, 163, 184, 186, 189, 212, 213, 219, 229, 240, 241, 278, 282, 301, 303, 317, 318, 322, 324

Printed in the United States
by Baker & Taylor Publisher Services